The World Cris

Volume V

Some titles are not available in North America.

The World Crisis

Volume V: The Unknown War

Winston S. Churchill

BLOOMSBURY ACADEMIC

LONDON • NEW YORK • OXFORD • NEW DELHI • SYDNEY

BLOOMSBURY ACADEMIC
Bloomsbury Publishing Plc
50 Bedford Square, London, WC1B 3DP, UK
1385 Broadway, New York, NY 10018, USA
29 Earlsfort Terrace, Dublin 2, Ireland

BLOOMSBURY, BLOOMSBURY ACADEMIC and the Diana logo are trademarks
of Bloomsbury Publishing Plc

First published by Charles Scribner's Sons 1931

Bloomsbury Revelations edition first published in 2015 by Bloomsbury Academic
Reprinted 2018 (three times), 2019 (three times), 2020, 2021 (twice), 2023
Reprinted with a new cover 2023

Cover Design by Ben Anslow

A catalogue record for this book is available from the British Library.

A catalog record for this book is available from the Library of Congress.

ISBN: HB: 978-1-4742-2342-3
PB: 978-1-4725-8703-9
ePDF: 978-1-4725-8705-3
ePub: 978-1-4725-8704-6

Series: Bloomsbury Revelations

Typeset by Deanta Global Publishing Services, Chennai, India
Printed and bound in Great Britain

To find out more about our authors and books visit www.bloomsbury.com
and sign up for our newsletters.

Contents

Maps and Illustrations

Table of maps, diagrams, etc.

In text

PREFACE

In the five volumes of the *World Crisis* and the *Aftermath* I have told the story of the War from the British standpoint, and particularly from those positions of authority which I held myself. The war at sea, the expedition to the Dardanelles, and the campaigns in France and Flanders filled the stage. It was only here and there that brief summaries of the struggles of Russia with Germany and Austria in the East could find a place. In this new volume the proportions are reversed. The tale both of the events leading to the War and of its battles is told from the Eastern theatre, and only brief, indispensable references are made to British and French affairs. I have attempted to give a general account of the whole War upon the Eastern Front, and the distant cannonade in France breaks only fitfully upon the ear. The primary theme arises in Vienna and covers the agonies of Central Europe. The familiar events in the West are seen only in their reactions upon the Eastern Front.

Although I had lived and toiled through the war years in positions which gave a wide outlook and the best information, I was surprised to find how dim and often imperfect were the impressions I had sustained of the conflict between Russia and the two Teutonic Empires. It was not until I studied its problems from this new angle that I began to see the tragedy in its completeness. I believe that British and American readers will also find the narrative of these events necessary to a true understanding.

The sources are abundant. Voluminous histories, memoirs, rejoinders, exculpations and official accounts, some only recently published, are available. Many have not been translated into French. Few have been translated into English. Others are technical, and interest chiefly military students. A whole library exists into which the English-speaking world has scarcely ventured. Yet our own fortunes were powerfully swayed by all that happened in the East, and it is there that we must look for the explanation of many strange and sorry turns in our fortunes.

I must acknowledge the assistance I have derived from the massive records of Conrad von Hötzendorf, the virtual Austro-Hungarian Commander-in-Chief; from the works of Hindenburg, Ludendorff, Falkenhayn and Hoffmann; from the Russian accounts by Danilov, Gourko and Sukhomlinov; from the successive volumes of the German and Austrian official histories; from the library of the Royal Institute of International Affairs; and from the long series of searching military monographs which have appeared from time to time in the *Army Quarterly*. I must also pay my tribute to the statement of the causes of the War by Professor Bernadotte E. Schmitt, of Chicago University, who has marshalled in masterly fashion the whole series of official and authentic documents in an impressive array.

Finally, I am deeply indebted to Lieutenant-Colonel Charles Hordern, who for more than a year has assisted me in the assembly and sifting of material with his excellent advice, and in making the necessary translations, and preparing the numerous maps without which the story would be unintelligible.

A list of some of the authorities consulted or cited will be found in Appendix II. In all cases I have sought to probe the original documents, and have had direct translations made from the German and Russian texts.

I have striven to make the operations of the Armies plain to the lay reader and to show also, as in previous volumes, what happened and why. Every effort has been made to simplify the terminology. Russian, Polish and Austrian names of men and places in great numbers are an inevitable deterrent to English-speaking readers. But the same difficulty would no doubt recur, if unhappily a great war were ever to be fought in Wales! For convenient brevity the word 'Austrian' is nearly always used to cover the Austro-Hungarian Empire. William II is described throughout as the Kaiser, and Francis Joseph as the Emperor. Other abbreviations and symbols will be introduced as the narrative proceeds. It is my hope that in the result the reader who will gaze attentively upon the simple maps and diagrams which illustrate and sustain the text will have at his disposal a continuous and compendious description of these vast and mournful episodes of human destiny.

Winston S. Churchill

CHARTWELL,
KENT,
13 *August*, 1931.

NOTE

The reference numbers printed against the more important quotations given in the text refer to the list of sources contained in Appendix III on page 271.

CHAPTER I
THE DUSK OF HAPSBURG

If for a space we obliterate from our minds the fighting in France and Flanders, the struggle upon the Eastern Front is incomparably the greatest war in history. In its scale, in its slaughter, in the exertions of the combatants, in its military kaleidoscope, it far surpasses by magnitude and intensity all similar human episodes.

It is also the most mournful conflict of which there is record. All three empires, both sides, victors and vanquished, were ruined. All the Emperors or their successors were slain or deposed. The Houses of Romanov, Hapsburg and Hohenzollern woven over centuries of renown into the texture of Europe were shattered and extirpated. The structure of three mighty organisms built up by generations of patience and valour and representing the traditional groupings of noble branches of the European family, was changed beyond all semblance. These pages recount dazzling victories and defeats stoutly made good. They record the toils, perils, sufferings and passions of millions of men. Their sweat, their tears, their blood bedewed the endless plain. Ten million homes awaited the return of the warriors. A hundred cities prepared to acclaim their triumphs. But all were defeated; all were stricken; everything that they had given was given in vain. The hideous injuries they inflicted and bore, the privations they endured, the grand loyalties they exemplified, all were in vain. Nothing was gained by any. They floundered in the mud, they perished in the snowdrifts, they starved in the frost. Those that survived, the veterans of countless battle-days, returned, whether with the laurels of victory or tidings of disaster, to homes engulfed already in catastrophe.

We may make our pictures of this front from Napoleon's campaigns. Hard and sombre war; war of winter; bleak and barren regions; long marches forward and back again under heavy burdens; horses dying in the traces; wounded frozen in their own blood; the dead uncounted, unburied; the living pressed again into the mill. Eylau; Aspern; Wagram; Borodino; The Beresina—all the sinister impressions of these names revive, divested of their vivid flash of pomp, and enlarged to a hideous size. Here all Central Europe tore itself to pieces and expired in agony, to rise again, unrecognizable.

* * * * *

In earlier volumes I have traced the remorseless growth of those antagonisms which in the last quarter of the nineteenth century converted Europe into an armed camp, and into two great systems of alliances upon whose equipoise the peace of the world was uncertainly founded. But this long process was studied and described primarily from the standpoint of the Western powers, and centred upon the abiding quarrel between France and Germany and the attitude of Great Britain thereto. We now re-ascend the streams of history to those sources of the World War which arose in central, eastern and south-eastern Europe. Even if Germany and France had never been rivals and enemies, or if England had never been estranged by Germany, the fountain-heads of wrath in the Austro-Hungarian Empire and the Balkan States would sooner or later have overflowed in a deluge of war. Without these eastern sources of trouble the mighty Western powers might have long dwelt in the sunshine of peace and progress. It was the fatal confluence of two powerful separate and self-moving sets of antagonisms that alone rendered possible the supreme catastrophe; and it was the course of events in the east that fixed the fatal hour.

The states and peoples of central and south-eastern Europe lay upon its broad expanses in the confusion left from ancient wars. The old battlefields were cumbered with the bones of bygone warriors, and the flags and trophies of far-off victories, and over them brooded the memories of many a cruel oppression and many a perished cause. In the main the empire of the Hapsburgs and the states of the Balkan Peninsula sate amid the ruins of centuries of struggle with the invading, proselytizing, devastating Turk. Here, long after they had ebbed and ceased in the west, the tides of warlike Islam had finally been dammed. After long-drawn struggles the Danube was liberated. For a while the Ottoman power reigned over the Christian races of the Balkans, and even in its decrepitude held them in a withering grip. One by one, aided mainly by Russia, these fierce races, hammered hard upon the anvil of Turkish misrule, shook themselves free; until finally the Turkish power was broken for ever. Roumania, Bulgaria, Serbia, Montenegro and Greece, relieved from the curse of bondage for five hundred years, stood erect, and gazed upon each other almost immediately with eyes of keen malevolence and rivalry. Each of them remembered that at one time or another the hegemony of the Balkans had been hers; and all began to gather up the tangled, severed threads of their conflicting national histories.

First among the champions of Christendom stood the empire of the Czars. If Austrian and Hungarian chivalry had stemmed the Turkish invasions, it was Russia who for two centuries had advanced upon Turkey, inspired to the deliverance of kindred races still in bondage, and impelled by other motives towards Constantinople and the warm, open waters of the Mediterranean. The feud between Russia and Turkey was as old and as deadly as that between France and Germany. But whereas Russia, animated by Peter and Catherine and other famous Romanov sovereigns, had waxed continually, the Ottoman power had waned and set. From the fourteenth to the eighteenth century the peril and preoccupation of central and eastern Europe was Turkish strength. During the nineteenth its danger was Turkish weakness.

The final retreat of invading armies, the freeing of virile races and wide domains, the decay and disappearance of a common foe, gradually relaxed or destroyed the bonds which had long united the races of the Dual Monarchy. The necessities which had induced the Teutons, Czechs, Magyars and Slavs to form a joint empire for security had stood the strain of a succession of disastrous wars and civil wars. As the external enemy faded and died, the army of the Austro-Hungarian Empire began to fall to pieces. Like the liberated states of the Balkans, the four constituent peoples of the Danubian plains began to think again for themselves about their past and their future. Hungary had in revolt and revolution almost torn herself away in 1848. Caught and crushed by Russian armies pouring through the passes of the Carpathians, she was led back captive by the Czar and chained once more to the throne of his brother Emperor. It was upon an orgy of blood and executions that the youthful Francis Joseph entered upon his long and fatal reign. Bohemia in the general resurgence of nationalism which marked the close of the nineteenth century fretted, chafed and struggled in the Austrian net. Perhaps she might have been reconciled if the Dual had become a Triple Crown. But this neither Francis Joseph nor Hungary would concede.

To the southward the problems of the Empire were even more acute. The southern Slavs lay astride the Imperial frontiers. The core of the race was in Serbia, but large numbers of Slavonic folk dwelt north of the Danube and in the provinces of Bosnia and Herzegovina. The sentiment and tradition of all the southern Slavs turned towards Serbia as to a magnet, and through Serbia far back across the ages to the once great Serb empire of Stephan Dushan. To revivify those glories and reunite the lands and peoples now sundered, became the persisting ambition of the Serbian people from the moment they had shaken off the Turkish yoke. This hardy warlike stock, 'the Prussians of the Balkans,' whose teeth were whetted in centuries of unrecorded ferocious struggles with the Sultan's troops, respected nothing that stood in their way. Reckless of consequences to themselves or others, fearing naught and enduring all, they pursued their immense design through the terrors and miseries of Armageddon, and have, in fact, achieved their purpose at its close.

All these disruptive forces were actively and increasingly at work within the Empire in the latter part of the last century. The progress of the western world, the advance of democratic ideas, the imperative necessity for universal education, the adoption of representative and Parliamentary institutions upon a wide franchise, the requirements of compulsory military service, all tended to aggravate the stresses. So long as education was a privilege gained with difficulty by the ardent few, questions of language and history were not disturbing; but when mixed populations and mingled religions took their obligatory seats in millions at the desks, every classroom, every curriculum in every village school became an arena. There was not in the declining Empire any force equal to that which has imposed throughout all innumerable national schools of the United States one single language and one universal secularism. Each race in the Dual Monarchy indulged its separatist tendencies to the full, and reviving ancient, even long-forgotten tongues, used these as weapons in ever-extending hostilities.

Vain to assemble such contrary elements in an Empire Parliament house. Vain to suppose that the processes and amenities of English House of Commons procedure would afford expression to such bitter divergencies. Parliaments can only flourish when fundamentals are agreed or at least accepted by the great majority of all parties. In the Parliaments of the Hapsburgs bands of excited deputies sat and howled at each other by the hour in rival languages, accompanying their choruses with the ceaseless slamming of desks which eventually by a sudden crescendo swelled into a cannonade. All gave rein to hatred; and all have paid for its indulgence with blood and tears.

These racial manifestations and their allied, though not coincident socialistic and proletarian tendencies were viewed with gnawing anxiety by the cultured, privileged, land-owning aristocracy, by the numerous hierarchies of officials and by the military classes upon whom the defence of property, the cohesion of the Empire and the maintenance of the monarchy depended. Three or four Irelands, at once Sinn Fein and socialistic, brawled together and wrenched at the structure of the Empire, while the powerful governing classes whose safety and prosperity were wrapt in its survival, watched the scene with wrath, fear and perplexity. Thus the twentieth century dawned upon the sixty million persons over whom the weary, stricken, tragic, octogenarian heir of the ages and their curses continued for a space to reign.

The spectacle of Turkish decrepitude, of Balkan ambitions and Austrian decay would not be complete without the Polish dream. While along the Danube the centrifugal forces gathered momentum, the centripetal preserved an undying energy on both sides of the Vistula. Here lay the famous kingdom of Poland, for one hundred and thirty years partitioned between the three military empires which surrounded it, but treasuring always the hope of freedom and reunion and capable of shaking to their very vitals every one of its three devourers. Deep hidden in the vaults of Warsaw reposed the old banners of the Polish nation. Helpless in the talons of the three Imperial eagles, closely woven into the texture of the three proud armies, liable at any moment to be marched against each other in compulsory fratricidal strife, twenty or thirty million Poles awaited the day when amid the ruins of Empires, their hidden flags would once again salute the daylight. Here too was a dream which has not failed.

* * * * *

The creaking and straining system of the Dual Monarchy revolved ponderously around the person of the aged Emperor. Francis Joseph had ascended his throne in 1848 amid executions, martial law and the rigorous suppression of revolt. He had sustained every kind of public tribulation and domestic tragedy. His brother the Emperor Maximilian had been executed in Mexico by a rebel firing party. His only son Rudolf, heir to the throne, had perished tragically in 1889. His wife had been stabbed through the heart on a jetty at Geneva by an Italian anarchist. He had never declared a foreign war he did not lose, nor bent himself to a domestic policy which was not evidently failing. In 1859 the fields of Solferino and Magenta had stripped him of north Italy. In 1866 the battle of Sadowa had transferred the hegemony of Germany from Austria to Prussia. Hungary against whom he had warred with severity asserted a challenging separatism in the heart of the Empire. Bohemia, whom he would never recognize as a partner, chafed bitterly under his hands.

However, he lived and thrived. He had sat on the throne for more than sixty years when King Edward VII died. At seventy-five he was not only well preserved, but vigorous. He walked far; he could still ride: his chief amusement was shooting boar and bears and deer. He had borne his bereavements stoically. He was jealous of his brother Maximilian; he did not love his wife; he had been on bad terms with all his family, some of whom had incurred a public notoriety which by his rigid standards was beyond any pardon;

he politely acquiesced in the existence of his nephew, the new heir, the Archduke Franz Ferdinand; but he could never forgive him for his love-marriage. General Marchenko, Russian Military Attaché at Vienna from 1905 to 1911, in memoirs which are a definite contribution to history, says that a colleague, Major von Bülow, the German Attaché (brother of the German Ex-Chancellor, and afterwards killed in Belgium), remarked upon the Emperor's troubles: 'He is used to all that. Without a misfortune in the day's work he would be bored.' Marchenko himself says that Francis Joseph 'regarded his defeats and reverses as sacrifices to fortune.' A courtly, sagacious, crabbed, disillusioned old gentleman, reared in the purple, harassed from youth up by awful public responsibilities, with an ever-present self-questioning about their adequate discharge.

In the closing phase of his reign he had become almost an automaton. He discharged routine duties without pleasure, indeed with distaste, punctually and assiduously, literally from dawn to dusk. He rose usually at four in the morning, and, dressed in his sky-blue uniform, drank his coffee at his desk amid official portfolios and files. His wish was to go to sleep not later than eight o'clock at night. He resented keenly all functions which interrupted this rule. When compelled to entertain company he dined as late as five or even six o'clock in the afternoon. Otherwise, although in Vienna the usual hour was between eight and nine o'clock, the Emperor took his evening meal between three and four. Alone upon his rocky pinnacle from which the tides of time had sunk, this venerable, conscientious functionary continued in harness pulling faithfully at the collar, mostly in the right direction, to the last gasp.

A living picture of the Court is given by Baron von Margutti who was for the last seventeen years of the Empire high in the Household. Francis Joseph lived in intimacy with a curious small coterie consisting of two septuagenarian aides-de-camp—Count Paar and Baron Bolfras, who was also chief of the military cabinet—and Count Beck, seventy years of age in 1906, and perhaps the Emperor's one trusted male friend. All these three men stood around the centre of power. They had dwelt there before most of Francis Joseph's subjects had been born. Their lives were wrapped up in the service of the Emperor. Paar, ably served by younger men, dealt with all the questions, great and small, of etiquette and a large part of patronage. Bolfras presided over the court side of the military sphere; but he brooded over higher matters of policy, had constant occasions to give his advice, and indeed claims to have both counselled and planned in 1878 the original occupation of Bosnia and Herzegovina. Beck, who had served the Emperor for fifty years in 1906, managed and looked after all the movements and public appearances of his beloved master. He knew exactly how he liked reviews, manœuvres, inspections of camps or garrisons, and every non-political public activity to be conducted. He studied the imperial wants and idiosyncrasies; he protected his Sovereign from every kind of minor annoyance; he also no doubt supplied him with a stream of antiquated opinion upon military matters, for he had been, in his day, Chief of the Staff of the Austro-Hungarian army.

Such was this ancient band of survivors eminently Victorian, unswervingly faithful, who surrounded the very old but clear-headed potentate in whose person all the loyalties of a disrupting Empire centred, and against whose régime all its hatreds welled.

The Emperor had one other confidante. Katharina Schratt, the daughter of a post-master in Baden, near Vienna, had been in the eighties a successful actress. Francis Joseph admired her beauty, charm and humour. The Empress welcomed her. She became associated with the Court. For over thirty years she was the Emperor's cherished friend. Whether at Schönbrunn or Ischl her discreet dwelling was always close at hand. Very early in the mornings the old gentleman would leave his palace by a private door and walking by carefully-secluded paths would breakfast with Frau Schratt, 'always good-tempered and smiling,' in an old-fashioned room 'with a white-clothed table, gay with flowers.' Here he found peace, happiness, and a window on the world, which none of his punctually-handled portfolios would have given him.

Frau von Schratt, as she came to be called, was extremely well informed upon all kinds of public and social matters. Ministers, bankers, nobles and actors found it both wise and agreeable to keep in touch with her. 'She was,' says Tschuppik, 'the link between the Emperor and the outer world. She was his newspaper; from her he learnt more . . . than from all his ministers put together: . . . it was often only from her that he learnt the truth.' Indeed on the tragic morning when the suicide or murder of the Emperor's only son had to be announced to him, it was to Frau von Schratt that the Empress Elizabeth turned, and the two women went together to break the news. This gifted woman, who had within limits the power to make and mar, remained always a private figure. She never abused her position to amass a fortune or aggrandize herself. She spoke to the Emperor on matters of State with tact and modesty. But she knew how to tell him what she believed was for his good; and he was always ready to listen and ponder on all she said. Her influence was jealously resented by the Court Chamberlain, the Count of Montenuovo, the guardian of etiquette and correctitude. He laboured continually to disturb the relationship between her and his Imperial master; but he laboured without success. This companionship was Francis Joseph's only happiness. He held tenaciously to it to the end.

It remains to be said that the Emperor, of course, was a strong Conservative. He thought that old-fashioned habits and methods and a conservative outlook were enjoined upon him by his position and by the complicated texture of his Empire. He did not conceal his abhorrence of innovation. He would never use a lift, avowed dislike for electrical appliances, detested the telephone, only rode in a motor-car to please King Edward, and disapproved of flying. All we can say with our superior knowledge is that in these unfashionable opinions he has not yet been proved wrong.

The death of the Crown Prince Rudolf in 1889 transferred the succession to the Emperor's brother Charles, and on the latter's death in 1896 it passed to his eldest son, the Archduke Francis Ferdinand.* The Heir-Apparent had the advantage of being educated without any expectation of the throne. He was a fine-looking man of moderate ability, simple tastes, tactless manners, a sincere character and a strong will. From his maternal grandfather, the 'Bomb King' of Sicily, he inherited a distrust of strangers and a tendency to believe himself disliked. It is said of him that he once remarked to his

---

*See Appendix, page 269.

Chief of Staff: 'You generally expect that every man will prove an angel. . . . For my part, I always assume that anyone I see for the first time is a scoundrel, and later on, if possible, I revise my opinion.'

At the castle of the Archduke Frederick at Pressburg he was a welcome guest, because it was hoped he might marry the eldest daughter-princess. However, it was gradually suspected that his interest was engaged by a young maid of honour, a German-Czech lady of honourable but not elevated parentage, Countess Chotek. Cross-questioned by her mistress the Archduchess Isabella, the Countess Chotek disposed of these rumours by a complete denial. But one day during a holiday by the Adriatic the Archduchess picked up by chance a locket dropped unwittingly by its owner. She opened the locket and found therein a miniature of Franz Ferdinand with the inscription 'Thine for ever.' She recognized the locket as usually worn by the Countess Chotek.

No time was lost in dismissing the maid of honour. The sequel startled the Austrian world. Franz Ferdinand, considering that he had compromised a young lady and involved her in disgrace and dismissal, gave full reign to the passion of his life. He announced at once that he would marry her. The old Emperor, who had planned to wed his new heir to the widow of his son Rudolf, the Crown Princess Stephanie, was deeply shocked; Vienna was thrilled, and the Dual Monarchy agog. A score of obstacles, arguments and vetoes were interposed. Franz Ferdinand crashed through them all. He signed an act of renunciation of any right to the throne for his future wife and children. He was ready to renounce it for himself, if need be. The marriage took place. This was the greatest, the happiest and the grandest event of his life. They were a devoted couple, inseparable in life—and death.

However, persistent and renewing complications disturbed the rigid etiquette of the Imperial Court. The Archduke Franz Ferdinand was a figure of the highest importance, and as the Emperor aged, he was bound to play an ever-increasing and almost dominant part in the politics and military affairs of the Empire. There was one key which always unlocked his regard. The ceremonial treatment accorded to his wife was for him decisive. She was by Hungarian law, whose generous principles considered only the fact of marriage, bound to become Queen of Hungary on her husband's accession to the Empire. In Austria, however, her precedence was lowly, and kept lowly, and embarrassing situations arose at every public function at which both sexes were present. With the birth of his children the Archduke found a new incentive. He looked back with remorse upon his oath of renunciation of their rights. 'Ease would retract vows made in pain, as violent and void.' To procure for his loved ones the recognition which he deemed their due became the paramount object of his life. The Countess Chotek fanned this flame incessantly. 'The woman's ambition,' said the suffragan Bishop of Vienna to Margutti, 'is unbridled and her unusual intelligence will soon show her the way to translate it into actual fact.'

The Kaiser William* was not slow to pick up the obvious key and fit it in the all-important lock. Before his marriage Franz Ferdinand was antagonistic to the Germans,

---

*For convenience in this account Francis Joseph is always referred to as "The Emperor," and William II as "The Kaiser."

hated the Kaiser and spoke of him with even more than his usual candour. But William II took pains. Whenever he passed through Vienna, it was to the Countess Chotek that he paid special attention. Friendship was soon established. Franz Ferdinand and his wife, invited to Berlin, were entertained with every possible honour. At the banquet the adoption of small round tables enabled the Kaiser to place the Countess at his side without departing from the rules. Compliments and courtesies were unceasing. The Countess Chotek, who was a charming woman, amiable, capable and discreet, became a German partisan. She spoke of the Kaiser in terms of the highest regard and admiration. She had no difficulty in carrying her husband with her. He discarded his former prejudices and from 1908 or 1909 onwards the two men were close friends. The old Emperor continued to disapprove the marriage, but as the weight of years descended upon him, resigned himself to events. Meanwhile the charge of the Imperial Army and the Navy devolved upon the Heir-Apparent and in spite of the prejudices and resistances of Francis Joseph and his ancient military cabinet, very considerable reforms were introduced into the army, especially in the artillery, and it was gradually Germanized, and furnished with new weapons and young leaders.

Foremost among these new chiefs stood—to give him for the first and last time his full title—General of Infantry Franz, Freiherr Conrad von Hötzendorf. In 1914 his name was scarcely known outside his own country. Even during the conflict his repute did not extend outside purely military circles. The large, agitated publics who devoured the war news in France, England or America never heard of him. Nevertheless he played a greater part in the World War and in its origins than any other of the sixty million subjects of the Hapsburg Empire. He was in fact the Commander of all their armies during the greater part of the war. He made the plans, he conducted the mobilization and fought almost all the battles. He went beyond these important duties. He was a diplomat as well as a soldier, a politician as well as a strategist. Indeed it is said by those who knew him that he was a politician first and a soldier second. He represented that most dangerous of combinations, a Chief of the General Staff absorbed in Foreign Policy. What Ludendorff became in 1917, Conrad was already some ten years earlier.

Born in 1852 the son of a Colonel of Hussars, Conrad mounted steadily the grades of the Austrian army. As a lecturer and a writer upon tactics and military training he was one of those apostles of the Offensive for whom machine guns and barbed wire had prepared so many disillusions. In 1906 the Archduke Franz Ferdinand entrusted him with the reorganization of the Imperial armies and marked him out for the first military position both in peace and war. Conrad was inspired in his duties by an intense realization of the dire and increasing peril of the Empire. He saw it racked at home by racial stresses and surrounded by fierce, powerful and hungry foreign foes. Russia, Italy, Roumania and above all Serbia, seemed to him enemies who waited but for the chance to fall upon the dying Empire and carve their fortunes from its body. Russia coveted Galacia, Roumania aimed at Transylvania; Italy sought the redemption of the Tirol and the Adriatic coast; while Serbia, aspiring to found with Russian sympathy a great kingdom for the Southern Slavs, seemed to Conrad the most malignant and hateful of all. It cannot be denied that when the time came all these countries proved themselves mortal enemies of the Austrian Empire, nor that they all invaded or threatened the provinces on which their hearts were set; nor that three out of the four have gained their objects in the main, if not to the full.

Studying these strategic problems as a soldier, Conrad convinced himself that if all his country's enemies combined, ruin was certain. He wished therefore to fight them one by one. 'We must,' he said, 'take the first opportunity of reckoning with our most vulnerable enemy . . . lest our foes . . . deliver a blow.' He was 'for . . . knocking out each enemy as occasion arose, so as to be sure that they would not all set upon Austria simultaneously.' He believed in preventive wars and was convinced Austria could fight two or three in succession; first Italy, then Serbia, and so on. For nearly ten years he laid siege to the Emperor. His persistency often offended his master, and his sincerity and ability won him renewed opportunities to offend. In the end he had his way. Constant dropping wears away stone.

His power of work surpassed his physical strength. Accustomed to mountain air from long service in Tirol, he felt stifled in his room at the Ministry of War. In the frosts of winter he worked with his windows open, and his visitors caught cold. He was stern with himself, that he might be more stern with others. He courted toil and privation, and inflicted them readily upon his troops. Indeed at the manœuvres a year before the war he pressed the army so hard that the Archduke was forced to remonstrate. 'It is not necessary,' said Franz Ferdinand, 'to teach the soldiers to die in time of peace.' This dark, small, frail, thin officer with piercing and expressive eyes, set in the face of an ascetic, austere in his way of living, fearless of men and events, devoted to his profession and to the Emperor, consumed with anxiety for his country, dwelt year after year at the very centre of Europe's powder magazine in special charge of the detonators.

* * * * *

The Alliance which Bismarck had formed in 1879 between Germany and Austria had broadened into the Triple Alliance by including Italy in 1883; but the Reinsurance Treaty of 1887 between Germany and Russia freed this formidable grouping from any offensive character. It was not until Bismarck had gone that the growth of Pan-Slav feeling in Russia and the unwisdom of German policy produced the rift between Russia and Germany which led eventually to the abyss. From 1892 when the Russo-French Alliance was declared, Europe was divided in a new sense between a Triple and a Dual combination. The Anglo-French agreement of 1904 not only ended the quarrels between Great Britain and France, but drew us in consequence closer to Russia. The gradual association of Great Britain with these two countries weakened the ties which joined Italy to the Triple Alliance. In neither case was there any overt or formal change. British Ministers still proclaimed the detachment of the British Empire from European combinations, and Italian statesmen reaffirmed their loyalty to the Triple Alliance. Nevertheless there had been a double simultaneous alteration in the European balance. The dawn of the sinister twentieth century revealed a distinct confrontation of Germany and Austria by France and Russia. Between these two pairs there were deep-seated antagonisms. Henceforward the clash of Russian and Austrian interests in the Balkans flowed along the same channel as the ancient unending quarrel between Germany and France. The sun still shone brightly and the weather was fair; but there was a sharp chill in the breeze.

The war between Russia and Japan cut across the rival groupings. At first the failure of the Russians and the British association with Japan seemed to weaken the Dual Alliance to an almost fatal extent; but the ever-rising power and assertiveness of Germany and the disputes about Morocco drew the nations back to their main alignments. France and Germany had during the last quarter of the nineteenth century acquired impressive colonial possessions. England had conquered and annexed the Boer republics. All these three Powers were actively establishing themselves along the north African shore from Egypt to Morocco. The French had waived their rights and interests in Egypt in consideration of British support in Morocco. But Germany, not consulted in the Anglo-French convention, resisted fiercely the satisfaction of French claims in Morocco. The apparition of England at the Algeciras Conference and her skilful intervention had left Germany isolated with Austria as her sole ally and supporter.

Efforts for peace and international agreement were not lacking. But neither the Hague Conference of 1907, nor its predecessor of 1899, were really Peace Conferences at all. Their contribution to the maintenance of peace—apart, perhaps, from the establishment of the Hague Court—was almost negligible. They occupied themselves mainly with the rules of war, and even here they were not successful in devising codes that could stand the test of reality. This engrossing concentration on particular aspects of war set every General Staff thinking, and fomented much suspicion. No small part of our own preparations at the Committee of Imperial Defence had their origin in the ambiguities of the Hague Conventions, which compelled us to decide what our own policy should be and opened up vistas of fields still unexplored in the work of war preparation.

These remorseless developments, which nothing in the organization of the old world could control, added to the burden which Germany already bore through her own expansion and ambitions, all the insoluble problems and obscure stresses of the decaying Austro-Hungarian Empire. From this time onwards the two central Empires made common cause, and each became perforce the undiscriminating champion of the other's aims. They had been allied; they were now combined. They were now shackled. Austria vaunting her fidelity looked to the might of Germany as her means of life; and Germany with the best and strongest army in the world knew that Austria was her only friend. This vicious, fatal degeneration made the peace and civilization of mankind dependent upon the processes of disintegration and spasms of recovery which alternately racked the Hapsburg Monarchy. The quarrel about Alsace-Lorraine was reopened in Bosnia and Herzegovina. The naval antagonism between Great Britain and Germany was fomented by the passions of races who had never seen the sea. The glory and safety of Europe hung, henceforth, upon its weakest link.

CHAPTER II
THE ANNEXATION OF BOSNIA

When the Emperor Francis Joseph looked back over his long life he grieved that the Hapsburg monarchy should have lost the fair Italian provinces during his reign. The wish for some compensating gain lay deep in his heart. This was not unknown to Aerenthal who became his Foreign Minister in 1906. Aerenthal, like Conrad, brooded over the growing dangers which beset the Empire. He hoped by dexterous diplomacy to revive its strength and gratify his master. After the Russo-Turkish war of 1878 the provinces of Bosnia and Herzegovina* liberated from the Turks had been placed in the care of Austria by the Congress in Berlin. For thirty years they had been ruled from Vienna under a mandate of the signatory powers which amounted to sovereignty in all but name. Formally, however, they were still part of the Sultan's dominions. The arrangement had worked fairly well. The Sultan had ceased to mourn his loss, and Europe had come to regard the provinces as part of the Austro-Hungarian empire.

This tranquillity was disturbed by the Young Turk revolution. A government appeared in Turkey, modernist, nationalist and aggressive. The whole of the Balkans and all countries intimately concerned with Turkey were forced to review their position. If the Young Turks succeeded in reviving their decadent empire and Turkey became a strong power, might she not reclaim her rights in more than one direction? Hitherto Bosnia had enjoyed paternal rule; but if Turkey established even only in appearance a Parliamentary constitution, would it not be argued that her former provinces in Austrian charge would certainly require institutions upon at least the same level? Bulgaria, though in fact independent, was also like Egypt, a tributary province of the Turkish empire. Prince Ferdinand had long cherished the hope of becoming a king and of proclaiming the independence of Bulgaria. He too saw in the change in the character of Turkey both the need and the occasion for self-assertion. All these issues came to a head in the autumn of 1908.

The misfortunes of Russia in her war with Japan had re-awakened the Russian feelings about the Dardanelles. If the Russian Black Sea fleet had not been prevented by Article 29 of the Treaty of Berlin from passing out through the Straits, they could have joined Admiral Rozhestvenski in his tragic voyage to the Sea of Japan. And the Russian argument, erroneous but sincere, was that the battle of Tsushima might then have had a different ending. When therefore Aerenthal began to sound Russia upon the revision of Article 25 which dealt with Bosnia, it seemed that both empires might derive satisfaction from modifications of the famous Treaty. In neither case was the issue of

---

*In future they will be mentioned as Bosnia.

much practical importance. Austria already had the provinces, and both the Bosphorus and the Dardanelles had been heavily fortified by Turkey. There was, however, open to both Powers the prospect of a sentimental gain. Austria had rendered a service to Germany at Algeciras. She had been, in the Kaiser's dangerous words, 'the faithful second on the duelling ground.' Might not she expect in her turn assistance in the gratifying of her own desires?

During the summer of 1908 Aerenthal addressed himself to the Russian Foreign Minister, Isvolski, and more than one secret conversation took place between them. Isvolski, a tall fine-looking Russian, was not a particularly wary negotiator. In principle he was well disposed to Aerenthal's ambitions and ready to discuss a plan whereby Russia would not obstruct the Austrian annexation of Bosnia, provided that Austria in return supported Russia in obtaining the right of passage for her Black Sea warships through the Straits.

The Austrian Ambassador in St. Petersburg, Count Berchtold, was naturally in the centre of these affairs. He arranged a meeting between Aerenthal and Isvolski at his château at Buchlau in September 1908. It was an important occasion both for the guests and their host. A friendly talk! A great chance for Aerenthal! Here was the Foreign Minister of the one Power of all others likely to be offended by what he wanted to do. Here he was in good will and in good faith ready to talk it all over like one man of the world to another. One may blame Isvolski for treating upon these grave matters with a lack of caution in a general and easy-going manner. When men speak for mighty nations they cannot always make the conversation smooth and agreeable. But far more must we blame Aerenthal. He conceded nothing to the fair play of the world. He took every advantage; he exploited every admission and even every courtesy. He left Isvolski under the impression that they were both working together, and the next day sold him up before the whole world. There is one set of rules for people who meet as declared opponents to argue, to bargain, or if needs be to strike; there is another set for gentlemen talking in a friendly way about matters in which they seek to collaborate. Here lay the offence of Aerenthal. It was a grave offence; it has definitely restricted the intercourse of nations. Every diplomat should study this story in its minute detail; but the moral that will be drawn is one which reduces the facilities of understanding between men and states.

The conversations ended; the Buchlau visit was over. Isvolski went upon his holidays; and Aerenthal returned to Vienna. He returned to Vienna with the feeling that he had involved the Russian sufficiently to compromise his obstructive power, and that Russia anyhow would not make serious trouble about the annexation. He prepared his dossier carefully; he loaded up his press; he told the Emperor that Russia had consented, and flung the annexation of Bosnia out upon the world.

It was a bombshell. Every Chancellory in Europe recognized it as an aggressive act done in an ill-conditioned manner. Germany, who had been told nothing, was astonished, but did not withhold her support from her ally. France was cynical; Italy surprised; Russia was indignant; Turkey offended, Serbia in a frenzy and England deeply shocked. To his very vitals Sir Edward Grey was outraged. All his cherished principles were challenged.

The Whig statesman, the monitor of the public law of Europe, the English gentleman and public-school boy—all these elements in his powerful character were equally affronted. A treaty had been broken. International instruments signed by many states had been set aside by one or possibly by two. The position of the other signatories was affected. They had a right to be consulted and to express their view. A little oblivious perhaps of some newly-turned pages in our own history, he took with confidence and even relish the highest line.

The Kaiser's official comment upon the event leaves nothing to be said by others. It is a striking example of how little justice or merits counted in German pre-war politics.

'Aerenthal's performance comes to look more and more like a subaltern's rag. He told us nothing about it, gave Isvolski and Tittoni such veiled hints that they regard themselves as entirely bamboozled, showed the Sultan, who is principally concerned, no consideration at all. He has thrust the appearance of connivance with Ferdinand, the breaker of treaties and of peace, on his Master: brought the Serbs to boiling-point; irritated Montenegro to the utmost; instigated the Cretans to revolt; thrown our Turkish policy, the outcome of twenty years' hard work, on the scrap-heap; exasperated the English and promoted them to our place in Stambul; infuriated the Greeks by his friendliness towards the Bulgarians; smashed the Treaty of Berlin into smithereens and thrown the concert of the Powers into the most unholy state of discord; annoyed the Hungarians because Bosnia was to have been incorporated with them; made the Croats furious because they had designs on the incorporation of Bosnia with themselves. That performance, viewed as a whole, is a European record such as no other diplomatist has ever put to his credit. He certainly is *not* a far-seeing statesman.'[1]

This did not prevent the whole force of Germany being exerted in Aerenthal's support. The new doctrine had become 'My ally, right or wrong!'

Europe now entered upon the second of the three grave crises which were the prelude to Armageddon. England, supported by France and Russia, proposed a Conference of all the signatory Powers to review the Treaty of Berlin, and at first Austria and Germany agreed. The dispute was then transferred to the subjects to be raised. Austria declared that the annexation itself was settled beyond recall, and could not be discussed. Many objections were found to the Russian desire to open the Dardanelles to her warships. Turkey claimed effective compensation. Months passed and the tension grew. The Turks organized a most injurious boycott of Austrian goods. The 'war of pigs' began between Austria and Serbia and the price of bacon throughout the Dual Monarchy was nearly doubled. Grey's righteous censures bitterly offended Vienna. The sharpest conversations occurred between the British Ambassador and Aerenthal. 'You are responsible,' exclaimed Aerenthal, 'for all this trouble.' 'Surely it was not we,' replied the Ambassador, 'who annexed Bosnia in violation of the Treaty of Berlin?' This retort incensed Aerenthal so much that he fell back upon abuse of the British conduct towards the Boers, which our representative could only remark was irrelevant to the point at issue.

The Czar showed himself profoundly discouraged and depressed. Marchenko has given a vivid account of his audience at St. Petersburg. 'I have there,' said the Czar, pointing to his writing-table, 'quite a lot of letters from the old man (the Emperor); but all are nothing but false-hood and deceit.' Isvolski, become Aerenthal's mortal enemy, hurried to Paris and London to express his wrongs. Serbian fury mounted steadily. Their future, they declared, had been blighted by a violent and unlawful breach of an international instrument, which if it were ever to be changed should reunite them and their kith and kin in Bosnia. Popular demonstrations, challenging speeches and considerable military activity continued in Belgrade. The Austrian preparations were upon a formidable scale. The three army corps opposite the Serbian frontier were raised to almost their war strength. Night after night large numbers of troops passed stealthily through Vienna on their way to the south. A strong development of Austrian forces became apparent opposite Russia in Galicia. Meanwhile diplomacy argued about the agenda of the Conference, and the newspapers, particularly in London and Vienna, carried on a wordy strife. So the winter passed.

In March the relations between Austria and Serbia were at the breaking-point and a frontier incident of any kind would have caused war. This grave word now crept into the dispatches from all the capitals. If Austria invaded Serbia, Europe would be set on fire, and where would the conflagration stop? Could the Czar, however peacefully inclined himself, however unready his army, hold back the popular surge in Russia which the chastisement of Serbia at Austria's law-breaking hands would certainly evoke? If Russia marched or was marched upon, what would Germany do? And France? The relations of the various alliances were limited on paper by important conditions. Germany was not bound to support Austria in an aggressive war, nor was France pledged to Russia in a quarrel which did not involve Germany. But the ties between Austria and Germany had grown stronger since the Algeciras Conference, and since the friendship of the Kaiser and the Archduke Franz Ferdinand. No one could feel any assurance that Germany would be anxious to find a technical excuse for not standing by her faithful ally. An alarming incident which had occurred between the French and Germans at Casablanca might serve as a ready pretext for widening the area of the struggle in harmony with what were believed to be the German military plans for a war on two fronts. Clemenceau ruled in France, and his conduct in these anxious weeks showed an iron composure; but it was certain that no direct challenge would be lightly offered to France while he sat there.

Sir Edward Grey had from the outset made it clear that Great Britain would not go beyond diplomatic action upon the dispute in the Near East. He declined absolutely to discuss what action Great Britain would take if the general European catastrophe occurred. In fact he made the same sort of moves as he was afterwards to repeat in July, 1914. This was the strongest policy open to him; for neither the Cabinet nor Parliament would have tolerated any decided declaration. For this reason, as we re-read the correspondence of this period, it may perhaps be argued that Great Britain sought to play rather too prominent a part upon a stage which had become so deadly. If we were not prepared to run the same risks as the other actors, ought we not to have stood more aloof? But all his action was loyal and skilful, and aimed only at peace and parley and the patient assertion of treaties.

In those days the two armed groups into which Europe was divided had not yet become camps. Neither the Triple Alliance nor 'the Triple Entente,' as the term ran, were knit together as they afterwards became, nor were they united upon the questions at stake. Great Britain, though resolute to support Russia diplomatically, was not enthusiastic about opening the Straits. Italy thought more of her antagonisms against Austria than of her membership of the Triple Alliance. France maintained an attitude of impenetrable reserve; but we may be sure that the most fateful contingencies were not those which were least present in the minds of her political and military chiefs. When we study this long-drawn crisis with after knowledge, we see how near Europe was to the abyss into which she was to plunge six years later. In March Aerenthal demanded of Serbia that she should cease her warlike preparations and forthwith publicly recognize the annexation of Bosnia. Serbia, encouraged by Russian sympathy, and to some extent by the countenance which Great Britain had given to her complaints, was by no means willing to submit. Nothing, it was said in Belgrade, could annihilate the Serbian race. Invasion, conquest, were lesser evils than the repudiation of its destiny. It was at this moment that Germany struck.

On March 22 Count Pourtalés, the German Ambassador in St. Petersburg, handed a brief written communication to Isvolski couched in urgent and peremptory terms. Unless Russia immediately recognized the annexation of Bosnia and persuaded Serbia to do likewise, Germany would let Austria loose upon Serbia, and a war would follow, in which Germany would sustain her ally to any extent that might be necessary. Isvolski, thunderstruck, hesitated to speak. 'Very well,' said the German, 'then it will be war.' Isvolski on this said he would consult his colleagues and the Czar. The Russian Council of State sat for four hours that same day. In the evening Russia submitted unconditionally to the German demand. She did not even consult with France or England. The Czar and his ministers believed probably with good reason that even a day's delay would be fatal. They saw themselves about to be attacked and invaded by Germany and Austria. Their army was still recovering from the disasters of the Manchurian campaigns. The revolutionary movement which had shaken the throne and the Russian state had scarcely subsided. This was no time to stand on dignity. Five years before France had dismissed Delcassé in the same dire plight. Now Russia in her turn must answer the stern Teuton summons, 'Obey or fight.' Russia obeyed.

When on the 25th a similar request somewhat differently framed was made by Germany to Sir Edward Grey in London, he handed the German Ambassador, Count Metternich, the following brief memorandum upon which the Liberal Cabinet had agreed:

'The assurance of a readiness to accept Baron d'Aerenthal's declaration respecting the annexation at a future conference affects only one of the various questions which have been raised by the action of Austria last autumn. At the present moment

His Majesty's Government are deeply interested in the preservation of the peace of Europe and therefore in a settlement of the Serbian crisis in particular. The assurance for which the German Government ask while involving an alteration of the Treaty of Berlin leaves the Serbian question unsettled and makes no provision for the solution of other questions relating to the Treaty of Berlin in which England and the other European Powers are equally interested. *His Majesty's Government are not disposed to give the assurance required until the Serbian question has been settled in a pacific manner on lines satisfactory to them and the other Powers and until a solution has been assured of other questions arising from the annexation of Bosnia by Austria especially the alteration of Article 29.** When this result has been obtained His Majesty's Government will be ready to agree to any peaceful settlement based on mutual good-will amongst the Powers.'[2]

Metternich read the paper with surprise and deepening gloom. 'This is a very grave decision,' he said, 'which imperils peace.' 'I replied,' said Grey, 'that this could only mean that Austria intended to attack Serbia, or to dictate terms to her, if we did not do what Austria asked. The British Government would never consent to act under pressure of this kind.' Thus for the first time the opposing wills of Germany and Great Britain met squarely. The two Governments seemed to look into each other's eyes. A silence followed. This action was taken by Great Britain with the knowledge of the Russian collapse, and without seeking aid from France. Girt with the sea and her naval supremacy as yet unchallenged, she could afford to preserve her self-respect if need be in isolation. She was not in the cage with the eagles.

None the less, all resistance to the wishes of the Teutonic allies was at an end. Sir Edward Grey could do no more than arrange the form of reply which Serbia would have to make to the Austrian demand in terms as little wounding to Serbia as possible. It was only with difficulty that Aerenthal was induced to allow Serbia to include the phrase '*sure of the peaceful intentions of Austria-Hungary*, Serbia will bring her army back to the condition of the spring of 1908.' He was anxious that it should be clear to all that she had submitted under duress. With this concession Serbia had to be content. She formally declared that she abandoned all protest against the annexation of Bosnia, and promised to live with Austria-Hungary in the future as a good neighbour. A convention was also drawn up between Bulgaria and Turkey in which Turkey recognized the independence of Bulgaria. All the Great Powers thereupon signified their agreement unconditionally to the modification of Article 25 of the Treaty of Berlin and recognized the annexation of Bosnia. No satisfaction of any kind was provided for Russia from Article 29. She was left to ponder upon events. Isvolski, deeply humiliated before Europe and blamed by his countrymen for exposing Russia to the worst rebuff she had suffered in living memory in time of peace, was only sustained by the indulgence of the Czar; and that only for a time. In 1910 he quitted the Ministry

---

*My italics. W. S. C.

of Foreign Affairs and became Ambassador in Paris. Here also he had a part to play. Aerenthal's triumph was thus complete.

Sir Arthur Nicolson, British Ambassador at St. Petersburg, writing while the impression of the Russian submission was strong upon him, said:

'After this easy victory, I should not be surprised if greater demands were made of Russia. . . . My firm opinion is that both Germany and Austria are carrying out a line of policy and action carefully prepared and thought out. Algeciras had to be revenged: the "ring" broken through and the Triple Entente dissipated. . . . The Franco-Russian alliance has not borne the test: and the Anglo-Russian entente is not sufficiently strong or sufficiently deep-rooted to have any appreciable influence. The hegemony of the Central Powers will be established in Europe, and England will be isolated. The activity in building up the German navy is significant; and the sudden entry of Germany on the scene here is also significant. When we have passed through the present *Sturm und Drang* period, I should not be surprised if we were to find both France and Russia gravitating rapidly towards the Central Powers, as neither of the former, distrustful of each other, feels that she can stand alone against the power of the central combination. . . . The ultimate aims of Germany surely are, without doubt, to obtain the preponderance on the continent of Europe, and when she is strong enough, and apparently she is making very strenuous efforts to become so, she will enter on a contest with us for maritime supremacy. In past times we have had to fight Holland, Spain and France for this supremacy, and personally I am convinced that sooner or later, we shall have to repeat the same struggle with Germany.'[3]

Such were the reflections of this eminent and accomplished diplomatist, soon after to become the head of the British Foreign Office. They were surely serious conclusions to spring from the trumpery change involved in converting Austria's sovereignty of Bosnia from fact into form. For all the evils brought to the structure of European peace by this episode, Aerenthal was alone to blame. He could have gained his point in all probability without serious friction. He could have carried Isvolski with him if he had treated him with ordinary consideration, or even good faith. His craft and ineptitude had made his victory dear-bought.

Some of the reactions expected by Nicolson were not to occur. Russia considered that she had a powerful friend to gain in Britain. The relations of the two countries became more intimate. The reorganization and expansion of the Russian army proceeded and her strategic railways, fed by French loans, grew steadily. The Czar undertook a journey of state to Italy by a route which in spite of pressing invitations meticulously avoided setting foot upon Austrian soil. His meeting with the King of Italy at Racconigi proclaimed that common interests existed between the two countries. Germany persevered with ever-increasing energy in her plan of building a fleet of which 'the strongest navy in the world' should stand in awe; and Great Britain, after some internal disputing, laid in the single year of 1909 the keels of no less than eight Dreadnought battleships unsurpassed for size and power. During that year the naval rivalry and its consequent tension between Germany and Great Britain became the dominant fact in Europe. The cleavages in the structure of Europe were no longer even concealed. Italy became noticeably detached from the Central Empires. Germany and Austria drew more tightly together; and France, Russia and Great Britain began to be united by individual injuries and common dangers.

CHAPTER III
TOWARDS THE ABYSS

Nearly five years intervened between the annexation of Bosnia and the crisis which led to the World War. They were years of acutely increasing tension marked at intervals by shocks and tremors. On two occasions, as we can now see, Europe must have come very near to the brink. The processes of decay or disruption in the Austro-Hungarian empire, the effort of Ottoman revival, and the growth of the power and assertiveness of the Balkan states were all continuous. The characteristic of this period is that Austria had now to deal with a Russia profoundly estranged. Beneath the surface of correct diplomacy and much superficial affability all the nations of Europe steadily and rapidly increased and perfected their armaments by sea and land.

In the spring of 1911 a French expedition occupied Fez. This development of the Anglo-French agreement about Morocco irritated German feeling. Some small German commercial interests were alleged to exist around a sandy bay on the Atlantic coast of Morocco called Agadir. The new German Foreign Minister, Count von Kiderlen-Waechter, brought these claims to the notice of the French government. The French declared with truth that there were no German interests at Agadir, nor in its hinterland— not a harbour, not a trading establishment, not a house, not a bale of goods, not a German! Nevertheless, recognizing that Germany had some grievance about French expansion in Morocco they were prepared to offer some territorial compensation in the Congo basin. As for Agadir they proposed a joint visit of accredited French and German representatives to the desolate spot in order to examine the facts or want of facts about the German interests there. Suddenly on July 1 it was announced that the German Emperor had sent a gunboat, the *Panther*, to maintain and protect German interests at Agadir. The *Panther* was already on her way.

The alarm which this abrupt, but otherwise trifling action caused throughout Europe is the measure of the strain of those times. The act of Germany might mean nothing or everything. If it meant nothing, why was it done? Clearly it was intended to raise large issues. July and August were dangerous months. By the middle of August the harvests of Europe are largely gathered and the stubble fields are cleared for war. If Germany intended to pick a quarrel with unlimited consequences July 1 was a convenient military date to choose for opening the debate. After the long story of Bismarck's calculated and successful wars and the various later episodes which have been here recorded, culminating in the summary treatment of Russia in April 1909 and the German Emperor's 'shining armour' speech about it, none of the Chancelleries or General Staffs of Europe could exclude the gravest possibilities from their minds. France became intensely alert and every German movement was watched with silent but profound attention. The British Admiralty, whose eye was already fixed upon German activities at Madeira and in the

Canaries, drew the notice of the Foreign Office to the effect which a German naval base on the Atlantic seaboard of Africa would have upon our food and trade routes between South Africa and South America. When Count Metternich mentioned the subject to Sir Edward Grey he was told at once that the situation was so important that it must be considered by the Cabinet; and on July 5 he was further informed that the Cabinet could not disinterest themselves in Morocco, and that until German intentions were made known the British attitude must be one of reserve. This vague but weighty declaration, all the more significant because of the small action which had called it forth, was received in absolute silence by the German Government so far as we were concerned. For some weeks not another word was spoken on the subject between the two countries.

Meanwhile the telegrams which passed to and fro between the different capitals became increasingly obscure and perplexing. Mr. Lloyd George, then Chancellor of the Exchequer, was gravely alarmed. Hitherto he had headed that section of the Cabinet which was predominantly opposed even to the consideration of war in any form. On July 21, however, with the agreement of the Prime Minister and Sir Edward Grey, he interpolated in his speech as Chancellor to the Bankers' Association at the Mansion House an extremely stiff warning to Germany of the dangers which might attend the further progress of her policy. The actual passage, the point of which was entirely lost upon his City audience, was as follows:

'If a situation were to be forced upon us in which peace could only be preserved by the surrender of the great and beneficent position Britain has won by centuries of heroism and achievement, by allowing Britain to be treated where her interests were vitally affected as if she were of no account in the Cabinet of nations, then I say emphatically that peace at that price would be a humiliation intolerable for a great country like ours to endure.'

Germany was not only startled but staggered by this challenging utterance. No government not separated by salt water from the German Army would have dared to utter such words. Following as it did upon the large increases in the British Navy, it revealed an unmistakable antagonism alike to German ambitions and methods. Accustomed to have French Ministers dismissed at his order, the Kaiser immediately sent a fierce and menacing protest through his Ambassador. 'After the speech of the Chancellor of the Exchequer, no explanation could be made by Germany. If France should repel the hand offered her by the Emperor's Government, the dignity of Germany would compel her to secure by all means the full respect by France for German Treaty rights.' 'Mr. Lloyd George's speech, to say the least, was a warning to Germany's address and had, as a matter of fact, been interpreted by the presses of Great Britain and France as a warning bordering on menace.' Sir Edward Grey replied at once that in view of the tone of the German communication he also was not prepared to offer any explanation. Orders were immediately given to secure the British fleet against surprise attacks.

There is no doubt that in the weeks that followed the Kaiser and his Government measured and weighed the issues of war and peace. They were not used to coming in contact with powers outside the sweep of their sword. They felt they had been openly confronted with a will as stern as their own. They decided eventually that the occasion was not propitious. But as August passed away there were so many reports of German military movements, particularly in the garrisons along the Belgian frontier, that both anxiety and suppressed excitement grew in the Foreign Office and the War Office. The Committee of Imperial Defence on August 23 made a prolonged examination of the military and naval problems likely to be raised by a General European War in which Great Britain might be engaged. This was the first time that such a possibility had ever been squarely faced by the Liberal Government. Colonel, afterwards Field-Marshal Sir Henry Wilson, the Director of Military Operations, explained in close detail, and, as it proved, with perfect accuracy, the German plan of invading France through Belgium, and the part that would be played by the British expeditionary army should Parliament decide to become the ally of France. He also gave an appreciation of the Russian military strength, plans and mobilization time-table which was found disappointing by those who had considered Russia an armed Colossus, but which also turned out to be true.

The British and French Staffs who had been in contact since the Algeciras Conference of 1908 remained in the closest association during these weeks. Most of the leading officers of the British Army had long been convinced that war with Germany sooner or later was certain, and all held that we should without hesitation stand at the side of France, if she were attacked. It was obvious that both the Foreign Office and the General Staff considered the position to be one of acute danger at the moment, and of increasing difficulty in the future. The Cabinet did not share these views and Parliament, unaware of the facts, would instantly have repudiated them.

By the end of September the situation became easier and an agreement between France and Germany was reached based upon territorial compensations in the Congo. It was plain from the resignation of the German Colonial Minister that there had been a severe internal struggle in the German governing organism. Differences of view were found to exist between the General Staff and the Admiralty and an impression was sustained by the Prime Minister and his Government that the disposition of the fleet at the beginning of the crisis had left much to be desired. As the result of these pressures I became First Lord of the Admiralty in October and thereafter devoted myself exclusively to the preparation of the fleet for war and to securing its instant readiness. The German Government announced its intention of making further important increases in the Army and Navy.

Sudden and grim as had been this confrontation of Agadir, in an odd way it improved the relations between Germany and Great Britain. As soon as the crisis was over, we set to work to bridge the gulf which gaped between the two countries. We did not wish the inevitable German naval expansion to become a further cause of dispute. We therefore arranged that Mr. Haldane should visit Berlin and explain our naval point of view and intentions to the Kaiser. We also sought to interest Germany in some colonial negotiations which would be to her advantage. All this was done to try to establish relations of mutual respect with even the hopes of goodwill. Amicable conversations ensued about the most delicate and serious naval issues. The policy to which I obtained the assent of the Cabinet was, in brief, to announce a five-years' programme of Dreadnought ship-building which would secure a superiority of sixteen ships to ten over any existing German naval programme, and an additional construction of two ships to every one that Germany should build under any new naval law. Dominion and colonial Dreadnoughts would be additional and we declared an intention to maintain our cruisers and flotillas at double the German strength. Alternatively we offered to have a naval holiday in which no British or German capital ship should be laid down for a year; or if possible to space out the programmes of both countries so as to leave a blank year between two annual quotas.

The naval holiday was rejected by Germany and she proceeded with her naval law. But in consequence of the frank and friendly talks which had taken place, both the German increases and our counter-building, which were punctually executed, caused no bickering. Indeed, they were accompanied year by year by the increasing retirement of the naval issue from Anglo-German controversies. I held strongly that the Germans would understand a plain, straightforward policy of this kind, courteously deployed and strictly carried out; that they would not resent the fact, but would accept it. This proved true. The Kaiser and Tirpitz realized that they would never have any chance of overtaking us, and that we were bent upon an overwhelming superiority at sea. They accommodated themselves to this, turned with interest to the colonial discussions and in all the troubles of 1912 and 1913 worked hand in hand with Sir Edward Grey to keep the peace. Never, in fact, had the relations of Great Britain and Germany been so little strained or indeed so promising as they were a fortnight before the great disaster. But for this détente Europe might not even have surmounted the unceasing strains and stresses which the next three years brought upon her from the Near East.*

On the other hand, France and Russia of course took note of the strong, independent, self-reliant attitude of Great Britain and began to reckon her as a real factor on which they could count in case of German aggression.

In this same July 1911, Italy exposed her intention of taking from the Turks the ancient Roman province of Libya known as Tripoli. During the Agadir crisis she continually pressed this demand upon the Turks. In September she sent an ultimatum and on October 5 an Italian expeditionary force seized the town of Tripoli and a strip of the seashore thereabouts. Turkey and Italy were thenceforward at war. Europe remained dumb in the face of this unjustified act. The Central Empires could not afford to lose the fact, nor France and Russia the prospect, of an Italian alliance. The Young Turks resisted the outrage with spirit. Enver himself made his way to Libya and animated the defence. Large Italian forces were for a long time held up on the beach. Here was the heaven- or hell-sent opportunity for which Conrad had waited so long. Here should be the first and most important of his preventive wars. Ever since 1899 when he went to command the garrison at Trieste, he had distrusted Italy and longed for the chance of regaining Venetia and Lombardy for the Empire. 'While Cabinets at Vienna and Berlin treated the alliance with Italy as a secure factor, I characterized it as a gross fallacy; I saw in Italy the enemy in all circumstances and compared the Triple

---

*A full account will be found in *The World Crisis, 1911–1914*.

Alliance to a three-legged table which must collapse if one of the legs gave way.' The antagonism was indeed profound: on the one hand the cause of *Italia Irredenta*, on the other the Austro-Hungarian Alsace-Lorraine. For years Conrad had persisted in urging a war with Italy. From the end of 1910 he became vehement. Italy, he declared, would be ready for war in 1912. It was folly to wait. Aerenthal rejoined that the Triple Alliance did not fall to be renewed till 1914. Conrad asserted that the alliance was a fraud. But now, seeing Italy compromised and entangled on the Libyan shore, he addressed a lengthy memorial to the Emperor declaring 'that Austria's opportunity had come and that it was suicidal to leave the opportunity unutilized.' Aerenthal, though patient with his fiery coadjutor, was at length aroused. He wrote to the Emperor that 'it was high time the foreign minister should remain competent and responsible for foreign policy. The duty of the Chief of the Staff was to make the military preparations requisite for the various possibilities of war, but without any right to influence as to which possibility should arise.'

The Archduke, by now hostile to Aerenthal, sustained Conrad's personal position, though he did not agree with his war policy. The full force of the dispute fell upon the Emperor. He had no doubts at all. He saw plainly that Austria's mainstay must be Germany and if Germany did not wish to quarrel with Italy, neither must he. Germany could not afford to estrange Italy. He could not afford to estrange Germany. On September 27 Baron Bolfras, by the Emperor's directions, interviewed Conrad. H.M. wishes 'to have order and normal intercourse' between Conrad and Aerenthal. Conrad should 'write a couple of lines to Aerenthal to say that he regretted that the matter had been thus set forth.' Conrad replied that before writing an apology to 'the Aerenthal' (*dem Ährenthal*) he would 'rather have his right hand cut off.'

He had always been upright and 'now in my old age I do not bow myself.' The furthest he would come was 'if H.M. requires peace between Aerenthal and me, I propose that we say, what has been, has been; a line will be drawn under it and the matter is then done with.' He added that he had never in his life had to apologize, and that the Archduke had strictly forbidden him to resign. Bolfras, after bewailing the stony path of mediators, reported the conversation to the Emperor and Conrad carried his tale to the Archduke. On October 8 Conrad handed a further memorial to the Emperor urging military measures against Italy and on the 17th he received a reply in brief and general terms of the sharpest character. 'His department,' he was told, 'was to strive for the utmost readiness for war,' while the Foreign Minister 'in knowledge of the same conducted his own affairs in accordance with His Majesty's will and in agreement with the two Minister-Presidents.' On November 15 Conrad was received by the Emperor, when the following conversation ensued.

The Emperor, 'very excited and very angry,' reproved Conrad.

H.M. I say at once, the continual attacks on Aerenthal—these pin-pricks—I forbid them.

Conrad. I beg Your Majesty to permit me to state my views as I now hold them; Your Majesty then decides.

H.M. These continual attacks, especially the reproaches regarding Italy and the Balkans which go on being repeated, are directed against Me; the policy is made by Me; it is My policy.

Conrad. I can only repeat that I wrote down my views just as I arrived at them. Your Majesty can of course mark them 'wrong.' That is in Your Majesty's power.

H.M. My policy is the policy of peace. To this policy of mine all must accommodate themselves. My foreign Minister conducts My policy in this sense. It is indeed possible that this war may come; probable too. But it will not be waged until Italy attacks us.

Conrad. If only the chances are then still in our favour!

H.M. So long as Italy does not attack us, this war will not be made. We have never had a 'War Party' at all hitherto.

Conrad. Those whose duty it is to see to it that all is ready if war breaks out, so that we do not come into a difficult situation from the outset, may not utter the word 'war,' for otherwise they will be accused of belonging to the War Party.

H.M. Prepared, one must be.[4]

The Emperor then proceeded to aim a shaft at the Archduke. He criticized the bellicose attitude which the German Crown Prince had revealed to the Reichstag. 'That will indeed not happen with us; but there are indications of it.'

This stormy audience could but be a preliminary to dismissal. A fortnight later Conrad, again summoned to Schönbrunn, was relieved of his post and transferred to an Inspector-Generalship of the Army. 'The reason,' said Francis Joseph, 'is well known to you and it is not necessary to talk about it.'

His Majesty, says Conrad, was pleased to say that our personal relations had become 'most friendly,' and he had sent for me in order himself to intimate my dismissal, because the direct way appeared to him the best.

His Majesty then paused, in the evident expectation that I should speak.

Conrad. I most humbly thank Your Majesty; I too have always only gone the direct way.

H.M. Then we have both acted alike and we part as friends.

Upon this I was dismissed.[5]

The Ballplatz lost no time in informing the Italians of Aerenthal's victory over Conrad, and all immediate tension ceased between the two allies.

In February 1912 Aerenthal died. His work was done; he had had a few months of excitement and triumph; he had secured a ceremonial satisfaction for his country; but the price was heavy, and through his own short-sighted sharp dealing, needlessly heavy. He could have gained all he sought far more easily by treating Isvolski like a gentleman. He had invoked the might of Germany against Russia upon a minor question. He had used a steam-hammer to crack a nut. Until 1907 he had followed the cardinal maxim of Bismarck, namely that every step taken by Austria in the Balkans should be preceded by agreement with Russia. In 1908 he had suddenly discarded this wisdom. He had embroiled Austria and Russia; he had poisoned the relations between the two neighbouring empires who could so readily with mutual advantage have disentangled and cherished their interests in the Near East. He had involved Russia in a public humiliation which the ruling forces constituting public opinion around the Czar would never forget. He was fortunate not to live to endure the outcome.

Aerenthal was succeeded by the late Austrian Ambassador at St. Petersburg, Count Berchtold, the owner of the château at Buchlau where the unlucky conversations with Isvolski had occurred. Berchtold was one of the smallest men who ever held a great position. His calibre and outlook were those of a clever Foreign Office clerk of junior rank, accustomed to move a great deal in fashionable society. Fop, dandy, la-di-da; amiable, polite and curiously un-self-seeking; immensely rich; magnate of a noble house; habitué of the Turf and of the Clubs; unproved in any grave political issue; yet equipped with the all-too-intensive training of a chess-board diplomatist; thus conditioned Berchtold fell an easy prey. He was allured by the glamour and force of the military men, and fascinated by the rattle and glitter of their terrible machines. We gaze with mournful wonder upon his doubting eyes and his weak, half-constructed jaw; we contemplate a human face in which there is no element of symmetry or massiveness. We are appalled that from such lips should have issued commands more fateful to the material fortunes of mankind than any spoken by the greatest sovereigns, warriors, jurists, philosophers and statesmen of the past. Berchtold is the epitome of this age when the affairs of Brobdingnag are managed by the Lilliputians.

Since her painful experience in 1909 Russia had lain low, but neither her military preparations nor her diplomacy had been idle. A war between Italy and Turkey seemed to favour a renewed Russian effort to obtain that privileged freedom of the Dardanelles for her warships which had so long been a prime object of Muscovite desire. Russia now offered Turkey in distress a defensive alliance modelled upon the Treaty of Unkiar Skelessi of 1833. Territorial changes likely to involve other Great Powers were excluded. The Russians offered to guarantee 'the maintenance of the present regime in the Straits of the Bosphorous and the Dardanelles. The Ottoman Government were to promise not to oppose the passage of Russian warships through the Straits provided that these ships did not stop in the Straits or only by agreement.' There was no basis for such an arrangement. Deep-rooted in the heart of the Turks was fear of Russia. In Russia they saw the probable destroyer of the Turkish Empire. In the Russian territories of the Caucasus they saw the greatest prize that Turkey could win by a victorious war. The Young Turk leaders were saturated with these ideas. Indeed they had already resolved that should the long-predicted European war break out, and Russia find herself at grips with Germany, they would invade the Caucasus with their principal armies. As this operation required the Turkish command of the Black Sea, it was necessary for them to become a naval power. They had already raised largely by public subscription the funds to purchase two Dreadnought battleships, the orders for which had been placed in England. They were therefore much embarrassed by the Russian proposal, and on learning that Great Britain and France were in no way pressing it, they rejected the overture with promptitude.

This second rebuff to Russian diplomacy led M. Sazonov, who had now succeeded Isvolski, into a remarkable change of front. Under his guidance Russia set herself actively to form a league of the Balkan states against Turkey. The elements for such a confederacy were certainly not lacking. History reeked with the wrongs which Montenegro, Bulgaria and Greece had suffered at Turkish hands. By the desperate struggles of generations they had freed themselves from Turkish yoke. Now the old oppressor still in control of many Christian provinces was in the toils. This was the moment to settle old scores and acquire new possessions. It needed only the influence of a Great Power which had long warred with the Turks to unite them in an effective alliance. Indeed it may well be that Russian diplomacy was only encouraging the Balkan states to do what they had already resolved.

On October 8, 1912, Montenegro declared war upon Turkey. Serbian, Bulgarian and Greek declarations followed in a few days. The hardy and dauntless men who had seized power in Turkey marshalled their utmost resources to resist this dangerous combination of their hated foes. The course of the war was swift and its results unexpected. To no class had the crushing Turkish defeats come with more surprise than to the military experts. Conrad had always thought poorly of the Serbians. The German General Liman von Sanders at the head of a military mission was actually reorganizing the Turkish army and the staff in Berlin were confident of Turkish successes. In high British military circles an inveterate distrust of the Greeks as fighting men lay joined with their traditional liking and partisanship for the Turks.

All these authorities were stultified by the event. The Greek army, which twenty years before had fled incontinently, now advanced with energy and speed in spite of heavy losses. The Bulgarians fought with the utmost skill and valour. But it was to the despised Serbians that the principal merit was ascribed. Not only did their troops fight skilfully and well, but their field artillery and heavy guns, trained and supplied by the French, played a decisive part both upon the battlefields and in the siege of Adrianople. By Christmas the Bulgarian army stood before the lines of Chatalja and King Ferdinand was dreaming of a triumphal entry into Constantinople. But while the Bulgarians had been fighting in Thrace, the Greeks had reached Salonica and the Serbians Cavalla. A general victory was no sooner assured than the conquerors were at each other's throats. Bulgaria, behaving in a most arrogant manner, found herself opposed by Serbia and Greece. Fierce fighting broke out in February 1913. The Greeks and Serbians fell upon their late ally. Overweighted by numbers and exhausted with her losses against Turkey, Bulgaria reeled before this onslaught. At this moment Roumania, which had taken no part in the war, invaded Bulgaria from the rear and conquered the Dobruja. Bulgaria, crushed and cowed by overwhelming strength, made such terms as were possible. She was deprived of almost all conquests, barred from the sea and stripped by Roumania of the very province from which her most famous and most heavily-smitten division of soldiers had come. In the confusion Enver Pasha had returned from Libya. He advanced with inexhaustible audacity and recovered Adrianople. On these accomplished facts the Treaty of Bucharest was eventually made.

All the reactions of these two Balkan wars were evil. The German Government and especially the Kaiser were most disagreeably impressed. Their long wooing of Turkey, their vaunted support, had only accompanied the Ottoman Empire to its greatest disaster. The fact that they had trained or at least had been the patrons of the Turkish army, while the French had supervised the technical preparations of Serbia and Greece, was unpalatable to the German General Staff. But the vexation of Austria was indescribable. The Serbians had not only proved their prowess in the field, they had doubled their area and increased their population by at least two-thirds. All the confident expectations of Vienna and Budapest that Serbia would be beaten by the Turks in the first Balkan war and by the Bulgarians in the second, were proved false. They found themselves face to face with the ambitions and hostility of that Greater Serbia whose very existence threatened the vitals of the empire. Russian elation inflamed the Austrian wrath. It was common talk in Vienna that a world war would come unless something happened to modify the 'unwholesome effect' of the Peace of Bucharest.

The Serbian troops in the course of the war had reached the Adriatic and the Serbian Government stridently proclaimed their intention of keeping the Albanian coast as their 'window upon the sea.' The Austrians refused to tolerate this, and although the Kaiser derided the idea of a war for a 'few Albanian goat-pastures,' war between Austria and Serbia was only averted by the prodigious labours of all the Great Powers assembled in London and especially by the co-operation of Great Britain and Germany.

Conrad, banished from the Council chamber to a military command, had no official influence upon the policy. He distributed to the principal personages in power a series of Essays by 'an onlooker' at 'epoch-making events which no patriot can view with indifference.' He strenuously urged war with Serbia simultaneously with mobilization against Russia. He acquired great influence with Berchtold. The war spirit which dominated the rank and fashion in Vienna during the winter of 1912 and throughout 1913 was favourable to him. In December 1912 he was once more appointed Chief of the General Staff by Imperial decree. He ceaselessly ingeminated war. On December 14: 'If the Monarchy means to resolve the question which touches its life interests, the best means appears to make war *now* against Serbia despite all qualms.' On December 23: 'Sole means to a solution: overthrow Serbia by war undismayed by consequences. . . . Though the Entente Powers together with Serbia may be strong enough jointly to threaten the Monarchy, yet we are powerful enough to confront these states with the choice of a general war of which the most important among them are in fact afraid.' On December 30 to the Archduke: 'We have reached the point where there is a trial of strength between the Monarchy and Serbia. It is a trial which must be seen through. All else—Albania, harbour question, consular question, trade agreements, etc.—are side-issues.' His appeals were supported by the new War Minister, Krobatin, and by Potiorek, the Governor of Bosnia, who wrote fatuously: 'But in God's name anyhow no rotten peace. Better a defeat on the battlefield in a struggle with a Great Power than that.' This was not in the end to be denied him.

However, the Hapsburg royalties did not share the excitement of their generals and statesmen. The Emperor remained immovable. Again and again he repulsed Conrad's demands, using such phrases as 'Even in politics one should stick to the rules of decency'; 'That would mean war, and I am against war'; 'That must not be done without a great deal of forethought'; 'We must do nothing without mature reflection.' With such replies did the vigorous, clear-headed octogenarian restrain the fierce currents of the times. In all these views he was supported by the Archduke. Francis Ferdinand's influence had restored Conrad to his post; but the Archduke would not accept his policy. His attitude in February was thus described to Conrad by his Equerry, Bardolff: 'The Heir to the Throne has sounded the retreat all along the line. In no circumstances will he have war against Russia. He will not consent to it. From Serbia, not a plum-tree, not a sheep. He demands demobilization of the reserves.' Berchtold under this august influence changed his own attitude with agility, and when Conrad came to him for sympathy and support blandly told him: 'I would never put my name to war against Russia. The Archduke Francis Ferdinand is absolutely against war.'

The cause of all this virtue and wisdom is not obscure. One single reason had decided the Emperor and his Heir. They had been left in no doubt that William II did not mean to fight. The Kaiser had conveyed this opinion to them both in the most forceful and confidential manner. They knew that without him they could do nothing. From their highest station and with their direct proprietary interests at stake, they viewed facts in truer proportions than their servants and advisers, and their control of the empire was effective. The peace of Europe during 1913 rested solely upon the Kaiser's 'No.' One hand only held the key that could unloose the deluge. From the moment that Austria had quarrelled with Russia, William II had the Dual Monarchy in his power. While his veto stood the world was safe.

It now remains to examine the causes and events which led to that veto being withdrawn.

CHAPTER IV
THE MURDER OF THE ARCHDUKE

The year 1914 opened cool and calm. The Anglo-German co-operation in Near Eastern affairs and the progress of the colonial Treaty had soothed the anxiety and suspicions of the British Cabinet. Indeed I had encountered in the previous autumn the most stubborn resistance to the Navy estimates necessary to fulfil our declared programmes against Germany. The Chancellor of the Exchequer, in the opposite mood from his Agadir speech, headed the formidable opposition of a majority of the Cabinet. I made it clear that unless the programmes were maintained, I should resign. Christmas brought an interlude to this sternly fought internal controversy. On January 3 Mr. Lloyd George published an interview in the *Daily Chronicle* in which he denounced the folly of expenditure upon armaments, referred pointedly to the resignation of Lord Randolph Churchill in 1886 on the subject of economy, and declared that the state and prospects of the world were never more peaceful. I had spent my holiday near Biarritz and returning through Paris met President Poincaré and some of the leading Ministers. I was impressed by a certain air of uneasiness in these circles. Mr. Lloyd George's interview seemed to have disturbed them.

As the year advanced the belief of our Cabinet that dangers were passing away grew steadily. I carried the full naval estimates through the Cabinet only by the fact that the adverse majority did not wish to face my resignation as First Lord of the Admiralty, and the violent agitation that would have followed, when they were about to be embroiled in the fiercest part of the Irish quarrel. Even the vigilant watch-dogs of the Foreign Office were at ease. Both Houses of Parliament comported themselves as if foreign affairs did not exist. The sanguine mood of the British Government found its counterpart in the French chamber. The Parties of the left held sway. Keen efforts were made to modify the law of Three Years' military service which had been passed in 1913. Indeed it was only maintained by a compromise which released the third-year soldiers while calling up two new contingents of recruits in their place. This year, for the first time since 1870, the French President dined at the German Embassy. This year, for the first time for nineteen years, we accepted a German invitation for the visit of a British squadron to Kiel during the regatta week in June. We confided four of our finest battleships to the Kaiser's hospitality. We sent at the same time four battle-cruisers to Cronstadt to pay a like courtesy to the Russians.

But under the surface the relationships of the Great Powers were ceaselessly hardening. The enlargements and improvements of the Russian army and the building of military railways proceeded apace. France had in one form or another consented to the enormous sacrifices of the Three Years' Law. Germany was not only increasing her army and navy, but by a capital tax of fifty millions sterling was purchasing war materials and manufacturing munitions and equipment with intense activity. The importations into Germany of all the rare metals needed for the hardening of steel and the making of the weapons and appliances of war—if we had only known it—tungsten, aluminium, vanadium, nickel, antimony, manganese, exceeded in 1914 alone the aggregate totals of the previous three years. Wordy battles were fought between German and Russian newspapers and professors in which all sorts of disagreeable and ugly recriminations were exchanged. The Russian War Minister inspired statements about the growing efficiency of the Russian armies. In the summer Sir Edward Grey asked me to arrange conversations between the First Sea Lord, Prince Louis of Battenberg and the Russian naval authorities similar to those which had taken place at intervals since 1906 between the French and British General staffs. The topics discussed were minor, but the event was significant, and meant to be significant. A good deal of vague war-talk was rife in German military circles. Still the forces of peace seemed to be more than holding their own, and both in Great Britain and France party politics and bitter faction held the stage.

* * * * *

The last few weeks of the Archduke Franz Ferdinand's life were filled with interest and action. In the middle of June he received the Kaiser as his guest at Konopischt. For three days the pair remained in close confabulation. According to the account which William II furnished to the German Foreign Office, the conversations turned mainly upon the Archduke's dislike of the Hungarians, for their mediaeval habits and oppression of other races within their bounds. He urged the importance of continually pressing Count Tisza not to maltreat the Hungarian Roumanians and thus foment dissension between the Triple Alliance and Roumania. The only other questions said to have been discussed were the relations between Greece and Turkey, Italy's conduct in Albania, and the replacement of the Hungarian Count Szögyeny by an Austrian Ambassador in Berlin. Rumour has extended this list. It has been asserted that the whole European position was surveyed in a sinister manner, and that the Kaiser said to the Archduke: 'If we do not strike soon, the situation will get worse.' It seems certain from what followed that he made no definite promise of German aid to Austria in any particular case.

The visit ended, the Kaiser proceeded to his villa at Corfu and Franz Ferdinand to the army manœuvres which were to be held in Bosnia. The schedule of his movements had been widely announced. Not only would the Austrian troops be exercising in great strength in the province coveted by Serbia, but thereafter the Heir to the Throne would pay an official visit accompanied by his wife to Sarajevo, the Bosnian capital. He would enter it upon June 28. This was the anniversary of the fatal Serbian defeat in 1349 at Kosovo Polye, 'the Field of Blackbirds.' All this was read and brooded upon in Serbia. This visit was also to be for the Countess Chotek, or Dutchess of Hohenberg as she had now become, the most formal assertion of her growing aspirations to ceremonial recognition. She was to join her husband at Sarajevo, and the arrangements for her separate journey were set out in that full official detail reserved for the journeys of the Emperor himself. Well might Count Paar, as he perused the programme, exclaim scandalized, 'What are we coming to?' Well might the Emperor accelerate his departure from Vienna to Ischl, to avoid either accepting or repulsing such pretensions!

The Serbian officers who had cut to pieces King Alexander and Queen Draga at Belgrade in 1903 had banded themselves together for mutual protection in a secret society called 'The Black Hand.' This deadly association nourished a fierce patriotism with the discipline of the early Jesuits and the methods of the Russian Nihilists. They were connected at many points with Serbian governing circles. It was even said that the Crown Prince Alexander, Pashitch the Prime Minister, and Putnik, the Commander-in-Chief, had at one time or another been with them; and their leader, Colonel Dimitriyevitch, was actually at this time the head of the Serbian Intelligence branch. Amid many obscurities there is little doubt that Dimitriyevitch organized the plot to murder the Archduke during his visit to Bosnia. A number of fanatical youths, most of them not yet twenty, were incited to go to Sarajevo. They were provided under his authority with bombs and Browning pistols which they were taught to use. They were given money for their journey and maintenance. They were given cyanide of potassium for suicide in the last resort. There seems no doubt from post-war revelations that Pashitch and several of his colleagues learned what was afoot. The Serbian Government at that time was at variance with the 'Black Hand' organization upon the administration of the newly-acquired Macedonian territory. It is said on their behalf that they sent orders to their frontier authorities to prevent the conspirators passing into Bosnia; but that these frontier authorities being themselves members of the Black Hand sped them on their way. It is also suggested that the Government endeavoured to warn Vienna that the Archduke would be in danger during his visit to Bosnia and Sarajevo. Indeed the Serbian Minister in Vienna, Yovanovitch, almost certainly made a vaguely-worded statement to one of Berchtold's subordinates to this effect. So far as this was regarded at all, it was regarded as an impertinence. The Archduke was alive to the dangers of his visit, and he attempted without success to dissuade his wife from coming with him. As a Prince and a soldier, he himself felt bound to fulfil his engagements.

In these circumstances it might have been expected that the most stringent police and military precautions would have been taken. Instead, the neglect and carelessness were such as to foster the insulting suspicion that the Archduke's life was not much valued in the highest spheres of the Austro-Hungarian Government. At this point General Potiorek presents himself for closer examination. After Conrad he was the leading military personage in the Austro-Hungarian Empire. Conrad himself when invited to become Chief of the Staff in 1908, had proposed Potiorek instead. A dapper, keen-looking soldier of almost monastic self-discipline, with a strong element of mysticism in his nature, and an intimate and carefully developed connection with the Emperor's aged court, Potiorek stood on firm ground. He was at this moment as the military Governor of Bosnia responsible above all others for the safety of the Heir-Apparent during his visit to its capital. Whether maliciously or through sheer incompetence, he grossly neglected this duty. His subsequent military record favours the more charitable view. But of course he knew how strongly the Court disapproved of Royal honours being accorded to the Duchess Sophie. It was understood she was not to be unduly exalted. Few police were imported, no troops lined the streets, no reserve of gendarmerie was at hand. The arrangements invited disaster, and, such as they were, they were muddled in execution.

On the afternoon of June 28 the Archduke and his wife entered Sarajevo. The murder had been carefully planned. At least seven assassins had taken their stations at various points upon the probable Royal route. Every one of the three bridges had its two or three murderers in waiting. The first attempt was made on the way to the Town Hall; but the bomb slid off the back of the motor-car and its explosion only wounded two officers of the suite. After the miscreant had been caught, the Archduke proceeded to the Town Hall and received in a mood of natural indignation the addresses of welcome. The police precautions had seemed to be lax, and the owner of the motor-car, Count Harrach, who sat beside the driver, accosted the Governor, Potiorek: 'Has not Your Excellency arranged for a military guard to protect his Imperial Highness?' to which the Governor replied impatiently, 'Do you think Sarajevo is full of assassins, Count Harrach?' The Archduke proposed to alter the return route and to visit the Hospital to which the wounded officers had been taken. When told that the bomb-thrower had been captured, he is said to have remarked, 'Hang him as quickly as possible or Vienna will give him a decoration.' A strangely bitter saying! Almost his last! Count Harrach wished to stand on the left footboard to protect the Archduke. 'Don't make a fool of yourself,' said Franz Ferdinand. The four cars moved out into the dense crowds in the original order, but at a faster pace. At the entrance to Franz Joseph Street the crowd, uncontrolled by the police, made a lane and by a fatal error the cars turned back to the original route, Governor Potiorek, who sat facing the Royal visitors, told the chauffeur that he had taken the wrong turning. The car slowed down and came close to the right-hand pavement. A young man fired two shots at three yards' range. The Archduke continued to sit upright; his wife sank upon his breast. A few murmured words passed between them. For a few moments no one realized they had been shot. But the Archduke had been pierced through the artery of his neck and the Duchess through the abdomen. Both sank into unconsciousness and expired within a quarter of an hour. The assassin, a Serbian student named Princip, was seized by the crowd. He died in prison, and a monument erected in recent years by his fellow-countrymen records his infamy, and their own. Such was the tragedy of Sarajevo.

In those days I was much concerned with the preparation of the Navy and with the creation of the Naval Air Force. I had spent the early hours of the morning at the Central Flying School at Upavon and motoring back to Portsmouth bought the newspapers at the ferry across the harbour. I remember I read the news while the car waited. I recall a sudden and vivid feeling that something sinister and measureless had occurred. I spent the afternoon in the dockyard where so many new ships were building and did not reach the Admiralty till late at night. Our Admiral telegraphed from Kiel that following the news of the murder the Kaiser had immediately quitted the scene and that the regatta and festivities were at an end. I reflected that it would be nice to get our great vessels back from the Baltic soon. They passed the Belts by June 30th.

* * * * *

The crime of Sarajevo roused widespread fury throughout the Austro-Hungarian Empire, and its various races were united with their government in rage and hatred of Serbia. To judge their feelings we must imagine our own in a similar case. Suppose that Ireland had been a republic growing in power and hostility; that it was not an island, but lay with frontiers actually joining Wales and Scotland; that there was a vehement, active pan-Celtic scheme to unite Ireland, Scotland and Wales into a separate foreign combination against England; that the Prince of Wales had gone to Carnarvon on official duty, and that he had been murdered by a band of assassins organized and sent by an Irish secret society and armed with weapons supplied from the Dublin Arsenal! That would have been a not-unfair parallel to the situation now created in the Hapsburg dominions. For some days the anger of the peoples of Austria expressed itself in violent demonstrations against Serbia and attacks upon Serbian representatives and establishments. The British Consul-General at Buda-Pest reported that Hungarian feeling was even more incensed. 'A wave of blind hatred for Serbia and everything Serbian is sweeping over the country.' The Hungarian nation he thought 'willing to go to any lengths to revenge itself on the despised and hated enemy.'

The Emperor, though shocked at assassination in principle, and loathing Serbia, was decidedly resigned and even cool upon the personal aspects of the tragedy. His first remark to Count Paar on hearing the news reveals his distinctive point of view. 'Horrible! The Almighty does not allow Himself to be challenged with impunity. . . . A higher Power has restored the old order, which I unfortunately was unable to uphold.' This, then, was the punishment administered by Providence as guardian of the Hapsburg dynasty to an Heir-Apparent who had fallen into a morganatic marriage.

The opportunity for which Conrad had waited so long and pleaded so often had now come. He demanded, as usual, immediate war upon Serbia. Mobilize at once and march in! Those who had restrained him in the past were gone. Aerenthal was dead; the Archduke was dead; and Conrad found in Count Berchtold not opposition, but agreement. Berchtold had already made up his mind. As Foreign Minister he was not, however, free to act alone under the Emperor. The constitution required that he should procure the agreement of the two Minister-Presidents of Austria and of Hungary. The Hungarian, Count Tisza, was an outstanding figure, a man of force and personality, clear-sighted, resolute, severe in speech, and with political influence far beyond the authority of his high office. On July 1 Berchtold told Count Tisza that he meant to make 'the horrible deed at Sarajevo the occasion for a reckoning with Serbia.' Tisza objected; he warned his colleague of the measureless consequences which might follow what he stigmatized as 'a fatal mistake.' He wrote to the Emperor the same day that Serbia's guilt was not proved and that if the Serbian government were able to furnish satisfactory explanations the Empire would have exposed herself before the whole world as a disturber of the peace, besides having to begin a great war in the most unfavourable circumstances. He insisted upon an inquiry. He dwelt upon the unsatisfactory attitude of Roumania. He advocated a treaty of Alliance with Bulgaria as a vital precaution before a breach with Serbia. On the other side, Conrad and the generals clamoured incessantly for war.

Conrad has given his own account.

'On July 1, I again spoke to Count Berchtold, who said that his Majesty also wished to await the result of the inquiry. Count Stürgkh and Count Tisza, said the Minister, pleaded for maintaining cool nerves. Tisza was against war with Serbia; he was anxious, fearing that Russia might strike at us and Germany leave us in the lurch. Stürgkh, on the other hand, expressed the opinion that an inquiry would provide grounds for going forward. I put forward the view that nothing but a powerful attack could prevent the danger threatened from Serbia. The murder committed under the patronage of Serbia was the reason for war. To Berchtold's anxiety lest Germany and Roumania should leave us in the lurch I replied that if that was how things stood with our alliance with Germany, we should in any case have our hands tied.

'The Minister said to me that he had prepared a memorandum in which he called upon Germany to secure Roumania for the Triple Alliance. I protested that we must ask Germany before all else whether she would or would not protect our rear against Russia.'[6]

* * * * *

On June 30 Tschirschky, the German Ambassador in Vienna, had reported to Berlin that he was taking every opportunity to 'advise quietly but very emphatically and seriously against too hasty steps.' The Kaiser's marginal comment upon this is celebrated. 'Who authorized him to act thus? That is very stupid; it is absolutely none of his business, for it is solely Austria's affair what she intends to do in this matter. Afterwards, if things go wrong, it will be said that Germany was not willing. Tschirschky will please stop this nonsense! The Serbians must be disposed of *and that right soon.*' On July 1 Count Hoyos, the permanent official at the head of the Ballplatz, received a German publicist, a Dr. Victor Naumann, who was in close touch with both Herr von Jagow, the German Foreign Secretary, and Stumm of the German Foreign Office. Naumann declared that not only in army and naval circles but also in the Wilhelmstrasse, the idea of a preventive war against Russia was not so entirely rejected as it had been a year ago. An agreement had been reached with England about Africa and the Portuguese colonies and the visit of the British fleet to Kiel had been arranged as a demonstration of the improved relations. Consequently they felt sure that England would not intervene in a European war. Stumm, he said, had spoken very earnestly to him of the danger of the Russian armaments. On account of many difficulties France would probably be compelled to work upon Russia in a pacific sense; but if nevertheless it came to a European war the Triple Alliance was still strong enough now. The Emperor William if he were spoken to in the proper way at the present moment 'when he is enraged over the murder at Sarajevo will give us every assurance and will hold to it even to the point of war, because he recognizes the dangers to the monarchical principle. The German Foreign Office will not oppose this attitude because they consider the moment favourable to bring about the great decision. . . . Austria-Hungary was lost as a monarchy and a Great Power if she did not make use of the present moment.'

This very strong hint enabled Berchtold when he received Tschirschky the next day to complain that Austria had been insufficiently supported in the past by Germany and did not know how she stood now. Tschirschky replied that this was due to the Austrian habit of expounding ideas without a definite plan of action. Berlin could make the Austrian cause its own only if Austria came forward with such a plan. To the Emperor on the same day Tschirschky, now fully abreast of the policy of the Wilhelmstrasse, declared that His Majesty could count on having Germany solidly behind the Monarchy whenever the question arose of defending one of its vital interests. The decision on the question of whether such a vital interest was at stake must be left to Austria herself. . . . 'My Emperor would stand behind every firm decision of Austria-Hungary.' It may well be believed that Francis Joseph drank this in with satisfaction. A more open incitement to an ally, whose people were already beside themselves with anger, cannot be imagined. On the one hand, therefore, at this stage we find both monarchs and both Foreign Offices ranged with Conrad on the side of violent action against Serbia, and only Count Tisza opposed.

Berchtold always had in mind the chastisement of Serbia as something sharp, swift and local. He pictured to himself an ultimatum and the immediate seizure of some Serbian town or district by Austrian troops at their peace strength without the delay or gravity of mobilization. He had pressed this upon Conrad in 1913 and the Chief of the Staff had explained repeatedly the technical impossibility of such an operation. Nothing could be done without mobilization. 'What are you thinking of!' he had exclaimed in October, 1913. 'If we mobilize, Potiorek will have 80,000 infantry, but now he has only 25,000, and they are scattered all over Bosnia.' But Berchtold persisted in this idea. He dreaded the sixteen days' delay which must elapse between the order to mobilize and the crossing of the Serbian frontiers. He feared what might happen in Europe in these sixteen days. It was one thing to march into Serbia and to occupy 'a sufficient bit of territory', thus confronting Europe with the accomplished fact; and quite another to set on foot the formidable process of mobilization. At this moment, undeterred by Conrad's objections, Berchtold still contemplated 'military action to be undertaken immediately, that is, without mobilization.' But to this again Count Tisza would not agree.

It was necessary above all things to make certain of German support and approval, and on July 4 Berchtold sent Count Hoyos, his trusted official confidant, to Berlin for a personal consultation with the German chiefs. Hoyos was armed with two documents, first a memorandum advocating the inclusion of Bulgaria in the Triple Alliance, as urged by Tisza, and secondly an autograph letter from Francis Joseph to William II. Neither of these documents mentioned the sudden inroad upon Serbia which was in Berchtold's mind, for this would have been contrary to Tisza's stipulation; but in addition Count Hoyos had verbal explanations to give. These explanations revealed Berchtold's definite 'firm plan' for which Berlin had seemed to wish. The Emperor's letter requires lengthy quotation.

'According to all the evidence so far brought to light, the affair at Sarajevo was not the bloody deed of an individual, but the result of a well-organized conspiracy, the threads of which reach to Belgrade; and even if, as is to be presumed, it will be impossible to prove the complicity of the Serbian Government, there can indeed be no doubt that its policy, which is directed towards the union of all Southern Slavs under the Serbian flag, incites to such crimes, and that the continuance of this state of affairs constitutes a permanent danger for my House and my territories. . . .

'The efforts of my government must in future be directed towards the isolation and diminution of Serbia. The first step in this direction should be to strengthen the position of the present Bulgarian Government, in order that Bulgaria, whose real interests are identical with our own, may be preserved from a relapse into a Russophile policy.

'If it is recognized in Bucharest that the Triple Alliance is determined not to forgo the adhesion of Bulgaria to it, yet would be prepared to induce Bulgaria to bind herself to Roumania and guarantee the latter's territorial integrity, perhaps people there will withdraw from the dangerous course into which they have been driven by friendship with Serbia and the *rapprochement* with Russia.

'If this succeeds, the attempt might further be made to reconcile Greece with Bulgaria and Turkey; there might then develop under the patronage of the Triple Alliance a new Balkan League, whose aim would be to set a limit to the advance of the Pan-Slav current and to secure peace for our countries.

'This, however, will not be possible until Serbia, which at present forms the pivot of Pan-Slav policy, has been eliminated as a factor of political power in the Balkans.

'You too, after the recent frightful occurrences in Bosnia, will be convinced that a reconciliation of the antagonism that now separates Serbia from us is no longer to be thought of, and that the maintenance of the pacific policy of all European monarchs will be threatened as long as this focus of criminal agitation in Belgrade is not subjected to punishment.'[7]

On July 5 Conrad had an audience with the Emperor at Schönbrunn.

'The discussion came at once to the political situation. His Majesty surveyed it in all its aspects and was perfectly clear as to its seriousness. I also expressed to His Majesty my view that war against Serbia was inevitable.

H.M. Yes, that is quite right. But how will you carry on a war if they all then fall upon us, especially Russia?

CONRAD. Surely Germany will protect our rear!

H.M. (looked at Conrad questioningly, and said). Are you sure of Germany?

Conrad here says that the Emperor had charged the Archduke Franz Ferdinand to ask the Kaiser at Konopisht whether Austria could in future count on Germany unconditionally and the Kaiser had avoided answering the question.

CONRAD. But, Your Majesty, we must know how we stand in that matter.

H.M. Yesterday evening a note was sent to Germany in which we called for a clear answer.

CONRAD. If the answer is to the effect that Germany is on our side, do we then go to war against Serbia?

H.M. In that case, yes. (After a moment's thought, he continued.) But if Germany does not give us this answer, what then?

CONRAD. Then, to be sure, we stand alone. We ought, however, to get the answer quickly, for the great decision depends upon it.

H.M. The German Emperor is on a journey to Scandinavia. In any case, we must wait for the answer.

'I had the impression that His Majesty did not feel sure of Germany and for that reason was deferring the decision.

'Whilst the audience so far had gone smoothly, His Majesty now was somewhat moved when I put forward the necessity of declaring martial law as a counter-measure to further Serbian attempts within the monarchy, and in this connection I pointed out that similar occurrences to those in Bosnia were also being prepared in other districts of the monarchy and might be directed against persons, headquarters or important objectives, such as bridges.

H.M. All that (i.e. martial law) will happen on mobilization.

CONRAD. It will then be too late.

H.M. No, that (i.e. martial law) is impossible.

CONRAD. There is nothing else for it, however.

H.M. But I do not do it.

CONRAD. As Your Majesty directs! I was obliged by my duty to propose it.

(On this, the Emperor became calmer again.)

CONRAD. But the least I ask is immediate steps to deal with bombs and the like and legal proceedings against those in possession of them.

H.M. Good. I will instruct the Minister-Presidents concerned in that sense.'

The audience ended upon a genial and holiday note.

'On Tuesday,' said the Emperor, 'I go to Ischl.' Conrad asked if he himself might go to Tirol. 'Of course,' said his master; 'you too must recuperate.'[8]

CHAPTER V
THE AUSTRIAN ULTIMATUM

When on the morning of Sunday, July 5, Count Hoyos reached Berlin he consulted with the Austro-Hungarian Ambassador, Count Szögyény, who asked forthwith for an audience of the Kaiser in order to deliver the letter of the Emperor Francis Joseph. The Kaiser invited the Ambassador to luncheon at Potsdam. Count Hoyos proceeded to the Foreign Office and had a lengthy conversation with Zimmermann. Meanwhile Szögyény reached Potsdam and delivered his letter and memorandum. The Kaiser read them both, and said at first that he had expected some serious step against Serbia, but that possible European complications made it necessary for him to consult the Imperial Chancellor before giving a definite answer. After luncheon, however, William II, without waiting for Bethmann-Hollweg's arrival, made the following momentous statement, which he authorized the Ambassador to convey to Francis Joseph as a personal message from Sovereign to Sovereign.

The Kaiser, according to the Ambassador, said that Austria might rely on Germany's full support. He must first hear the opinion of the Chancellor; but he did not in the least doubt that Herr von Bethmann-Hollweg would agree with him, especially in the matter of the action against Serbia. It was the Kaiser's opinion that this action must not be delayed. Russia's attitude would doubtless be hostile, but he had been prepared for this for years; and should it come to war between Austria-Hungary and Russia, Austria could be assured that Germany would stand by her side with her accustomed loyalty. As things stood to-day, however, Russia was in no way prepared for war, and would certainly think twice before appealing to arms, although she would incite the Powers of the Triple Entente against Austria, and add fuel to the fire in the Balkans. "He understood very well that it would be hard for his Imperial and Royal Majesty, with his well-known love of peace, to march into Serbia; but if we had really recognized the necessity of war against Serbia, he would regret it if we did not make use of the present moment, which is all in our favour."

It did not take Count Szögyeny very long to return to Berlin and telegraph these declarations to Vienna.

The Kaiser was under no illusions upon the gravity of the step he had taken. He had, in fact, decided to court the general European war. He had urged Austria to invade Serbia and had promised to defend her against Russian interference. As the German defence of Austria against Russia meant the immediate German invasion of France and violation of Belgian neutrality, the whole fearful panorama was unrolled. Of course he hoped it would not come to war. Austria would punish Serbia, and be once more indebted to Germany. France and England, in fear of war or love of peace, or from moral or material unpreparedness would persuade Russia to stand aside; and Russia, convinced at last of the worthlessness of their friendship or alliance, would abandon the Triple Entente. The Central Empires would tower up, united and triumphant over a bloodless field. For the future they would have only isolated opponents to confront. The 'mailed fist' and the 'shining armour' would once again have done their work, and he, the Kaiser, would have proved his mettle to the satisfaction even of his most exacting subjects. But if not, so much the worse for them all!

He was to leave at 9.15 the next morning upon his yachting cruise in the Norwegian fjords. Before that, there was much to do. He had already summoned the Chancellor and the heads of the fighting services. General von Falkenhayn, the Prussian Minister of War, arrived at 5 p.m., Bethmann-Hollweg at six, and Captain Zenker, representing the Naval Staff, a little after seven. Admiral von Capelle, representing the Admiralty in the absence of Tirpitz, and General von Bertrab, the senior General Staff Officer then present in Berlin, arrived between eight and nine the next morning. Baron Krupp, head of the armament works, was commanded to dine with the Emperor at Kiel the following night. To each of these functionaries the Emperor spoke separately, and all of them have recorded their impressions of what he said. On July 5 Falkenhayn wrote to Moltke the Chief of the Staff who was taking a cure, that His Majesty had informed him that 'Austria-Hungary appears determined not to tolerate any longer the plots hatched against Austria in the Balkan peninsula, and if necessary to accomplish this end, to begin by marching into Serbia; even if Russia will not tolerate this, Austria is not disposed to give way. . . . Considerable time will elapse before the treaty with Bulgaria is concluded. So Your Excellency need hardly curtail your stay at Carlsbad. Nevertheless I thought it desirable, although I have had no instructions to do so, to let you know that the situation is acute, in order that you may not be quite unprepared for surprises which in the end may come about.' To the Kaiser's direct question whether the army was ready for all contingencies, Falkenhayn had replied briefly and unconditionally that it was ready.

Bethmann-Hollweg merely expressed his concurrence with the Emperor's views, as recorded by him in more guarded language. Captain Zenker reported to his naval superiors: 'His Majesty informed me . . . that the Austro-Hungarian *chargé d'affaires* [*sic*] had inquired of him whether Germany would fulfil the obligations of her alliance in the event of an Austro-Hungarian conflict with Serbia and the strained relations with Russia that might perhaps result. His Majesty had promised this, but he did not believe that Russia would intervene on behalf of Serbia, which had stained itself by an assassination. France, too, would scarcely let it come to war, as she lacked the heavy artillery for the field armies. Yet, though war against Russia and France was not probable, nevertheless the possibility of such a war must be borne in mind from a military point of view. Still, the High Seas Fleet was to start its cruise to Norway as had been planned for the middle of July, and he was going to start on his journey according to schedule.' Admiral von Capelle recorded that the Kaiser 'did not believe that a great war would develop. In his opinion the Czar would not associate himself with the murderers of princes. Besides that, neither France nor Russia was prepared for war. The Emperor did not mention England. On the advice of the Imperial Chancellor, he was going to start quietly on his journey to the north, in order not to rouse any apprehensions. Nevertheless, he wished to inform me of the strained situation, in order that I might consider it further. General von Bertrab's evidence is almost identical. Baron Krupp informed a colleague on his board of directors on July 17 that 'the Emperor had spoken to him on the conversation with the Austrians, but had characterized the affair as so secret that he (Krupp) would not have ventured to communicate it even to his board of directors. . . . The Emperor had told him personally that he would declare war immediately if Russia mobilized. The Emperor's repeated insistence that in this matter no one would be able to reproach him again with want of resolution had produced an almost comic effect.'

These interviews have been made the basis for the report that the Kaiser held on July 5 a Crown Council at Potsdam on the question of peace or war. William II has been at pains to repel this suggestion. Actually the action he took was at once far more autocratic and more slipshod than any Council or Conference. He only saw his Chancellor and officers separately and handled the whole business in a purely personal manner.

On the morning of July 7 the Imperial Yacht *Hohenzollern* sailed away to Norway and for three weeks the mighty potentate, upon whose word the lives of countless millions hung, took no part in European affairs. 'Mischief, thou art afoot. Take thou what course thou wilt.'

The measures taken by the various German authorities after the Kaiser's departure were discreet. Moltke's deputy at the General Staff, Waldersee, deposed at the post-war Parliamentary investigation: 'There was nothing to initiate . . . the Army was, as always, ready.' And at the time (July 17, 1914) he wrote to Jagow—a strange official intimacy between the Foreign Secretary and a subordinate military officer: 'I shall remain here ready to jump; we are all prepared at the General Staff; in the meantime there is nothing to do.' Krupp, after a preliminary inquiry, learned that the munition works had sufficient materials on hand to guarantee the activity of all factories for quite a long time 'even if fully shut off [from outside sources].' The Navy required more attention and seems to have had a sharper realization. After a secret conference of the highest officials summoned by Admiral von Capelle it was decided to hasten the construction of all nearly-completed small craft; to increase the fuel supplies; to provide fleet auxiliaries and store ships; 'to put into shape' the naval flying forces; and to send a battleship on a test trip through the now-just-deepened Kiel canal. Warnings were also sent to the cruisers in foreign stations. Admiral von Spee, commanding in the Pacific, was told on July 6 to remain with the *Scharnhorst* and *Gneisenau* at Ponape 'in certain and constant communication.' On the 9th he was told that war between Austria and Serbia was possible and that the Triple Alliance might become involved, and on the 10th that England might be involved 'if it came to a general war.' The *Goeben* was ordered to Pola and workmen sent from Germany to hasten repair of her boiler-tubes, and Admiral Suchon was informed that the situation was not free from anxiety. Lastly the little gunboat *Eber*, which was being repaired in our dockyard at Capetown, was warned to adjust the work to the political situation. She curtailed her repairs forthwith. Of this last item a report reached the British Admiralty. It was not quite clear why the *Eber* had changed her programme of work. The indication was however too slight for conclusions to be drawn. After all, we too were always ready.

When Lord Granville became Foreign Secretary on July 6, 1870, he was informed by his official adviser that 'he had never known during his long experience so great a lull in foreign affairs and that he was not aware of any important question that the new Minister would have to deal with.' A few days later the Franco-German war had begun. Now in 1914, on this very July 6, Sir Arthur Nicolson himself wrote that 'apart from Albania we have no very urgent and pressing question to preoccupy us in the rest of Europe.' Thus history repeats itself.

Early on the morning of the 7th Count Hoyos returned from Berlin with the fateful answer. It exceeded the rosiest dreams of Conrad and of Berchtold and the rest of the war party at Vienna. The Austrian envoy brought back the joyous tidings which Conrad records in the following terms: 'Germany would stand on our side unconditionally, even if our advance against Serbia let loose the great war. Germany advises us to set matters in motion.' Perhaps never in the history of the world has so vast an obligation been entered into so incontinently. The Vienna Cabinet was given a blank cheque valid against the whole resources of the German Empire to fill in at pleasure, provided only that it set to work without delay.

* * * * *

By noon the Ministers forming the Cabinet of the Austro-Hungarian Empire were assembled in conclave. The eight men gathered around the table represented four nationalities and five governments. Berchtold, as Foreign Minister, presided. Count Stürgkh, the Austrian Prime Minister, Bilinski, the joint Finance Minister, von Krobatin, the War Minister, Conrad the War Lord and his naval colleague Admiral von Kailer, Hoyos, and last but by no means least Count Tisza. Very complete accounts of this meeting have been made public.[9]

Berchtold began by saying that the ministerial council had been summoned 'to advise on the measures to be adopted for the restoration to a healthy basis of the bad internal political conditions in Bosnia and Herzegovina in connection with the Sarajevo catastrophe. . . . It must be decided whether the moment had not come to render Serbia for ever innocuous by a manifestation of power. A decisive stroke of this kind could not be effected without diplomatic preparations, therefore he had consulted the German government. The discussions in Berlin had led to a very satisfactory result, for both Kaiser Wilhelm and Herr von Bethmann-Hollweg had given assurances with all emphasis of the unconditional support of Germany in the event of a warlike complication with Serbia. . . . He was clear that a passage of arms with Serbia might have war with Russia as the consequence. Russia was pursuing a policy which, on a long view, had for its object the consolidation of the Balkan States, including Roumania . . . against the Monarchy. In the face of such a policy their situation must continue to grow worse. . . . '

With one exception the Cabinet was spellbound with relief and thankfulness. Indeed, we cannot wonder at their mood. Imagine struggling for years against external menace and internal disruption; imagine the rage and hatred for a deadly foe stifled for years;

and then imagine an armed and invincible giant, a genius, superhuman in force and warlike skill, suddenly placed for the first time, perhaps for the last, at your absolute disposal! Rub the lamp, utter the incantation, and you have him at your service! Nay, for ever at your service, provided you do not fear to invoke him now. Now or never!

Count Tisza alone stood forth in direct opposition. 'I shall never consent to a surprise attack on Serbia without previous diplomatic action, as seems to be intended, and to have been also regrettably discussed in Berlin by Count Hoyos. We shall in that case be in a very bad position in the eyes of Europe, and must also reckon on the hostility of the whole of the Balkans—except Bulgaria—without even the latter, now so much weakened, supporting us effectively. We must formulate demands on Serbia, and only send an ultimatum if Serbia does not accept them. These demands should indeed be hard, but not unfulfillable. If Serbia accepts them, we shall have a resounding diplomatic success to proclaim and our prestige in the Balkans will rise again. If our demands are not accepted, then I, too, will be for warlike action; but I must here make plain that even in this event our aim should be the diminishing, but not the annihilation, of Serbia. Russia would never consent to this without a life-and-death struggle, and as Hungarian Minister-President I will never consent to the Monarchy annexing a part of Serbia.' Then follows a significant sentence showing the positive pressure which the Kaiser and his Chancellor were applying to Austria. 'It is not Germany's affair to judge whether we ought or ought not now to launch action against Serbia. I, personally, am of opinion that it is not at the moment absolutely necessary to make a war. The agitation against us in Roumania is very strong. In face of the excited public opinion there, we must reckon with a Roumanian attack, and will in any case have to hold a considerable force in Siebenbürgen to overawe the Roumanians. Now, when Germany has happily freed the way for Bulgaria's accession to the Triple Alliance, there opens to us a promising field for a successful diplomatic action in the Balkans through the inclusion of Bulgaria and Italy in the Triple Alliance. . . . France's strength compared to Germany's will grow even worse from her lower birth-rate, and Germany consequently will in future years have more and more troops available against Russia.' . . . Thus Tisza, but he was isolated. The others resolved that 'unacceptable demands must be addressed to Serbia, so that war would be inevitable,' and this conclusion was conveyed to the Emperor.

After the Cabinet Tisza sent a memorial to the Emperor.

'Such an attack upon Serbia would, in human possibility, provoke the world war, in which case I—despite all optimism in Berlin—should be obliged to regard Roumania's neutrality as at least very questionable. Public opinion there would passionately demand war against us, a pressure which the present Roumanian Government could not resist at all and King Carol only with great difficulty. In this war of aggression the Russian and Roumanian armies would have to be counted as in the enemy's camp, which would make our prospects very unfavourable. . . .

* * * * *

'To summarize what I have said, a war provoked by us would probably have to be fought under very unfavourable conditions, whereas a postponement of the breach to a later date, if we make good diplomatic use of it, would result in an improvement in our relative strengths. If in addition to these political aspects I take into consideration the financial and economic situation—which would make the conduct of the war immensely (*kolossal*) more difficult and would render the sacrifices and suffering involved in it almost insupportable for the community—I cannot, after painfully conscientious reflection, share the responsibility for the proposed military aggression against Serbia.'[10]

Strange indeed that this man should have perished at the hands of an assassin who believed he was avenging mankind upon one of the prime authors of its miseries!

To make sure there was no mistake Tschirschky, the German Ambassador, smarting from a rebuke his earlier prudence had earned him, called upon Berchtold next day. At the close of the visit Berchtold reported it to Tisza.

'He told me,' wrote Berchtold, 'that he had received a telegram from Berlin according to which his Imperial Master instructed him to declare here with all emphasis that in Berlin an action against Serbia is expected, and that it would not be understood in Germany if we allowed the opportunity to pass without striking a blow.'[11]

Berchtold and Conrad now proceeded to fill in the blank cheque. They made it out for all the assets of the German people and appointed a speedy date for payment. In the pigeon-holes of the Ballplatz there lay a document prepared three years before for use against Serbia should occasion arise. This was the celebrated ultimatum. It expressed all that Austria felt against its foe and all that she had never until now dared to say aloud. Only a few minor changes in the wording were necessary to bring it up to date and make it fit the circumstances of the hour.

* * * * *

In the course of July 8 Conrad, too, visited Berchtold. He found with him Barons Burian and Macchio, and Counts Forgach and Hoyos. He writes:

'I received information as to the demands which were to be handed to Serbia in an ultimatum with the short time-limit of either twenty-four or forty-eight hours. It was to be expected that Serbia would refuse the demands, so that on the expiry of the time-limit, mobilization for war would ensue.'

BERCHTOLD. What happens if Serbia lets things go as far as mobilization and then gives way all along the line?

CONRAD. Then we march in.

BERCHTOLD. Yes—but if Serbia does nothing at all?

CONRAD. Then Serbia remains occupied until the costs of the war have been paid.

BERCHTOLD. We will not hand in the ultimatum until after the harvest and after the close of the Sarajevo Inquiry.

CONRAD. Rather to-day than to-morrow, so long as the situation is what it is. So soon as our opponents get wind of it, they will get ready.

BERCHTOLD. Care will be taken that the secret is kept most carefully and that no one knows anything of it.

CONRAD. When is the ultimatum to go out?

BERCHTOLD. In fourteen days—on the 22nd July. It would be a good thing if you and the War Minister would go on leave for a time, in order to preserve the appearance that nothing is happening.

We then spoke about the attitude of Roumania and the possible intervention of Russia.

CONRAD. As to whether we are to go to war with Russia we must be perfectly clear at once. If Russia orders a general mobilization, then the moment has come for us to declare ourselves against Russia.

BERCHTOLD. If we enter Serbia and have occupied sufficient territory—what then?

CONRAD. With the occupation of territory nothing has been attained; we must proceed until we have struck down the Serbian army.

BERCHTOLD. And if it retires?

CONRAD. Then we demand demobilization and disarmament. Once things have got that far, the rest follows.

BERCHTOLD. Only take no measures now which could give us away; nothing must be done which would attract attention.[12]

Sentence of death had thus been signed, sealed and delivered upon the Empire of the Hapsburgs, upon the Russia of Peter, and of Catherine the Great, and upon the Germany of Bismarck. The end of the world of Queen Victoria was at hand.

* * * * *

But now it is summer time and all over Europe families of every class are looking forward to their holidays. The Kaiser is cruising among the fjords of Norway; his generals and ministers are at watering places, salt or medicinal. Francis Joseph rests in his shooting lodge at Ischl. Conrad, as arranged, departs for Tirol. Russian royalties and generals preen themselves at Homburg or Marienbad. The French President and his Premier are banqueting and parading with the Czar at St. Petersburg. London and Lancashire folk are thinking of Margate or the Isle of Man. Only the English Cabinet is tethered to Westminster by the Irish troubles, and the Admiralty is busy with its test mobilization, about which it had been fussing, and with the Royal Review of the entire British fleet appointed for the third week in July. All is calm and the skies are blue and the weather genial. Nevertheless a certain piece of foolscap covered with typewriting is lying in Berchtold's portfolio. It will be despatched to its address on July 23.

* * * * *

Whole libraries have been written about the coming of the war. Every government involved has laboured to prove its guiltlessness. Every people casts the odium upon some other. Every statesman has been at pains to show how he toiled for peace, but was nevertheless a man of action whom no fears could turn from the path of duty. Every soldier has found it necessary to explain how much he loved peace, but of course neglected no preparations for war. Whereas the causes of old wars are often obscure from lack of records, a vast fog of information envelops the fatal steps to Armageddon. A hundred reasons are offered to show why all the governments and potentates acted as they did, and how good their motives were. But in this cloud of testimony the few gleaming points of truth are often successfully obscured. In the mood of men, in the antagonisms between the Powers, amid the clash of interests and deep promptings of self-preservation or self-assertion in the hearts of races, there lay mighty causes. Then came a few short sharp individual acts, and swiftly the final explosion. It is these acts and their doers that we must seek to discern.

There was the man who fired the shots that killed the Archduke and his wife in Sarajevo. There was the man who deliberately, accepting the risk of a world war, told the Austrian Emperor that Germany would give him a free hand against Serbia and urged him to use it. There was the man who framed and launched the ultimatum to Serbia. These men took the fatal decisive steps. Behind them hundreds of high functionaries laboured faithfully and energetically in that state of life unto which God had been displeased to call them; and each has his tale to tell. But no one except the doers of these particular deeds bears the direct concrete responsibility for the loosing upon mankind of incomparably its most frightful misfortune since the collapse of the Roman Empire before the Barbarians.

CHAPTER VI
THE FRONTS AND THE COMBATANTS

This fortnight of sunshine and peace was the last which many millions of men and women were ever to enjoy. It was the respite of the nations. Let us look beneath the fair-seeming surface of Europe, into those chambers and recesses in which the agencies of destruction have been prepared and stored. Let us survey the regions about to be rent by the explosion. Let us measure the forces gathered during the generations of wealth and science for the torment of mankind, and describe the conditions, combinations and directions under which when liberated they will work their will.

Let us first examine with a military eye the theatre of impending action. The prime characteristic is its size. In the West the armies were too big for the country; in the East the country was too big for the armies. The enormous masses of men which were repeatedly flung at each other were dwarfed and isolated by the scale of the landscape. Sixteen or seventeen armies, each approaching two hundred thousand men, were in constant movement against the enemy, sometimes grouped in twos and threes, sometimes acting in convergent combination, yet always separated by wide gaps of undefended and almost unwatched country from one another. Everywhere and always the flanks and often the rear of these huge organizations were exposed to hostile strategy or manœuvres. No large force on either side could advance far without intense and growing anxiety, lest some other powerful body were advancing swiftly from an unexpected angle and would suddenly manifest itself in unknown strength, marching upon the vital communications. Each of these armies comprised the population of a large city, consuming men, food and highly-refined, costly manufactures at an incredible rate. None could live for more than a week without a copious flow of supplies. The capture by surprise of some key fortress, the cutting of an important railway line, a blown-up bridge or a blown-in tunnel, the seizure of some mountain pass or gap in a chain of lakes, might spell not only the failure of gigantic operations but the ruin and disintegration of larger and far more highly organized forces than Napoleon had led from Europe into Russia.

Here was War in all its old unlimited hazard, but on an unexampled scale. No endless succession of trench lines, range behind range, fortified with every device or carefully studied for eventual defence, all backed by a prodigious artillery and batteries everywhere supporting each other, all laced together by a close network of railways—none of this reduced the liabilities of the commanders or set bounds to the consequences of a victory. There were all the dramatic, dumbfounding situations, all the movement, all the disproportionate forfeits of accident and chance of the campaigns in the Shenandoah Valley. It was the same fierce, primordial game multiplied fifty-fold and with whole ponderous armies instead of mobile brigades as counters. No long-prepared, elaborately mounted offensives, no months of preparation for resistance as in the West: here it was 'catch as catch can,' as in the wars of Marlborough, Frederick and Napoleon. But the pitch was also raised by the strong, multiplying power of railways, capable of producing now here, now there, an irresistible development of hostile forces. In this wide scene and amid these dire conditions Austria flagged, Russia toiled, suffered and finally collapsed; while the German Titan, equipped with science and armed with terror, darted from point to point with cruel, flashing sword.

The eastern frontiers of the combatants seemed to be devised to set the hardest problems to the generals. The reader who gazes on the map—and if he will not gaze, he should not read further, for he will comprehend nothing—will readily discern the governing factor of the Eastern Front. The Polish salient, a bulge of territory 230 miles long by 200 miles wide, thrust itself deep into the structure of the central allies. Its western edge abutted upon the highly-important industrial and mining areas of Silesia. At its extreme point Russian territory was only 180 miles from Berlin. No natural frontiers, no broad rivers or mountain chains or desert tracts separated the Slav and Teutonic Empires. Painted wooden posts, notices in different languages, a change of gauge in the railways, the military and political decisions of by-gone generations, the history of warring races, alone divided the three great Powers.

Diagonally across the salient flows through a sunken bed the broad, deep, sluggish, muddy current of the River Vistula. In the middle lay the city and fortress of Warsaw. This extensive, fortified region was the greatest repository of Russian military supplies and establishments. It was a city of eight hundred thousand persons, replete with barracks, hospitals and magazines, guarded by a circle of forts nearly as wide and as highly reputed as those of Antwerp. After Moscow, it was the second railway centre of Russia with six main lines of railway, several of them double, radiating from it. To this

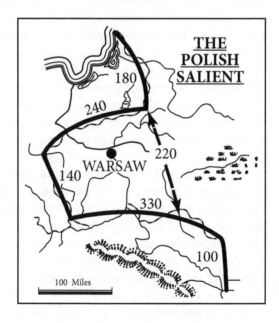

point all the military strength of the Russian Empire through Kiev, through Moscow, through St. Petersburg, could, if necessary, be drawn.

Russian Poland is 'The Land of the Plain.' West of the Vistula it is an open, undulating expanse of poor soil, 300 to 400 feet above the sea-level, nourishing the sugar-beet industry and a sprinkling of industrial towns. To the southward, upon the plateau of Lublin, wheat and orchards abound. East of the Vistula the country becomes increasingly marshy and wooded, until seventy or eighty miles east of Warsaw an invader is confronted with the 300-mile barrier of the Pripyat Marshes. Here is a region as large as Scotland of primeval bog and forest. The roads, few and far between, are causeways, and villages rise as separate islands amid bottomless, impassable swamps. The Pripyat Marshes, the cradle of the Slav race, the last sanctuary of the Aurochs, have now in the orientalization of Russia become the dividing gulf between Europe and Asia. The Polish salient is flanked on the north by the projecting tongue of East Prussia, stretching along the Baltic shore. Its western face fronts Silesia and Posen. On the south it is embraced by Galicia. Each of these regions requires a separate view.

East Prussia, reaching beyond the Niemen River, is a land of lakes and marsh, of forest and woodland, a country of soft though monotonous beauty, but cultivated, drained and roaded by Prussian industry to a degree far above that of Russia or Russian Poland. The main military feature of East Prussia was the chain of lakes and fortifications known in this war as the 'Angerapp Line,' thirty miles within the frontier and running north and south for nearly sixty. This strategic obstacle, held together by the minor fortress of Lötzen in its middle, formed an impenetrable shield. It could not be pierced: it could be avoided by a Russian march along the Baltic shore towards the port and fortress of Königsberg, or by an upward thrust from Warsaw in the direction of Danzig at the mouth of the Vistula.

The Angerapp Line and East Prussia generally was but an outwork in Germany's eastern defences. Their main rampart lay along the Vistula from Danzig to the fortresses of Graudenz and Thorn and thence, quitting the Vistula, by Posen and Breslau. These last three strong places all carried powerful local garrisons, rising to thirty or forty thousand fortress troops apiece on mobilization. All were elaborately prepared military centres, able to act as bases for armies. All were linked together and to Central Germany by a magnificent system of commercial and strategic railways, second in efficiency only to those of the Western Front. Upon the German eastern frontier, therefore, the reader must bear in mind the following factors, which will frequently play their part in this account: First, the projecting tongue of East Prussia, with its Angerapp Line, parting a wave of invasion like a breakwater; secondly, the crescent of the four fortresses and entrenched camps of Königsberg, Thorn, Posen and Breslau; thirdly, the German Vistula dividing the beloved outwork of East Prussia from the main homeland; and lastly—and most important of all—the reticulation of the German railways joining the fortresses to the Fatherland and to each other, and enabling great numbers of men to be moved in the shortest time from north or south, from one end of the crescent to the other.

On the south the Polish salient is flanked by Galicia, which is a wooded, rolling, well-watered region from 700 to 1,200 feet above sea-level. The Austrian frontier indents upon the salient in a wide 330-mile arc. Across the chord of this arc from Cracow to the Roumanian frontier run the Carpathian mountains from 4,000 to 8,500 feet high, crossed by six lines of rail and several easy passes, and descending on their northern slopes by numberless terraces and spurs to the great plains of Russia. Owing to the general level of the plateau from which they rise, the Carpathians are hardly recognizable on the spot as a mountain range. The three principal cities of Galicia—Cracow, the heart of Polish nationalism and culture; Przemsyl, the military, and Lemberg, the cosmopolitan and commercial centre—were all fortified and formed a line of strongly defended bases and depots facing north, and a strategic structure for the counter-invasion of the Polish salient by forces of the greatest magnitude.

In these surroundings the defence of the Russian salient against an Austro-German attack was a problem of the utmost difficulty. Indeed it was realized that the defence of its western extremity was impossible. All the Russian forces deployed west of Warsaw were exposed to being struck from the north and the south in flank and rear by Teutonic armies marching towards each other from well-prepared military areas at opposite points of the compass. Even more impracticable, as we shall see, was a Russian invasion of Silesia so long as East Prussia and Galicia remained under German and Austrian control. The Russians had therefore sought to protect themselves by an elaborate defended line withdrawn at all points a long way within their own frontier. Their fortress system extended from Kovno, through Warsaw to Dubno. This system comprised four distinct groups of fortresses. In the north opposite East Prussia the fortresses of Kovno, Olita and Grodno defended the line of the River Niemen. Next in order Osovets, Lomja, Ostrolenka, Rojan, and Pultusk defended the line of the River Narev. In the centre lay the triangle Warsaw, Ivangorod, Brest-Litovsk, with its subsidiary system Warsaw, Novo Georgievsk, Zegrzie. To the south facing Galicia was the smaller Volhynia triangle formed by the fortresses of Lutsk, Dubno, and Rovno. Of all these strong places, Warsaw, Novo Georgievsk, Ivangorod and Kovno were at the outbreak of the war in the course of being modernized. The remainder were out of date and many indeed largely dismantled.

To sum up, the Russian frontier stretching 900 miles from Memel on the Baltic to the Bukovina was in the highest degree vulnerable by combined Austro-German invasion. Unless in such a war the Russians successfully took the offensive or evacuated Poland, they must expect to be continually attacked and invaded from deadly and unexpected directions. On the other hand, no general advance was possible for them until they had first of all conquered East Prussia in the north and reached the summits of the Carpathians in the south. Until their armies stood in one line from Danzig to Cracow, and also held the passes of the Carpathians, no advance into Germany or Austria was possible. To gain this line by overwhelming numbers and thus straighten their front was the first indispensable Russian objective. To hold East Prussia and Galicia and thence to grip and harry the Polish salient constituted the obvious strategy of the Teutonic Powers.

* * * * *

All the opening events in the East were dominated by German strategy in the West. In his plans in 1890 for a 'war on two fronts,' the first Moltke intended to stand on the defensive against France and throw the main strength of Germany against Russia. There has recently been published upon the authority of the Reichsarchiv, the German official history department, a most important memoir drawn up by the second Moltke, undated, but certainly written after February 1913. The nephew, already Chief of the German Staff, explains why the plan of his uncle could no longer be followed. In the twenty-three years that had passed Russia had improved her communications and quickened her mobilization. The French army was much stronger and better trained. It was by no means certain that a French offensive, if made, would be towards Alsace-Lorraine. Germany could not relinquish all initiative and offensive in the West. The invasion of Russia would be frustrated by the retreat of the Russian armies into the depths of their country. The war would therefore be a long one. If the offensive were taken against France on the other hand, both armies would be close to the frontier and a 'decision would be rapidly reached.' If Germany were successful, the German armies would soon be free to turn eastward.

These were the main grounds which led Count Schlieffen to reverse the strategy of the first Moltke. He drew up the celebrated 'Schlieffen Plan' in which the whole strength of Germany was to be directed from the outset with the utmost rapidity upon France by means of a wheeling movement through Belgium. This would avoid the long system of fortifications which guarded the French frontiers from Switzerland to Verdun, and would lead directly into the heart of France. If the superior numbers of the Germans were used in this way, the French armies would be defeated and driven south or actually caught and destroyed within six weeks. Count Schlieffen developed his scheme with ruthless logic. Every sacrifice should be made and every risk accepted in order to ensure the overpowering weight of the German advance through Belgium. If Alsace-Lorraine were invaded, if East Prussia and even Silesia were overrun, if Belgian neutrality were violated and England brought in as a hostile force, still everything should be staked upon a single, simple, vast operation which if successful would end the war with France almost as soon as it had begun.

All this has long been well known; but it was not until the publication of the 1913 memoir of the second Moltke that anyone realized to what extreme conclusions Count Schlieffen was prepared to press his thought. He proposed literally that 'the whole German army should be deployed in the West and nothing left against Russia.' The second Moltke continues:

'The Field-Marshal (Count Schlieffen) states that in 1866 Prussia left nothing to oppose France and directed the whole of her force upon Austria. Similarly in 1870 Germany left nothing opposite Austria. First Prussia in 1866 against Austria, and then Germany in 1870 against France, by employing superior forces achieved rapid and brilliant successes; and France in the first case, and Austria in the second did not dare to cross the frontiers thus left open.'

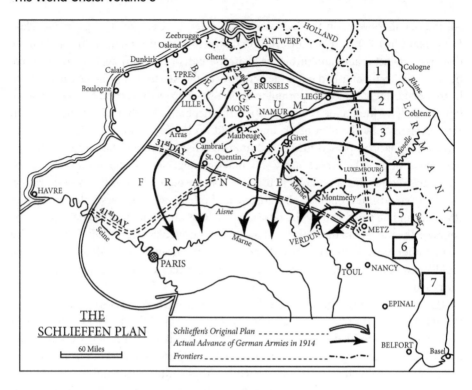

THE
SCHLIEFFEN PLAN

60 Miles

Schlieffen's Original Plan _ _ _ _ _ _ _ _ _ _ _
Actual Advance of German Armies in 1914
Frontiers _ _ _ _ _ _

Having thus given absolute effect to the clarity of his conceptions, Count Schlieffen died.

The German General Staff adopted his plan and cast aside the work of the first Moltke. France in 1866 and Austria in 1870, they observed, were neutral states free to await the result of the opening battles before committing themselves to the war. But Russia is now

'bound beforehand by treaty to take the part of France and will mobilize at once, before a decision has been reached. Thus it is not clear how Russia would be prevented from crossing over our open Eastern frontier by German successes in the West.'

'Austria too . . . if left unassisted by Germany, would in view of Russia's great numerical superiority remain on the defensive, and give Russia complete freedom of action. If the Russians were marching on Berlin, France, even if heavily defeated, would be spurred on to an extreme effort and finally German forces would have to be recalled to defend the capital.'

These reasonings seem sound; but they constitute the first inroad upon the integrity of the Schlieffen plan.

Time passed; the first Moltke was dead; Schlieffen was dead; and the second Moltke addressed himself to the facts of 1913.

'It is not pleasant,' he wrote, 'to begin a campaign by violating the territory of a neutral neighbouring State. But when it is a matter of the existence of our State, all regard for others must drop into the background.'

He saw no hope of coming to any diplomatic arrangement with Belgium for permission to cross her territory. He stated definitely

'the violation of Belgian neutrality will also make England our enemy. . . . Even if Germany gave the most solemn assurances that she would voluntarily evacuate Belgium after a successful campaign against France, no single person in England would believe such assurances.'

The provocation to Great Britain was not however deemed important,

'as England will actively take part in the war on the side of our adversaries, whether we march through Belgium or not . . . for she fears the German hegemony and true to her policy of maintaining European equilibrium will do all she can to hinder the increase of German power. We shall have therefore to reckon England among the number of our enemies.'

He continues:

'No help from Italy is to be expected. She was to have sent 5 corps and two cavalry divisions to the Upper Rhine but in the late autumn of 1912 she declared that, hindered by the occupation of Libya, she could not send this army.'

Lastly he weighed the consequences of marching across the narrow strip of Dutch territory called in the pre-war discussions of the British General Staff 'the Limburg appendix.'

'Dutch neutrality would be violated and Holland also would join our enemies. The disadvantage of this is not so much that we should have to reckon with four Dutch divisions, about 70,000 strong, as the following: In a war of the Triple Alliance against the Entente, not only the German coast would be blockaded, but more or less the Austrian and Italian. Import of provisions would be extremely difficult for Germany. So long as Holland remains neutral, importation through that country under the American flag will be possible. If we make Holland our enemy we shall stop the last air hole through which we can breathe.'[13]

If the first principle of the Schlieffen plan was NUMBERS, the second was SPEED. From this arose a feature which governed German military thought, and when the crisis came paralyzed all efforts to prevent war. The turning movement through Belgium could not begin effectively till the city of Liége had been captured and its four lines of railway put in working order under German control. Liége guarded the bottle-neck through which two whole German armies must pass before they could deploy fan-wise and then swing round to the Southward. Its railways were the only means by which they could live once they were in action. Everything therefore turned upon the seizure of Liége immediately upon a declaration of war with France. The mobilization of European armies took weeks. Liége was a question of days counted in hours. Its capture could not wait for mobilization. Six brigades of infantry and a mass of artillery with cyclists and motor-cars had therefore been held year after year near the German frontier on a peace footing of permanent readiness to strike. Nearly three weeks before the main shock of the armies could begin, these six German brigades must storm Liége. It was this factor that destroyed all chance that the armies might mobilize and remain guarding their frontiers while under their shield conferences sought a path to peace. The German plan was of such a character that the most irrevocable steps of actual war, including the violation of neutral territory, must be taken at the first moment of mobilization. Mobilization therefore spelt war. None of the Governments except the German and French, and none of the Sovereigns seem to have understood this; nor have historians yet brought it home to the public in any country. We shall see in the next chapter how powerless were the efforts set on foot in the closing days of the crisis to avert the catastrophe. Here was the cause.

Surveying the scene the second Moltke decided to adhere to the Schlieffen plan with modifications. He left an army in East Prussia besides strong garrisons of second-line troops belonging to the German eastern fortresses. In this, no doubt, he was justified. He proceeded however, from motives of so-called prudence, to alter the proportions of the German troops who were to face the French fortress line and those who were to invade France through Belgium. He added approximately one-fifth to the strength of the defenders of Alsace-Lorraine and reduced by one-fifth the forces of the Great Invasion. But this was not the Schlieffen plan any more. It was a compromise which defaced and in the event destroyed the original conception. Had the shade of Schlieffen risen before the second Moltke's table and given his counsel, he might well have said: 'Unless you succeed in your invasion through Belgium, you will have lost the war. Unless you are prepared to stake overwhelming strength upon it, do not call it my plan. If you are not going to follow my plan, had you not better go back to the designs of your uncle? Let the French break their strength upon the German fronts. Avoid ranging Belgium and probably England in the ranks of your enemies. Establish yourself and your ally Austria victoriously in the East. Gather to you Bulgaria, Roumania and Turkey. Hold Italy to her engagements by the strength which you will have given to Austria; and later on we will make a fresh plan for France.'

Although these various alternatives were present in the mind of the French and Russian staffs, they could only guess which would be adopted, and with what emphasis in any quarter. But Austria was Germany's ally. In the conversations which Conrad had held with Moltke (we have now finished with his uncle) in Berlin in

March 1909 it had been agreed that Austria should withstand the Russian offensive while Germany marched against France in so-called accordance with the Schlieffen plan. Conrad expected, however, that seven or eight German army corps would be left in the East, and that the Germans would be strong enough to aid him by a considerable offensive from the north into the Polish salient. Both in conversation and in correspondence the name of Syedlets, a town a hundred miles to the east of Warsaw, recurs. This name played a persistent part in Conrad's thought. He imagined a Napoleonic scheme in which the Russians in millions would be massed in the Polish salient, while he, Conrad, would advance northwards from Galicia and joining hands with the Germans near Syedlets cut the whole lot off. This was his dream and prepossession.

Apart from such visions Austria would surely have been wise at the outset to stand in the main upon the defensive. The streams and rivers running northward from the Carpathians offer a succession of positions well adapted to an obstinate delaying defence. But Conrad had set his heart upon an attack. He knew that the Russians must be hampered by the long distances through which many of their divisions must move. He hoped to attack and defeat them more or less piecemeal and, in any case, before their whole enormous strength was marshalled. In the elaborate calculations of the Austrian staff it was assumed that Russia would deploy against Austria about 31 divisions with 11 cavalry divisions by August 18, the twentieth day of mobilization, and that this would grow to 52 divisions by the thirtieth day, August 28. Against these, Austria could present 30½ divisions plus 10 cavalry divisions by the twentieth day, increasing to 38½ divisions by the thirtieth day. It seemed therefore to Conrad that Austria's best chance was to come to grips as soon as possible, and that unless this were done the balance would turn heavily against her as the weeks passed.

Very similar tales were told us at the time of the Agadir crisis in 1911 of the French plan of rupturing the German invasion by an offensive between the eleventh and thirteenth days of mobilization, when they expected to have a temporary superiority. All these calculations are so disturbed by unknown and unknowable factors that they ought not to be taken as more than a rough guide. Although general staffs present the results of their labours in simple and precise assertions, these are no sure foundations upon which to make intricate plans depending upon a few days or a few divisions one way or another. Both the French and the Austrian forecasts were gravely wrong not only as to the strength employed by their antagonists at the outset, but still more as to the arrangement and direction of the invading masses. The general staffs and those who speak for them are prone to emphasize the importance of forestalling the enemy in the beginning of great wars, and statesmen are at their mercy on such questions. Even Time, that precious talisman of war, may be bought too dearly if it leads to the wrong placing of the masses, to the erroneous training or organization of the troops, or to an untrue conception of the character of the war, or of the values and proportions of its physical and moral factors. It is with the greatest reserve that we thus throw doubts upon the sovereign virtues of celerity in striking the first blow. Nevertheless as the scale of the war rises in magnitude, celerity and forestallings at particular points and for particular brief periods seem to become less effective. After all, the supreme study is the general battle and everything should be subordinated to that. Both the French and Austrians would have fared better if they had allowed the invaders of 1914 to test for themselves the then unmeasured power of modern firearms. Both were nearly destroyed at the very beginning of the war by the precipitate offensives which they launched in complete misconception of the numbers and movements of their enemies and of the power of their own rifles, machine-guns and artillery.

* * * * *

We must now turn from the camps of our enemies to those of our allies. The relations of the French and Russian Staffs authorized by long-proclaimed alliance had every year become more intimate. At the Conferences of 1911, 1912 and 1913 France had been represented successively by General Dubail, General de Castelnau and General Joffre. Since 1906 both Russia and France had been bound 'on the first news of German mobilization to mobilize all their forces without previous discussion.' Both parties believed that Germany would use her main force against France and only a minimum against Russia. Both agreed that their armies should take the offensive at the earliest moment, and that the destruction of the German Army was their first and chief objective. In 1913 General Joffre stated that France would concentrate 1,500,000 men by the tenth day of mobilization, and would begin operations on the eleventh. General Jilinsky declared that Russia would in 1914 be able to move against Germany by the thirteenth day with 800,000 men (apart of course from the forces deployed against Austria). The Russians hoped to be able to hold at least five or six German Army Corps in the East, and with this the Frenchmen appeared content.

General Sukhomlinov had been since 1909 Russian Minister for War. His military career had been long and distinguished. He had fought at Plevna in 1877 and had risen steadily through all the grades of his profession both in commands and in the General Staff. He was a soldier of ability and self-restraint. At the outbreak of the Manchurian war when invited by Kuropatkin to become Chief of his Staff he refused, as he did not know the theatre well enough; but he offered to take a subordinate command. After the Manchurian war was over and after several years of futile attempts to reconstruct and reform the Russian Army by committees of Grand Dukes and other notables, Sukhomlinov was called in. In 1908, the Czar invited him to become Chief of the Russian General Staff, an appointment at that time equal in status and authority to the Minister of War. Sukhomlinov accepted only on the condition that he should be subordinate to the War Minister, as the dual authority was clearly an unsound system. The next year he became Minister of War. He was then sixty-one.

For five years he had laboured to improve the Russian Army. He set before himself, according to his account, four main objectives: first, the reduction of the three weeks' start which the German mobilization arrangements had over the Russian; secondly, the technical and scientific progress of the army; thirdly, the revival of its spirit after the defeats in Manchuria; and fourthly, the organization of the supplies and reinforcements of the army in war. He made recruiting truly territorial. He reduced the lavish fortress garrisons, out of which he formed an extra six divisions besides heavy artillery, balloon, and wireless units. He multiplied the number of machine guns, added 250,000 men to the annual quota of recruits, increased the number of officers and improved the food and clothing of the Russian soldier.

General Sukhomlinov was, as is well known, removed from his post in May 1915, and arrested and tried in 1916 on charges of neglect in the war-preparations, of treacherous relations with the Germans and Austrians during the war, and of the acceptance of bribes. He was found guilty and sentenced to imprisonment for life. Released during the revolution by Lenin in the general amnesty of Czarist prisoners, Sukhomlinov betook himself to Germany. He survives there to this day, and vindicates himself in able memoirs. He was certainly the scapegoat of disaster. There is no doubt that the Russian Army of 1914 was incomparably superior to that which had fought the Manchurian war. The whole military system had been reorganized; the extensive rearmament and equipment programmes prescribed in the agreement of 1911 with France had been carried out. Copious French loans—104 millions sterling in 1913 alone—had provided quantities of war material, and the five-year plan of strategic railways upon and to the western frontiers had already made substantial progress. Thus the mobilization of the whole armed strength of Russia and its assembly in the battle zone did not break down. The prodigious task was punctually accomplished.

* * * * *

Such were the plans and compacts which underlay the civilization of Europe. All had been worked out to the minutest detail. They involved the marshalling for immediate battle of nearly twelve million men. For each of these there was a place reserved. For each there was a summons by name. The depots from which he would draw his uniform and weapons, the time-tables of the railways by which he would travel, the roads by which he would march, the proclamations which would inflame or inspire him, the food and munitions he would require, the hospitals which would receive his torn or shattered body—all were ready. Only his grave was lacking; but graves do not take long to dig. We know no spectacle in human history more instinct with pathos than that of these twelve million men, busy with the cares, hopes and joys of daily life, working in their fields or mills, or seated these summer evenings by their cottage doors with their wives and children about them, making their simple plans for thrift or festival, unconscious of the fate which now drew near, and which would exact from them their all. Only a signal is needed to transform these multitudes of peaceful peasants and workmen into the mighty hosts which will tear each other to pieces year after year with all the machinery of science, with all the passions of races, and all the loyalties of man.

Yet it should not be supposed by future generations that much direct compulsion was required. Of all the millions who marched to war in August 1914, only a small proportion went unwillingly away. The thrill of excitement ran through the world, and the hearts of

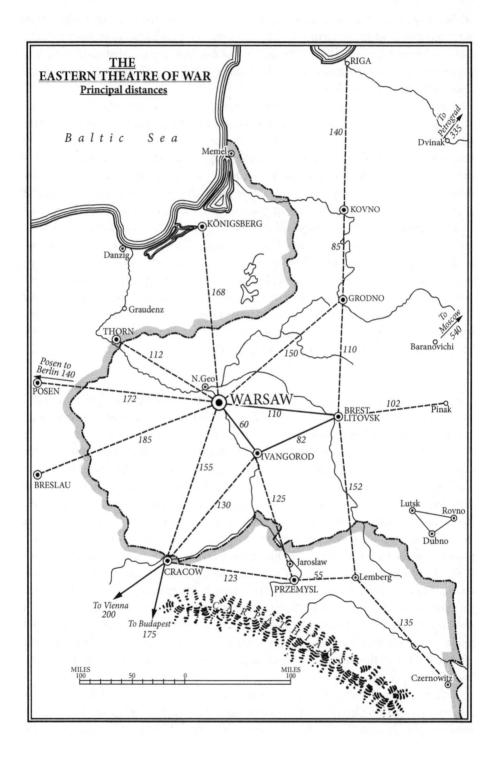

THE
EASTERN THEATRE OF WAR
Principal distances

Baltic Sea

RIGA

To Petrograd 335

Dvinak

Memel

KOVNO

KÖNIGSBERG

Danzig

85

168

GRODNO

Graudenz

To Moscow 540

THORN

Baranovichi

112

150

110

Posen to Berlin 140

N.Geo

POSEN

WARSAW

BREST LITOVSK

102

Pinak

172

110

60

185

82

IVANGOROD

BRESLAU

155

152

Lutsk

Rovno

130

125

Dubno

CRACOW

Jaroslaw

123

55

Lemberg

PRZEMYSL

To Vienna 200

135

To Budapest 175

MILES 100   50   0   MILES 100

Czernowitz

even the simplest masses lifted to the trumpet-call. A prodigious event had happened. The monotony of toil and of the daily round was suddenly broken. Everything was strange and new. War aroused the primordial instincts of races born of strife. Adventure beckoned to her children. A larger, nobler life seemed to be about to open upon the world. But it was, in fact, only Death.

CHAPTER VII
DECLARATIONS OF WAR

Count Berchtold had ordered the ultimatum to be presented to Serbia at six o'clock in the evening of Thursday, July 23. Originally it had been five o'clock; but Berchtold delayed delivery for one hour in order to make sure that President Poincaré and the French Prime Minister, Viviani, should have actually left St. Petersburg on their journey home. The German Chancellor and Foreign Secretary did not see the text till the afternoon before. They were startled by its character; but nevertheless did not recall or alter the German circular note, already dispatched to guide their Ambassadors in London, Paris and St. Petersburg, declaring that the Austrian demands were 'moderate and proper.' The ultimatum required compliance by Serbia within forty-eight hours.

Whole libraries have been written upon the next eight days and their chronicle is far beyond the limits of this book, which can but notice the salient points. The many sincere efforts made by statesmen and ambassadors to keep control of the situation, the desperate resistances of the Czar to war, the eleventh-hour repentance or awakening of the Kaiser, the paroxysms into which the Cabinets of the Parliamentary countries were thrown, the despairing agitations of the Socialists in every land, counted as nothing compared to the mechanical processes of mobilization and the outbursts of national fervour and excitement. The Austrian ultimatum had fired the train which led to a mine loaded by the vice and virtue of half-a-century. The flame ate remorselessly along the fuse.

Europe was thrown at once into convulsions. In a dozen capitals the leading political, diplomatic, military and editorial personages felt themselves at once in the presence of danger. The rasping terms, the humiliating conditions, the parade of mortal hatred could have no other meaning than war. It did not seem possible that any state however small, however in jeopardy, could make the necessary abject acceptance. When on the Friday afternoon of July 24 the British Cabinet, assembled to discuss the Irish quarrel, then at a pitch, heard Sir Edward Grey read the text of Berchtold's document, nearly every one felt that we had entered a new world. I remember that we had to go abruptly to the House of Commons to vote in a routine division. Behind the Speaker's chair I met my great friend and political opponent Mr. F. E. Smith, afterwards Lord Birkenhead. We had been trying to reach some party reconciliation about Ireland, and he asked me anxiously whether I had any news to impart. I said: 'None of this matters now. In a week all Europe will probably be at war.'

After voting I went back to the Admiralty and reviewed the naval situation with Prince Louis of Battenberg, the First Sea Lord. There was very little to be done. At no moment in a hundred years was the Navy more conveniently disposed. It was, in fact, actually undergoing a test mobilization and assembled in its entirety for the review. Out of 525 war vessels under our direction, there were only five large ships in dockyard hands in any part of the globe. All the rest could proceed to their war-stations without a moment's delay. However, on Saturday the reserve men who were required for the oldest and weakest ships would be going back to their homes, and on Monday the whole battle fleet assembled at Portland would separate for exercises, training ashore, or leave. Every hour or day of dispersal would require about the same time for reassembly. The First Fleet, comprising practically all our modern strength, was permanently upon a war footing. We decided that as everything was completely in our control within the time-bracket, we need not take any alarmist action. We could afford for forty-eight hours to go on with the dispersal of the Fleet as if nothing had happened. After all no one had the right to assume that because Austria wished to chastise Serbia, all the greatest nations and empires would go mad. They might; but they might not.

Sunday morning, July 26, showed that Serbia had submitted. Her leaders understood only too well that argument or protest would be answered by cannon. But then during the day it was learnt that the Serbian obeisance was not acceptable to the Austro-Hungarian Government. There were, it appeared, some reservations. The Austrian Minister, Baron Giesl, had quitted Belgrade; and the invasion of Serbia by Austria was imminent. Serbia, under no illusions, had mobilized at the same time she bowed. By Sunday night excited crowds filled the streets of St. Petersburg, Vienna and Berlin. All the Sunday newspapers published evening editions in triple-leaded type. Reports that the German navy was mobilizing came in from many quarters, official and unofficial. We continued to allow the reservists to go to their homes; but we held the First Fleet together at Portland and kept all the Second Fleet ships lying alongside the quays where their balance crews lived and trained. Near midnight, after consultation with Sir Edward Grey, I published this fact in the newspapers. This exceptional procedure was intended by the Foreign Office to intimate to all who might be concerned that the British Empire was not detached from the European situation.*

Difficulties had been expected in obtaining the Emperor's signature to the Declaration of War against Serbia. When Margutti handed the necessary document to Count Paar, the Count remarked: 'This may be all right, but all I can say is that men of eighty-four years of age don't sign war proclamations.' Count Berchtold had therefore fortified himself by laying before his master at the same time a report that the Serbians had already fired upon Austrian troop steamers on the Danube and that hostilities had in fact begun. The text submitted to Francis Joseph ended with the words 'the more so as Serbian troops have already attacked a detachment of Imperial and Royal troops at Temes-Kubin.' This was not true; and Berchtold, after the Emperor had signed the Declaration, erased the sentence, explaining the next day that the report was unconfirmed. But he did not give the Emperor any chance to review the decision. His policy was perfectly clear. He meant at all costs by hook or by crook to declare war on Serbia. In the whole world that was

---

*A fuller account of the British naval precautions may be read in *The World Crisis, 1911–1914*.

the only thing that counted with him. That was what Germany had urged. That he must have; and that he got. But he got much more too.

The Serbian reply had been handed to Giesl in Belgrade at 6 p.m. on Saturday, the 25th. Its submissive character was known all over the world on Sunday morning. Its actual text was not officially telegraphed. It reached London, Paris and Berlin by post early on Monday, the 27th. The Serbian Minister in Berlin gave it to the German Foreign Office in the morning, and about noon it was handed to Herr von Jagow. All this is certain. The Kaiser had returned to Germany from his cruise in the Norwegian fjords on the night of the 26th in a very warlike mood. The intemperate minutes which he had scribbled upon the telegrams received at sea convict him of this. At three o'clock in the afternoon on the 27th he held a conference of his executive officers of state and war. The Chancellor was there and the Chiefs of Staff. Jagow was there; but he had not brought the Serbian reply with him. The Emperor was told verbally that 'it agreed on nearly all the points including the punishment of the officers.' He was not told in such a way as to make any decided impression upon him in the general stress. The conference concerned itself with military measures and precautions and separated in a spirit of resolve to 'fight the business through, cost what it may.' [*die Sache, koste es was es wolle, durchzufechten.*][14] This at least was the information conveyed to Falkenhayn, not himself present at the meeting. Jagow returned to Berlin and during the evening received M. Jules Cambon, the French Ambassador, who asked him about the Serbian answer. He said that he 'had not yet had time' to read it. Nearly forty-eight hours had already passed since it had been rendered in Belgrade.

During the evening of the 27th the Wilhelmstrasse completed their arduous task of making a fair copy of the document for the Kaiser. This was sent off by special messenger at 9.30 p.m. to the palace at Potsdam, 18 miles away. Incredible as it may seem, the Kaiser, as we are assured on all hands, did not read it until late in the morning of the 28th. When he did so, he was staggered. In fact, he was completely capsized. Already since his return he was beginning to be uneasy at the attitude of England. He was relieved and delighted at the Serbian submission. He wrote in the margin of the despatch: 'A brilliant performance for a time limit of only forty-eight hours. This is more than one could have expected! A great moral victory for Vienna; but with it every reason for war is removed and Giesl ought to have remained quietly in Belgrade. On the strength of this I should never have ordered mobilization.'[15]

Wilhelm II now thought he had gained what he wanted most of all—a great diplomatic triumph without a shot fired. Once again the Czar would be rebuffed; once again the Austrian alliance would have been cemented by faithful German support. This time, at least, his reputation in German military circles for firmness could be under no reproach. Regicide Serbia would be chastened in due course with the acquiescence of the Powers. There need be no war. He expressed himself ready to negotiate on the basis of a temporary Austrian occupation of Belgrade. He wrote at once to Jagow: 'I am convinced that on the whole the wishes of the Danube monarchy have been acceded to. The few reservations that Serbia makes in regard to individual points can in my opinion well be cleared up by negotiation. But it contains the announcement *orbi et urbi* of a capitulation of the most humiliating kind, and with it every reason for war is removed.'[16]

If these words had been written twelve hours earlier, they would certainly have stopped the War. But now they were too late. At eleven o'clock on this same morning, Tuesday 28th, almost while the Kaiser was writing his minute and congratulating himself that the danger was passed, Count Berchtold telegraphed to Belgrade that 'the Royal Serbian Government not having answered in a satisfactory manner the note of July 23, 1914, presented by the Austro-Hungarian Minister at Belgrade ... Austria-Hungary consequently considered herself henceforward in a state of war with Serbia.'

There can be no doubt that the German Chancellor and Foreign Minister, led up to a certain point by the Kaiser, had made up their minds to bring about a state of war between Austria and Serbia, with the intention of confronting the Powers of the 'Triple Entente' with an issue on which they must fight or fall apart. They believed and also no doubt sincerely hoped that their rivals would choose the latter alternative. They had braced themselves however for the worst contingencies. They knew the impulsive character of the Emperor. They knew his fear of War. They did not intend to give him the opportunity of back-sliding at the critical moment. Hence the routine formality and inexplicable delays at Berlin; hence the decision, speed and energy at Vienna. But there must have been some special art practised to keep the text of the Serbian reply from the Kaiser till the sands had run out. It is on this point that William II should speak. He was by no means supine in the transaction of business. On the contrary he discharged his duties with punctilio and super-abundant energy. Now if ever was the moment in his reign when these qualities were required. This, of all of the innumerable documents he had dealt with in his reign, was the one which deserved them. How was it that the contents of the box delivered by messenger at Potsdam on the night of the 27th did not meet his eye till a further fatal twelve hours had passed? Confidential secretaries, personal aides-de-camp, Court officials—someone—must have been pressed into the service of the Wilhelmstrasse. Was the Kaiser a victim of the same manipulation which in different forms was applied to both his brother autocrats in Russia and Austria? The searchlights of post-war inquiry, which have lighted more brightly the events of this week than any period in history, should be directed to this dark and carefully-shaded spot. The facts remain that the Serbian reply was not read by the man on whose decision the fate of the world still hung, until nearly sixty hours after it had been delivered at Belgrade; and that before he could act upon it, the irrevocable declaration of war had gone forth from Vienna.

The Austrian declaration of war upon Serbia ended the first phase of the outbreak of Armageddon. The griefs and hatreds of these two countries against each other could now obtain satisfaction by arms. The second phase was the dispute between Germany and Russia about the mobilization of their armies. The first quarrel was petty but real; the second measureless but technical. Until the Austrian cannon bombarded Belgrade, the control of German policy lay with the Kaiser and his Ministers. Once fighting had begun even in this obscure corner of Europe, the German and Russian General Staffs predominated. Military reasons cut across and ruptured every diplomatic situation.

Moltke and Falkenhayn towered above Bethmann-Hollweg and Jagow, just as the warlike Grand Dukes and Generals at St. Petersburg took charge of the Czar. Henceforward the prescribed war plans of the German and Russian empires and the execution of the successive stages of their mobilizations became the over-powering theme in both countries. Kaiser and Czar alike felt themselves morally gripped by firm seconds who led them remorselessly to the duelling-ground, cautioned them against betraying weakness or nervousness on the field of honour, handed them the pistols and gave the signal to fire upon each other to their mutual destruction. This second phase occupied four days. It ended at 6 p.m on August I when Germany declared war upon Russia.

During this period immense efforts, led by Sir Edward Grey, were made to retrieve the situation. Nearly all the Ambassadors in all the great capitals strove earnestly for peace. As this movement developed a spontaneous force, it affected both Bethmann-Hollweg and Jagow. When it became increasingly plain to them from the reports of the German Ambassador in London, that a general war would find the British Empire ranged with France and Russia, both lent themselves to action which a few days earlier would have dispersed the crisis. The Kaiser now desperately shaken by the imminence of the explosion, and the Czar sincerely clinging to peace, interchanged a series of personal telegrams unique in the story of nations. But neither they, nor their Ministers, nor all that Grey might do, could regain control of the purely technical measures and counter-measures which the chiefs of armies demanded and took. The first war, between Austria and Serbia, was about a murder. The second war, which absorbed it, was a war between Germany and Russia about precautions. The third and greatest of all wars, beside which the others were but trivial, the war between Germany and France, was merely consequential and happened almost as a matter of form. The German plan for this third war required the invasion of Belgium, and the invasion of Belgium brought the British Empire united to the field. Nothing in human power could break the fatal chain, once it had begun to unroll. A situation had been created where hundreds of officials had only to do their prescribed duty to their respective countries to wreck the world. They did their duty.

War having broken out on the Danube, various levers of precaution or preparation were pressed throughout Europe. At five o'clock we ordered the whole British First Fleet, comprising our thirty-eight best capital ships, to its northern war-station at Scapa Flow. It left Portland at 7 a.m. on the morning of the 29th, passed the Straits of Dover during darkness with all precautions, and by midday on the 30th was safely through the narrow seas and in blue water. This movement, which was kept secret, till accomplished, from all except the Prime Minister, was in no way provocative. The Fleet was actually steaming farther away from Germany. Nobody could object to that; but it made us quite secure whatever might come. We were in the fortunate position that the one essential step which our own safety required, while it increased our diplomatic influence, did not endanger the immediate safety of others.

Up till this stage it had not been certain that Germany and Austria would not gain another bloodless victory such as had rewarded Aerenthal five years before. But on this occasion Germany found herself almost immediately in the presence of a sombre fatalism in the 'Entente' Powers. There was a feeling in Paris and London that Germany meant to have war and meant to have it now. If she did not, it was easy to find half-a-dozen solutions. Grey indefatigably proposed a conference of the Powers and begged all parties to be reasonable. France abstained from every form of provocation. But there the British and French governments came quite definitely to the end of their resources. If Germany intended war, nothing could stop her. If she was bent on so directing events that the long-threatened, long-dreaded hour must strike, then she would have her way. There could not, for instance, be any question of France begging Russia to give in for the sake of peace, or of Great Britain telling France or Russia that they would certainly be left alone if they chose to fight. The two great western Powers felt that if Germany would relieve them of all responsibility and would of her own initiative and at her own moment bring successively Russia, France and Great Britain into one united front against her, they could not help it. They must face whatever was coming to them. Believing themselves about to become the objects of deliberate aggression, and seeing their all-powerful opponent putting himself hopelessly in the wrong, the one thing they would not do was to repudiate each other. To do this might avert the war for the time being. It would leave each of them to face the next crisis alone. They did not dare to separate. They awaited with bated breath but stern hearts the further steps that Germany might choose to take.

The scene must now be shifted to St. Petersburg. We have seen how nicely Berchtold had timed his ultimatum so as to make sure that President Poincaré should have sailed before news of it arrived in Russia. Monsieur Sazonov, the Russian Foreign Minister, had however a premonition. Instead of going to bed after the leave-taking he drove to the Foreign Office, where he learned that a most important despatch from Vienna was being deciphered. It was the ultimatum.

The next morning found Russia and Austria face to face. The deepest feelings of the Slav race were aroused. The wounds of the Bosnian crisis five years before still ached. The visit of the French President, gone but yesterday, gave confidence. Russian society, military and political, was gathered in the capital and large numbers of notables thronged the court at Tsarskoe Selo. Nevertheless, the decisions of the Ministerial Council held on the 24th were studiously restrained. No military steps were taken; but the Minister of War was authorized to prepare in case of necessity orders for a partial mobilization against Austria. A manifesto was published declaring that Russia could not remain indifferent to the fate of Serbia; and Vienna was earnestly asked to extend the time-limit of forty-eight hours to enable discussion to proceed. The German Ambassador, still Pourtalès of the Bosnia crisis, informed Sazonov that Austro-Hungary 'could not accept interference in her differences with Serbia, and Germany also on her side could not accept a suggestion which would be contrary to the dignity of her Ally as a Great Power.' Sazonov rejoined: 'We shall not leave Serbia alone in her struggle against Austria.' The next day arrived the Austrian refusal to extend the time-limit. On this the Czar, presiding over his Council of State, ordered immediate proclamation of the preparatory state, corresponding to Germany's *drohende Kriegsgefahr* ('threatening danger of war') and to our own 'precautionary period,' and of martial law in fortresses and on the frontier. He also authorized his Foreign Minister to issue, when he deemed it necessary, the orders already in preparation for partial mobilization against Austria.

But now occurred one of those technical difficulties of which statesmen should be better informed beforehand. The Russian General Staff was horrified at the form of partial mobilization sanctioned by their Government. They exclaimed that it would derange their plans for general mobilization if, as they believed, war with Germany as well as with Austria should ensue. Even against Austria alone, the Southern Districts would provide thirteen corps only, instead of the sixteen their war-plans required. In particular the mobilization of the Warsaw region not hitherto ordered must be included in any coherent precautions against Austria. They complained vehemently that the partial mobilization which had been approved was a political measure which bore no relation to military requirements; it would confuse their railway movements and be deeply injurious should the supreme danger supervene. General Yanushkevich shook Sazonov with his solid arguments. He was supported by all the principal Staff Officers and by the Quarter-Master General,* Danilov. It was agreed that two ukases should be prepared for the Czar to sign—one for partial, the other for general mobilization—and that final decision which to use should be held in suspense. On this Yanushkevich warned Jilinski, the commander at Warsaw, that July 30 would be announced as the first day of Russian general mobilization.

On the expiry of her ultimatum and the departure of Baron Giesl from Belgrade on the evening of July 25, Austria had ordered the mobilization of eight corps—half the Imperial Army—against Serbia, with the 28th as the first day of mobilization. Although this measure was aimed solely at Serbia, it affected military districts in the north of the Empire like Prague, from which troops were to move to the Serbian frontier.[†] Thus the Russians had grounds for believing that preparations were also on foot against them. The Austrian declaration of war following these disturbing reports determined Sazonov to act upon the discretion accorded him three days before. He therefore sanctioned the partial mobilization, and informed the German Government, with many disclaimers of any hostile intent towards them, that the Odessa, Kiev, Moscow and Kazan military areas would begin to mobilize on the 29th. Jagow had stated on the 27th both to the British and Russian Ambassadors in Berlin, that 'if Russia mobilized only in the south, Germany would not mobilize, but if she mobilized in the north or if Russian troops entered Austrian territory, Germany would have to do so too.' Thus Sazonov had not only reason to take precautions against Austria, but the right to believe that these would not involve Germany in counter-measures.

Meanwhile the temperature was rising fast. On the afternoon of the 29th the news that the Austrian monitors had begun the bombardment of Belgrade roused Russian public and official opinion to fever heat. About the same time the German Ambassador Pourtalès informed Sazonov 'that further continuance of Russia's measures of mobilization would force Germany to mobilize, and that a European war could then scarcely be

---

*i.e. Deputy Chief of the General Staff.
†See map, page 75.

prevented.' The situation of the Russian minister was painful in the extreme. Austria had rejected all his proposals. Germany forbade all pressure upon her Ally. Every word of encouragement or comradeship had been studiously avoided by England. The military chiefs, on whom the life of Russia might depend in a few days, were unanswerable in their technical sphere. Germany had retracted her promise to remain impassive if the Russians mobilized only against Austria. The guns were firing on the Danube, and the attack upon Serbia had actually begun. M. de Sazonov resisted the military men no more. There remained only the Czar.

Late on the night of the 28th the Czar had sent his personal telegram to the Kaiser:

'Am glad you are back. In this most serious moment I appeal to you to help me. An ignoble war has been declared to a weak country. The indignation in Russia shared fully by me is enormous. I foresee that very soon I shall be overwhelmed by the pressure brought upon me and be forced to take extreme measures which will lead to war. To try and avoid such a calamity as a European war, I beg you in the name of our old friendship to do what you can to stop your allies from going too far. NICKY.'[17]

On the morning of the 29th he received a telegram from the Kaiser sent independently a little before his own, saying that the Kaiser fully understood how difficult it was for the Czar and his government to face the trend of public opinion. Therefore

'with regard to the hearty and tender friendship which binds us both from long ago with firm ties, I am exerting my utmost influence to induce the Austrians to deal straightly to arrive at a satisfactory understanding with you. I confidently hope you will help me in my efforts to smooth over difficulties that may still arise. Your very sincere and devoted friend and cousin, WILLY.'[18]

Both these telegrams were in English. They seemed to offer a new hope of peace. But even this intimate tie of the sovereigns, each with his throne and dynasty at stake, could not withstand the hourly increasing strain of the military measures. Some time during the morning of the 29th both ukases for mobilization, partial and general, were presented to the Czar by General Yanushkevich. It seems probable though not certain that after long and strenuous arguments the Czar signed both. At any rate, Dobrorolski, the Chief of Mobilization, during the afternoon of the 29th obtained the signatures of the various high authorities as prescribed by the Russian constitution to an order for general mobilization approved by the Czar. This task was not completed till eight o'clock, and the General having cleared the telegraph lines was about to give the decisive signal, when he received a definite order from the Czar cancelling general mobilization and authorizing only partial mobilization.

Nicholas II was still struggling for peace. He had telegraphed again to the Kaiser thanking him for his conciliatory and friendly messages, and ending 'it would be right to give over the Austro-Serbian problem to the Hague Conference. Trust in your wisdom and friendship.' At 9.40 p.m. on the 29th the reply of the Kaiser to the Czar's first telegram arrived. It suggested that Russia should 'remain a spectator of the Austro-Serbian conflict, without involving Europe in the most horrible war she ever witnessed.' He advocated a direct understanding between the Russian and Austrian governments and promised to promote it. Although this was no concession at all by Germany on the main issue, it had affected Nicholas II sufficiently to induce him to countermand the general mobilization. He even tried to stop the partial mobilization; but both Sazonov and Yanushkevich convinced him that this was impossible. At 1.20 a.m. he replied to the Kaiser:

> 'Thank you heartily for your quick answer. . . . The military measures which have now come into force were decided five days ago for reasons of defence on account of Austria's preparations. I hope from all my heart that these measures won't in any way interfere with your part as mediator which I greatly value. We need your strong pressure on Austria to come to an understanding with us.'[19]

None of these internal Russian perturbations were apparent to Berlin. The German General Staff had full and punctual information of most of what was being done in the various Russian military districts. Although the formal order even for partial mobilization was not dispatched till midnight on the 29th, the commanders concerned, warned informally by the General Staff, in their professional zeal and lively expectation of war, were already making all kinds of preparations in anticipation of the order which they expected momentarily to receive. All such preparations were reported to Berlin. They involved, for instance, the Warsaw area, as well as the southern commands of which Germany had been officially informed by the Russian Government. Since the 29th Moltke had urged the sending of an ultimatum to Russia, and Falkenhayn had demanded the proclamation of '*drohende Kriegsgefahr.*' When on the 30th the Russian formal announcement of the partial mobilization was received, the Kaiser agreed to this. 'Threatening danger of war' was proclaimed. This measure was virtually equivalent to the first two days of general mobilization, that is to say it set in motion a vast number of processes that would in any case have been taken upon a decree of general mobilization. It must not be supposed, however, that the military commanders throughout Germany had remained inert during the last three or four days. Like their Russian counterparts each wished to be forward in every preparation, and all the military centres were humming with activity. Reports of all this, carried back to Russia, decided Sazonov and the military authorities that general mobilization could be delayed no longer. By an immense concerted effort they prevailed upon the Czar at 4 p.m. on July 30 to sign a new ukase of general mobilization, and an hour later all the military centres were so informed.

Shortly before noon on July 31 the news of the Russian general mobilization reached Berlin. At 3.30 p.m. an ultimatum was sent to Russia declaring that if Russia did not 'within twelve hours cease every war measure against us and Austria-Hungary and make to us a definite declaration to that effect,' the German mobilization would be ordered. This summons was delivered at midnight on July 31. At 6 p.m. August 1 Germany declared war on Russia. It is strange to reflect that on this very day Sir Edward Grey had at last reached a complete agreement with the German Foreign Office upon a form of direct negotiation between Austria and Russia. The cause of quarrel had disappeared on paper at the same time as the fighting all over Europe began.

The British preparations kept pace with these grave developments. At the Cabinet on the morning of the 30th, moved by Captain Hankey,* the Secretary of the Committee of Imperial Defence, I asked and obtained sanction for the putting into force of the 'precautionary period'; which the War Office ordered at 2.10 p.m. At the same time as this was done I authorized the Admiralty to send the 'Warning telegram' to the fleets. This last had become only a formality. Apart from the recall of the reservists of the Third Fleet ships, all our naval arrangements so far as we could foresee them were complete.

* * * * *

The war of Austria upon Serbia about the murder of the Archduke and other grievances had begun. The second war of far graver character had broken out between Germany and Russia about the mobilization of the Russian armies against Austria. The Eastern Front was aflame. But now the third and greatest spread of the conflagration must follow. The German General Staff had no fears about Russia at the outset. They could easily have waited for two or three days before taking any measure against her. All their thoughts were turned on France. Since the war had come, they must attack France without delay. The six brigades straining at the leash beyond the frontier must violate Belgian neutrality and seize Liége from the second day of mobilization. Not a moment could be lost. Accordingly Germany on July 31 informed France of her ultimatum to Russia and asked the French Government to declare within eighteen hours whether it intended to remain neutral in a Russo-German war. Belgium was also invited to afford clear passage to the German armies about to invade France. There was of course no quarrel between Germany and France, and a treaty of guarantee between Germany and Belgium. These difficulties had to be surmounted promptly. The German Ambassador in Paris was therefore instructed, if contrary to expectation France should declare an intention of remaining neutral, to 'demand the surrender of the fortresses of Toul and Verdun as a pledge of neutrality.' This demand—like asking Great Britain to hand over Portsmouth and Dover—was intended to make sure that there could be no backing out by France. Any such improper behaviour on her part would have been most embarrassing to Germany, whose armies had already started. The French Prime Minister, M. Viviani, however, replied forthwith, according to the formula agreed upon in his Cabinet, that 'France would act according to her interests.' 'You have a treaty of alliance with Russia, have you not?' '*Parfaitement*' [quite so], replied Viviani. Nothing could be more correct and debonair, and the German Ambassador was thus relieved from delivering the second and contingent part of his message about Toul and Verdun. Monsieur Viviani escorted his visitor to his car. Nothing more of significance passed between the two countries. Germany declared war

---

*Now Sir Maurice Hankey.

on France at 6.45 p.m. on August 3; and the next morning the German vanguards broke into the Duchy of Luxembourg, in contravention of the various treaties which protected it, on their way to march across Belgium to the invasion of France. The Belgian king and people, threatened with instant assault, appealed for aid to Great Britain and France as joint guarantors with Germany of her neutrality.

When these events became apparent to the British Cabinet and Parliament during August 2 and 3, an ultimatum was sent to Germany forbidding her to violate the Belgian frontiers, and requiring her to withdraw at once any troops who might have done so. Answer was required by midnight on the 4th. The answer was a refusal and the continued march of the German armies. At midnight therefore by German time on August 4 Great Britain, in full unity with all the Dominions and dependencies of the British Empire, declared war upon Germany.

* * * * *

It is impossible to recount these events in the light of all we know without once again trying to apportion responsibility. We have described the slow half-conscious growth of European antagonisms in the quarter-century before the catastrophe. We have seen how the mine was slowly loaded. We are now concerned with the guilt of firing it. After all, it need never have been fired. A war postponed may be a war prevented. The combinations of States vary as years pass. The Ententes or Alliances of one decade may have lost their savour in the next. Time and peace solve many problems, and men's thoughts move on to new spheres. Terrible before the history of a thousand years is the burden of those who let this blast of misery and devastation loose upon the thoughtless world.

We must not allow ourselves to be baffled by the immense volume of knowledge now accessible upon the immediate coming of the war. Everything has been laid bare. The Gooch-Temperley official documents reveal the whole conduct of Great Britain. Even the German writer Ludwig affirms that there is no substantial discrepancy between these full post-war disclosures and the voluminous Blue Book published within a few months of the beginning of the struggle. The archives of the German, Austrian and Russian Empires have been ruthlessly exposed by revolutionary Governments, each anxious to condemn the old regime or at the least unconcerned to protect it. Not only dispatches and telegrams, but office memoranda, the records of informal conversations between diplomatists or military men, the marginal scribblings of the Kaiser, all are now in world-open print. There is no lack of material. Indeed, it is its plethora that obstructs judgment.

To read many modern writers one would suppose that the war came by itself, and that no person in authority ever thought of such a wicked thing. Berchtold did this and Conrad that, and Jagow was on his honeymoon, and Tschirschky was snubbed by the Kaiser, and Bethmann-Hollweg did not understand the situation, and the Russians got excited and Moltke alarmed, and then all of a sudden all the greatest nations in the world fell upon each other with fire and sword. It was a case of spontaneous combustion. The theory that it all happened by itself, that Germany carelessly gave Austria a blank cheque to correct Serbia, that Russia was indignant at the spectacle, that Germany was alarmed because Russia mobilized, that France and England did not tell Russia she must give in, that England did not tell Germany in time that she would fight, that all Berchtold wanted was his little private war with Serbia, that all Germany wanted was not to be forced to desert her ally, that all the Kaiser wanted was a diplomatic triumph—all these cases find ample documentary support. Still certain stark facts which no elaboration can veil stand forth for all time.

Berchtold and his circle meant to use armed violence upon Serbia. The Kaiser encouraged and urged them to do so. Both parties knew that such an event must arouse not only the Czar and his government, but the Russian nation. Both decided to accept this risk and whatever else it might entail. The Kaiser, having given Berchtold and Vienna a free hand, deliberately absented himself until the ultimatum to Serbia had been dispatched. The German Chancellor and Foreign Secretary instructed their Ambassadors to declare that Germany considered the ultimatum right and proper, before they had even seen its terms. When the Serbians returned a soft answer, Jagow and others delayed the presentation of this document to the Kaiser until it was too late for him to prevent Austria declaring war upon Serbia. Berchtold issued his declaration of war with precipitate haste and obtained its signature from the Emperor Francis Joseph, partly under false pretences. Every request for delay was refused by Vienna. Every proposal, whether for conference of the Powers or direct negotiations between Austria and Russia, was refused or resisted until too late. At St. Petersburg the Russian Government, Court and military men extracted first a partial and then a complete mobilization decree from the reluctant Czar. Germany fastened upon Russia a deadly quarrel about her mobilization. Germany sent an ultimatum to Russia requiring her to cancel it within twelve hours. At this moment the German mobilization, although not officially proclaimed, was already in progress. Germany declared war upon Russia. Germany summoned France to repudiate the terms of the Franco-Russian Alliance and hand over to German keeping her key fortresses as gages of faithful neutrality. Germany declared war upon France. Germany violated the treaty protecting the Duchy of Luxembourg. Germany violated the neutrality of Belgium. When Belgium resisted, Germany declared war upon Belgium, and marched across Belgium to the invasion of France. It was not till then that Great Britain declared war upon Germany, and we are still disinclined to say that she was wrong.

CHAPTER VIII
THE MOBILIZATION INTERVAL

The mobilization of all the armies proceeded apace. The peoples of Europe were smoothly and swiftly drawn into the cogwheels of a long-prepared, all-powerful and intricate machinery of whose existence they had hitherto been only vaguely aware. The patiently elaborated plans of all the general staffs for the various wars that might have to be fought had been put into operation by a few simple decisions, and by every road and railway more than twelve million men were moving towards the battlefields. Censorship and secrecy cast their palls over the scene, and a strange hush descended upon Europe. The silence was broken only by the crackling of the German advance guards breaking into Belgium, and by the Austrian invasion of Serbia. These two small countries at the opposite ends of the battle fronts were the first to feel the edge of the Teutonic swords. In each case compelling motives actuated the invaders. The capture of Liége and the opening of the four lines of railway which passed through it were indispensable to the deployment of the German right wing. The rapid overrunning and subjugation of Serbia was no less urgent for Austria. If this could be accomplished in a three-weeks' campaign, as was generally believed, the bulk of the troops used against Serbia would be in time for the later phases of the opening battles with Russia. But a speedy, decisive victory over Serbia promised other consequences even more important.

Germany had good hopes when the crisis began of gaining other adherents. The Triple Alliance included Italy, and a military convention was based on this fact. She was a party to Austria's secret treaty of alliance with Roumania. She had a close understanding with Bulgaria cemented by an identity of animosities against Serbia. She had considerable expectations of Greece, arising from the connection of the Royal Families. Lastly, on August 2 she had contracted an offensive and defensive alliance with Turkey. Thus the whole of south-east Europe was by presumption vowed or inclined to the Teutonic cause. Over all these confident expectations the apparition of the British Empire as the ally of France and Russia had thrown a paralyzing chill. Italy had been the first to fall away. By a secret condition in the original treaty of the Triple Alliance Italy had stipulated that she should not be obliged in any circumstances to go to war with England. The Austrian designs upon Serbia prejudiced Italian interests, and immediate claims for compensation in the Trentino were advanced. The historic feud and clash of interests between Italy and Austria came plainly into view. The position of the Italian army in Libya, and indeed the life of Italy itself, would be jeopardized in a war in which the command of the Mediterranean was lost or seriously endangered. On July 31 Italy, deaf to all appeals from Berlin and Vienna, explained that as Austria was the initial aggressor against Serbia, the *casus foederis* did not arise, and declared that she would remain neutral. The decision of Italy affected profoundly the attitude of Roumania. King Carol, with his pro-German sympathies, pleaded the text of the secret treaty in vain. Opinion in Bucharest had been estranged by the terms of the Austrian ultimatum to Serbia, nor could Roumania contemplate without alarm an increase of Bulgarian territory at Serbia's expense. Although as late as August 9 the Roumanian Chief of the Staff inquired from Conrad at what points it would be convenient for the Roumanian army to concentrate, the decision to remain neutral had already been taken. King Carol, overruled by statesmen of all parties, among whom Mr. Take Jonescu, always a sincere friend of England, played a prominent part, bowed in grief to the inevitable. Greece could not dissociate herself from Great Britain or from British sea-power. The Young Turks, whose plans for a war with Russia and conquests in the Caucasus were completed, found their hopes of gaining the command of the Black Sea destroyed by the impounding of the new-built Turkish battleship about to sail from the Tyne. Turkey was also affected by the sudden unexpected problems which a war with Great Britain would bring upon her. Bulgaria alone was found willing, under important reservations, to promise to march with the Central Powers when an opportune moment arrived; but the danger of offending Roumania made the Central Empires hesitate to avail themselves of this aid. Thus the whole combination which a generation of German diplomacy had been building dissolved in a vapour of hesitations and polite disclaimers. The action of Great Britain also determined the attitude of her small but ancient ally, Portugal; and at the other side of the globe the empire of Japan, although the Anglo-Japanese alliance was not invoked, prepared herself to extirpate German influence in the Far East. Certainly the long-gathered associations and slowly woven ties which the influence of the British Empire had established were impressively effective.

All the more important was it for Austria to clarify the Balkan situation by a speedy conquest and elimination of Serbia. The defeat of Serbia and her collapse might be the signal which several at least of the neutral States seemed to await before answering to the long-drawn and several times repeated trumpet-call.

* * * * *

Conrad had already taken his first military decision. It was a capital error and its consequences were inexorable. The Austrian plans, like those of other countries, had been drawn for various contingencies. Plan **B**, 'Balkan,' the smaller and more probable, was for war against Serbia and Montenegro while Russia remained neutral. In **B**, three out of six Austro-Hungarian armies were to invade Serbia, the Fifth and Sixth from Bosnia and Herzegovina, and the Second across the Save and Danube, while the other three armies took up precautionary defensive positions against possible Russian hostility in Galicia. Plan **R**, 'Russia,' on the other hand, contemplated a war with Serbia and Russia simultaneously. In this case only the Fifth and Sixth armies, much weaker than the others and amounting to twelve divisions, were to invade Serbia from the west, while the Second Army was to join the main Austrian concentration in Galicia. Which to choose? On July 25, when Austria ordered mobilization, Conrad had chosen Plan **B**, 'Balkan.'

The origins of this surprising decision are found in the conversations and councils which have already been described at which the chastisement of Serbia was resolved. The German blank cheque had arrived; it must be filled in at once and cashed, lest it should be stopped. To act promptly and with enormous force against Serbia was what the Germans had invited. It offered a chance of a rapid sudden success and a campaign over before Europe had recovered from her shock, and while diplomacy might still be endeavouring only to limit the conflict. This idea of an immediate decisive striking down and punishment of Serbia in a private war while the rest of the world was talking or keeping the ring had taken possession of Berchtold and his colleagues, and Conrad viewed the problem through their eyes. His own account is revealing.

'The diplomatic activities took as their goal only a war against Serbia, consequently mobilization and assembly for this must ensue. To break this off or to diminish the strength employed on account of the possibility of Russia's intervention was not feasible. It might well be—and diplomacy counted on it—that the action against Serbia would be completed without an interruption by other Powers. This was the more likely to occur if a rapid thorough success against Serbia forestalled the intervention of other Powers. It followed that strong forces should be directed against Serbia from the outset; that is, that the complete mobilization "**B**" and the assembly against Serbia involved in it should be ordered.

'This necessity was imposed upon us by the diplomatic action.'

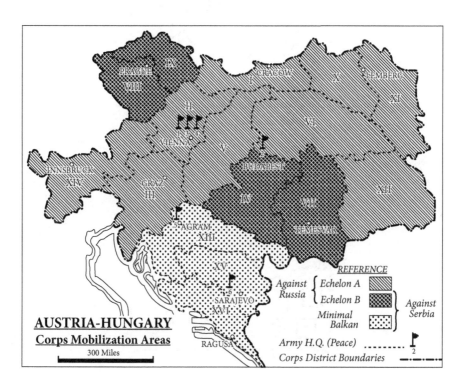

AUSTRIA-HUNGARY
Corps Mobilization Areas
300 Miles

He proceeds:

'Meanwhile there was the danger that Russia would seize Austria's upraised arm, might threaten war or even actually resort to it. From a military point of view therefore the most desirable thing would have been to take the initiative against this danger and to treat the war against Serbia as a side-show. But to do this on the strength merely of the possibility of Russian intervention was out of the question, since if Austria acted thus the obligation on the part of her allies to co-operate would lapse. Moreover, Austria would thereby incur the grave charge of letting loose a world war, whereas the war against Serbia was merely a brutally imposed action of self-defence.

'For the diplomats the situation was clear. It was otherwise for the Chief of the General Staff, who on the one hand must keep before him the rapid and decisive war against Serbia, but on the other must be prepared suddenly to divert everything towards a war with Russia. This was a dilemma involving in itself the gravest responsibility and a most unfavourable situation from the point of view of operations. . . . '[20]

These reasons may be true or partly true; but they are not convincing. Conrad had misjudged what Russia would do and ignored the true proportions of the military problem. Already on July 25 the effects of the Austrian ultimatum to Serbia were apparent in every capital. By the 26th the German government was conscious of a stern spirit in the Powers of the Triple Entente. The Russian agitation was intense; the French had shown an icy calm; England had declared in the most public manner that her First and Second Fleets would remain concentrated. A situation of terrific intensity had been created. The idea that Austria would be suffered to invade and crush Serbia while all the other Powers remained spectators was fantastic. Yet under the prepossessions of a fortnight before, when Germany was believed to be wishing for vigour against Serbia, and in spite of the new vast peril of the situation, Plan **B** was put into operation and carried out in a purblind integrity.

It is vain for Conrad to shield himself behind 'diplomacy.' Nothing could supersede the military situation for which he was responsible. The life-and-death fortunes of the Austro-Hungarian Empire depended upon the Russian action. If Russia invaded Austria, every man would be needed. Until a battle had been fought between Russia and Austria no entanglement of Austro-Hungarian forces in Serbia could be tolerated. If on the other hand Russia, confronted with the armed might of Germany, lowered her sword, the chastisement of Serbia would be easy and sure. A very few days would settle the question one way or the other. Conrad had only to reply to those who pressed him to strike down Serbia: 'We shall know very soon whether it is to be Plan **B** or Plan **R**, and I insist upon that delay, even if we lose our advantage against Serbia.' But impatient to strike the detested enemy, he underrated the chances of Russian action, and though the briefest pause would have given him certainty, launched the Imperial armies on an erroneous premise.

On July 31 the general mobilization of Russia was in full progress. On the same afternoon the Kaiser telegraphed to the Emperor as follows:

'The preliminary mobilization of my entire army and of my navy which I have ordered to-day will be followed in the shortest possible time by definite mobilization. I count the 2nd August as the first day of mobilization and am prepared, in fulfilment of my duties as an ally, to begin war against Russia immediately. In this momentous struggle it is of the greatest importance that Austria should direct her main forces against Russia and should not divide her forces by an offensive against Serbia. This is the more important as a large part of my army will be tied by France. In the battle of giants into which we are entering shoulder to shoulder, Serbia plays quite a subsidiary part, which calls only for such defensive measures as are absolutely necessary. A successful issue of the war, and with it the existence of our monarchies, is only to be hoped for if both of us move with our full strength against our new and mighty opponents. I beg of you further to do all you can by meeting her wishes to induce Italy to take part. All else must be subordinated to the entry of a united Triple Alliance into the war.—WILHELM.'[21]

So here is the whole web of illusion torn to pieces and Conrad and the Austrian leaders are face to face with a hideous reality of an immediate Russian invasion which their Ally is urging them to meet with their fullest strength. On paper, Plan **B** was automatically superseded by Plan **R**. It was now necessary to send the Second Army to the north. However, it was already in its trains for the opposite direction. A spring had been released and the highly complicated process was in active progress. To arrest the movement of the Second Army in mid-transit would throw the whole organization into confusion. No course was open but to allow its eight divisions to complete their journey to the Serbian frontier, detrain at their appointed sidings, proceed to their assembly points, and then in their proper order of arms and units re-enter their trains and be carried to Galicia. This return journey could not begin effectively till August 18. There was the consolation that the mere arrival of this army on the Serbian frontier would draw off a proportion of the Serbian forces and thus aid the Fifth and Sixth Austrian Armies. Conrad was thus forced to pretend a necessity where none existed, and to make a virtue of it, if possible. He says:

> 'The First, Third and Fourth Armies were on the way occupying all assembly transport routes towards Galicia, while the Second Army was arriving, to start with, on the Save and Danube and would not follow the above-named armies until after the lines of approach to Galicia had become free.
>
> 'If these orders, imposed by necessity, had the advantage that until the Second Army was withdrawn from the Save and Danube the enemy would find himself threatened there and would be compelled to hold forces to oppose them, yet there was also the danger that the forces of the Second Army might become involved in hostilities against Serbia. The great river barrier, of course, diminished this danger.'[22]

He felt the need of offering some explanation to his military colleague upon the strange peregrinations to which his Second Army was condemned. He wrote to Moltke on August 1:*

> 'YOUR EXCELLENCY,—
>
> 'At this fateful moment I am impelled to place myself in direct relations with you in order to make certain of that full unity which I have always kept as my objective. We hoped to wage this as a localized war without further complications. The endeavour of all the Powers to localize the war strengthened us in this belief. It is natural that we should assemble for this [localized] war sufficient forces to hold out a prospect of success by weight of numbers. When Russia by mobilizing her southern military districts showed herself hostile to the Monarchy, we turned to Germany with the request that she would declare that this step taken against

---

*Dated August 2.

us would also be unacceptable to Germany. At the same time, mobilization of the remainder of the army was ordered, for their assembly in Galicia was envisaged. At this stage we were obliged—as, indeed, Germany also urgently wished—to declare openly that our hostile measures were only directed against Serbia and that further mobilization was merely a measure of protection against the threat from Russia.

'It was hoped that these measures, in conjunction with the energetic diplomatic pressure of the other Powers, more especially Germany, would restrain Russia from hostile action against the Monarchy, and would also afford to the latter the possibility of carrying through her action against Serbia.

'Such being the case, we could, and must, hold fast to the idea of the offensive against Serbia, the more so since we had to bear in mind that Russia might merely intend to restrain us from action against Serbia by a threat, without proceeding to war against us. While, however, the Powers—and, above all, Germany—were only intervening diplomatically, Russia did not discontinue her mobilization, but made it general. Meanwhile, our movements destined against the South began to take place. From the diplomatic activities of that time it was, in our opinion, apparent that Germany, if we were attacked by Russia, would, indeed, fulfil her duties as an ally, but that she would rather avoid a Great War. Thus, we were obliged to hold to our intention to proceed with our action against Serbia, and to entrust our protection against Russia—against whom we could not by ourselves initiate an offensive war—to our troops which were to assemble in Galicia and to the German threat to Russia and the influence of the remaining Powers.

'It was not until July 31 that there came suddenly the decided declaration of Germany that she herself was now willing to carry through the Great War against France and Russia. This produced an entirely new situation. It was immediately reckoned here that we must put in the preponderating mass of our forces in the North, and I beg Your Excellency to accept the assurance that, in spite of the great complications caused by our transport of troops to the South which has already been completed, this will be carried through.'[23]

'*Qui s'excuse, s'accuse! Qui s'explique, se complique!*'

* * * * *

The full force of 'Plan **B**' had been put into operation against Serbia concurrently with the Austrian mobilization on July 25. The Dual Monarchy declared war upon Serbia on the 28th and three Austrian armies moved towards the Serbian frontier. The position of the Serbians seemed forlorn. Northern Serbia is lapped and bounded on three sides by the Danube and its tributary, the Save, into which the Drina flows. Belgrade, the capital, stood actually upon the Danube at the frontier and was undefendable. Three army corps comprising eight divisions of the Austrian Second Army began to deploy along the northern frontier while the Fifth and Sixth Austrian Armies, each comprising two corps, about eleven divisions, advanced to invade Serbia from the West. The Serbian Commander-in-Chief, the Voivode Putnik, could not tell whether the main hostile advance would be made from the North or the West. He did not know, as we know, that the Austrian Second Army detraining to the northward was from August 2 under orders to scramble back into its trains and hurry to the Russian front in Galicia. All he saw was the marshalling and deployment of powerful forces upon both frontiers. Indeed, he believed that the main invasion would come upon him from the North. The Serbian army consisted of 11½ infantry divisions and one cavalry division, in all 180,000 rifles, 8,500 sabres and 500 guns. To the southward in the mountainous and broken country behind the upper Drina, the Montenegrins gathered, 40,000 strong. The Serbian forces were divided into three so-called Armies, each of which, however, was little stronger than an Austrian Army Corps. Leaving detachments to observe the frontier and delay the invasion, General Putnik assembled his three armies in the centre of Northern Serbia, facing North with their left upon the town of Valjevo and with covering troops along the rivers. These prudent dispositions, although facing north in error, enabled the front to be easily and swiftly changed to meet the real attack from the West.

The deployment of the Austrian armies around the Serbian frontiers marshalled some 19 divisions against the Serbian 11½, and these by their geographical position seemed able to advance now from one side, now from the other, to turn the flank or rear of any position occupied by their weaker antagonists. In addition, behind all, low down on the eastern border, Bulgaria waited, armed and silent, with memories of recent unutterable injuries to avenge. But the Serbians, seasoned, war-hardened men, inspired by the fiercest patriotism, the result of generations of torment and struggle, awaited undaunted whatever Fate might bestow.

The command of the two armies destined to invade Serbia was confided to General Potiorek, whom we have already met as Governor of Bosnia on the fatal day of Sarajevo. Potiorek had a strong position with the Court. He had served under Baron Bolfras for some years. He was intimate with the Emperor. His favour had survived unharmed the many indignant comments which the faulty and neglectful police arrangements of June 28 had excited. His nerves were however seriously affected by the tragedy. Throughout his campaigns against Serbia he kept himself closely within his guarded headquarters. Thence he directed the operations and used his influence with the Emperor to procure the largest number of troops for the longest possible time—regardless of the general situation. In particular he clamoured unceasingly for the use of the Second Army; and Conrad was soon engaged in a serious dispute with him about it.

Potiorek knew that the Second Austrian Army was strictly forbidden to cross the Save-Danube line and must begin its departure for Galicia on the 18th. Nevertheless he ordered his Fifth and Sixth Armies to invade Serbia upon two widely separated and divergent lines. The Fifth Army advancing on August 12 was to reach Valjevo on the 17th; The Sixth Army to the southward, starting between August 14–18, would move on Uzhitse. Meanwhile the Second Army would demonstrate especially against Mitrovitsa and Shabatz and threaten to cross the Save from the North. It followed from this plan that the Austrian Fifth Army would have to fight practically the whole of the Serbian forces single-handed; for the Second Army was soon departing, and the Sixth Army was out of contact to the southward, preoccupied with maintaining the loyalty of Bosnia, and wandering off to engage the Montenegrins, and 1½ Serbian divisions coming from Uzhitse. The relative strength of the combatants was thus transformed. The 6 Austrian divisions of the VIIIth and XIIIth Corps might expect to meet the bulk of the Serbian army, actually 10 divisions, somewhere between the Drina and the Kolubara, or behind the latter river itself. Potiorek hoped, of course, that the threat of the Second Army from the North and the Bulgarian danger in the East would lead the Serbians to disperse their forces. General Putnik, in what may well have seemed to him a desperate situation, found safety by running risks. He kept his three armies together in his central position, determined to hurl their whole strength at whichever of the foes who encircled his country first exposed themselves to battle.

On August 12 the Austrian Fifth Army began its advance, and crossed the Drina between Zvornik and Liuboviya, meeting determined resistance from the Serb covering troops as they fell back slowly. The IVth Corps from the Second Austrian Army entered Shabatz almost unopposed. The direction of the invasion being now defined, Putnik swung his Third and Second armies to face west behind the Dobrava and Jadar rivers, while his First Army followed them up. By August 15, the right of the Austrian advance had reached the neighbourhood of Krupanj and Zavlaka on the Jadar, while its left approached the Dobrava which flows into the Save below Shabatz. Their centre was still an hour from the township of Tekerish at nightfall. A heavy storm in the evening brought all movements to an end. Meanwhile Putnik, marching swiftly forward from the Kolubara, placed his Second and Third armies ready for battle from the Save below Shabatz to Krupanj. He held his First Army in reserve to guard against the attacks which he must fear from the Second Austrian Army across the Save between Shabatz and Obrenovatz.

On August 16 what has been called the Battle of the Jadar began. Fierce fighting ensued on a front of about thirty miles. The Serbian left, threatened on both flanks by the advance of Potiorek's XIIIth Corps, retired beyond Krupanj. But in the north among maize-fields and thick, intersected blind country, the Austrian advance from Shabatz was repulsed with heavy loss. Even worse were Austrian fortunes on the front of the VIIIth Corps in the centre. The 21st (Schützen) Division, composed mostly of Czechs, met with grave disaster and were driven in rout from the key position of the whole battle. Treachery and cowardice were imputed to these unwilling soldiers, who, after a prolonged disorderly flight, reassembled beyond the Drina only 3,000 strong. Night fell with the Austrian centre broken and driven back upon the Drina, and with the Austrian left repulsed with heavy losses, and also compromised by the disaster in the centre.

That same night Conrad, with the titular commander-in-chief, the Archduke Frederick, left Vienna for Przemysl, his headquarters against Russia. Here, on August 17, he learned Potiorek's unpleasant news. It raised a poignant issue. The Second Army, already so long delayed, was due to leave the Serbian front on the 18th. There was not an hour to lose. But its departure at this moment might well entail the complete defeat of the Fifth Army and the failure of the whole plan against Serbia. On the other hand, its intervention promised an almost certain victory, which would or might bring in Bulgaria and Turkey. Already, during the night of the 16th, Conrad had consented to allow the Second Army

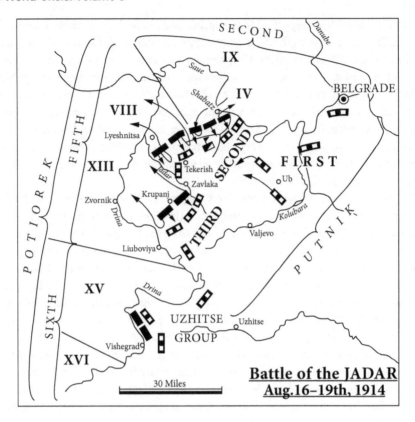

Battle of the JADAR
Aug.16–19th, 1914

30 Miles

to demonstrate in force along the Save to conceal the fact of its impending departure and to pin down the enemy. Now Potiorek demanded its full support; and a few minutes later the Second Army itself reported the retreat of the Northern Wing of the Fifth Army, and that its own IVth Corps was advancing towards Shabatz to their assistance. Meanwhile beyond the frontiers of Galicia, the Russian masses must be gathering in enormous strength and the battle of the nations drew near. Tossed on the horns of his self-created dilemma, Conrad allowed the Second Army to throw the IV Corps in towards Shabatz, if this was judged necessary, in order to achieve success. But that evening came a further wire from Potiorek. His demands had increased with his distresses. 'The intervention of the Second Army in driblets might,' he declared, 'lead to a reverse; they should cross the Save in force not only at Shabatz but lower down. Until they had to depart to Galicia surely they could not remain passive onlookers.' The Second Army themselves wired: 'Are we to leave IV Corps behind, or to move as arranged?' Conrad thereupon ordered the departure in principle of the Second Army, but agreed that the IVth Corps might remain until the Shabatz situation was resolved.

The fighting continued on the 18th and 19th. The Austrian IVth Corps drove back the Serbian right and the Serbians fell back behind the Dobrava. But the Serbian Second Army, reinforced by a division from its First Army, threw back the remainder of the Austrian VIIIth Corps on Lyeshnitsa, while their Third Army held its own in the south.

The whole of the Austrian Fifth Army was now in a grievous position. A week's hard fighting in hot weather and difficult country against a hardy enemy and with poor artillery support had exhausted its strength. Supplies, both of ammunition and food, were running low. Its centre and left were hard-pressed and retiring. Its left flank was about to be exposed by the withdrawal of the Second Army. In these circumstances its commander (Frank) ordered the general retirement of the Army beyond the Drina river. Potiorek's report on the evening of the 19th ended 'Fifth Army in retreat . . . one division of VIIIth Corps has been dispersed and the other has suffered very heavily. The XIIIth Corps is intact. The IVth Corps at Shabatz is engaged with equal numbers of the enemy. Result not yet known. The help asked for,' he added ungraciously, 'came two days too late.' Conrad and the Austrian Headquarters now took a hard decision. They determined to cut the loss in Serbia and at all costs to prevent the Second Army becoming involved there. Potiorek challenged this ruling. 'If the Second and Sixth Armies cannot forthwith take the offensive, as a set off to the defeat of the Fifth, my task of keeping the Serbs off the soil of the Monarchy will be very difficult,' and further that he was 'holding the three divisions in readiness.'

He now exerted all his influence at Vienna. The Emperor's military Cabinet intervened. Berchtold on Potiorek's side invoked diplomacy and the prestige of the Monarchy in the Balkans. Despite the appeals of the Archduke Frederick, Conrad and the Austrian Headquarters were overruled by the Emperor, and Potiorek was placed in independent command of 'All the Army Corps engaged against Serbia and Montenegro.' He was to lead them to further disasters. It was not until August 30 that Conrad was able to disentangle the missing IVth Corps.

* * * * *

The Austrian entry into the field illustrates once again the commonest of all the great military errors. It is the error most easy to perceive in theory and most difficult to avoid in action. There are two enemies and two theatres: the task of the Commander is to choose in which he will prevail. To choose either, is to suffer grievously in the neglected theatre. To choose both, is to lose in both. The Commander has for his guides the most honoured principles of war and the most homely maxims of life. 'First things first!' 'Being before well-being!' 'What you do, do well!' 'Always be strongest at the point of attack!' It is the application of these simple rules to the facts that constitutes the difficulty and the torment. A score of good reasons can be given not only for either course, but also for the compromises which ruin them. But the path to safety nearly always lies in rejecting the compromises. We have seen how Conrad was led astray by forces and reasons which seemed to him irresistible. We shall presently see Moltke and his successor Falkenhayn succumbing under the same pressures. We shall also watch their effects upon Lord Kitchener and the British War Committee.

Until Conrad pressed the button which set Plan **B** in motion, he had the choice of two sound operations. The first was to neglect Serbia and concentrate every man and gun (apart from troops needed to prevent or even merely to delay the Serbian invasion of Austria) upon his long-weighed offensive against Russia. The second was to crush

Serbia, invading from every side at once in overwhelming force, and thus probably bring Bulgaria and Turkey, if not indeed Roumania, at once into the field as allies. But this entailed standing on the defensive in Galicia. He must retire, fighting delaying actions for as long and as far as might be necessary, yielding mile by mile the soil of the Monarchy till Serbia had been annihilated. Of these two plans, the former was the more magnificent; but the latter offered great prizes. Moreover a delaying strategy by Austria at the beginning of the war consorted naturally with the Schlieffen Plan. The Germans hoped to be victorious in the West within six weeks from mobilization, and would then return to the East with ample power. If Conrad could keep alive and unbeaten against Russia for that period, he had every right to count on strong German aid; and with this aid, even if the Russians had crossed the Carpathians, all could quickly have been regained. Meanwhile he would have settled with Serbia and perhaps have gained Turkey and Bulgaria.

From the moment that he had given the order which irrevocably sent his Second Army to the Danube and kept it out of the opening battles in Galicia, only this latter alternative was rightly open to him. It was his paramount duty to make the Second Army fight *somewhere* at the crucial moment. It could no longer reach Galicia in time to fight there. It must therefore fight in the station into which it had got, and win a decision there. It followed that Conrad must renounce his offensive against Russia, about which already he had so many misgivings, and adopt dilatory tactics till the Franco-German issue was declared. But in fact he did neither. He fooled away the power of the Second Army in both theatres. It left Potiorek before it could win him a victory. It returned to Conrad in time to take part in his defeat.

CHAPTER IX
THE ASSEMBLY OF THE EASTERN ARMIES

The Austrian plan for a war against Russia contemplated the assembly of their forces in the Galician plain behind the San and Dniester rivers, and in front of the Carpathians. This was well suited for an immediate advance into Russian territory, but threatened many dangers in the event of defeat. The Austrian line of retreat lay either south and south-west through the passes of the eastern Carpathians or westward through Przemysl and Cracow into Bohemia, or possibly into German Silesia through the narrow corridor between Russian Poland and the western Carpathians, called 'The Moravian Gate.'

Since, in making his war plan against Russia, Conrad had resolved upon a forestalling attack, his mishandling of the opening movements becomes all the more blameworthy. Plan **R** had counted upon four Austrian armies to support his offensive, in which case his superiority to the Russians between the twentieth and the thirtieth days would have been substantial. But Plan **B** had tripped up Plan **R**, and only three armies, and at the best a bare equality, were available to sustain a most ambitious scheme of war.

* * * * *

It was perhaps with some compunction that Moltke acquainted Conrad on August 2 with his general dispositions. He certainly endeavoured to state in the most favourable terms the German contribution to the Eastern Front. General von Prittwitz, the Commander-in-Chief of the Eighth German Army in East Prussia, was ordered to contain as strong forces of the Russians as possible, so as to keep them away from the Austrian Army and lighten its task in the first fighting.' 'Should the Russians undertake a premature offensive against East Prussia with forces greatly superior to the [German] Army of the East, an Austro-Hungarian victory will thereby be facilitated, and the more so, the earlier the A-H. army enters upon its advance towards Russia. Should no such premature and greatly superior Russian offensive against Germany north of the Vistula take place, the Army of the East will advance in the direction which brings greatest relief to the A-H. Army.' In addition a German Landwehr corps formed from the fortress garrisons was assembling opposite Chenstokhov under General von Woyrsch. This Corps would invade Russia on the twelfth day of mobilization (August 13) marching in the direction of Radom, and 'keep in mind tactical co-operation with the Austrian left.' 'The Austrian Army,' concluded Moltke, 'can consequently count with certainty upon a tactical support of its offensive against Russia by the whole of the German forces assembling in the East. The earlier and more continuous the advance towards Russia, the greater will be the combined success.'

Conrad, on the other hand, continued to count on and urge the fulfilment of what he believed Moltke had promised in the pre-war conversations, namely that the Germans, simultaneously with his drive to the north, would make a downward stroke in strong force from East Prussia southward and south-eastward towards this same area between Warsaw and Brest-Litovsk which he was attacking from the opposite quarter. Again and again he repeats in his telegrams and letters to Moltke and Prittwitz the name of Syedlets. He announced to Moltke on August 3 his intention to take the offensive with his left-wing armies eastward and northward on August 20; but he added: 'It is in any event desired that the offensive of the 4½ Corps under General von Prittwitz should take place in the direction of Syedlets.' Conrad also was forming from his garrisons in the neighbourhood of Cracow under General Kummer an improvised force called an 'Army Group.' It consisted of a cavalry division, cyclists, and 44 infantry battalions with artillery. These would press on without halting into Russia, 'shoulder to shoulder with the German Corps.' This operation of Woyrsch and Kummer was of course intended to be no more than a raid into Russian territory in an area where it was believed to be almost entirely undefended. It would create a diversion while the regular forces were assembling. It could not seriously influence events. About Conrad's request for the southward advance of the 4½ German Corps from East Prussia to Syedlets, Moltke maintained a complete silence. His orders to Prittwitz commanding the Eighth German Army, the sole defence of the eastern frontiers of Germany, were that he should not advance into Russia unless the Russians stood on the defensive. But this was not imparted to his Ally. On other matters the German Chief of the Staff was voluble, and his letters may serve us as a chronicle of events which only indirectly concern this account.

Moltke to Conrad.

August 5, 1914

'The assurance of Your Excellency that Austria-Hungary will carry through in sure fidelity to her alliance the struggle which has been begun, confirms me on a point on which I never had any doubt. I did not need it, my dear comrade, and I would rather doubt my God than the fidelity which we have established between us. The struggle will be a severe one for us, since England, too, has ranged herself on the side of the murderers and of the Russian knout. We hope, with God's help, to carry it through, even so. Our advance in Belgium certainly is brutal, but for us it is a matter of life and death and whoever stands in our way must take the consequences.

'We must tackle France in the open field; we cannot involve ourselves in a prolonged war of position before her barricaded Eastern frontier, for the decision must be obtained as quickly as possible. To that end we require Liége and the direct route through Belgium. I am sorry that blood should flow, but Belgium has rudely rebuffed all our most far-reaching assurances. The news from Russia sounds favourable. On our front in the East they have retired in confusion behind the Narev; they are, it seems, evacuating the whole of Russian Poland.

'This war, which sets almost the whole of Europe alight, will probably cost us our fleet, but the decision will be reached on land. The spirit of our people is excellent. Every man knows that the existence of Germany is at stake and all are ready to give their utmost for the Fatherland. The troops can hardly find accommodation for the mass of volunteers. The entire country—men, women and children—is ready to act. There is an angry bitterness against faithless Russia; our mobilization is developing like clockwork. Not a single hitch has so far occurred. Once the assembly has been successfully completed, the struggle which will decide the course of world history for the next hundred years can begin. It is an inward joy to me to be able to take part with you in this struggle.

'With God, my comrade!'

The chief of the German staff added three postscripts: first, that Italy's felony would be revenged in history: secondly, that Roumania would probably be friendly to the Central Empires: and thirdly, that Turkey very likely would declare war against Russia within the next few days.

He concluded in a strong vein.

'Assemble your whole force against Russia. Even Italy cannot be such a dirty dog as to fall upon your rear. Let the Bulgarians loose against Serbia and leave the pack of them to tear each other to pieces. There must now only be one objective—Russia. Thrust the knout-carriers into the marshes of the Pripyat and drown them there.'[24]

It was easier said than done. Indeed, Moltke's next letter, written on the 9th, offered little but verbal encouragement to the Austro-Hungarian Monarchy, now plunged out of its depth in the deluge.

Moltke to Conrad.

August 9, 1914

'Any action by Italy against Austria at this difficult time—against her allies hitherto— after having taken upon herself to break faith, appears to me so horrifying that so far I cannot believe in it. If this felony, which will be the culminating point of rascality, really takes place, then, in my view, there is nothing for it except for Austria forthwith to close the jaw of the hungry beast of prey [*i.e.* to cede territory as a bribe for peace]. . . .

'The point is to wage war successfully against Russia and to defer everything else for a later arrangement.' . . .

Then follows a bleak notification.

'Dear friend, we ourselves here are in so difficult a situation with four enemies against us that we cannot spare anyone, willingly though we would do so. We have already gone to our utmost limit and we have already fallen back on our Landsturm.

We must have a decision in the West; that is a question of life for us. You know yourself how willingly I would help; it cannot be done.' . . .

The end of this letter—rather an excited screed for the directing mind of the Schlieffen plan—is narrative.

'We have to-day taken the first Russian battery from a cavalry brigade. The Russians attack most stupidly and are shot down everywhere. Everywhere are small, scattered attacks by cavalry brigades and small detachments of infantry. We already have over five hundred prisoners, who are glad to get something to eat. The Belgians are quite negligible, incapable of attack. They had five brigades in Liége, which was strongly entrenched, and our six peace brigades stormed it with nothing but the resources of the field army. Four to five thousand prisoners! The forts on the Northern front alone have not yet surrendered, but from to-morrow onwards they will be under fire from the rear. The crossings of the Maas are in our hands intact. Our cavalry is pushing on towards Brussels and Antwerp. The fight has cost us some blood—not overmuch—and it has paid us. We are now waiting for the English.

'With God, dear friend! A thousand thanks for the heavy artillery—may I be able to reciprocate!'[25]

Conrad now addressed himself to Prittwitz direct.

Conrad to Prittwitz.

(Telegram.)

August 14

'Offensive of our left wing towards Lublin and Cholm will start on August 22.

'The general situation indicates that an offensive by German Eastern army in direction of Syedlets is of decisive importance and it is urgent that Syedlets be reached as quickly as possible. I request information by return as to intention of H.Q. German army of the East.'[26]

Captain Fleischmann (Austrian liaison with Prittwitz) to Conrad.

(Telegram.)

August 15. 10 *a.m.*

'At the moment enemy is entering E. Prussia from Kovno, Olita and south thereof. A blow is about to be struck against this move which should succeed in the next few days. Only after that can operations be begun in direction of Syedlets. German Eastern Army is already drawing important forces upon itself and believes that it is thereby freeing the way for the Austrian offensive.'[27]

This news was anathema to Conrad. He regarded the German advance towards Kovno as an 'eccentric' (i.e. divergent) operation useless for his purposes and wrong in itself.

Conrad to Prittwitz.

August 15, 1914

... 'Only by co-operation can success against Russia be achieved.

'On August 14 I communicated through Captain Fleischmann ... I renewed the request ... for the offensive ... in the direction of Syedlets.

'An exchange of views is desired to explain to your Excellency why I ascribe to the advance of the German Army of the East against Syedlets a decisive importance for the general success.' ...

And after a lengthy exposition

'It thus appears to me that the task of warding off a Russian advance against Berlin and thus protecting the rear of the main German forces fighting against France, while at the same time co-operating with the A-H. Armies in the defeat of the common enemy, can only be carried out reliably by handing over the defence of East Prussia against Russian invasion to Reserve divisions and Landwehr, supported by the fortresses, while at the same time the main forces of the army under your Excellency's command begin the offensive in the general direction of Syedlets.

'I gather from Captain Fleischmann's report of August 14 that your Excellency (contrary to the above view) is now (striking against the invader towards Kovno—Olita) and will not begin the operations against Syedlets ... until after (that stroke).'[28]

In a romantic mood he suggested at least the advance of two or three divisions a hundred miles into the hostile territory crowded with Russian troops of unknown strength. The Germans in East Prussia, who were expecting to be attacked from two directions, by nearly two and a half times their numbers, had neither will nor means for such adventures.

According to his Spartan code, Conrad made his headquarters at Przemysl in a barrack-room with straw as his bed and an oil lamp for light. He had need to mortify the flesh. His Second Army could only arrive in the decisive theatre ten days late and after the main shock of battle, upon which Conrad counted so much, had already clashed. The German help from the north was plainly not forthcoming. Thus two all-important factors in his combination had already disappeared. Should he in these circumstances persist in his offensive? Still resolute for the offensive, he nevertheless left Vienna without deciding finally upon its direction. His left-wing army would not be ready to move before the 21st; perhaps the Germans would have beaten the Russians in the north by then and would be able to send him aid or at least make a helpful diversion. At any rate, Conrad decided to keep his option open for a while. On August 18 he told General Auffenberg, who commanded the Fourth Army, to be prepared to strike either N., N.E., or E.

Before leaving Vienna he had despatched the greater part of the Austro-Hungarian cavalry north, north-east and east to reconnoitre the whole of the frontier from the Dniester to the Vistula on the general line Mohilev—Lutsk—Lublin. This ambitious programme was far beyond the capacity of his ten cavalry divisions. The width of the frontier to be searched was 250 miles (the distance from London to the Scottish border) and its depth was over 90 miles. The time available was only four days. It had been expected that the Russians, according to their custom, would herald their advance by clouds of Cossack cavalry. Ivanov, however, had no cavalry screen. He preferred to use his cavalry to bridge the gaps between his four armies as they closed in westward from their 300-mile front. In consequence the Austrian horsemen found little or nothing before them until here and there they came up against covering parties of Russian infantry whose fire, drawn by the bright reds and blues of their peace-time uniforms, caused heavy local losses and speedy retirements. The results of the Austrian cavalry reconnaissance were worthless. The Austrian saddle, owing to its excessive padding, proved unserviceable for such long marches in August weather. So many of the horses had sore backs that a number of regiments returned on foot leading their steeds. Entire divisions could not move for a week. The Austrian aeroplanes, nominally 42, most of which were soon unserviceable although matched by equally infantile Russian aviation, procured no news of any value.

* * * * *

The order for general mobilization signed by the Czar at mid-day on July 30, 1914, involved in European Russia and the Caucasus 30 corps with a total of 96 infantry and 37 cavalry divisions (about 2,700,000 men) in addition to 900,000 special reserves and fortress troops. The arrival of the various Asiatic army corps from the thirtieth day onward would raise the total to 1,830 battalions, 1,250 squadrons and 6,720 cannons, in all roughly 5 million men, of which about two-thirds were combatants.

If Austria and Germany had to fight on two fronts, Russia had to fight two enemies on one wide front. The Russians had alternative mobilization plans for war with the Central Empires. **G**, 'Germania,' envisaged the bulk of the German forces massed against Russia. **A**, 'Austria,' contemplated Germany on the defensive in the east. In both cases the field armies were to be divided into the North-west group consisting of the First and Second armies and the South-west group consisting of the Third, Fifth and Eighth armies. The Fourth Army was to be added to the North-west in the event of **G**, or to the South-west in the event of **A**. The Sixth and Seventh armies protected the flanks and the line of battle stretched from the Baltic and Finland to Roumania and the Black Sea. In either alternative all Russian Poland west of the Vistula was to be evacuated on the outbreak of hostilities in order to ensure an unhurried concentration. The North-west group of armies was to assemble along the East Prussian frontier and the South-west along the Galician frontier of Austria.

These primary arrangements were common to both plans. If Germany took the offensive in main force at the outset in the East both groups of Russian armies were to retire alike towards a line running north and south through Brest-Litovsk and behind the Pripyat marshes, abandoning the whole of Poland, Warsaw and all the fortresses of the Vistula and the Narev. If necessary the strategy of the Moscow campaign of 1812 would be repeated. The Russian line would retire still farther to gain time at all costs for the arrival in three or four weeks or more of the Asiatic troops (5½ Siberian and 2 Turkestan corps), and the complete assembly of the whole resources of the Empire before attempting a decisive counterstroke. So much for 'Germania.' If, on the other hand, Germany remained on the defensive in the east, both groups of Russian armies were to attack at once, the North-west group invading East Prussia and the South-west Galicia, to conquer these two bastions preparatory to re-assembling east of Warsaw for a combined advance into the centre of Germany.

* * * * *

The Grand Duke Nicholas, uncle of the Czar, had assumed command of all the Russian Armies against Germany and Austria upon the declaration of war. By August 6 the Russian General Headquarters—in future called the Stavka—learned definitely that the German main forces, including those along its eastern frontier from Pomerania, Posen and eastern Silesia, were entraining for the French front. 'Germania' was not going to happen, and Plan **A**, as had been generally expected, would come into force. The Fourth Army therefore joined the three armies in the South-west group facing Galicia. All these preliminary movements had been minutely concerted and came into operation in response to the simplest gestures.

But now France with nearly the whole might of Germany pouring down upon her began to raise strident cries for help. In the arrangements concerted from 1911 onwards between France and Russia a violent irruption into Germany with the object of relieving France from German pressure was to be made by Russia from the outset, if Germany threw her main weight to the west. Now that this was clearly happening, the French Government, going much further than the pre-war protocols, urged Russia to march directly against Germany. This would have involved great changes in the carefully preconceived plans. Moreover, the Grand Duke Nicholas although by no means over-rating the Austrian armies, was not prepared to march past them into Germany, leaving them behind his left shoulder, without quelling them—at least for the time being. To show Russian goodwill and sincerity towards her imperilled ally, he ordered between August 7 and 10 the formation of two more armies, the Ninth and Tenth, at Ivangorod and behind Warsaw, with the German frontier of Thorn, Posen and Breslau as their eventual objective. Moreover, in order to accelerate the formation and advance of these armies, the Stavka decided to skip some important preparatory stages and had devised a

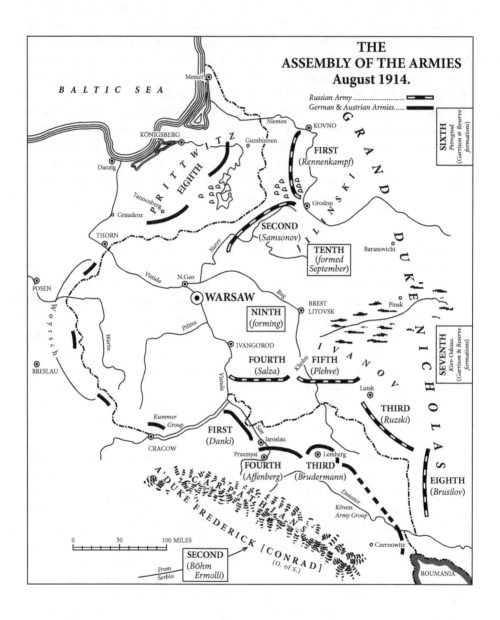

THE ASSEMBLY OF THE ARMIES
August 1914.

Russian Army ....
German & Austrian Armies......

BALTIC SEA

Memel

Niemen

KOVNO

KÖNIGSBERG

Gumbinnen

PRITTWITZ

EIGHTH

Danzig

FIRST
(Rennenkampf)

GRAND

Tannenberg

Graudenz

Grodno

THORN

Narev

SECOND
(Samsonov)

DUKE

VILINSKI

Baranovichi

TENTH
*(formed
September)*

Vistula

N.Geo

POSEN

Bug

WARSAW

BREST
LITOVSK

Pinsk

Woyrsch

NINTH
(forming)

NICHOLAS

Pilitsa

Wartu

IVANGOROD

IVANOV

BRESLAU

FOURTH
(Salza)

Kholm

FIFTH
(Plehve)

Lutsk

Vistula

THIRD
(Ruzski)

Kummer
Group

San

FIRST
(Danki)

Jaroslau

CRACOW

Przemysl

Lemberg

EIGHTH
(Brusilov)

FOURTH
(Affenberg)

THIRD
(Brudermann)

CARPATHIANS

Dniester

Kövess
Army Group

A' DUKE FREDERICK [CONRAD]
(O. of S.)

0   50   100 MILES

SECOND
*(Böhm
Ermolli)*

From
Serbia

Czernowitz

ROUMANIA

SIXTH
*Petrograd.
(Garrison & Reserve
formations)*

SEVENTH
*Kiev-Odessa.
(Garrison & Reserve
formations)*

form of 'forward mobilization' which at a serious cost in efficiency gained eight or nine precious days. It was expected in all the War Offices that the main struggle in the west would be in full progress from August 19 onwards, and history will recognize the intense loyal efforts made by the Czar and his generals to make their onfall with the greatest possible strength at the same time.

CHAPTER X
AUSTRIA AGAINST RUSSIA

In its broadest outline the immense composite battle of Lemberg was fought by three Austrian against four Russian armies during three weeks from August 23 to September 12 along a 200-mile front facing north-east between the Vistula and the Dniester rivers. From the beginning of September onwards each side was joined by an additional army. At first the two northern Austrian armies defeated the two Russian armies opposite to them. They were robbed of their victory by the easterly advance of the two southern Russian armies upon Lemberg, which overpowered the third Austrian army before an additional Austrian army could be recalled from Serbia, whither it had been sent in error. The whole Austrian front was thus driven back 150 miles and only reformed behind the Wisloka river. This prodigious military event comprised seven separate hard-fought battles between individual armies each lasting several days, reacting upon each other, involving the engagement of 648 Austrian battalions against 720 Russians, and causing in the aggregate to both sides the loss or slaughter of between five and six hundred thousand men. This mighty episode must now be described.

By August 20 the three Austrian armies of Dankl [First], Auffenberg [Fourth] and Brudermann [Third] were ranged in line, with the 'Army group' of Kummer, supported by Woyrsch's German corps, protecting their left, and the 'Army group' of Kövess their right flank. Conrad's expectation that the main Russian force would be found in Poland between Lublin and Kholm led him to discount the chance of any heavy attack upon Lemberg from the east. He was strong in his old prepossession that, by advancing northward into Poland, he would break up and cut off large Russian masses assembled in the salient. He was still hopeful that the Germans would move southward from East Prussia to meet him. At any risk he felt bound to attempt to forestall the full development of the Russian strength. The situation as he saw it was grim.

'In Serbia, the offensive a failure, and considerable portions of the Second Army destined against Russia involved; in E. Prussia the German army in retreat; the stroke towards Syedlets not to be counted on; Roumania fallen away, and her intervention on the Eastern wing not come about; Russian troops on that wing thus set free; Bulgaria and Turkey in passive expectancy; Italy tending to turn hostile; in Vienna, forces behind the scenes at work, agitating against **A.O.K.**;* and before us the Russian superiority of force gathering to strike an annihilating blow.

---

*Armee-Ober-Kommando: the Austro-Hungarian G.H.Q.

'Nevertheless I held fast to taking the initiative in the North, for the enemy there must be grappled, so that he should not disturb the victorious advance of the German armies against France, so that the German Eastern army should not be given over to face a blow in isolation, and finally so that Russia should not gain time to gather together her full numerical superiority.'[29]

On the 22nd therefore he ordered Dankl, who now lay south of the woods and marshes of the Tanev valley, to advance northwards in the general direction of Lublin, to cross the Tanev river and occupy the high ground beyond. He ordered Auffenberg on Dankl's right to move a day later in the direction of Kholm. He ordered Brudermann to stand in front of Lemberg and cover these movements from any interference from the east. Conrad expected—and events did not belie him—that all three armies would come into contact with the enemy on the 26th. He did not feel in immediate danger from the east; he hoped to find his prey in the north. All was now ready; he could wait no longer. With many misgivings and heart-searchings, veiled or deadened by a fatalistic mood, he gave the signal. Forward, then! And forward went the Imperial and Royal Armies over the broad rolling landscape, their gay uniforms vivid in the August sunshine, their many races and divergent loyalties held together by the discipline and mechanism of war and caught in the momentum of events.

* * * * *

The command of the Russian South-west front was entrusted to General Ivanov. The four armies of Salza (Fourth), Plehve (Fifth), Ruzski (Third) and Brusilov (Eighth) deployed in that order from north to south along the Galician frontier from Ivangorod to Roumania. Together they comprised nearly 1,200,000 men. The Russian high strategy was clairvoyant. The Stavka was acutely sensible of the peril being struck at from both sides of the Polish salient. The basis of General Ivanov's plan against Austria was the advance of a mass attack not from the north but from the east. Brusilov's (Eighth) and Ruzski's (Third) armies with 8 corps assembled in the Lutsk, Dubno and Proskurov areas were to march westwards across the east Galician frontier with their right on Lemberg and their left on the Dniester. This straightforward invasion beginning on August 18/19 and crossing the frontier by the 22nd was expected to cause the Austrians to assemble their main strength about Lemberg and give battle there facing east. Meanwhile Plehve's army with 4 corps was concentrating at Kholm some sixty miles to the north-west facing south. It was to leave its concentration zone about the 22nd to be in time to come down upon the Austrian northern flank when the battle towards Lemberg began. Salza's army with 3 corps, still further to the west between Kholm and the Vistula, was to move south about the same time as the Fifth towards the line of the San River and beyond. It would thus be ready to cut off the enemy's probable line of retreat westwards by Przemysl and Cracow. Their retreat southwards across the Dniester and the Carpathians would be prevented by Brusilov on the left or southern flank. To sum up, Ivanov expected that Conrad would seek to invade Russia in an easterly direction and that he would speedily encounter front to front the armies of Ruzski and Brusilov who were advancing to meet him. Meanwhile the armies of Salza and Plehve would swing steadily round from the north and strike the advancing Austrians on their left flank and rear.

Both Commanders were, as we see, equally in the dark about each other's plans. In fact their assumptions were in each case exactly contrary to the facts. The Russian right seeking to turn Conrad's left met his main offensive, and Conrad's right wing was soon overweighted by the advance of the two armies of the Russian left.

The Battle of Krasnik

General Ivanov had not intended Salza's Russian Fourth Army to leave its concentration zone about Lublin until its mobilization was completed and all its transport had arrived. The Grand Duke, believing that the Austrian main force was about Lemberg ready to advance eastward, did not expect that Salza would encounter any serious opposition. The remainder of the transport and late arrivals could overtake the army on the march. He ordered it, therefore, against Ivanov's judgment to advance across the San River to a position west of Przemysl, where it could cut any retreat of the Austrians westward through the Cracow corridor. By the afternoon of the 22nd Salza reached the line of the Wyznitsa stream. Although not a single man of his reserve divisions had yet come up, his army resumed its southward march at daybreak on the 23rd, and his advanced guards soon reached that same high ground overlooking the Tanev valley up which Dankl's Austrians were already toiling. This direct collision head-to-head of the Austrian First and Russian Fourth armies led to the battle of Krasnik. The line of contact ran very nearly east and west. The country was open and the troops on both sides were eager to engage. The long-stored-up peace-time ammunition was plentiful, the infantry fighting was at 1,200 or 1,500 yards, and the troops were on the top of the ground manœuvring without trenches in an encounter battle such as most of the generals of all the countries had pictured to themselves would occur at the outset of a great war.

As the Austrian centre and left reached the high ground they encountered the leading troops of the XIVth Corps forming the Russian right. Severe fighting followed with heavy losses to both sides and without appreciable gains to either. But during the afternoon the Austrian left (the 1st Corps) came into action: and by this preponderance the Russian XIVth Corps was beaten back upon Krasnik, involving in its retreat the 13th Cavalry Division between Krasnik and the Vistula. Meanwhile the Xth Corps on the Austrian right had reached its destination without meeting the enemy forces in its front, for these had halted for the night in the valley of the Por three or four miles farther north. Such was the first day.

Both armies renewed the battle on the 24th. General Salza, persisting in his orders to cross the line of the San as soon as possible, ordered his centre and left Corps, the XVIth and Grenadiers, which had not yet been engaged, to storm the high ground north of the

Tanev. Here they met Dankl's Vth and Xth Corps in stern conflict. The Austrian left had meanwhile continued its attack upon the Russian XIVth Corps and the whole force of both armies was thus in action. By nightfall the Austrian superiority of numbers—144 battalions to 104—bore the Russians backwards and darkness found the Russians still clinging tenaciously to the high ground about Krasnik, having been driven back about 3 miles.

Taking advantage of the success of his 1st Corps and keeping in mind also the dominant intention of forcing the enemy eastwards, General Dankl, whose conduct of the battle was skilful, ordered his right and centre corps to hold fast on the 25th while his left continued its advance across the Wyznitsa, and then to turn east to attack the flank and rear of the Russian resistance east of Krasnik. Under this pressure and threat of envelopment of Russian XIVth Corps at last gave way and the Austrians' further advance eastward caused in turn the rapid withdrawal of the Russian XVIth Corps followed by the Grenadier Corps, to a new line 4 miles in rear. So far the victory in this hard-fought battle rested with the Austrians. They had turned the enemy's right flank and in straightforward open fighting had driven him back at least 7 miles. These two armies, each of nearly 200,000 strong, had now fought all day for three days, and had lain exhausted on the ground at night. The slaughter had been severe. At least 40,000 men had been killed or wounded, and in addition the Russians had lost more than 6,000 men taken prisoners and 28 guns.

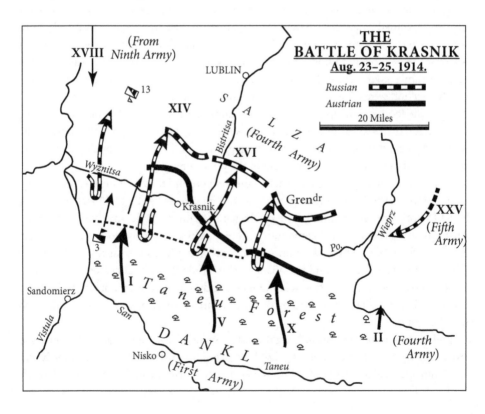

The news of heavy and adverse fighting around Krasnik caused bewilderment at the Stavka. The Grand Duke and his staff, although their forces were far better disposed strategically, were under as complete a misconception of the situation as was Conrad. Neither the Grand Duke nor General Ivanov could believe that the enemy were still unconscious of or ignoring the advance of the main Russian mass of attack across the East Galician frontier towards Lemberg. At both Russian headquarters it was believed that the Fourth Army had merely run into an isolated Austrian force of unexpected strength posted to protect the northern flank of a main Austrian battle-front facing east. They believed that at least two and possibly three Austrian armies were ranged about Lemberg, or were perhaps even advancing to meet the armies of Ruzski and Brusilov. There could not therefore be any important surplus available to support the Austrian army which had taken Krasnik. Accordingly it was decided to encircle and crush that army. The Russian Ninth Army newly forming at Ivangorod for the advance into Germany was ordered to send its XVIIIth Corps southwards to reinforce the right of the Fourth Army and turn Dankl's left. The Russian Fifth Army, Plehve's, on the immediate left of the Fourth, was ordered to make a right-wheel against the flank and rear of the unexpected opposition in front of its neighbour. The blame for the defeat at Krasnik was laid on General Salza. He had failed to reconnoitre the wooded country of the Tanev before involving himself in it; he had made bad arrangements for intercommunication; he had failed to use the Vistula as protection for his right flank. It is always easy to cite errors of this kind after a reverse, but it is probable that the undue haste with which the Grand Duke Nicholas himself had sent forward this Fourth Army before its concentration was complete and thus exposed it to battle against markedly superior numbers played at least as large a part in its misfortune as the faulty tactics of its unlucky Commander. Be that as it may, General Salza on the evening of the 25th was superseded in the command of his Army by General Ewarth.

The news of Dankl's success at Krasnik inspirited Conrad's already audacious and sanguine temperament.

> 'This,' he writes, 'was a joyful and welcome beginning, but I knew only too well that
> it was only a beginning and that the momentous decisions were yet to be taken. . . .
> The basic idea was an offensive to give a decision between the Bug and the Vistula;
> and repel the blow threatening Lemberg from the east and north-east, but also to
> prevent the Russians in the Brody direction from turning their forces against the
> Fourth Army from which I looked for a decision.'[30]

The Austrian Fourth Army under General Auffenberg was now almost in line upon Dankl's right, and its intervention the next day might be decisive. Conrad, bidding high for victory, actually drew on the night of the 25th three divisions from his already weak Third Army under the Archduke Joseph Ferdinand, to support, prolong and protect the right of Auffenberg. He was still without any serious apprehension of the Russian attack impending from the east upon Lemberg. The few Russian corps reported crossing the East Galician frontier he regarded 'as a passing episode.' His view was shared by

General Brudermann who on the 25th proposed to attack and envelop the northern Russian columns approaching Zloczov. Conrad agreed and Brudermann ordered his reduced Third Army, together with the bulk of Kövess's 'Army group,' to march north and east on the 26th. There are two parallel tributaries of the Dniester river called the Gnila- and the Zlota-Lipa respectively. Brudermann set his whole available force in march across the former to meet the Russians on the latter. The Austrian Second Army was only now beginning to arrive around Stanislau in the south. Thus we see the Third Austrian Army, the sole defence of the whole of the right flank and communications of Dankl and Auffenberg, not only giving a quarter of its strength to aid the northern battle, but eagerly and confidently advancing northward and eastward against what their leaders regarded as a weaker foe. At this moment the armies of Ruzski and Brusilov, with eight army corps comprising 336 battalions, 264 squadrons and 1,214 guns, were rolling forward slowly and with every precaution at about 8 miles a day upon an 80-mile front. The heads of their columns too would reach the Zlota-Lipa on the 26th. When properly closed up and fully deployed they were more than two and a half times the strength of Brudermann's army.

From the 26th onwards therefore two new separate battles began, and raged simultaneously some 30 miles apart, reacting continually one upon the other. The scale of the conflict was trebled and the whole Austrian front was in action.

The Battle of Komarov

In the North each antagonist brought an entire new Army into action. The battle of Krasnik continued, and upon its right the battle of Komarov began. The opening was remarkable. As Plehve's Fifth Army, in pursuance of the Grand Duke's orders, swung right-handed like a door on its hinges to strike Dankl upon his right and rear, he exposed his own flank to the Fourth Austrian Army, which under Auffenberg was now coming up on Dankl's right. Auffenberg believed that only three Russian divisions were in front of him and that the enemy's main body was at least a day behind. Plehve was not aware that any strong Austrian force was marching upon him. Auffenberg decided upon an immediate attack, and set his three corps (VI, IX and II) in line in touch with Dankl, his centre directed upon Komarov, and his left on Zamość.

Auffenberg's advancing divisions clashed almost immediately with the left flank guards of Plehve's army on its westward march. The Austrian cavalry divisions soon came in contact with the Russian Vth Corps marching westwards towards the river Huczwa. Fighting dismounted, they compelled the Russians to deploy; but, as is always the case, the cavalry carbines were no match for the infantry rifles, and before noon the horsemen had had enough and withdrew from the field. One after another Auffenberg's corps collided with the Russian troops marching across their front, forcing them to turn and fight under quite unforeseen conditions. West of the Tomaszov-Zamość high-road four Austrian divisions in a strong mass caught the Russian XXVth Corps in the act of wheeling, and after heavy fighting in the woods south and south-west of Zamość,

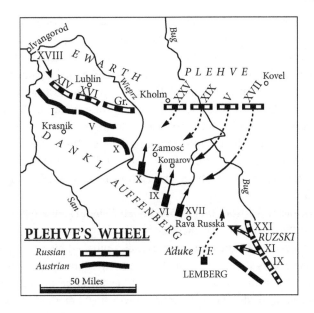

PLEHVE'S WHEEL

Russian ▭▭▭▭
Austrian ▬▬▬▬

50 Miles

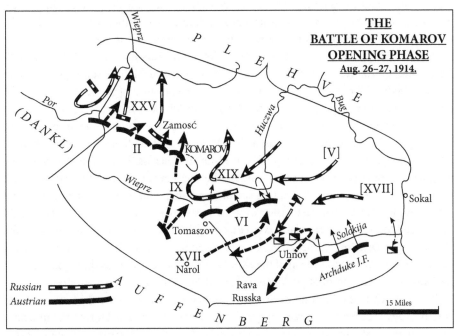

THE
BATTLE OF KOMAROV
OPENING PHASE
Aug. 26–27, 1914.

Russian ▭▭▭▭
Austrian ▬▬▬▬

15 Miles

forced them back to the walls of the town. By the evening of the 26th the two flanks of the Austrian Fourth Army were thus 5 to 10 miles in front of its centre and Auffenberg indulged hopes of surrounding the enemy, whom he still rated at only three or four divisions. Plehve, equally misinformed, ordered his four corps to continue the westward wheel against Dankl. Confused fighting and a series of disconnected clashes marked the 27th. Each side found their enemy far stronger at every point than was expected. The Austrians' attack was prejudiced by the misfortune or misconduct of its cavalry. Before dawn a Russian Cossack detachment broke into the bivouacs of the 10th Austrian Cavalry Division at Uhnov, unguarded by outposts, and raised a panic from which the Division was only rallied after a flight of 10 miles. The 6th Austrian Cavalry Division in the contagion of the alarm also fell back 6 miles, towards Narol. The Austrians' VIth Corps advancing across the Huczwa to begin their closing-in movement north-westwards counted on these same cavalry to protect their right flank. They were now attacked from this quarter by Russian troops in strong force, and could make no further progress. After long fighting in the centre, the Austrian IInd Corps carried Zamość village and the high ground about it.

In spite of the heavy Austrian attack upon his left General Plehve felt strong enough to persevere on the 28th in his original intention of marching westward against Dankl's right; and Auffenberg, cheered by the capture of Zamość, pursued his enveloping operation. But now on Auffenberg's extreme right the three divisions of the Archduke Joseph Ferdinand had reached the battlefield. They had been delayed throughout the 27th by an order and a counter-order the significance of which will presently appear. They were on the 28th about to come into action on the right of the VIth Corps and with what it was hoped would be overwhelming strength complete the envelopment. Meanwhile the whole of the rest of both Austrian armies engaged the Russians on their front.

August 28 began with an Austrian disaster. The right flank division (15th) of the VIth Corps, still unprotected by the cavalry, had been ordered to fall back during the night to the south side of the Huczwa to join in later with the advance of the Archduke Joseph's division when they came up level with it. The 15th Division in recrossing the swampy valley shortly after midnight marched into and through the outpost line of the Russian Vth Corps which had penetrated thus far. The Russians waited till the mass of the division was crowded upon the long stretch of banked-up road across the swamp. A devastating fire was then opened upon it from all sides. The division was at once thrown into utter confusion. Its Commander committed suicide, and after suffering four or five thousand casualties the remnants of the division escaped westwards leaving 4,000 prisoners and 20 guns in Russian hands. In the alarm consequent upon the annihilation of this division, the 27th Austrian Division on the left at once deployed facing east. The panic spread during the darkness to the 26th Division of the IXth Corps in the centre. Thus the whole attack of Auffenberg's centre and right was deranged and delayed till late in the afternoon.

But meanwhile the Archduke's three divisions were moving up to the Solokija river, and their advance from so threatening an angle became effective. During the morning they took the 61st Division of Plehve's left Corps (XVIIth) by surprise in flank and rear while it was still marching westwards. It fled in disorder across country to the north, leaving many prisoners and 40 guns in the Archduke's hands. His centre was however arrested by heavy Russian artillery fire shortly after crossing the river, and his left, crossing at Uhnov, hurrying forward without waiting for its guns, was brought to a standstill by Russian infantry. General Auffenberg now threw in a division he had held

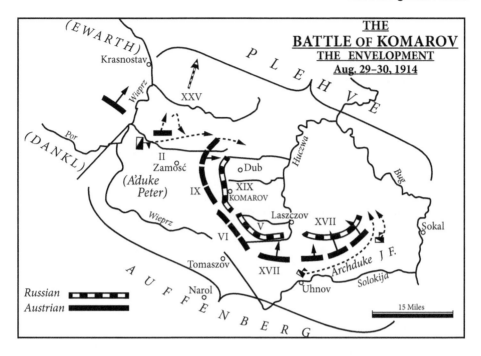

THE
BATTLE OF KOMAROV
THE ENVELOPMENT
Aug. 29–30, 1914

in reserve, which, crossing the Solokija west of Uhnov after fighting lasting into the night, forced the left flank guard of the Russian Vth Corps back on to the main body about Laszczov.

General Auffenberg's encircling movement was now reaching its climax. The XVIIth, Vth and XIXth Russian Corps were in the net which he was striving to draw around the Laszczov-Tomaszov-Zamośc battle zone. The whole of both Austrian armies renewed the battle on the 29th. The Archduke's divisions swung left-handed westward towards the Huczwa stream, the XVIIth and VIth Corps pinned the enemy between that stream and Tomaszov. The IXth Corps continued its attack upon Komarov while the IInd Corps bent eastwards from Zamośc towards the north of Dub. Meanwhile Dankl pressed forward against Ewarth.

Thus far the Austrian plans in the north had prospered.

'One cannot be certain,' says the Russian official history, written under the Soviet, 'whether what was intended was a general offensive, or a sort of *attaque brusquée* endeavouring to make up by rapidity for a marked numerical inferiority. This impetuosity and this idea of a sudden violent thrust disconcerted our Fourth and Fifth Armies whose movement was slow and long-drawn out, and which were in no way prepared for an encounter battle.'[31]

Leaving this struggle to approach its climax, we must now turn to the Lemberg front.

CHAPTER XI
THE BATTLE OF LEMBERG

The Battles of the Gnila-Lipa

The battle of the Gnila-Lipa has two phases. The first began on the 26th. The three Austrian corps (XIIth, IIIrd and XIth) advanced in high hopes to the Zlota-Lipa expecting to crush the heads of inferior Russian forces. But the Russians were not only vastly superior; they were moving forward very slowly with the utmost precaution. They were expecting at any moment to come in contact with the main force of the Austrian army, and the heads of all their columns were therefore substantially deployed. The Austrian attacks all miscarried. Under the influence of the doctrine that the offensive was the only form of war, the Austrian divisions were launched to

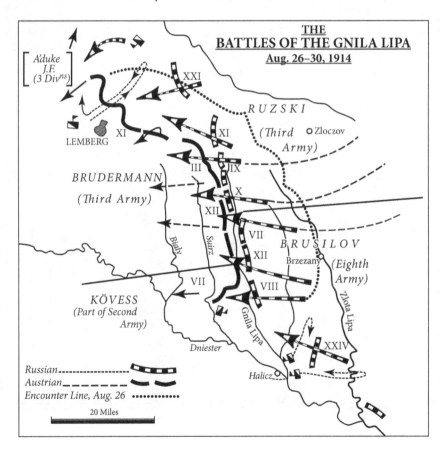

THE
BATTLES OF THE GNILA LIPA
Aug. 26–30, 1914

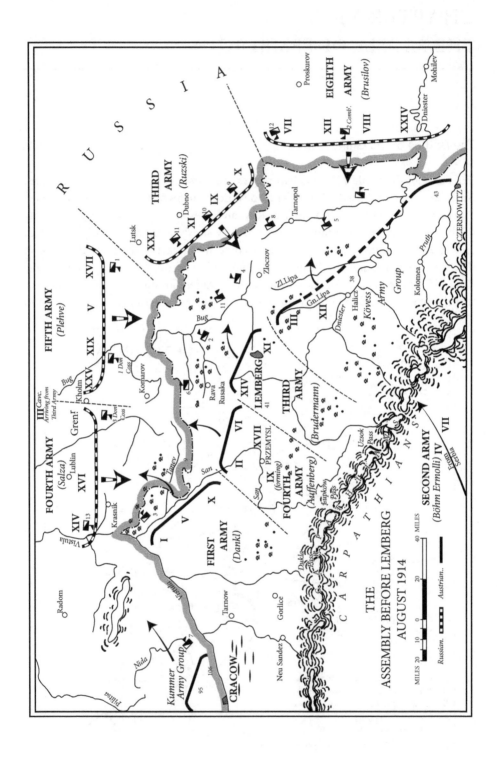

THE
ASSEMBLY BEFORE LEMBERG
AUGUST 1914

the attack, frequently disconnected from each other and without artillery preparation. Everywhere they were repulsed. Not only defeat, but panic overtook a large portion of the Third Army. The Russian front, growing stronger every hour, overlapped as well as outweighed the Austrian line. The shock of collision was all in favour of the heavier Russian attacks. By nightfall the whole of the Third Army was in retreat. Two whole divisions, indeed, were driven in such disorder and terror from the field that they only rallied in Lemberg, 25 miles from the scene of the battle. Masses of routed Austrian troops streamed into Lemberg throughout the night. The next morning it was clear to **A.O.K.** that their Third Army had sustained a brutal and shattering blow. At the same time all reports now carried to headquarters the news of enormous Russian columns far exceeding any forces dreamed of in this quarter coming up abreast of the Zlota-Lipa throughout its entire length. At 8 a.m. on the morning of the 27th Conrad ordered the retirement of the whole Third Army to a line close in front of Lemberg. He also ordered Auffenberg, now just becoming deeply involved in the battle of Komarov, to return the three divisions of the Archduke Joseph in motion towards his right flank. Both these measures were justified by the facts. However, less discouraging reports from the Third Army led Conrad to sanction their remaining on the line of the Gnila-Lipa, and at Auffenberg's insistence he permitted the Archduke Joseph to continue his march on the flank of the northern battle.

Actually the Third Army was outnumbered by nearly three to one. Along the Gnila-Lipa the Russians employed 292 battalions, 162 squadrons and 750 guns against 115 Austrian battalions, 91 squadrons and 376 guns. But it must be remembered that General Ivanov presumed that he was about to meet the main strength of the Austrian army, and that hitherto he had only encountered their leading forces. He thought he had their weight in front of his left wing. In a country with few roads like Galicia the movements of these great armies involved columns of 25 and 30 miles long on every practicable route. Thus the rear half of the army was at any given moment two days' march from the fighting-line. So far the Russians had conquered with their heavy advance guards alone. Now they must prepare for battle on the greatest scale. They therefore halted for two days to allow their columns to close up and deploy. In these two days the Austrian Third Army managed to get into a fighting posture along the Gnila-Lipa.

It is said that if the Russians had swept down on the 28th and 29th, they could with their great superiority have routed finally the Austrian Third Army. The Grand Duke, preoccupied with the position of Plehve's army in the battle of Komarov, and judging more accurately than Ivanov the strength of the Austrians in front of Lemberg, ordered Ivanov to cancel his orders for the halt for deployment, and to press on at once with his troops towards Lemberg and the enemy. These orders had to be obeyed. Nevertheless it was more than forty-eight hours before the Russians were again in movement. The Grand Duke was both right and wrong. But the Commander-in-Chief of the south-west front and his powerful staff had no intention of being hurried into a disaster. They bowed, and they delayed until their arrangements were complete. This brings us to the second battle of the Gnila-Lipa or second battle of Lemberg as it is sometimes called, which opened on August 30.

When the Russian advance was resumed it was irresistible. From daylight on the 30th Brusilov's artillery bombarded the Austrian position, and at about 10 a.m. the Russian infantry in overpowering strength assaulted and broke the whole front of the XIIth Austrian corps. The disordered and panic-stricken troops attempted vainly to reform after a retreat of 7 miles; but a Russian cavalry division threw them again into flight. Similar scenes were enacted along the whole front. All the roads leading back to Lemberg became a seething mass of terror-stricken troops, guns, wagons and vehicles of every kind, intermingled with the fugitive inhabitants. By nightfall the Austrian Third Army seemed in dissolution. It had fled from the field in rout and ruin and had only been halted after 18 miles. Now and henceforward the mere cry '*Kosaken kommen*,' 'the Cossacks are coming,' was sufficient to throw regiments and brigades into confusion. All these harsh and insulting phrases are drawn from the Austrian official history.

We now leave for a moment these battlefields drenched with blood upon which for a week seven armies together comprising at least two million men have been in deadly grapple, for agonies no less intense in Conrad's bleak headquarters at Przemysl. Since the morning of the 26th two great battles had been thundering beyond the northern and eastern horizons. As Conrad's hopes in the north brightened steadily his anxieties from the east mounted to a monstrous scale. The fiery commander was torn between the opposite stresses of the two fields, the promise of victory and the threat of ruin. The first shock of the defeat of the Third Army on the 26th had led him on the 27th to suspend the northward movement of the Archduke Joseph's three divisions. But later reports had shown that Brudermann had managed to reform along the Gnila-Lipa and that the Russians were not pursuing. So Conrad had allowed the Archduke to proceed and he was soon crucially involved in the battle of Komarov. Meanwhile the bad condition of the Third Army and the enormous masses of Russians now plainly closing up for a decisive onslaught were obvious. Ruzski and Brusilov were already within a day's march of Lemberg and within three days' march of the communications of both the Austrian armies fighting in the north. Conrad was like a man about to seize a prize behind a dyke which was about to burst. On the 28th he again demanded the return of the Archduke's divisions; but Auffenberg, who now saw what he hoped was a decisive victory within his grasp, argued stubbornly, and again in the end Conrad yielded. The truant Second Army was now assembling in strength to the southward. Conrad decided to increase his hazards. Eight of the ten days between the twentieth and thirtieth days of Russian mobilization during which he had counted on winning a great victory, had gone. The Russian armies were now reaching their full establishment and the weight of numbers became daily more adverse to the Austrians. To Bolfras he wrote for the Emperor's eye a letter so full of interest and self-revelation that it may be allowed to interrupt the military narrative.

August 27.

'In the gravest moment of my life I am in receipt of your much-appreciated letter of the 24th and 25th. I hasten to answer it, but wish only to add that, as I write, the general battle is proceeding, which will decide the fate of the Monarchy. . . .

'There is not much to say about our successes compared with those of the Germans, mainly because the German victories have been gained at our expense; for of the hundred divisions which Germany is forming she has given only nine regular and three landwehr divisions to the Eastern theatre, and sent all the others to the West. Thus the enormous weight of the Russian Army is thrown upon us, and moreover we have the war against Serbia and Montenegro to conduct. In this we lack the assistance of Roumania, which was always counted upon for the war against Russia, and in addition Italy's defection has led to Germany sending five promised reserve divisions not to the East, but to the West.

'With the policy which has led to this result I have nothing to do (*kann ich nichts*). Foreseeing the events which have now arisen, I advised a course of action in 1909, and again in 1912, but in vain. It is a malicious freak of Fate that it is I who now have to bear the consequences of that neglect.

'The enclosed copy of a report by Potiorek gives an authentic picture of the failure in Serbia. That a complete infantry division should simply scatter, and abandon its guns and material, was the less to be expected as our troops otherwise are everywhere fighting just as gallantly as the Germans, who are engaged *not against Russians, but only against Frenchmen*.'*

After this striking exposure of his standard of values, Conrad continues.

'The transfer of the IVth Corps to the north is an urgent necessity, the more so when it is realized that Russia, besides her first-line divisions, will from now on bring her reserve divisions also into the field. Our troops are to-day already engaged with these. It was thus high time for us to take the offensive, for we should otherwise be opposed by a crushing superiority, and so must set the dice rolling before the IVth Corps are here. And moreover, the enemy advancing from all sides has left us no more time for delay.

'The offensive which began with the victorious battle at Krasnik on the 23rd, 24th and 25th August has to-day led to the general battle. The troops are suffering heavy losses, especially from the superior Russian artillery. What the outcome of this battle of giants will be lies in the hand of Fate, we have here the conviction of having fulfilled our obligations to the best of our knowledge and conscience; that must suffice us.

'Thank you for your kind inquiry after my sons. . . . Whether they are still alive, I do not know. . . . '[32]

Both sets of pressures upon Conrad now increased. The shattering defeat of his Third Army on the 30th was matched by the hope and prospect that Auffenberg was about to surround Plehve and gain a tremendous victory. The ordeal shows us the measure of

---

*My italics.—W.S.C.

Conrad's force of will. He resolved to secure for Auffenberg two more days in which to conquer, and to endure for that space the hourly increasing peril from the East. This was his greatest decision. Nor did it fail. The Russians advanced but slowly and with every precaution. They took two days to traverse the 18 miles which the Austrians had yielded so hurriedly on the 30th. It was not till September 1 that they came into contact with the new Austrian front before Lemberg. Formed of the fragments of routed divisions and of exhausted, nerve-broken troops in much confusion, it was only a shadow. Nevertheless it seemed from the enemy's side a line of battle in position. The two days which Auffenberg had demanded had been accorded him. Let us see what use he was able to make of them.

August 31 was to be Auffenberg's great day. Ever since the 26th he had been fighting his way forward on both flanks of Plehve's army which was now enclosed on three sides. On the 30th Dankl's army, pressing hard towards Lublin, had captured Krasnostav, thus threatening to separate Ewarth from Plehve. Plehve's position was critical. His three corps about Komarov might well be surrounded altogether. On the night of the 30th he had issued orders for their immediate retreat. But was it not already too late? Here then was the prize for which Auffenberg had fought so hard and skilfully, and for which Conrad was running such desperate risks at Lemberg. The Austrian plan was simple, obvious even. On the right the Archduke Joseph with his three divisions and two cavalry divisions was to advance westward to the Huczwa and also to destroy the bridges on the Bug. On the left the Archduke Peter with a similar infantry force marching from the neighbourhood of Dub was to turn and envelop the Russian right. Meanwhile the centre of the Austrian army would press at every point the wavering Russians. The net which had been cast around the three Russian corps seemed about to close. One more thrust on either flank and the encirclement of 100,000 men would be complete. Nor were there any other Russian troops near enough to interfere.

Fortune was now to play a mischievous trick. By an extraordinary coincidence the movement of both the Austrian wings was paralyzed by exactly the same kind of accident. An aeroplane reported to the Archduke Joseph on the right that a Russian division was marching up behind him from the east. Cavalry patrols reported to the Archduke Peter that Russian battalions were encircling the northern flank of his turning movement. The division in front of him and the cavalry had already retired; his own flank was compromised. In fact however the Russian battalions did not exist, and the Russian division on the opposite wing was only a few squadrons of cavalry and horse artillery scouting forward on the extreme northern flank of General Ruzski's army. But both the Archdukes took similar action on the false reports. The Archduke Joseph sent back both his cavalry and parts of two of his infantry divisions to the Solokija river to protect his rear, and was not strong enough to advance with the rest. The Archduke Peter fell back 7 miles to Zamość. Thus at the moment when the steel doors were about to clang together and imprison three-quarters of the Russian Fifth Army, they swung wider than ever on their hinges, and through the gap of 20 miles Plehve's army marched in good order to safety. Here died the last Austrian chance of victory. It was not until the morning of September 1 that Auffenberg realized what had occurred. With fierce anger and dismay he ordered the advance to be resumed, and his whole army set off in hot pursuit. They were masters of Komarov and the enemy's position. They had captured thousands of prisoners and many guns. Their seven days' bloody fighting had won them the honours of the field. It had won them little else.

Let us return to Conrad's headquarters at Przemysl, where the sum of all these events, accidents and apprehensions is computed from hour to hour. Conrad had hoped that his battered and demoralized Third Army would nevertheless be able to maintain itself in front of Lemberg till Auffenberg had triumphed. But on the night of September 1 panic broke out in a Hungarian brigade which rapidly spread, and the whole division fled in disorder into the city. On the right the Cossacks stampeded the 11th Austrian Cavalry Division which did not draw rein for 12 miles. The Russian line, gathering constantly in weight, extended round both flanks of the quavering Third Army, and Brudermann with Conrad's reluctant assent yielded Lemberg and fell back 20 miles to a line of lakes and marshes along the Vereszytsa. By September 1 all illusions had been swept away. The veil was now lifted from the theatre of war and the general situation of the masses on both sides was now plain to the Austrian headquarters. The weight and peril of the Russian advance from the east was now insupportable. In these straits Conrad's courage and resource did not desert him. Had he commanded German troops or even fresh Austrian troops, he might have drawn from the very collapse of disastrous battle the means of victory. He rose to the occasion in his headquarters, but his soldiers, asked for more than they could perform, did not rise with him.

Certainly the plans which he produced in the intense stresses of these events command respect. His Third Army had retreated behind Lemberg and it was to be expected that the Russian centre would press forward at their heels through the city. He had observed that the general tendency of the Russian advance was inclining constantly to the northward

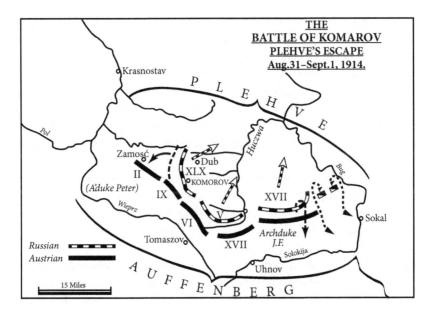

THE
BATTLE OF KOMAROV
PLEHVE'S ESCAPE
Aug. 31–Sept. 1, 1914.

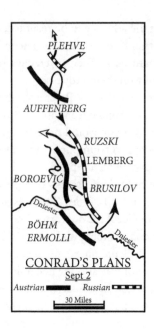

and that his Second Army, at last in line, overlapped their left in the south. He now ordered this army to advance upon the Russian left and rear. He ordered Auffenberg to abandon the pursuit of Plehve, to turn his Fourth Army right-about and march south instead of north, their rear covered by the Archduke Joseph, now become rearguard instead of heading the pursuit. By so doing he sacrificed all hope of further successes in the northern battle. On paper at least his plan was formidable. The southward march of Auffenberg would bring his army down upon Ruzski's right flank and rear. The Second Army wheeling up from the south would strike the Russians from the opposite quarter and while they pressed forward through Lemberg towards the Third Army on the Vereszytsa they would be smitten simultaneously on both sides. We must honour his spirit and mental resiliency; we may admire his conceptions; but the materials at his disposal were not strong enough to convert them into reality. In fact he would have been a wiser and a better general if he had without more delay ordered on September 1 or 2 a general retreat of all the Austrian armies to the San. However, the orders went forth from Przemysl and the weary and battle-strained Austrian armies set themselves in motion accordingly.

We must now repair to the Russian headquarters. The Stavka had by this time accurately divined the general situation and knew where the Austrian masses were. The Grand Duke had no intention of pressing any further advance from the east. On the contrary, the longer the Austrians remained on the Vereszytsa, and as far forward as the neighbourhood of Lemberg, the greater his chance of destroying them. His new Ninth Army descending the Vistula from Ivangorod was now coming down upon Dankl's left and rear, while Ewarth attacked him in front. Here was the decisive strategic thrust, and the one he had intended from the first. Moreover on the night of September 1–2 tidings calculated to shake the strongest nerve had reached him. Something had happened in East Prussia, something appalling, incomprehensible and measureless in its terrible significance! Something had happened which invested the Austrian efforts to envelop Plehve with new menace. He was deeply anxious for Plehve and did not know whether or in what condition he would escape. He therefore ordered Ruzski's whole army to turn from westward to north-westward and march to Plehve's aid. He ordered the greater part of Brusilov's army to incline to the north in touch with Ruzski, leaving only two corps around Lemberg in front of the Austrian right. In short, the Russian armies were to sideslip to their right, withhold their left hand, and press for a vast strategic entrapment with their right.

The Battle of Rava Russka

All these movements on both sides now began to operate simultaneously, and a curious situation resulted. Auffenberg's army, marching south to fall on Ruzski's right and rear,

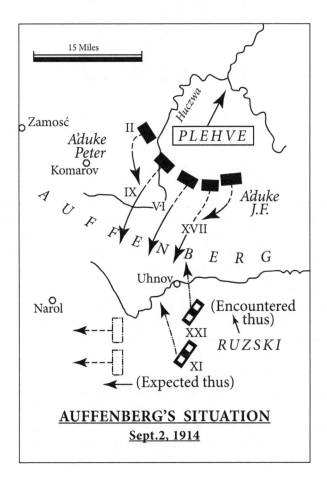

AUFFENBERG'S SITUATION
Sept.2, 1914

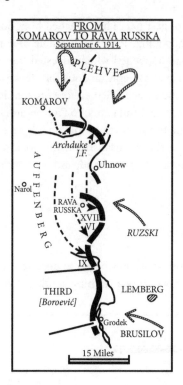

FROM
KOMAROV TO RAVA RUSSKA
September 6, 1914.

PLÉHVE

KOMAROV

Archduke
J.F.

Uhnow

Narol

AUFFENBERG

RAVA
RUSSKA

XVII
VI

RUZSKI

IX

THIRD
[Boroević]

LEMBERG

Grodek
BRUSILOV

15 Miles

began to brush with their left elbows, as it were, against Ruzski's army marching north upon the opposite course. Neither commander could understand what was happening. Auffenberg had expected to attack Ruzski in flank and Ruzski to attack Auffenberg in rear. As the true position gradually dawned upon them, Ruzski faced west to fall upon Auffenberg, and Auffenberg under the pressure of this attack pivoted his whole army on its left, and in two days with much difficulty and considerable skill formed front against him. At the same time in the south the Austrian Second Army, dragged about in and out of trains for so many days, arriving amid disasters and an atmosphere of panic, made no headway against the weak Russian southerly flank, and eventually took station along the Vereszytsa on the right of its maimed companion, the Third. By September 8 as the whole scene clarified, the Fourth, Third and Second Austrian armies stood at last in a single line facing east to resist the attack of only two Russian armies in their front, but with no other guard for their northern flank and line of retreat than the hard-pressed Dankl from whom they were separated by a gap of 40 miles. Opposite this gap, as yet unconscious of its existence, stood the whole of Plehve's army in good order and the cavalry corps of General Dragomirov.

On the evening of the 9th Conrad, still undaunted, demanded a final effort of his worn-out troops. He realized that the whole of Ruzski's army was now in front of Auffenberg and that consequently he had only Brusilov in front of his Second and Third armies. He was therefore in superior strength on the southern part of the front. He ordered both these armies to advance, wheeling as they did so, to take Brusilov in flank simultaneously with renewed attacks by Auffenberg upon Ruzski. He had penned these orders when a message arrived from Dankl that he was forced by the general situation and his own to order the retirement of his army behind the San river. Still Conrad persisted in his plan. September 9 was therefore the greatest battle-day yet seen upon the eastern front. Both sides had marched far and fought long and hard, and both attacked simultaneously. Conrad motored to Grodek and close to the battlefront endeavoured to inspire his troops by his presence. But the attacks of the Second and Third armies, despite their local superiority, made no progress and very severe fighting which lasted the whole day left the fronts unchanged. Both Ruzski and Brusilov, however, reported that the Austrian line in front of them was too strong to be broken. They thus paid their joint unconscious tribute to Conrad's tenacity.

The final blow was now to be delivered from the north. General Dragomirov's cavalry corps had penetrated deeply into the gap between Auffenberg and Dankl. Plehve, whose army was not, as Conrad had assumed, a disorganized mass, but in good fighting order, followed corps by corps behind them, leaving the three divisions of the Archduke Joseph on their left hand. The whole of this great force was already in rear of Auffenberg's right and their march on the 11th would have involved his complete encirclement. He had already in the nick of time drawn in the Archduke Joseph's divisions southward to strengthen his own left wing. But neither he nor Conrad had any idea how powerful were the Russian forces now traversing his rear, or what fatal points they would reach on the 11th and 12th. Fortune, whose caprice had robbed Auffenberg of his victory on the 31st, now made him a handsome amend. For this purpose she had previously bestowed upon the Russians a powerful wireless apparatus. Early in the morning of the 11th this instrument lifted up its voice and in clear tones, unmuffled by cipher, ordered the two left corps of Plehve's army to reach the two hamlets Cieszanow and Brusno that day.

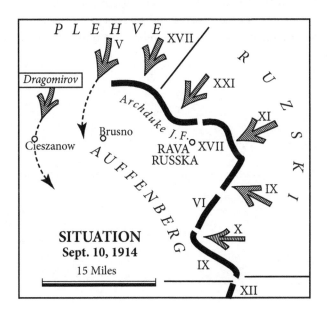

115

The unexpected message amazed both Austrian commanders, and showed them as by a lightning flash the extent of their peril.

Conrad, still hoping against hope, ordered the Archduke Joseph to march against the intruders 'and make more room to the rear.' But Auffenberg, who knew that these divisions, which had been marching and fighting continuously for eighteen days were now reduced from over 50,000 to barely 10,000 men, did not pass the order on. Without losing an hour he began his retreat south-east, and guided by further Russian wireless messages extricated his army from its mortal danger. Conrad's orders to the Second Army 'to attack without halting, with energy and regardless of loss' were likewise not passed to the troops by its commander, Böhm-Ermolli. The limits of human nature had been reached and the Commander-in-Chief's orders for further battles fell on empty air. Late on the afternoon of the 11th Conrad bowed to Fate.

'The advance of the Second and Third armies' [he writes] had brought no effective decision. On the contrary the risk of a break-through by two Russian corps behind the left wing of the Fourth Army threatened to place it in a catastrophic situation. . . . In the circumstances there was only one course of action which had to be brought on with all speed, namely to break off the battle and withdraw all the armies behind the San river.'[33]

The order which had been wrung from him by terrible and torturing events was issued from Przemysl at 5.30 on the afternoon of the 11th. Almost on the very same hour Moltke acknowledged his defeat at the battle of the Marne and ordered through Colonel Hentsch the retirement of all the German armies of the centre and the right. Thus both on the Eastern and Western fronts the first mighty onslaught of the Central Empires upon which almost their all had been staked ended simultaneously in failure.

We must now proceed to East Prussia and study at close quarters the events whose mere report on the night of the 1st September so profoundly affected the Russian headquarters.

CHAPTER XII
THE INVASION OF EAST PRUSSIA

The command of the Russian north-west front was entrusted on the outbreak of the war to General Jilinski, who in the capacity of Chief of the Russian Staff had a year before made the final secret arrangements with the French for the co-operation of the two Allies in such a war as had now begun. General Jilinski from his headquarters at Bialystok controlled from the twelfth day of mobilization at least ten army corps and ten cavalry divisions. It was his intention to invade East Prussia and overwhelm its defenders without losing a single hour. He divided his troops into two nearly equal armies. On August 17 he ordered the advance of his First Army from the Niemen line and two days later that of his Second Army from the line of the Narev. It was known that the German forces in East Prussia were comparatively weak and the rapid conquest of this northern bastion was confidently expected.

One good look at the map of East Prussia will reveal the main conditions of its attack and defence. This long strip of German territory, stretching from the Vistula nearly to the middle Niemen River, is penned between the Baltic shore and the frontiers of Russian Poland. It is exposed to attack from the east by a Russian army based on Vilna

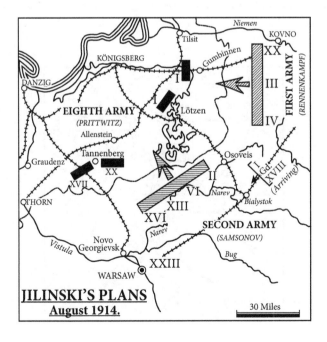

and from the south or south-east by equally or even more important forces advancing from Warsaw or from the Warsaw-Vilna railway line.

The Generals who were to lead the two armies upon what the Russian High Command in its expansive moments called a 'gigantic raid' had been chosen for their reputed energy and resolution. Rennenkampf commanded the first or Vilna army and Samsonov the second or Warsaw army. Both these Generals were supposed to be the pick of the Russian Service. Both had distinguished themselves as dashing cavalry leaders in Manchuria. Unhappily they had been personal enemies since the Manchurian campaign, when a fierce altercation, descending to fisticuffs on the Mukden railway platform, had occurred between them about an alleged failure of Rennenkampf to support Samsonov at a critical moment. The responsibility for concerting the movements of these two armies and of ensuring the best relations between their leaders devolved with peculiar weight upon General Jilinski.

All the troops of these great armies had left their various concentration areas by the 13th or 14th and were diligently marching westward and north-westward to the invasion of Germany.

The defence of East Prussia in this grave hour had been, as the reader will remember, entrusted to General von Prittwitz. His nickname '*der dicke Soldat*' 'the fat soldier,' was not impressive. He had at his disposal the 1st, XVIIth and XXth Corps and the 1st Reserve Corps, with one additional division and one cavalry division, and he could draw from the garrisons on the Vistula and from the fortress of Königsberg perhaps four or five detachments of partially mobile troops each equalling about a brigade. These forces constituted the German Eighth Army, which must now sustain the assaults of Russian hosts two or three times its numbers. The difficulties of Prittwitz were aggravated by the fact, obvious from the map, that whatever troops were sent to attack or arrest Rennenkampf in the north ran the risk of being cut off by the advance of Samsonov from the southwest. But for this, as for other problems, Schlieffen had left a plan. At a

certain stage in their advance the Russian armies must find themselves inevitably divided by the 50-mile chain of the Masurian Lakes. At this point they would have no lateral communication and would be for several days entirely separate entities. The German plan, according to Schlieffen, was to throw the whole army at this juncture at whichever of the two Russian armies came first within effective striking distance, and then using the superbly organized railway system of East Prussia to go round and strike the other. Many a war game, with all its attendant railway time-tables, had been played upon this well-known theme in the years before the war. Here too on a smaller scale the Germans had a war on two fronts. Whatever happened in these serious preliminary battles it was Prittwitz' duty not to be cut off, or so mauled at or near the frontiers that he could not, if the worst came to the worst, form a continuous fighting front behind the Vistula. A situation at once delicate and momentous, requiring the highest qualities, but offering also the most brilliant opportunities to a Commander-in-Chief! The task was one in which Marlborough, Frederick the Great, Napoleon or the Lee-Stonewall Jackson combination would have revelled, but in which General von Prittwitz felt himself from the outset overweighted.

He compromised therefore by sending his XXth Corps to await the Warsaw army and his 1st Corps to delay Rennenkampf, while holding the rest of his forces in a more or less central position. The Commander of his 1st Corps, General von François, ultimately to prove as we shall see the real hero of Tannenberg, was a man of independent and unruly temperament. He could not bear to yield up the sacred soil of the Fatherland to the Cossack hordes. The streams of refugees, the lines of burning villages aroused him and his soldiers in an intense degree. He vehemently urged Prittwitz to allow him to strike Rennenkampf as soon as he had crossed the frontier and to send all the rest of the Eighth Army to his aid. There would be time afterwards—just time—to get back and turn on Samsonov. For this counsel he could indeed cite the letter and the spirit of this particular Schlieffen plan. After cruel heart-searchings Prittwitz allowed himself to be persuaded by his adventurous and half-defiant subordinate. He compromised again by leaving the XXth Corps to wait for Samsonov and allowed his other 5 divisions to join François for the battle.

This was not long delayed. During the 17th and 18th Rennenkampf's masses poured across the frontier and after a fierce preliminary encounter at Stallupönen drew up for battle on the 20th before the town of Gumbinnen. That day was fought a battle between 7 German and 8 Russian divisions* which, though it passed almost unnoticed in the pandemonium of Europe, set in motion several chains of causation violently and even decisively affecting the whole course of the Great War. Very few people have even heard of Gumbinnen, and scarcely anyone has appreciated the astonishing part it played. The fortunes of the day were piebald. François with his 1st Corps surprised the Russian right at dawn and beat it back for 7 miles in disorder. The single German cavalry division, passing under the noses of the inert Russian cavalry corps, swept right round the

---

*A Russian division was larger than a German one, 16 battalions to 12, but had fewer field-guns, 48 to 72, and no heavy guns as the German had.

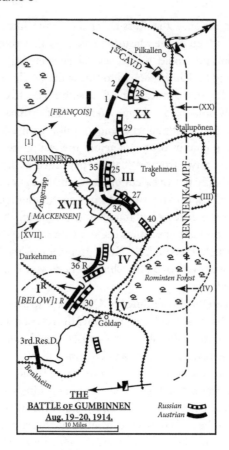

THE
BATTLE of GUMBINNEN
Aug. 19–20, 1914.

Russian
Austrian

broken flank and created a panic among the masses of Russian transport. General von Bülow's 1st Reserve Corps at the other end of the line made some progress and was hopefully expecting the arrival of an additional German division for action the next day. But General von Mackensen with the XVIIth Corps, encouraged by François' success, had attacked in the centre impetuously, frontally and without surprise, and sustained a sudden and most disconcerting repulse. The Russians were entrenched. Mackensen had made little or no artillery preparation. His men were mown down; the crowds of wounded drifting to the rear were soon joined by numerous stragglers; then whole troops appeared retiring together, at first in order and presently in disorder. The white-haired Mackensen himself, quitting his headquarters, endeavoured personally to stem the rout, and thus ceased to function as a corps commander. His example was followed by his principal officers. It was in vain. The XVIIth Corps was afterwards to fight in these same operations with the utmost courage and effect, but the German accounts of Gumbinnen contain almost without exception the insulting word 'panic.' This disorder entailed the arrest of the German right, and night fell upon tumultuous scenes of victory and defeat in which both armies had equally shared.

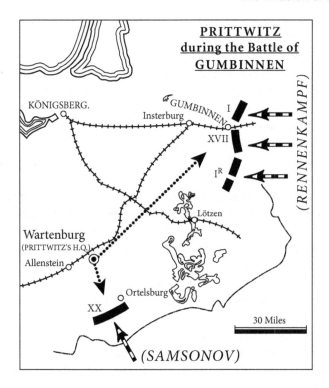

PRITTWITZ during the Battle of GUMBINNEN

Now came the crucial episode. General von Prittwitz had commanded this battle of only 7 divisions from his headquarters at Wartenburg, nearly 75 miles away. He has awaited with great anxiety, and even we must say nervousness, the result of this first important collision with the mysterious and incalculable Russian power. The impressions which he sustained were most unfavourable. To comprehend his position we must think of a man with his left arm stretched out to its fullest possible extent and his fingers caught in grinding machinery, while his right hand (XXth Corps) is drawn up close to his shoulder to ward off another blow which he fears is going to be struck by a new antagonist from another quarter. He had throughout been fearful of this great extension of his left arm. He had let himself be dragged forward by François, he dreaded that his arm might be cut off, or that he himself with his single XXth Corps might be butted into and overwhelmed by his enormous new assailant advancing from the direction of Warsaw.

The Battle of Gumbinnen has been fought. François has had his way—but thank God, reflects Prittwitz, the XXth Corps was kept back: and what are the results? They are certainly not good. At the best the battle is drawn. In his kind of strategic position Prittwitz cannot afford drawn battles. He must bring his troops back while time remains. For what is the Battle of Gumbinnen, good and bad taken together, compared to this blow which he sees impending upon him from Warsaw? He sees in nightmare mood the advance to the Baltic of a new vast Russian army from Warsaw, overwhelming his XXth

Corps and cutting off the rest, entangled in doubtful fighting 100 miles to the north-east. He knows he is confronted with forces at least twice his own strength, and amid all these dangers there gleams one safe, indispensable refuge to reach which is at once his heart's desire and his supreme responsibility—the line of the Vistula. And then at 6.30 p.m. this same day the definite news arrives that long, heavy columns of the Russian Southern army have been seen streaming across the frontier near Mlava.

The actual information was 'The Russian army from Warsaw with a strength of 4 to 5 army corps has begun to cross the German frontier opposite the front Soldau-Ortelsburg.' His staff were doubtful about imparting this last formidable item to their chief. Among their number was a remarkable man with a trained intelligence of the first order—General Hoffmann, Chief of the Operations Section. His knowledge of his profession was profound, and to it was added an outlook as wide as the war itself. No clearer brain or more discerning eye could be found in the élite of the General Staff. His was the mind behind most of the German plans on the Eastern Front. We shall often recur to his sagacious wisdom. General Hoffmann has recorded an illuminating conversation which he had with his colleague, Grünert, upon the unpleasant news from Mlava.

'Too stiff a dose for our venerated leader!' says Hoffmann—or words to that effect. 'Impossible to withhold such information from a Commander-in-Chief!' opined Grünert. It had moreover already reached him.

'I suppose, gentlemen,' said General von Prittwitz, when he had summoned them to his office, 'you have also received this fresh news from the Southern Front?' and then he added in vehement decision, 'The army is breaking off the battle and retiring behind the Vistula!'

Hoffmann and Grünert were for renewing the fighting at Gumbinnen on the 21st. François and the other Generals on the field were furious at the idea of breaking it off; they felt sure they could turn both the Russian flanks and beat Rennenkampf soundly on the second day 'even though the XXth Corps has been denied us.' But Prittwitz had made up his mind. He was determined to break off the battle and to retreat by a long night march out of all contact with the enemy.

Had Prittwitz relied upon his competent staff and acted only with them, he might yet have been carried through his perils. But at this moment he took independent action. In his agitated state he went to the telephone, and without informing any of his officers, cleared the line to the German Main Headquarters at Coblenz. Moltke is called to the receiver. It is for him also an hour of superhuman stress. All the German armies in the west from Belfort to Brussels are either in deadly grip, or about to enter into battle on French and Belgian soil. The impression which Prittwitz gave Moltke over the telephone was that of a man unequal to his task. To fall back precipitately to the line of the Vistula was bad enough, but worse was threatened by Prittwitz.

'At any rate,' said Moltke, 'you must at all costs hold the Vistula'; to which Prittwitz replied that even that could not be guaranteed without reinforcements. The river was low. It was fordable in many places. 'How shall I hold the Vistula with my handful of men?' This remark closed his military career, for no sooner had the receivers been replaced, than Moltke was looking for his successor. In this search we will join him.

In Moltke's laden mind arose a now famous image. Away in Hanover there sat at this moment the massive figure of a retired general, a man of Sadowa and Mars la Tour who had passed from the service some years before. Now all the supreme events for which his life-training had prepared him were rushing to their climax. The whole of the Prussian army, the fate of the German Empire, nay the dynasty itself, all were cast into the scale, and for him there was as yet no place. There he sat in his civilian clothes, brooding on the scraps of information which the newspapers afforded, wondering whether the call would come to him. After all, he knew East Prussia. Mile by mile he knew it. Even if others were to gather the laurels in France, surely against the Russian hordes there was something for Hindenburg to do!

He records his emotions quite simply in his memoirs. 'Would my Emperor and King need me? Exactly a year had passed without my receiving any official intimation of this kind. Enough younger men seemed available. I put myself in the hands of Fate, and waited in longing expectation.' And then at 3 o'clock in the afternoon of August 22 a telegram from the Emperor's Headquarters! Was he prepared for immediate employment?—'I am ready.' But even before his reply could have reached Main Headquarters, he received a further despatch stating that his willingness to serve was assumed, and that he was to command an army in the East. He was even told the name of his Chief Staff Officer.

Moltke in his necessity had had another idea. When the Germans after violating the Belgian frontier had on the night of August 6 sent six brigades to carry Liége by a *coup de main*, the attackers blundered and came to a standstill. A situation of strange confusion arose. In the darkness and disorder the columns making their way between forts not yet surrendered lost their direction and hung on the verge of disaster. At this moment a Staff Officer—long immersed in the inmost secrets of the General Staff and of the impending war, a man whose opinions had been so strongly expressed that it had been thought expedient a year before to remove him from Berlin to a brigade—had suddenly appeared from the gloom. He took command of one column which had lost its general, and of all the forces within reach, found the right road, led the troops forward, entered the city; and with the early light of morning single-handed smote upon the gates of the citadel and procured its surrender with its entire garrison. Here surely was a man versed in every aspect of Staff work, acquainted alike with its largest and smallest propositions, and now showing qualities of action and audacity in actual contact with violent events. Join his force and knowledge to the prestige and character of old Hindenburg, and East Prussia would surely not lack stout defenders.

Accordingly on the 22nd, a motor-car has already brought the imperious Ludendorff from his Deputy-Quartermaster-General's post with the invading armies to Headquarters. From here, as he is careful to tell us, he issued direct orders to the troops upon the East Prussian Front. These orders were however actually confined to the following points: First some reinforcements from the eastern fortress garrisons were to join the Eighth Army. Secondly the Army Staff was to meet him at Marienburg—a long way back; and thirdly the various army corps were to be handled independently until the new Commander-in-Chief had arrived upon the scene. He then entered his special train and, picking up

Hindenburg, who was waiting in the 'well-lit station hall' at Hanover, rumbled off to the East.

Of all this—of Prittwitz' telephonings, of what he had said, of what had resulted from it—the Staff of the Eighth Army had not the slightest inkling. But if we return to their headquarters at Wartenburg we shall see that meanwhile events have not stood still. While General von Prittwitz was telephoning to Coblenz on the night of the 20th, Hoffmann and Grünert had been in energetic discussion with the Chief Staff Officer, Waldersee. This is the same Waldersee who as Moltke's deputy was waiting during the month of July 'ready to jump' at any moment. His opportunity has come. Something of this sort passed.

'It is all very well to say "retire to the Vistula," but you cannot get there without fighting another battle. The Warsaw army is 80 miles nearer the Vistula than our troops that fought to-day at Gumbinnen.'

This argument was decisive. Waldersee bowed to it. Prittwitz reappearing was persuaded that he must fight another battle even to retreat. He became more composed. Under the impulse of Hoffmann a series of movements was planned which would strain to its utmost the long-prepared organization of the East Prussian railways, but which practically without alteration marshalled the forces for the Battle of Tannenberg. All the troops which had fought at Gumbinnen were to break contact with the enemy and retire fast as possible. François with his victorious 1st Corps, and the 3rd Reserve Division also, were to entrain 20 miles west of the battlefield. And these troops in forty-eight hours were to be carried round the railways towards the right flank of the XXth Corps watching the Warsaw Front. Mackensen, with his somewhat smirched XVIIth Corps, and Bülow with his 1st Reserve Corps were to retire by march as fast and as far as possible with a view to turning southward to join the left of the XXth Corps, if circumstances should require or permit.

Thus on the night of the 20th Prittwitz' decision to retire behind the Vistula has already been cancelled by him, and every move made by his staff has well and truly laid the foundations of a tremendous military event. But mark what follows. Prittwitz did not tell his staff what he had told Moltke. He did not tell Moltke that he had changed his mind. He left the Supreme Command under the impression that retreat to the Vistula was his final word, and since no contradiction or explanation came from his staff, it was assumed that they were all in agreement with their chief. This, apart from Prittwitz' agitated manner, emphasized to Moltke the gravity of the position. He acted immediately and did not think it worth while to impart his decision either to the moribund Commander or his discredited Army Staff. They would know soon enough. Thus from the 20th to the 22nd, when Prittwitz received the abrupt news of his dismissal, neither Moltke nor Prittwitz knew what the other was doing, though in fact it would have been deeply interesting to both.

When on the evening of the 23rd Ludendorff bustled into the decapitated headquarters of the Eighth Army which he had summoned to meet him at Marienburg, he received from General Hoffmann the report of the troop movements actually in progress. He agreed with them all. He found nothing to add and nothing to take away. He had expected to find a paralyzed staff and a drifting army. He found the board set with rare skill and decision for immediate battle.

'I found him,' says Hoffmann, 'extremely surprised to learn that all the instructions and orders necessary for the intended attack on the Russian Warsaw army had already been given.'

This assertion of General Hoffmann has not been challenged by any of the voluminous writings which Ludendorff has given to the public. It was natural that an officer called from the exciting scenes of Liége and newly considering the problem on the Eastern Front should wish to reserve his opinion till he arrived at his new headquarters. Ludendorff would have been most imprudent to have prescribed a battle combination from a distance. But the facts are clear, namely that upon his arrival with Hindenburg at the new Eighth Army Headquarters all the movements necessary to the Battle of Tannenberg were already in progress. Let us in a nutshell repeat what these movements were. Three of the seven German divisions which fought at Gumbinnen were railed round to the right and left of the XXth Corps opposite the invasion from Warsaw. The other four were marching westward so as to be able to take their positions upon its left. Hindenburg and Ludendorff found themselves with nine divisions spread or about to be spread in

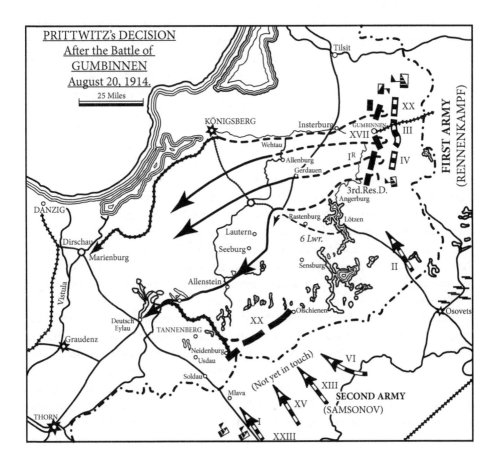

a crescent formation facing south-east, and into the midst of this crescent the Russians from Warsaw were steadily marching.

After all these perturbations, alarums and excursions among the Germans, we must now return to the Russian side.

Rennenkampf and his Generals had been staggered by the Battle of Gumbinnen. They had felt the grip as it seemed of a terrible foe closing upon them. Suddenly, for no reason which they could perceive the grip had relaxed. The Germans had retreated; they had vanished completely away; they had abandoned the field leaving their dead and wounded behind. Where had they gone? That might be found out later. Why had they gone? There, was the mystery. But there was one explanation; an explanation gratifying to Russian sentiment, comforting to their highest hopes. The repulse, the heavy losses of Mackensen's corps had communicated a panic to the German army. They knew they were beaten. They had accepted the fact that they were absolutely outnumbered by the might of Russia. They were retreating with all speed and preserving their forces for a struggle far inside their own country. A surge of intense relief and elation rose in the Russian Command. Henceforth they had beaten troops in front of them; troops who had not merely lost a battle, but thrown away a victory almost in their grasp; troops obeying an inexorable strategic compulsion to retreat.

Let us then sum up the consequences of Gumbinnen. It induced Prittwitz to break off the battle and propose a retirement to the Vistula. It provoked Moltke to supersede Prittwitz. It inspired Moltke to appoint Hindenburg and Ludendorff, and thereby set in motion the measureless consequences that followed from that decision. It procured from Hoffmann and the staff of the Eighth Army the swift and brilliant combination of movements which dictated the Battle of Tannenberg. It imparted to the Russian Command a confidence which was in no way justified. It gave them an utterly false conception of the character, condition and intentions of their enemy. It lured Jilinski to spur on Samsonov's marching army. It lured Samsonov to deflect his advance more to the West and less to the North, i.e. farther away from Rennenkampf, in the hopes of a greater scoop-up of the defeated Germans. It persuaded Rennenkampf to dawdle for nearly three days on the battlefield in order to let Samsonov's more ambitious movement gain its greatest effect, and it led Jilinski to acquiesce in his strategic inertia.

But far wider and more fateful consequences followed in the general war. If Jilinski, Rennenkampf, Samsonov underrated the Germans in East Prussia, Moltke formed the impression from Prittwitz' alarming message that he himself had hitherto valued the Russians far too low. If a German army of seven divisions could be so smitten in a single day of straightforward battle that the army commander with the agreement, which was naturally assumed, of his trusted and deeply instructed General Staff Officers, including the hitherto cherished Waldersee, thought only of retreating to the Vistula, obviously all the calculations of the strength necessary to defend the Eastern Front must be revised. This conviction seems to have dominated Moltke's mind during the five or six days' convulsion which followed in France. He had already a tender conscience about his pre-war arrangements with Conrad. At the first moment when he could see daylight in France, he must transfer large reinforcements to the East. More than that, he

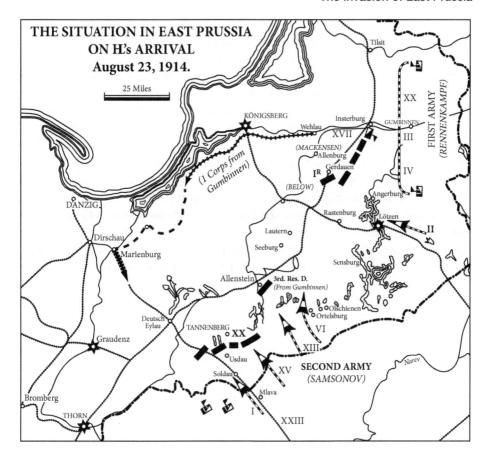

THE SITUATION IN EAST PRUSSIA
ON H's ARRIVAL
August 23, 1914.

25 Miles

must insist upon an immediate offensive by the Austrian armies. 'On the 21st August in consequence of the breaking off of the Battle of Gumbinnen and the beginning of the retreat in the direction of the Vistula,' General von Freytag-Loringhoven, the German Military plenipotentiary at the Austrian Headquarters, represented to Conrad 'that an early relief of our weak forces in East Prussia by an offensive of the Imperial and Royal armies as arranged is desirable.' Conrad, whose mood and situation have been described, had consented to order the advance 'with a heavy heart.' 'Instead,' he remarks, 'of the support hoped for from the Germans, the position was reversed,' and he saw himself 'obliged to relieve them by an offensive the success of which, in view of the numerical superiority of the enemy, was doubtful.'

The greatest has yet to be told. Up to the 25th everything appeared to be going well for the Germans in France. The French offensive in the Ardennes had been decisively broken. The wheel through Belgium was driving all before it. The French army of the left and the British army were retreating and being pursued as fast as men could march. Says Tappen, chief of the Operations Section at Supreme Headquarters, 'The favourable reports which came in from all sides daily up to and including the 25th in combination with the great victories of the Sixth and Seventh Armies in Lorraine during the 20th to the 23rd August awoke in the Supreme Headquarters the belief that the great decisive battle of the West had been won. Under the impression of this decisive victory the Chief of the General Staff, in spite of considerations to the contrary, on the 25th August decided to send forces to the East. . . . Six corps were allotted for this purpose, among them the XIth and the Guard Reserve Corps. . . . The Commanders of the Second and Third Armies, in full confidence of having won victories, raised no objection to parting with these two named corps, and as they had been engaged in the investment of Namur, they were immediately available. The other four corps, two from the centre and two from the left wing, could not be sent at once as they had to be disengaged.' Thus the wheeling wing of the Schlieffen plan was weakened at its most critical moment by the withdrawal of the two corps which would otherwise in a fortnight have filled the fatal gap at the Marne.

It is now necessary to describe the last of the consequences that followed from Gumbinnen, namely the astounding Battle of Tannenberg, the Cannæ of the World War, and its follower the Battle of the Masurian Lakes. These operations are of interest even to the non-professional reader from the scale of the tragedy which they presented and from the personal contentions for their laurels which are still proceeding.

CHAPTER XIII
THE BATTLE OF TANNENBERG

Few men have written with more penetration on the Great War than M. Jean de Pierrefeu. His task of drafting the official communiqués of the French Army during the whole struggle ensured him the fullest knowledge of what happened in France. His high intelligence and literary qualities used this knowledge in the most effective manner. But when he makes an excursion to the Russian front and attempts to describe the Battle of Tannenberg, he merely repeats in an attractive form some of the popular delusions which have gathered round that battle. His opening paragraphs illustrate at once the situation and his misconceptions of it.

Ludendorff at grips with the Russians! Two Russian armies have invaded Eastern Prussia: in the east that of Rennenkampf, a mass of 24 infantry divisions at more than full strength, preceded by a numerous cavalry: in the south that of Samsonov, less important but still alone superior to the sole defence of East Prussia—the Eighth German Army. To face this double enemy it must be divided. But the march of Samsonov endangers the troops in front of Rennenkampf beyond the Masurian lakes. They run the risk of being ground between the two armies. Moreover Moltke has contemplated a general retreat to the west on the line of the Vistula. A prudent solution indicated already by Schlieffen in his plan! However Ludendorff without hesitation adopts the solution of audacity. At a glance the position of the two Russian armies in Eastern Prussia evokes in his Staff Officer mind familiar with the themes of celebrated campaigns, the plan of a famous manœuvre which so many great Captains have used. It is the classical manœuvre: *to surprise successively two adversaries who are separated (before their junction) and beat them one after the other.* In this case to fall upon Samsonov with united strength, then to turn against Rennenkampf before the latter has time to go to the help of the former. Such is the plan of the campaign which is about to open. Point by point events unfold exactly as Ludendorff has foreseen them. As Rennenkampf, marching slowly through Eastern Prussia from east to west, reaches the line of the Masurian lakes, Ludendorff withdraws from before this sluggish enemy the bulk of the German forces confronting him. He joins these forces to the fraction of the Eighth Army opposing Samsonov. He then attacks Samsonov and beats him. As above all by a stroke of genius he has directed two corps withdrawn from the Masurian lakes upon the rear of Samsonov's army, this army collides with them in full retreat, and disaster culminates in ruin. 'There is Tannenberg!' '*Voilà Tannenberg!*'[34]

The reader who is acquainted with the story of the Battle of Gumbinnen, with the times and circumstances, of Ludendorff's appointment and with the orders which he gave or did not give or found already given, will see at a glance the monstrous perversions of fact which underlie this sprightly and compendious narrative. That so shrewd and authoritative a commentator should five years after the armistice have given such a travesty to the world, makes it a public duty to expose the truth.

We will proceed to trace the real part which Ludendorff played in this tremendous battle. In so doing we shall not deprive him of any credit which is his due as a brave and skilful officer faithfully bearing an immense responsibility. We shall strip him only of the legendary trappings which ignorant rumour has offered him, and which he has shown himself so eager to take and keep.

* * * * *

While the affairs described in the last chapter have been unfolding on the German side, the Russian hosts have been toiling on. The tragic figure of Samsonov now flashes for its brief moment in the light of history. Cavalry leader in Manchuria, Governor of Turkestan, on sick-leave in the Crimea at the outbreak of war, Samsonov on August 8 arrives at Bialystok to command the Second, the southern Russian Army. This army of more than 5 corps and 5 cavalry divisions is to march from the Bialystok-Warsaw railway line north-west towards the Baltic. It will pass south of the chain of Masurian lakes and strike the Germans more or less in the direction of Allenstein, and by so doing will cut off in flank and rear every German soldier opposing the advance of the First Russian Army under Rennenkampf.

Strategically it was a deadly thrust. It might have been much more deadly. With that sorry wisdom that judges after the event, one may ask why the Russian strategic plan ever contemplated an advance of two separate armies, with all the advantages it gave to the Germans with their breakwater of lakes and fortifications and their network of railways. Why was it not open to Russia to have moved with one united army, advancing south of the lakes on a broader and stronger front? Could they not have afforded to leave the area between Kovno and the frontier untenanted, indeed to lure on the German forces into it? The one fatal punch to which the Germans were exposed by geography was a north-westward advance from the Warsaw-Bialystok line towards the Vistula. Such a march intercepted all communications, traversed all railways, dislocated all prepared plans, swept out of existence all German schemes for ringing the changes from one flank to the other, wiped out a score of grave anxieties and obligations. It was a pincer attack in which all the available strength could be employed on one half of the pincers, the other being fixed naturally and for ever by the sea.

Moreover, the massing of the entire Russian forces on this southern line would eliminate the fortress of Königsberg as a factor in the operations. That powerful place, mysterious and formidable to an army advancing like Rennenkampf's with its right hand on the Baltic, would simply have ceased to count in a single massed Russian advance from the south-east. It would have been left behind and cut off with whatever else the Germans might think fit to hold in the long and dangerous military promontory of East Prussia. No need to fight at Stallupönen and Gumbinnen, no need to trouble about the lakes and the Lötzen fortress in their midst!

But this simpler method had been deliberately prevented by the decisions or neglects of pre-war strategy. Only two lines of rail—both single—crossed the frontier—Bialystok-Lyck and Warsaw-Neidenburg. This sandy, trackless border had purposely been left roadless and desolate to guard against a German offensive. Now their own offensive war-plans for a different situation had to be made within the limitations they had themselves created. They were condemned to improvisation and the second-best.

Nevertheless, with its great preponderance the Russian offensive was sufficiently formidable; and we find Samsonov striding forward with his five corps in this same menacing direction in conjunction with Rennenkampf's advance and crossing the German-Polish frontier on a broad front continuously during the 21st and 22nd.

RUSSIA'S
STRATEGIC ALTERNATIVE

50 Miles

Let us look at the condition of this new Russian army at the moment it begins its invasion of Germany. The five army corps of which it consists have been marching without rest for 8 or 9 days along sandy tracks in the burning heat of August. Jilinski in his eagerness to intervene in the general war drama at the earliest moment has set Samsonov's forces in movement before their transport arrangements have been completed. He has by repeated telegrams urged the weary columns forward. He has refused all appeals for a halt and in consequence these fourteen divisions—a mass of over 200,000 men—are now about to come into contact with their German foe, reduced by sickness and straggling, wearied by many severe marches, weakened from scanty rations through trying to live on a barren country, with their regimental reserves of food already heavily drawn upon, and their communications so unorganized that no supplies can reach them from the rear. We may picture these brave troops already hungry, worn and footsore, their ardour checked by leaden fatigue, wandering forward through the broad landscape of sombre pine forests, innumerable tawny lakes, infertile stubble fields with squalid hamlets few and far between. They are about to encounter the best trained troops in the world, local men fighting on their native soil, soldiers whose kith and kin are flying for safety under their very eyes, with hearth and home at their backs, and with all the terrors of scientific war at their command.

The Russians can hope to have on their side one advantage, and one advantage only—overwhelming numbers. If this is denied them, their ruin is certain. Will they have this advantage of overwhelming numbers? Only if they are combined. But will they be? To learn this we must go back to the battlefield of Gumbinnen where Rennenkampf is still rejoicing in his victory.

General von Prittwitz's decision to break off the battle and the movements ordered by his staff on the night of the 20th had been executed with extraordinary celerity. When night fell seven German divisions were in contact with Rennenkampf's army. When morning broke they were nowhere to be seen. The XVIIth and Ist Reserve Corps are already 15 miles away to the south-west. François with three divisions is already entraining 20 miles away for the most part on the lengthy sidings towards Königsberg. The day is fine and warm and the Russian chiefs, who the night before were far from sure where the advantage of the battle lay, gave themselves up to optimism and rejoicing. It was not until the third day (the 23rd) that the ponderous mass of the First Army got itself again into motion and by leisurely marches rolled forward westward along the Baltic shore.

What explanation can be offered for this? Many have been forthcoming. De Pierrefeu does not hesitate to accuse Rennenkampf of treachery. He uses the expression 'sold to the enemy.' He points to a second disaster later in the war when Rennenkampf fell under suspicion so grave that he was removed from his command. We shall examine this charge further presently. Hoffmann can only suggest jealousy and personal spite. He recalls the old feud between Rennenkampf and Samsonov in the Manchurian war. But Jilinski has not been charged with treachery. Jilinski had had no quarrel with Samsonov. Jilinski was the immediate authority by whom both the Army commanders were directed. It is Jilinski who is playing the hand. Why then did he acquiesce calmly, nay cordially, in Rennenkampf's delays, while at the same time he urged Samsonov ruthlessly forward? Obviously because he was deceived about the German fighting power. He had convinced himself that they could not withstand the double attack. Henceforward his aim was not merely their defeat, but their destruction, and this destruction would only be complete if Rennenkampf did not drive the Germans back before Samsonov was ready to cut them off. The reasoning was sound: it was the facts which were wrong.

But anyhow there can be no excuse for Rennenkampf's total loss of all contact with the enemy. However the strategic movements might be planned, it was vital to know where the Germans were. There were only four or five corps to be accounted for. Whatever was not in front of Rennenkampf, might be moving to attack Samsonov, and *vice versa.* Rennenkampf had no less than five Cavalry Divisions—20,000 horsemen—none of whom had taken any serious part in the battle. They had only covered 48 miles in the previous 3 days and their transport was complete. Reconnaissances of even 30 miles would have revealed during the 21st and 22nd at any rate the rearguards of the German XVIIth and 1st Reserve Corps.

But Rennenkamp had lost the German army. He had no idea where they were or what they were going to do. He gladly assumed that the bulk had taken refuge inside the fortress

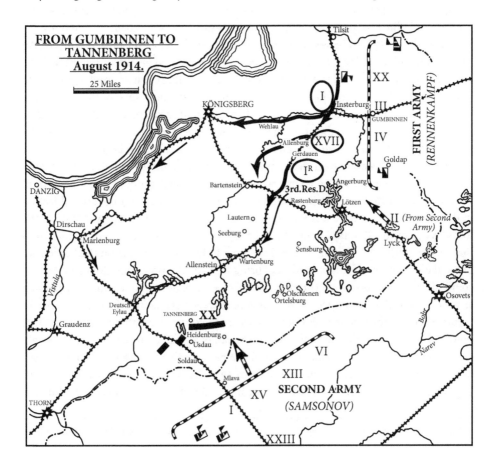

of Königsberg and that the rest were hurrying back towards the Vistula. Even on the 26th when a circle of steel and fire was about to close round Samsonov, Jilinski complacently ordered Rennenkampf to provide two corps for the investment of Königsberg and to march on with the rest towards the Vistula. In fact Prittwitz's panic-stricken decision to break off the battle at Gumbinnen had created a deception of the Russian mind which no ruse, however carefully planned, could have effected. Henceforward Samsonov will be left alone to face all the German forces in East Prussia and to engage his weary troops against an enemy incomparably superior in organization, communications, quality and morale, who may now bring to the decision 180 battalions against his 150, and who possesses artillery half as strong again in numbers and double his weight in metal. In these circumstances the great battle which followed could only have one result.

During the 23rd the three corps of Samsonov's centre (XIIIth, XVth and XXIIIrd) advancing north-west began to come in contact with the reinforced German XXth Corps.* The three divisions which had been sent round by rail from Königsberg were not yet in position, and the XXth Corps which had been facing south, partly by pressure, partly by design, gradually hinged back on its right through a quarter circle until two days later it faced east. It was as if a door had swung open invitingly. Into it the Russians marched. So far everything seemed to promise success. Samsonov was confident, Rennenkampf slothful, and Jilinski unperturbed. Only Samsonov's troops were exhausted and hungry.

The battle of the 23rd between the Russian centre and the XXth Corps was severe. All through the 24th and 25th the Russians despite their fatigue and privations fought well and their great numbers pressed heavily upon the slowly recoiling German front. By the night of the 25th the XXth Corps had completed its backward wheel. One of the reinforcing divisions had come into line on its left. No further withdrawal could be allowed; orders were given to fight it out to the death in the positions then occupied, and the battle of the two centres—7 Russian divisions against 3½ German—was about to begin.

The issue was awaited with deep anxiety at the German Headquarters. A battle at odds of two to one, against an enemy whose quality had not yet been put to the proof, was in itself a grim event. Yet this battle was only one, and that not the crucial feature in the combination. Where was Rennenkampf, and what would he do? Although in the four days since the 20th his columns spread fan-wise have only advanced 15 miles, and that in a westerly direction, he has still the time to join his comrade on the battlefield. Three days' marches, if unopposed, will bring him to Allenstein; his clouds of cavalry could already have been overrunning the narrowing region between the two Russian armies. What is there to stop him? The corps of Mackensen and Bülow, with the German cavalry division, though he does not know where they have gone, stand in his path. This powerful body which the German accounts speak of as 'the Eastern Group' is probably capable of warding Rennenkampf off until the battle with Samsonov is over. But then its forces cannot take part in that battle themselves. They must be either engaged with Rennenkampf or awaiting his attack. Meanwhile as they face north and east the Russian

---

*It had been joined by a Landwehr division and a fortress detachment equal to a Brigade, i.e. it was in all 3½ divisions.

20 Miles

Alle

Allenstein

Osterode

(3rd.Res.D.)

I Corps arriving

TANNENBERG

XX

Gilgenburg

Usdau

VI

XIII

Neidenburg

XV

Neide

SECOND ARMY
(SAMSONOV)

Soldau

I

2nd.D.
(XXIII)

oMlava

SAMSONOV'S ADVANCE
Aug. 23–25, 1914

Russians

GERMAN XX CORPS:
Original Line
Eventual Line

VIth Army Corps guarding Samsonov's right will as it advances be traversing their rear, and if Rennenkampf attacks they will be taken between two fires, as well as fighting against double their numbers. So here is another possibility loaded with peril. All therefore depends on Rennenkampf. If, even now, he converges towards Samsonov by forced marches, the whole German army in East Prussia will be fighting simultaneously at odds of two to one. What then will Rennenkamp do?

It was this that tormented Ludendorff and his Chief from the moment when at 2.30 on the afternoon of August 23 they learnt from Hoffmann the whole situation. To leave 'the Eastern group' as a shield against Rennenkampf, was to avoid the gravest risks, but to reject all the prizes. On the other hand, to ignore Rennenkampf, to take the chance of his advancing and to bring them southward, offered first of all the certainty of striking the isolated VIth Corps—not two Russians to one German, but two Germans to one Russian—thus intervening in the most terrifying manner upon Samsonov's rear.

On the night of the 24th Hindenburg on Ludendorff's resolve ordered both Mackensen and Bülow to go south by 'enormous forced marches' and strike the VIth Corps. 'From the point of view of the High Command,' says Hoffmann, 'the position that evening was the most difficult in the whole battle.' Even now Ludendorff did not make up his mind finally—and who shall blame him?—about Mackensen's corps. It should start south, but at any moment it might have to turn back and help the solitary German cavalry division in delaying the advance of Rennenkampf's mighty host. Still the orders were given, and the whole Eastern group was marching southwards throughout the 25th.

At this moment the story of the crisis of Lemberg repeated itself in the astounding event which, coupled with Rennenkampf's inertia, has given rise to the accusations of foul treachery. The Russians had inadequate telegraph and signal arrangements and all their communications were awkward and tardy. But, as we know, they possessed their radio service. Their radio now with bland simplicity proclaimed to the world in two uncoded messages exactly what Rennenkampf and exactly what Samsonov would do or not do on the 25th and 26th. The German wireless station in the fortress of Königsberg listened to these amazing disclosures. In the early morning the first message told them that the Russian First Army would not reach the line Gerdauen-Allenburg-Wehlau until the 26th, thus making it certain that Rennenkampf's army could not take part in Samsonov's battles. In the afternoon the second message revealed all Samsonov's projected movements. It showed that he believed the rearward wheel of the XXth Corps was part of a general German retirement and that he had only to pursue. This was immensely reassuring. It showed that Samsonov's attack on the XXth Corps would probably not take place until the 26th. 'In addition to this,' says Hoffmann dryly, 'the order confirmed the information we already had as to the strength of the Russian forces, and apart from this we were very glad to know the exact objectives of the individual enemy corps.' Thus Fortune cast her mischievous foreknowing smile on General Ludendorff at this birth moment of his memorable career. When he arrived on the 23rd, as he believed, and as the world has long believed, to restore order out of chaos, to retrieve disaster and stem the rout, she had presented him with a splendid opportunity ready-made and requiring only his nod of approval. On the 25th when he hung on the double tenterhooks of Rennenkampf's menace and Samsonov's impending battle with the German XXth, Corps, she reassured him on both accounts. Rennenkampf may for two or three days be disregarded, so that all the troops of the German Eastern group may fall upon Samsonov's right, and Samsonov himself will not attack seriously until the 26th, by which time the whole of the Eighth Army—François on the right and Morgen's Division deflected to the threatened left—will be in line. Nor need he fear a trap. The movements described by the intercepted radio can be checked by the ordinary contacts and reconnaissances of the field and are found generally to correspond. This is the way to make war.

The German High Command passed the night of the 25th in comparative mental comfort. General von François with his Ist Corps supported by various detachments equal to another division was rapidly arriving on the German right. In order to help the threatened XXth Corps in what was expected to be a hard-fought battle on the 26th, Ludendorff demanded that he should attack the Russian left at dawn. François protested vehemently. Only part of his fighting troops had detrained. Very little of his artillery and none of his ammunition columns had yet arrived. The task set him was severe. Samsonov had guarded his left flank by a new Russian army corps—the Ist—which was now entrenched upon the ridge of Usdau; and its left was prolonged almost to the

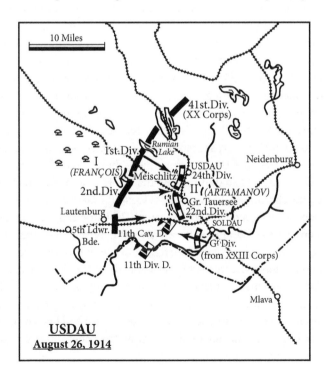

Polish border by a Guard division, a rifle brigade and two cavalry divisions. François, in attacking the Ist Corps as directed, would have to expose first his left shoulder and finally his back to the rest. He wanted to find the true flank of the enemy and make a still wider turning movement. Convinced at length that for this there was neither the strength nor the time, he fell back on a more solid objection. He disliked frontal attacks. Anyhow he would not make one without the fullest artillery preparation. 'Remember what happened to Mackensen last week at Gumbinnen.' Ludendorff, determined from the outset to assert the authority of the new command over a competent but notoriously unruly subordinate, curtly insisted. Hindenburg, who presided at this fierce discussion, maintained an august silence. So severe was the tension that he himself felt it necessary to visit François and enforce the orders with his whole personal weight. Under this pressure François adopted a policy of passive resistance. He obeyed—but in such a manner as to make sure he had his own way.

No one could say that he did not attack on the 26th; but in fact he so delayed his movements and restrained his troops that scarcely any progress was made. Indeed, to be blunt, he played with the army staff from dawn till dusk. That this was a calculated and deliberate frustration of their will and not merely the slothfulness of reluctance, is proved by the fact that the wily François asked the XXth Corps on the night of the 25th whether they were really so hard pressed that he must make an attack without artillery support and before he was ready, in order to save them. The XXth Corps replied reassuringly that they were all right, and that there was no need for him to compromise his preparations. Ludendorff passed the morning of the 26th in great impatience, but also in complete uncertainty as to what François was actually doing. It was not until the evening that he realized that he was being fooled. But by the evening other things had happened.

The two corps of 'the Eastern Group' had collided with the Russian VIth Corps protecting Samsonov's right flank and rear. It was an encounter battle. The Russians had no apprehension of any serious danger. They thought that some portion of the retreating German army might be marching back parallel with, but at a considerable distance from them, while other retreating units would be following on behind them through Rastenburg. Samsonov's orders drew this picture for them. However, early in the morning of the 26th the Russian VIth Corps received the unexpected news that an enemy brigade was at Lautern and later that it was occupying Seeburg. Full of ardour they attacked these forces with a division, and thus ran into the whole Eastern Group (two army corps and the 6th Landwehr Brigade) who were descending upon them from the north as fast as desperately determined men could march. The battle exploded immediately. The attacking Russian division found itself hopelessly outnumbered. It defended itself bravely till the evening. Its companion counter-marching to help it was involved in its ruin. The Russian corps commander became demoralized. During the night and the next day the whole corps fled southwards, and its divisions did not stop till they reached Olschienen and Wallen, 21 and 25 miles respectively from the battlefield. The first of the blows which destroyed Samsonov had been struck. His right flank guard had been broken down; and this vital information was not imparted to him by the general concerned except in a confused manner and after a delay of many hours.

During this momentous 26th François' artillery had arrived, and he declared himself ready to attack at daybreak on the 27th. Hindenburg and Ludendorff proceeded to an eminence at the foot of Lake Gilgenburg, on which amid fir trees an aerial perch had been erected whence a clear view could be obtained. They were enormously cheered at 6 o'clock by the news that the Usdau position had already been stormed. This however proved to be false. The fighting troops had mistaken the village of Meischlitz, 2,000 yards to the south-west, for that of Usdau, and the real attack on the latter did not begin till 10 o'clock.

This engagement, which some have called the battle of Usdau, repeated upon the Russian left the disaster which the day before had befallen their right. The whole of François' artillery, strengthened by heavy guns withdrawn from the fortresses, opened terrific fire upon the Russian entrenchments facing west on the Usdau ridge. These entrenchments, hurriedly dug in continuous lines without traverses or covering rifle pits and thickly manned, were soon choked with dead and wounded, and the Russian corps, to whom the vital protection of the left flank of Samsonov's army had been confided, showed themselves unable to withstand the artillery storm; the division on the right, followed by that on the left, quitted their trenches before it was even necessary to launch the German infantry assault, and streamed back southward in considerable disorder by the way they had come, in the direction of Soldau. Thus on two successive days both the flanking corps which protected the advance of the Russian centre had been routed, and for Samsonov on the night of the 27th only one flickering hope remained—immediate retreat.

* * * * *

We will pass the night of the 27th at Samsonov's Headquarters in the little town of Neidenburg. His right-hand corps (the VIth) has already been hurled back in shocking disorder by powerful forces which can only have come from Rennenkampf's front. His Ist Corps has run away from the Usdau position on his left. In the centre, far in advance of these two faithless guardians, his valiant XVth Corps with a division from the XXIIIrd on its left has been for three days in heavy action with the German centre, and his XIIIth Corps finding little opposition in front has actually stretched forward as far as Allenstein. On both flanks rout, and in the centre, far advanced in danger's jaws, a doubtful battle and hideous lack of food! How did he re-act to these impressions?

It is inconceivable that an experienced commander would not by this time have realized the mortal peril which confronted his whole army. Immediate orders to the XIIIth, XVth and XXIIIrd Corps to retreat, and to his flank corps to attack, offered the only possible chance of escape. But a sombre spirit of fatalism—characteristically Russian—seemed to have overpowered the doomed commander. He had been misled. He had supposed he had only a beaten foe to deal with. But the die had been cast, fate must decide; better perish than retreat. Perhaps there would be better news to-morrow. An awful psychic lethargy descended upon his weary being; and at midnight on the 27th Samsonov ordered his centre corps to continue their attack. But, as Hindenburg remarks, 'they were no longer seeking victory, but destruction.'

At dawn on the 28th the whole German army counter-attacked. The XXth Corps reinforced on its left by the 3rd Reserve and Goltz's Divisions advanced in increasingly successful onslaught upon the Russian centre. Mackensen (XVIIth) and Bülow (I. Res.) were moved westward with the double purpose of helping the XXth Corps and also reaching some position to defend the rear and flank against Rennenkampf who had at last belatedly begun to appear. But the decisive action took place upon the German right, and here again there occurred one of François' grand disobediences. The 28th did not see Ludendorff at his best. He felt that the battle was won; he sought no decisive victory. Provided he was secure against an attack from Rennenkampf, he was ready to be content with small results. His orders to Mackensen and Bülow, repeated on the 29th, prevented these powerful forces from taking any very effective part in the battle, or from closing the wide gap which was open to the Russian retreat in the south-east.

No one can blame him for taking precautions against Rennenkampf. But it is his orders on the 28th to François which have the worst appearance in the light of further knowledge. François pursuing eastward with vigour all through the 28th had entered Neidenburg by nightfall. He was ordered by Ludendorff to change his direction to almost due North and advance in the direction of Lahna. Now these orders implied the virtual abandonment of any serious attempt to round up the enormous masses of the Russian centre. It moreover condemned François to plunging his corps into the forest area with the certainty that he would become dispersed, would not get far or do much. The order

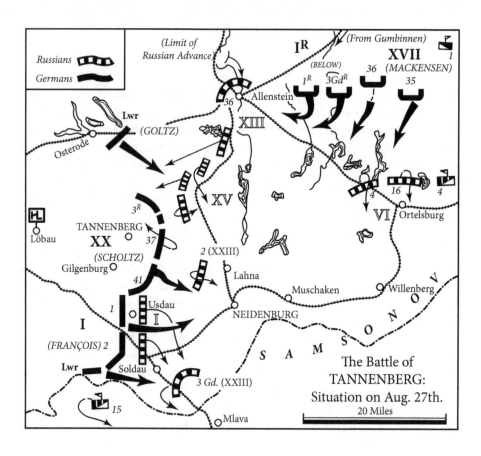

The Battle of
TANNENBERG:
Situation on Aug. 27th.
20 Miles

was sent in terms of exceptional impressiveness. It concluded with a solemn adjuration that the corps 'could render the greatest possible service to the army if these intentions were duly carried out. All depends on the Ist Corps.' But General von François had quite different intentions. His advance troops were already half-way along the road from Neidenburg to Willenberg. This road running due east was in every way convenient for his purpose. It ran in open country within good rifle shot of the edge of the forests. Along this road therefore during the whole of the 29th General von François hurried his troops, building up as he went, a long line of posts and pickets, to block in the Russian masses. By nightfall François' line was completed. With 25 battalions he had strung himself out over a length of 50 kilometres. By the night of the 29th, in spite of a further order to advance north-eastward, he had this thin single line of posts between the Russian masses struggling to escape from the forests and whatever hostile troops might be set in motion against it from the direction of Warsaw. Again Ludendorff acquiesced in the decisions imposed upon him by this audacious officer.

* * * * *

We have now reached the last act of the tragedy. The British liaison officer in Russia, General Knox, had been attached to Samsonov's staff. In the morning of the 28th he

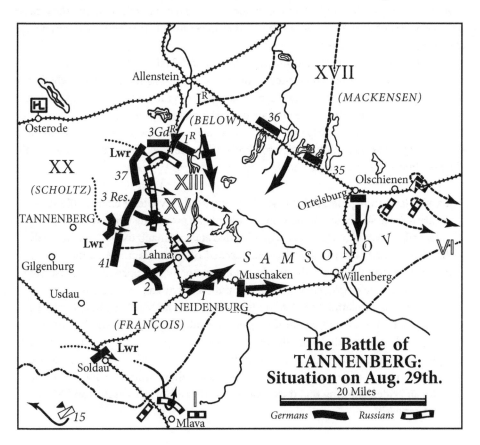

The Battle of
TANNENBERG:
Situation on Aug. 29th.
20 Miles
Germans   Russians

motored up from Neidenburg to join the Commander-in-Chief. He found him by the side of the road studying his maps surrounded by his staff officers. Suddenly Samsonov rose, ordered his Cossack escort to provide horses for himself and his staff, and was about to ride off in the direction of the XVth Corps. General Knox prepared to mount and accompany him, but Samsonov took him aside. The situation he said was very critical. He did not know what was going to happen. He did not wish a foreign officer to accompany him. Even if the worst happened here, it would not affect the ultimate course of the war. With that he said good-bye and rode off. Knox adds that both he and his staff were calm. They said 'The enemy has luck one day, we will have luck another.' Knox went back with a long train of motor vehicles and just got through Neidenburg in time.

We may accompany General Samsonov a little further. He spent the night of the 28th with the headquarters of the XVth Corps. Throughout the 29th the dissolution of the Russian centre proceeded and large masses of men in utmost confusion surged aimlessly about in the forest. At length the General and his 7 staff officers are alone. Night comes on; they dismount from their horses; they struggle eastward. The General, asthmatic, exhausted, brokenhearted, is supported by his officers. At last he can go no further. Murmuring to himself 'The Emperor trusted me,' he turns aside from the others. He is alone. Three days before he had commanded a quarter of a million men. The officers hear a single shot; they search for his body; they never find it. They resume their journey, and some escape to tell the tale.

The closing scenes continued during the 30th and 31st. All beaten armies tend to retreat along the path by which they have advanced. But as the Russians, whether as stragglers or in formed bodies, attempted to escape from the southern edge of the forest, they were met by the pitiless fire of François' cordon and driven back. Again and again by day and night the most desperate efforts were made to escape. Often bands of soldiers, following the cross held aloft by a priest, broke from the woods and rushed towards the German line; but none reached it.

Says a German regimental history: 'With morning grey a long enemy column of all arms came slowly out of the woods without any protecting troops and offered a target which would never have been permitted at peace manœuvres. Unfortunately fire was opened on it too soon by some excited riflemen; upon which the general fire of both battalions and the machine-gun company was opened. This last was for the first time employed as a complete unit, and with all its six guns it opened continuous annihilating fire. A more fearful effect could hardly be imagined. The Russians tried to take refuge in the woods, abandoning vehicles and horses. The frightened and wounded animals rushed aimlessly over the country, wagons were upset, there was soon wild chaos. The units which were still armed sought to take positions on the edge of the woods, but very soon they exhibited white cloths on poles and rifles, showing that they regarded further advance as useless and wished to surrender.'[35]

During the 31st they surrendered in enormous numbers. A single battalion of General von François' corps captured 17,000 prisoners. Large bodies of troops were seen from the air assembling in various open spaces, and alarm was caused at the German Headquarters until it was realized that they were only prisoners and that the bayonet glints were only those of their German escort. The Army Command had no idea how many they had cut off in the forests. Hoffmann on the 30th put the number at 40,000, but Grünert was sure it did not exceed 20,000. Hoffmann offered to pay him a mark for every one under 20,000 if Grünert would pay a mark for every one above. Hoffmann expresses a well-founded regret that this wager was not accepted. In all 92,000 unwounded Russian prisoners and 30,000 wounded Russians were collected by the victors. Of these 92,000, 60,000 were the well-earned prize of François' corps.

By the evening of the 28th Ludendorff was so satisfied that the victory was complete, that he was already building up a line against Rennenkampf, whose cavalry divisions were now at last approaching Allenstein and could almost overlook the battlefields where their comrades had perished. It was to be their turn next.

* * * * *

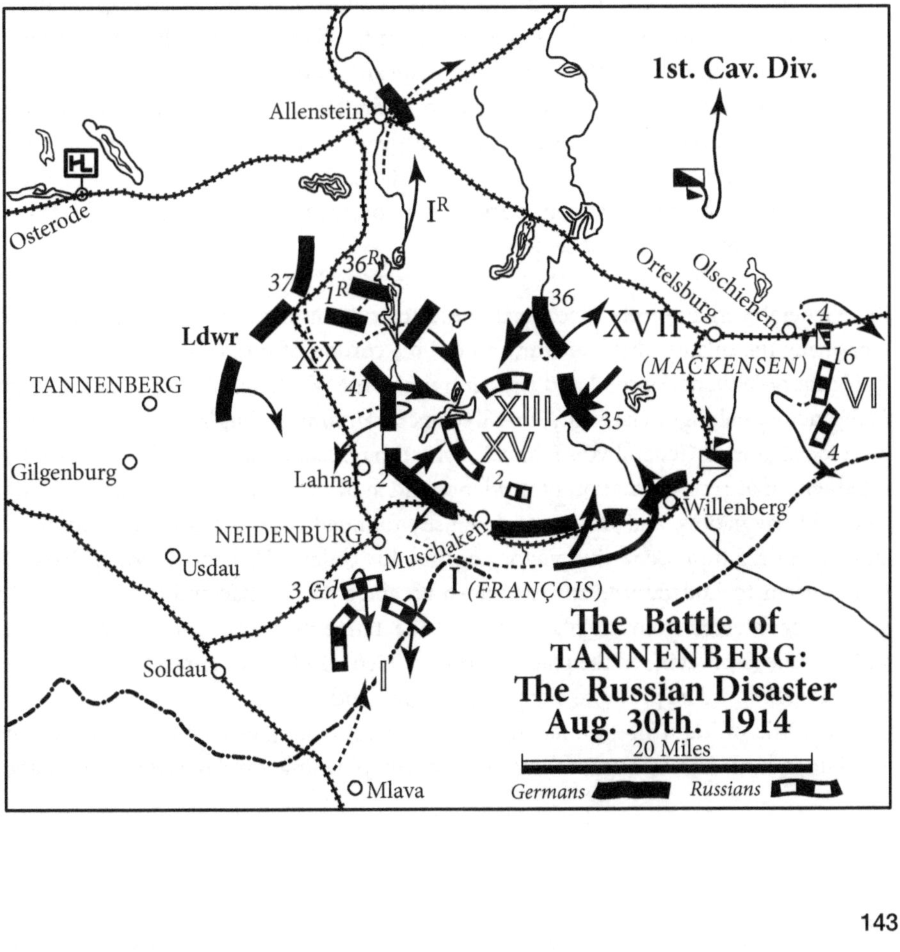

The Battle of
TANNENBERG:
The Russian Disaster
Aug. 30th. 1914

20 Miles

Germans ▰ Russians ▭

The glory of Tannenberg was during the war and for some years afterwards successfully appropriated by Ludendorff. It was the stepping-stone by which he rose to the effective control of the whole German War. Hindenburg made no personal claims. He was content to allow Ludendorff's statement to pass unchallenged. It was as follows:

'General von Hindenburg had always agreed to my suggestions and gladly accepted the responsibility of consenting to them.' But facts which are no longer in dispute prove first that all the movement which concentrated the Eighth Army against Samsonov had already been ordered by Prittwitz' staff on the initiative of Colonel Hoffmann, and these movements were approaching completion at the moment when Ludendorff arrived at the Army Headquarters. Secondly, that the only orders issued by Ludendorff *en route*, apart from those relating to minor reinforcements, were to withdraw the headquarters of the Eighth Army as far back as Marienburg and to authorize the various corps to act independently pending his arrival. Both these interventions were unfortunate and led to loss of precious time. During the course of the battle Ludendorff on the 25th endeavoured to force François into a premature attack which if checked would have enabled Samsonov's army to escape before disaster overwhelmed him. François disobeyed him with magnificent results. On the 28th Ludendorff resigned himself to the escape of the Russian centre. In a fit of nerves he prevented the XVIIth and Ist Reserve Corps from effectually closing the gap to the eastward; and on the same day ordered François to advance in a direction which undoubtedly would have enabled the mass of the Russians to escape to the south-east. In fact Hindenburg, no doubt at Ludendorff's suggestion, telegraphed on the night of the 28th to the Supreme Command: 'The battle is won; pursuit will continue. The surrender of the two Russian corps *may well not be achieved.*'

But General von François disobeyed these instructions and at great risk, yet truly measuring the quality of the enemy, ran out his cordon of posts and pickets along the Neidenburg-Willenberg road and thus entrapped the whole Russian centre. The credit of the victory belongs in large measure to General Hoffmann, but its glory must for ever be associated with General von François, who though commanding only a single corps acted with that rare alternation of prudence and audacity which is the characteristic of true soldierly genius, and who upon his justly founded convictions defied Ludendorff and gained for him a dazzling victory against his orders. That this opinion, harsh as it may seem to Ludendorff, has now been accepted in German military circles, may perhaps be inferred from the photograph of the Tannenberg decennial celebrations, in which François is accorded the place of honour, even Hindenburg himself, the President of the Republic, being proud to sit upon his right hand.

The Battle of Tannenberg inaugurated the memorable partnership of Hindenburg and Ludendorff. Hindenburg in loyal and courtly phrasing has described it as a happy marriage. Ludendorff has given more definite and less graceful descriptions. It stands among the renowned associations of Great Captains in history. Nothing can rob it of its glamour. To avoid the constant repetition of these two names which will occur so often in our story, it will be a convenience to express the combination by the cabalistic symbol '**HL**'.

CHAPTER XIV
THE FIRST MASURIAN LAKES

The double battles of the Eighth German Army under Hindenburg and Ludendorff against the two superior armies of Samsonov and Rennenkampf are not only a military classic but an epitome of the art of war. One of our finest officers, General Ironside, has devoted an entire volume to the first thirty days in East Prussia which certainly no military student should neglect. Here our pages must be confined to a general account of the operations, placed in their relation to the whole European scene.

By the night of September 1 the victors of Tannenberg were already turning to their new task; nor was there the slightest doubt what that task should be. Says Hoffmann laconically: 'Samsonov's army had been practically destroyed. Of his five-and-a-half Corps three-and-a-half were either dead or prisoners, the remaining about one-and-a-half Corps had to be sent back into the neighbourhood of Warsaw for re-formation. Our hands were free to act against Rennenkampf.'

With fierce and confident hope the Germans made their plans. They were freed now from the anxieties of a converging attack by superior forces. Their problem was simplified. Many unknown factors had disappeared. They had tested the quality of their troops and organization in every kind of fighting against their foe. They knew that whether in attack or defence he was no match for them. Moreover, the two fresh army corps (Guard Reserve and XIth), so improvidently withdrawn from the German right wing in France, had arrived in East Prussia. Hindenburg and Ludendorff disposed of seventeen divisions (the original nine, the four auxiliary, and the four from France). This powerful force, braced by success, was entitled to feel itself superior to Rennenkampf's army, whether that comprised twenty or twenty-four divisions.

Nor was the method of setting about him far to seek. He must be attacked on his front from the sea to the lakes. While thus gripped, his flank must be turned and if possible his retreat cut off by a right-handed Northward movement through the line of the lakes. Here the immense strategic advantage of this line of water, marsh and German fortifications presents itself. The small fortress of Lötzen stood in the gap between the northern and southern lakes. Its resolute Commander had made no answer to a Russian summons to surrender but to fire upon, wound and capture the officer and trumpeter sent upon that audacious mission. The Russians, having overlooked in their plans for the invasion of East Prussia the need of a few heavy howitzers to reduce Lötzen, could do nothing against its permanent defences. Lötzen was therefore a bridge-head and a fatal sally-port through which the flank and communications of Rennenkampf's army could be assailed. The gap, only a mile wide, was traversed by a good military road and by the railway-line to Lyck and beyond the Russian frontier. South of Lötzen the chain of lakes continued for another 30 miles to Johannisburg with a number of gaps between them defended by field works none of which had passed out of German hands during the crisis of Samsonov's invasion. If the Germans could advance in force through the Lötzen and the other gaps between the lakes while Rennenkampf was held to his positions by a frontal attack, the capture or destruction of his entire army was a reasonable expectation.

The point for decision was not the method but the relative strength to be assigned to the frontal and to the turning movements. It must be remembered that the turning movement as it progressed would expose first its right shoulder and later on its rear to the attack of any Russian forces in Warsaw or along the Narev. The remains of Samsonov's army were not perhaps immediately formidable, but the Germans could not know what other resources the Russian Empire might not have marshalled in their great railway centre of Warsaw or behind their fortified river line. It would be necessary to ward off or delay such interventions until Rennenkampf was beaten. The shorter and sharper the operation, the less would be the risk. '**H**' decided to send eight divisions against Rennenkampf's front, to provide five together with the two cavalry divisions for the turning movement through the gaps, and to use the remaining three to ward off the Russians from the south. There were, and are still, two opinions upon this distribution. François, to whom the leading rôle in the turning movement was confided, naturally and perhaps rightly pressed for an additional corps. But Hoffman points out that **H** were not entitled to ignore the possibility that Rennenkampf himself might take the offensive with his great mass against any Germans on his front, and would in such circumstances have a superiority of more than two to one.

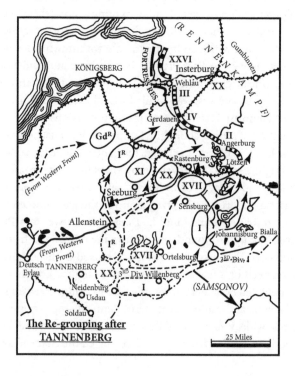

The Re-grouping after
TANNENBERG

25 Miles

Thus then it was settled. The XXth, XIth, 1st Reserve and Guard Reserve Corps moved against Rennenkampf's front; the Ist and XVIIth Corps, and the 3rd Reserve division with the cavalry were assigned to the envelopment. It took four days to re-group the German forces in accordance with these orders, and on September 5 their general advance began.

What meanwhile of Rennenkampf and his Russians? And what of Jilinski? Up till August 27 Jilinski still had a picture of his Second Army advancing northwards, but he felt uneasily that it required help from Rennenkampf. Late that day he had wired to him that German troops were being transferred from Rennenkampf's front by rail and were strongly attacking Samsonov. 'Co-operate,' he said, 'with the Second Army by moving your left flank as far as possible towards him.' But Jilinski's order displayed no disquietude about the Second Army and he seemed content with Rennenkampf's movements of three Corps two moderate marches to the south-west. In the evening of the 29th at 7 p.m. a more urgent order arrived. 'In view of the heavy fighting in the Second Army the C.-in-C. orders you to move two corps to its support. The cavalry should be sent forward to Allenstein,' and at 11 p.m. 'The Second Army has withdrawn,'—certainly no over-statement—'therefore the C.-in-C. orders the forward movement of the two corps to cease.' And on the 30th: 'General Samsonov has suffered a complete defeat and the enemy has now full liberty to turn against you. You must take every measure to interrupt the railway lines by which the enemy may move troops against you. Be careful that the enemy does not take measures against you through Lötzen.'

Even now, however, the Commander of the North-West Front had not abandoned the idea of blockading Königsberg, and on September 1 his staff were still forming a reserve corps for this purpose. The reaction of Tannenberg upon Jilinski and Rennenkampf was the same. Both expected that the Second Russian Army would now have to bear the full weight of the German attack. Rennenkampf decided to withdraw all his forces and concentrate on the general line of Insterburg, and on September 2 he issued orders which placed the bulk of his army in an entrenched position with the sea on one flank and the lakes on the other. The next three days were occupied in fortifying this line, which but for the Lötzen gap and turning movements farther to the south was secure. Acutely sensitive of the Lötzen danger, he assigned an entire Corps to watch its exits. Jilinski approved these arrangements. He ordered his First Army to 'maintain its present position at all costs against superior forces of the enemy which may be brought against it.' His Second Army which he was able to re-inforce by the XXIInd, the IIIrd Siberian, and the Ist Turkestan Corps—a new Army in themselves—was to cover the approaches to the lower Narev in such a way as to threaten, though somewhat remotely, the very turning movement which the Germans had designed.

But on September 4 the two-and-a-half German divisions which under von der Goltz were to ward off Russian interventions from the southward advanced on Mlava and seized the town. Jilinski thereupon leapt to the conclusion that the Germans, instead of throwing their weight against Rennenkampf, were going to strike at Warsaw; and he now became anxious for Rennenkampf to take the offensive. He developed a grandiose scheme for another great concentric offensive in which his First Army, the remains of the Second and the three new Corps were to take part. This offensive was to begin on September 14.

Such were the orders of General Jilinski on the night of September 4. They dealt largely in phantom armies and with an imaginary situation. They were brushed aside by reality. During the 5th, 6th and 7th the four German Corps constituting the main attack upon Rennenkampf advanced by easy marches and drew up before the Insterburg entrenchments. They did not begin their battle until the 9th. Meanwhile the turning movement had made great progress. François, with three divisions and a cavalry brigade, drove weak Russian forces out of Bialla on September 7; and at dawn the next day took the town of Arys, which like Bialla was held only by six Russian battalions and a few batteries of artillery. The two German divisions employed, fighting upon their own peace-time training ground, knowing every yard, quickly routed these detachments; and thereupon François turned due north with his own Ist Corps towards Rennenkampf's communications. He sent his third division to capture Lyck in order still further to widen the envelopment.

At the same time Mackensen and the XVIIth Corps had marched through the Lötzen gap and deployed beyond it. Here they encountered the Russian IInd Corps drawn up to receive them, and a serious engagement began. During the 8th the Russians stopped the gap. They were strongly entrenched between various lakes, and no local means could be found of turning their flanks. The two German cavalry divisions which were to have passed the gap after the XVIIth Corps, found themselves hopelessly blocked by its transport. Two additional Russian divisions arrived during the day, and when darkness fell the Russian front was everywhere secure.

September 9 was a day of general battle. Hindenburg with four Corps attacked the Insterburg line. The XVIIth Corps strove to get its shoulder through the Lötzen gap. The Russians withstood them all stubbornly. The deep trenches they had now constructed gave them protection from the German artillery. They were not blown out of them as Samsonov's left flank guard had been from its shallow ditches on the morrow of Tannenberg. Enough Russians were left alive after the bombardments to arrest the infantry attacks; and the Germans had not the ammunition for the pulverizations customary upon the Western Front. Indeed the night of the 9th closed with the German forces everywhere engaged and the Russian front everywhere intact.

But nothing could stand against the turning movement from the south. François had played a part on this day as decisively and brilliantly successful as at Tannenberg. At day-break (3.30 a.m.) on the 9th his two indefatigable divisions broke upon the left and rear of the Russians resisting the XVIIth Corps and rolled, crumpled and scooped them up. The whole Russian line opposite the Lötzen gap broke into confusion. The best part of four divisions, hard-fought in front, turned in flank and attacked in rear, were routed and fled the field leaving sixty guns, 5,000 prisoners and all their impedimenta in François' hands. Hard indeed, cruel and unfair, are those malignant turns of war by which events far beyond their view and utterly outside their control rob brave soldiers of all the fruits of their sacrifices and their success. General Ironside has calculated that François' two divisions had covered 77 miles in four days, with deployments and fighting on two of them. They therefore deserved at least some of the rewards which fell into their hands.

During these events François' third division had in a combat of equal strength defeated the Russians in Lyck. The flank of Rennenkampf's left army was now turned, and two German Corps with two cavalry divisions had only to march steadily northward through Gumbinnen, upon Stallupönen or Vilkoviski, to cut off the retreat. Thus ended for the day the fierce and bloody fighting in East Prussia of September 9.

But now Rennenkampf acted with desperate vigour. Without troubling to inform Jilinski, he resolved to fly while time remained. He fled and he flew. No sooner had the news of the disaster to his troops in front of the Lötzen reached his Headquarters than

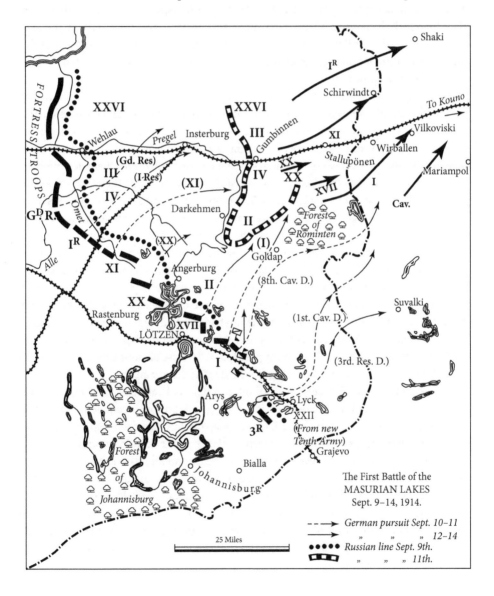

The First Battle of the
MASURIAN LAKES
Sept. 9–14, 1914.

---→ German pursuit Sept. 10–11
——→   „   „   „   12–14
●●●● Russian line Sept. 9th.
▭▭▭   „   „   „   11th.

he issued orders for the immediate general retreat of his whole army, covered by the counter-attack of two divisions. 'It was,' says General Ironside, 'most gallantly executed by the 40th division of the IVth and the 26th division of the IInd Corps. It was perfectly successful in its purpose.' This counter-attack occupied September 10. The German XXth Corps was brought to a complete standstill with surprising losses. It staggered before the blow. It was forty-eight hours before it could set itself again in motion. Russian military annals should not forget this feat of arms. Under its audacious protection Rennenkampf and the Russian First Army set out for home. Fast they went and faster still. Due east, back again along the track they had covered three weeks before in such overweening hope. Every risk was run in order to escape. Divisions marched parallel on either side of a single road, occupied by interminable columns of transport. They marched all night, they marched all day and all the next night and on still. The main bulk of the army actually covered 55 miles in 50 hours while still remaining in the ranks. On still they marched or stumbled and staggered away from the foe whose art was more terrible even than his flaming sword.

But none of this wise promptitude and speed would have availed the Russian army if François and Mackensen had been allowed to march in their original direction. They must have cut in upon the line of retreat between Gumbinnen and Vilkoviski and broken everything into chaos. Speed in flight was vital; but by itself it would not have gained salvation. It was the counter-attack of the two brave divisions, nameless men and commanders unnoticed by history, who saved the army. They left their mark upon the German XXth Corps. They made a more important impression upon Ludendorff's mind. This great soldier and genius in whom so many fine qualities were embodied suffered from the very liveliness of his own perceptions. Dwelling at the heart of the plan, receiving and reacting to all the events and news, true or false, which flowed in from minute to minute, Ludendorff sustained a sinister impression from the Russian counter-attack. Instead of letting Mackensen and François swoop out north-eastward, he pulled his right hand in for close participation in the battle which he expected to develop around Darkehmen on the 10th. Thus as the 10th wore on after the sun had climbed high in the heavens, and the long columns of Mackensen and François were streaming northwards to deploy upon the tactical flank of the Russian Insterburg position, it became obvious they were clutching only at the skirts of a Russian retreat or even indeed at the vacant air.

By the night of the 10th the chance of interception had vanished. Nothing remained but a stern chase, and in this the Russians had even a greater incentive to speed than their ravening pursuers. After the 13th the German pursuit slackened, and the enormous mass of Russian troops and vehicles, nearly choked by a block in Stallupönen, streamed eastward and homeward by every route, track and footpath. The last fighting was at Vilkoviski. Here the Russian rearguard had to stand at bay to gain a few more hours for the masses in rear to liquidate themselves. Rennenkampf decided, perhaps rightly, that nothing should be done to extricate the rearguard. They fought to the end and were destroyed. But with a loss of 45,000 prisoners, about 200 guns and perhaps 100,000 casualties, Rennenkampf's army escaped to the Niemen from the steel jaws which had already devoured Samsonov.

15 Miles

Insterburg
Stallupönen
Gumbinnen

Russian Retreat

Originally intended pursuit

I^R

XI
Darkehmen

Angerapp

Goldap

Paulswald
Benkheim

XX

XVII
Lötzen
I (FRANÇOIS)

(MACKENSEN)

Positions Sept. 9th.
" Sept. 10th.
Limit of Advance
set for Sept. 10th.
Approximate Line of
Russian Rearguards,
Sept. 10th.

1st. MASURIAN LAKES
Effect of the Russian Counter attack
Sept. 10, 1914.

For nearly a week Jilinski had been issuing orders to the void. The Germans, who read on the wireless with almost hourly punctuality his mental excursions, were baffled by the flood of secret matters imparted to them. It was impossible for them to learn any more from the orders of the Russian High Command, even when laid in text before them, since these had now ceased to have any contact with reality. It sounds magnificent to have the command of the Russian North-West Front; to poise there high at the summit, moving a million men and the pieces of a gigantic chess-board. But what mental torture could exceed the measure meted out to Jilinski as he sat each day during this fatal month at his desk in Bialystok. His two Army Commanders were famous national warriors with wide freedom of action. The orders which he could rightly issue were broad and few and far between. The information which reached him was voluminous when little was happening, and scanty or nil when supreme events were in progress. Jilinski had given his lifetime to the military service and was esteemed a soldier of the highest professional skill. In thirty days this wonderful chance of his had flared up in utter catastrophe. There he sat at the same desk in the same room with the same ceremony and decorum around him, a failure, a byword in history, a cause of his country's undoing—all because he had sent telegrams from time to time as was his duty, and events had belied these telegrams. There were the maps, there were the telegrams, there was the quiet room, there was the horrible disaster. And this was the glamour of a high Command—almost the highest— in modern war! This was what was supposed to equal the opportunities and experiences of the great Commanders of history. What a swindle, what a mockery! They at least rode their horses in the battle smoke and shared the perils of the soldiers they actually led.

But here all around were only the maps and the jiggling flags, the counterfoils of telegrams, all read by the enemy, and incoming disconnected tidings of ruin, and glum staff officers slouching in with more.

The military critics have glared upon Jilinski's various orders, but few of them with their present-day knowledge of the values and proportions of the campaign in East Prussia, would care to have such opportunities offered to them. At the end he was furious with Rennenkampf. Just as Samsonov during the four days of his agony had ceased to hold the slightest communication with his Chief, so Rennenkampf, from the hour when he scuttled with such commendable promptitude and fortunate effrontery from the Insterburg line, had not bothered about anything except getting his army away—unless indeed it be getting his own headquarters away. For these last moved very rapidly. They changed repeatedly, sometimes three or four times a day, until the crisis had passed, and thereafter he betook himself to Kovno 'far from the madding crowd.'

Jilinski, neglected and marooned, but still accountable, poured out his resentment to the Grand Duke and the Stavka. 'General Rennenkampf has thought more about the safety of his staff than of directing the movements of his army, which he has not in actual fact commanded for several days. He reports that he is moving to Vilkoviski and that he is withdrawing the IIIrd and XXVIth Corps eastward, leaving the remaining Corps of his army to their fate. His staff has gone with him. The behaviour of the Army Commander had made all direction of operations impossible. He has altered the position of his Headquarters four times in the last twenty-four hours, each time completely breaking off communication.' The Stavka, which had at any rate the victory of Lemberg to live upon, received these protestations coolly. They replied that 'it was quite in the nature of General Rennenkampf to wish to direct his troops personally' and suggested that Jilinski should 'try to get in touch with him' at Vilkoviski. He was already in Kovno.

On September 17—the day Rennenkampf's rearguard was sacrificed at Vilkoviski, Jilinski was relieved of his command and General Ruzski from the successful Galician theatre was placed in charge of the North-West Front. He rallied the First Army in front of the Niemen river. Says Hoffmann in his diaries: 'Well, well; up till now with inferior numbers we have defeated about fifteen Russian Army Corps and eight cavalry divisions and we are not finished yet. Now for it once again.'

* * * * *

Meanwhile what have been the fortunes of the Austro-Hungarian Empire?

General Conrad von Hötzendorf had fought the battle of Lemberg to the last ounce, the last inch and the last minute which his armies could sustain. When on September 11 he was forced to give the hateful signal to retreat there was very little fighting power left. The retreat was terrible. Auffenberg's army in escaping from the Russian claws had to traverse and impinge upon a large part of the communications of the Third Austrian Army. Transport vehicles of every kind marched four-abreast upon roads also encumbered with civilian refugees. 'Extraordinary rains pretty generally follow great battles,' and the infantry plodded across sopping fields. The guns drove their way somehow through the traffic blocks. Few and devoted were the soldiers of the rear-guards. Many were the alarms and panics which the dreaded cry 'Kosaken kommen' started. Vast interminable processions of misery—physical suffering of every kind, weariness, grief for friends and comrades dead, grief for battles lost beyond recall—trailed across the landscape. These rivers of the Inferno flowed sluggishly; but they flowed ceaselessly; they flowed homewards. They flowed faster than the Russians could follow. The power of the modern rifle, of a few machine-guns, of a battery or two of field artillery, to delay the pursuer, to make him await his artillery, nay, to kill him if he is impatient, may perhaps for the first time have been inculcated in the minds of the Imperial and Royal Armies. At any rate they toiled on; they struggled on; but they continued to get away; away from the fire of the foe and the ghastly battles and the hopeless sense of being overpowered.

Przemysl was a first-class fortress. A wide circle of detached forts guarded the military area and the many roads, each crawling with humanity and wagons, which converged upon it. Inextricable congestion ensued. Przemysl itself became for some days a solid block of guns and transport. On the roads leading to it all wheels presently ceased to turn. Meanwhile the Russian cannon growled behind, and rifle-shots as well as shells smote the paralyzed columns. In the end there was no recourse but to unyoke the horses and leave miles of laden transport four-abreast to be the poor but not unwelcome prize of the victors.

Still Przemysl gave some relief. An army corps was left to hold the fortress besides its own special troops. The rear-guards disappeared within the spacious perimeter. The cannon of the forts fired upon the Russians, and they had to halt or go a long way round. But the retreat continued. When the San was reached on the 16th, the state of the armies was such that Conrad realized the impossibility of turning there. He ordered the retreat to proceed to the Dunajetz, which flows into the Vistula more than 130 miles west of Lemberg.

'Day and night' [reads the Austrian official account] 'behind a gigantic train of transport-wagons marched the infantry, with bowed heads, yet undiscouraged; the artillery, sinking in up to their axles in the morass of the roads, worked their way forward; the cavalry regiments, like horsemen of the Apocalypse, in molten confusion, made their way on, their presence often betrayed from afar by the penetrating smell given off by the festering galls of hundreds of led horses.'[36]

After the passage of the San the Russians' pursuit, for reasons which will presently appear, slackened, and by September 26 Conrad found it possible to form a front before reaching the Dunajetz stream. Of the 900,000 Austro-Hungarian troops who had taken the field in August in Galicia six weeks before considerably less than two-thirds had repassed the San. Says the Austrian official account:

Austrian Line Sept. 11th. ▩▩▩
    ,,   ,,   Sept. 28th. ◼◼◼
Russian Cavalry Screen ••••••••

50 Miles

**THE AUSTRIAN RETREAT
AFTER LEMBERG
September 1914.**

'The Russians did not exaggerate when they claimed in their message of victory that the enemy had lost 250,000 dead and wounded and 100,000 taken prisoners.'

But this was not the worst of the injury to the military power of the Austro-Hungarian empire. The Imperial and Royal army was composed like no army in the world. Mutual jealousies, the arrogance of the Hungarians, the pan-Slav ambitions of the Czechs, Croats and Slovenes, the questionable sympathies of the Tirolese, created a doubtful loyalty in at least one man in four. The personnel of the army was 25 per cent German, 23 per cent Magyar, 17 per cent Czecho-Slovak, 11 per cent Serb, Croat and Slovenes, 8 per cent Polish, 8 per cent Ukranian, 7 per cent Roumanian and 1 per cent Italian. In order to prevent collective disaffection a considerable mixture of races had been arranged in many units, but the pre-war cadres of the army contained about 75 per cent of officers of German race and this proportion was followed very largely in the permanent staff of under-officers and sergeants. There were eighty words of command in German which effected the drill and control of the whole heterogeneous mass. Outside the German frame-work many officers did not even know these. It was this permanent Teutonic staff and structure that held the whole army together. These courageous, resolute professionals had exposed themselves with ardour. Their losses had been out of all proportion to those of the rank and file. More than half had perished. They were irreplaceable. Never again could the great masses of brave and docile manhood, which the Dual Monarchy could still command, be guided by the Teutonic element. The need of employing very large numbers of new officers of Czech, Roumanian or Croat nationality offered positions of authority to many who hated the Teutonic race and cared nothing for the House of Hapsburg. This mutilation of the Austro-Hungarian army in the terrible battle of two nations called Lemberg ranks with the turn at the Marne as the most important and irrevocable result of the war in 1914. It is the supreme condemnation of Conrad's narrow military creed, tense, sincere, lion-hearted as it was. His finest qualities were the cause of his country's undoing. Of all the campaigns that were ever fought the Austro-Hungarian campaign in Galicia required most of all the use of Time. Of all the armies that have ever existed since Hannibal marched into Italy, the Austro-Hungarian army needed the most careful handling. Conrad broke their hearts and used them up in three weeks. Had he sat in the seat of Moltke with the Schlieffen plan to execute and the German armies to direct, he might to-day be the outstanding captain of history books different from those which will now be printed.

CHAPTER XV
THE SECOND ROUND

By the middle of September what may be called 'the first round' of the World War was over. The Battle of the Marne was decided, and the great thrust on Paris, embodied in the Schlieffen Plan, had definitely failed. The expulsion of Rennenkampf from East Prussia had ended the Russian invasion of Germany. Almost simultaneously the Battle of Lemberg had resulted in a Russian victory. France had survived the onslaught; Germany had destroyed the Russian invasion; and the whole Austrian army had suffered defeat. The slaughter of these battles, in which all the best-trained troops of the warring nations had been desperately engaged, had exceeded anything which history records of the past and was destined to surpass any other month even of the Great War itself. The antagonists, gasping and streaming with blood, but still possessed of unmeasured resources, their full wrath unloosed, paused for a moment to rearrange their armies and refill their ranks, to replenish their ammunition and shape their plans anew.

The twin defeats on the Marne and around Lemberg had been decisive in their influence upon the neutrals. Roumania had actually decided at the beginning of September to make proposals to the Central Powers for alliance. During the critical hours of the nth Count Czernin, the Austro-Hungarian Ambassador in Bucharest, had telegraphed to Vienna that Roumania was prepared to take an active part against Russia if the territory of Suczawa were ceded to her in reward. Conrad in his extremity had clutched at this. But under the decisions of the battlefields in France and Galicia the offer was suppressed before it could be accepted. Bulgaria, the spectator of the Austrian repulse by Serbia, wrapped herself in impenetrable reserve. We shall come to Italy later.

Even as early as August 10th Moltke's quality had been judged inadequate; and his successor was openly discussed. Now on the 12th of September he was dismissed from the supreme command, and Falkenhayn, who at the outbreak had been War Minister, ruled in his stead at Supreme Headquarters. The dismissal was veiled in secrecy and pretence. No public proclamation was made. Moltke became ill; he dropped out; and gradually it was understood that a change had occurred.

The new Commander was a soldier of ability and distinction. He was comparatively young. He had passed through all the grades. He had a high degree of personal charm and the broad outlook of military statesmen. Many good judges consider him the ablest soldier that Germany produced during the whole war. He had been a convinced adherent of the Schlieffen Plan in its integrity. He had watched with misgivings and even disapproval the cumulative weakenings of the right-hand wheel which had marked Moltke's concessions to the pressure of arguments and events. To these he attributed the miscarriage. His first resolve on assuming power was to restore the Schlieffen Plan to its original form, and in spite of all the changed conditions to carry it through with his utmost resources. For this purpose he ordered the greater part of the Sixth and Seventh armies to be transported from the Alsace-Lorraine front to strengthen with overwhelming force the German right; and thither also he proposed to direct the four new army corps of youthful volunteers which had been formed upon a strong professional framework in the first enthusiasm of the war.

Opportunity, however, had gone. Indeed, but for Joffre's slowness in making up his mind, the German right flank would itself have been turned at the very outset of Falkenhayn's command. Maunoury's army which from September 10 faced east had only to be marched north, to begin an outflanking movement in which all the priorities rested with the French. Nevertheless, as Joffre gradually and tardily perceived the situation, he began to reach out his left hand, and corps after corps, withdrawn from his right wing, was sent to prolong the French line to the northward. Thus in succession the German Corps arriving from Alsace-Lorraine found themselves confronted at each point by the similar movement from south to north which was taking place on the French side. This process quickened every day and developed into a series of would-be out-flanking encounters known to history as 'The Race to the Sea.' By the end of September Falkenhayn realized that the day of the Schlieffen Plan was gone for ever.

His second resolve was the great drive against the Channel ports. Most of his Sixth and Seventh Armies had by now been employed in filling the newly-extended German front from the neighbourhood of Noyon, where its right had rested on September 10, to the neighbourhood of Lille, where it was established by the 20th of the month. There remained however the four new corps from Germany, the IIIrd Reserve Corps and detachments investing Antwerp, together with various other forces gathered from the front or released by the capitulation of Maubeuge. Falkenhayn's new plan was to secure his right flank by taking Antwerp and settling once for all with the Belgian army, and thereafter to thrust in about La Bassée and strike in the direction of Boulogne. Between these two horns of attack, one driving through Antwerp along the coast, the other converging westward from La Bassée, Falkenhayn hoped to catch the remains of the Belgian army and any French or British troops in the Pas de Calais, and at the same time become master of all the sea-ports from the mouth of the Scheldt to the mouth of the Seine by which British aid could come to France and Belgium.

However, a succession of unforeseen and untoward events obstructed this design. The British army had begun to withdraw from the Aisne at the wish of the British Government and Sir John French in the first week of October. After some delays through its trains having to traverse laterally the railway communications of the French front, it began to arrive in the neighbourhood of St. Omer. Here it was joined by its cavalry which had marched behind the French lines. This army, now made up to rather more than full strength, advanced from St. Omer and deployed along the very front from La Bassée to Ypres upon which Falkenhayn's new offensive was about to fall. At the same time the British Cabinet showed itself strongly disposed to aid and stimulate the Belgian defence of Antwerp, whose forts were falling one by one under the enormous howitzers lent by Austria. The Royal Naval Division arrived in the threatened city, and its evacuation by

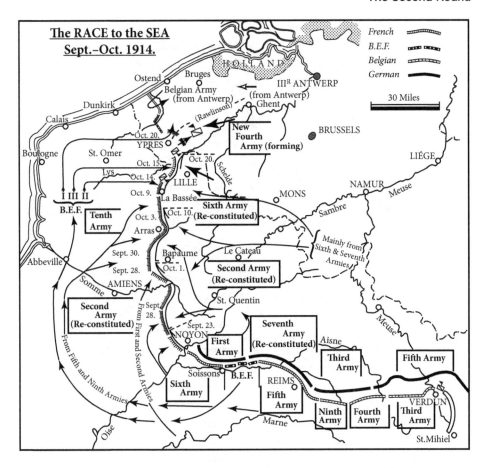

The RACE to the SEA
Sept.–Oct. 1914.

the Belgians was delayed by five days. Lord Kitchener, exerting himself for the salvation of Antwerp, sent the last available British regular division (the 7th) collected from the fortresses of the Empire, together with a cavalry division and a brigade of Fusiliers Marins and a territorial division obtained from the French, all under General Rawlinson, to the neighbourhood of Ghent.

Both sides were in equal ignorance about each other's intentions. Lord Kitchener and his colleagues had, of course, no knowledge of the powerful forces which Falkenhayn was about to loose. Falkenhayn and the Supreme Command were perplexed by unexpected contacts around Bruges and between Ghent and Antwerp with British regular cavalry and the advance troops of well-known British regiments. The British army was missing from the Aisne and French troops had replaced them in their old positions. There seemed more than a possibility of a strong British thrust being delivered from the sea coast against the right flank of the intended German advance. It was judged necessary, therefore, to delay the march of the four new German Army Corps which were now detraining in Belgium until the coast from Antwerp and Ostend had been cleared of the Belgian army and its British allies of uncertain and unmeasured strength. It was not until October 9, the day the Germans entered Antwerp, that the general advance

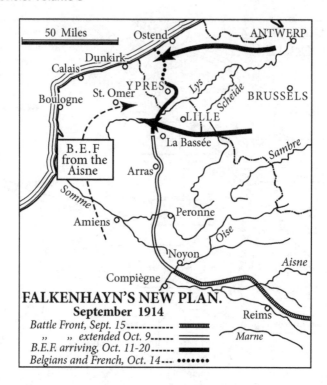

FALKENHAYN'S NEW PLAN.
September 1914

Battle Front, Sept. 15
„   „ extended Oct. 9
B.E.F. arriving, Oct. 11-20
Belgians and French, Oct. 14

southward began, and not until October 11 that the German troops opposite La Bassée and Armentières came into collision with the advance guards of the British IInd Corps under Smith-Dorrien. Close, fierce fighting immediately began and neither side could make any progress. The British IIIrd Corps, under Pulteney, which came into the line near Armentières, was equally held. The downward advance of the four new army corps towards Ypres and Dunkirk would have turned the left of the British battle now raging from La Bassée and Armentières. But Sir John French, with soldierly daring, sent his Ist Army Corps under Haig to Ypres to meet these enemies of unknown strength, and trusted to fortune, to the cavalry, and to the arrival of further detachments to skin over the wide gap between his two main bodies. At Ypres Haig found Rawlinson with the 7th Division and his cavalry, and a new collision with the German masses of a most bloody and desperate character occurred. Farther to the north again King Albert and his army, aided by the heroic Fusiliers Marins of Admiral Ronarc'h, and by the monitors and other bombarding vessels with several flotillas from the British navy, turned to bay along the line of the Yser. Along this whole front from La Bassée to the sea an intensifying battle now flared. The Belgians under British impulsion opened the sluices, and the sea poured over the flat ground, causing large inundations and bringing the advance of the German right (IIIrd Reserve Corps) to an absolute standstill.

No progress could be made therefore by either horn of the German attack. Falkenhayn then reduced the scope of his plan and from the 20th October onwards aimed only at a break through in the centre at Ypres and Armentières. He encountered an unyielding

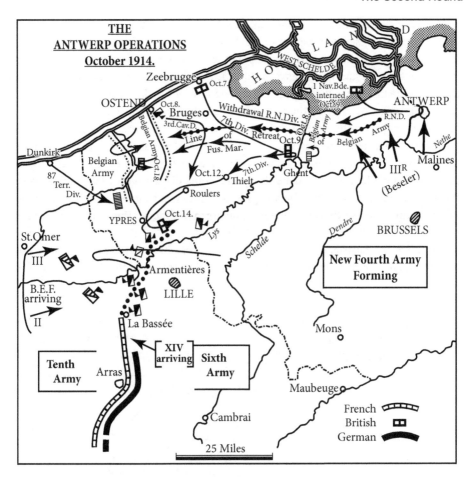

THE ANTWERP OPERATIONS October 1914.

resistance. By October 30 he was forced to restrict his ambitions to the mere capture of Ypres. Upon this task his new army corps were launched in all their youthful ardour. Supported by bombardments of their heavy artillery the flower of German youth and patriotism advanced in seemingly overwhelming numbers, often in close order, hand in hand, singing their national songs. They were met by what had now become little more than a picket line of long-service British regulars skilled in the use of the rifle and with a very few machine-guns, crouching in deep disconnected holes which they were unable or unwilling to quit. Appalling slaughter was inflicted upon the German masses. Attacks renewed again and again with patriotic devotion withered before the well-directed rifle fire. But Falkenhayn and the Kaiser, who had now come to regard Ypres as a trophy indispensable to the prestige of the German army, persisted obstinately, and not till after the middle of November did they finally accept the fact that the fronts in the west were stabilized from Switzerland to the North Sea.

These memorable events have been thus briefly recounted for the purpose of showing their repercussion in the East. The driving of the Russians from East Prussia gave **HL** the chance to take stock of the position of their southern ally. The Imperial and Royal

Austro-Hungarian armies re-gathering, mutilated, disorganized and discouraged far behind the San, presented a woeful spectacle. Falkenhayn found himself confronted not only with the Austrian demands for help, but with the acrid reproaches of Conrad that the guaranteed aid had not arrived in time. The condition of the Austrian armies and the ever-present danger that Vienna, if deserted, would make a separate peace, added arguments of greater weight than complaints or pledges. Nevertheless Falkenhayn, at first set on reviving the Schlieffen Plan, and later absorbed in 'The Race to the Sea', continued obdurate to the Austrian appeals. He would not at the moment send troops from the west. Any aid to Austria must come from the forces of which Hindenburg and Ludendorff already disposed. Accordingly after some discussions by telephone between the two German Headquarters four corps were withdrawn from the Eighth Army, railed swiftly southwards and deployed in the region north of Cracow. Thus was constituted the new German Ninth Army which should form along the Silesian frontier a force capable of sustaining the Austrians on their northern wing. **H.** directed the movements of both the Eighth and Ninth Armies and for the time being assumed direct command of the

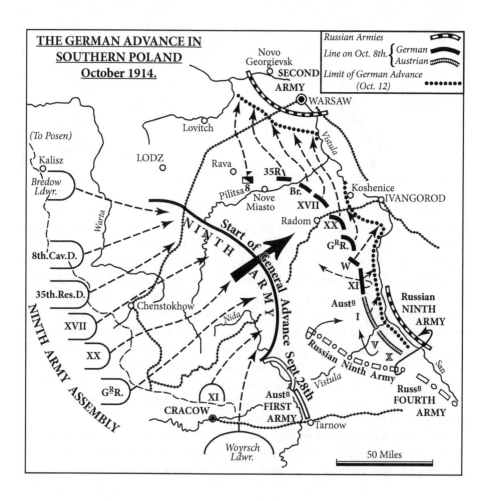

THE GERMAN ADVANCE IN
SOUTHERN POLAND
October 1914.

Ninth. So expeditious was the transportation that in the third week of September the Ninth German Army, formed largely of troops who had been fighting in East Prussia a week before and comprising perhaps a quarter of a million men, stood along a hundred-mile line from the south of Posen to the east of Cracow. This army, as the map will show, faced the original gap in the Russian front from the south of Warsaw to Ivangorod, which has been already mentioned. The new thrust was ready, and it was aimed at what might well be a deadly spot.

Russia in the first shock had experienced chequered fortune upon a gigantic scale. In the south a great victory had been gained by a million and a quarter Russian soldiers. In the north armies of nearly a million had been torn to pieces and hurled in confusion back against the frontiers they had invaded.

It was in this situation in mid-September that the French Government made formal requests through diplomatic channels that the Russian armies should be brought to the left bank of the Vistula and assembled for the direct invasion of Silesia. This was, no doubt, the shortest path to the heart of Germany. The southern bastion of Galicia and the Austrian armies which defended it were greatly reduced, but the triumphant grip of the German power on the northern bastion of East Prussia still exposed the longed-for operation to deadly peril from the north. The Grand Duke and the Stavka, who had little to learn upon this problem, resented the requests which reached them through their Foreign Office instead of from one Headquarters to another, as an intrusion by the French Government into Russian strategy. They would like nothing better than to invade Germany. This had been their intention from the outset. They were doing their best; but they alone must be judges of the time and the method. The Grand Duke, in rejoinder, asked various questions of Joffre. First, what did he propose to do in France if the Germans transferred the bulk of their forces from the West to the East; and secondly, whether his object was only to clear France and Alsace-Lorraine, or to advance to the Rhine, or indeed to penetrate to the centre of Germany. Joffre replied on September 20 that the German army was in fact already tied to the west by the battles which had been fought and their resulting situation, and that the operations then in progress (i.e. 'The Race to the Sea') would have the effect of keeping them there. As for the advance into Germany, it would of course be unlimited. Sazonov returned a reply to the French Government which, though tactfully couched, was by no means encouraging. The French under their stresses became sharply critical, and the Russian Ambassador in Paris (Isvolski) appealed to his Government to make further efforts to reassure them.

On September 22 the Grand Duke held a conference at Kholm. Here it was decided to re-group the Russian armies in the Polish salient behind the Vistula as a preliminary to a general advance of the Russian centre into Germany in spite of the danger they would run from the north. This must be warded off, and at first it was hoped that Ruzski with the First, Tenth and Second Armies, now ranged behind the Niemen and the Narev, would be sufficient for this purpose. But after Ruzski and Rennenkampf had portrayed the injuries which had been received, their armies were judged unequal to the task. The Grand Duke therefore decided that the Fifth Army (Plehve) should be sent to Warsaw to reinforce the North-West Front, now facing almost north, for its responsible task.

This having been settled, the assembly in the centre began. By the end of September the Grand Duke had set in motion the immense displacement of his forces hitherto ranged against Austria, and during the first fortnight of October three whole armies moving northwards by march and rail filled the front from the confluence of the San with the Vistula up to Warsaw. The Ninth, by march, took the southernmost situation. The Fourth, by road and rail, filled the centre round Ivangorod, and the Fifth joined hands with the Second Army round Warsaw. Thus the Grand Duke drew up four armies comprising one and a quarter million men either to favour the advance into Germany, or to meet an impending German attack aimed at what had hitherto been the weakest part of the Russian line.

These movements were however only in their early stages when on September 28 the German Ninth Army, drawing with it in its forward movement the First Austrian Army on its right, began its advance eastward and northward towards Ivangorod. Up till now the Stavka had no knowledge of the swift formation of this new army on the Posen-Cracow line and still less of its actual advance. All had passed behind the screen. On September 30 a pocket-book taken from a dead German officer revealed to them the significant fact that only two German corps remained in East Prussia. Where were the other four? Had they come South? This confirmed various nebulous indications which had for some days past reached the headquarters of the South-West front that German troops were being transferred by rail to the south. The Stavka therefore rightly

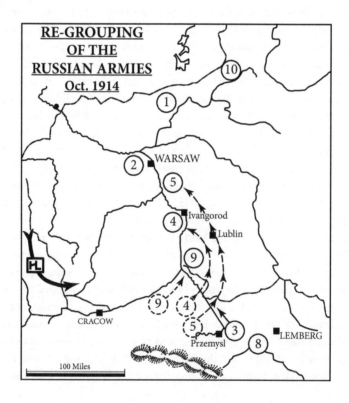

divined that a considerable movement was in progress against them by a German army working closely with the Austrian left. All the dispositions already made were singularly appropriate to this revelation.

The German advance was swift and steady. Driving back the covering Russian forces in six long marches, the Germans were already approaching the Vistula at the end of the first week of October. The object at which **HL** aimed was to seize and hold all the crossings of the Vistula from its confluence with the San to Warsaw and, thus protected, strike at the central fortress itself. They knew from the enemy's wireless, which continued to babble unsuspectingly, that important Russian movements northwards were already in progress; they could not measure their scale. The magnitude of the Grand Duke's operations, begun quite independently of the German offensive, far exceeded the anticipations of the German High Command. But on October 9 an order found on a corpse near Grojec revealed the plan. Says Hindenburg:

'From the confluence of the San to Warsaw it appeared that we had four Russian armies to cope with, that is, about sixty divisions against eighteen of ours. From Warsaw alone fourteen enemy divisions were being employed against five on our side. That meant 224 Russian battalions to 60 German. . . . The enemy's superiority was increased by the fact that as a result of the previous fighting in East Prussia and France as well as the long and exhausting marches of more than 200 miles over indescribable roads our troops had been reduced to scarcely half establishment and in some cases even to a quarter of their original strength. And these weakened units of ours were to meet fresh arrivals at full strength . . . the Siberian Corps, the elite of the Czar's Empire! The enemy's intention was to hold us fast along the Vistula while a decisive attack from Warsaw was to spell our ruin. It was unquestionably a great plan of the Grand Duke Nicholas Nicholaievitch, indeed the greatest I had known, and in my view it remained his greatest until he was transferred to the Caucasus.'[37]

It required, indeed, all the confidence of dazzling victories, all the resources of iron will and cool audacity, to induce **HL** to press on into the gigantic arms which the Russian bear was spreading for the hug. On they went; few episodes in German military history show a more generous effort to relieve an ally, or a more just measure of their sense of superior quality over the Russians. It was perhaps the most 'sporting' operation which has ever been admitted to the spheres of Teutonic strategy. But every precaution was taken for escape in the case of failure. No army ever advanced so resolutely with such complete arrangements for retreat. Bridges and tunnels were mined at the same time as they were repaired. The whole of the communications of the advancing army were organized so as to make the swiftest recoil possible. Thus prepared for the extremes of fortune the Ninth Army, clasping Dankl's Austrian First Army encouragingly with its right hand, came squarely up against the line of the Vistula.

The Grand Duke must have been well content to see how conveniently he could convert the combination in progress of all his armies for the invasion of Germany into a trap for the new and—as it must have appeared to him—desperate German offensive. It was with justifiable hopes that the dispositions so forcibly described by Hindenburg were carried into effect. As Hindenburg advanced he found himself opposed by ever-gathering masses, and these masses continued more and more to reach round his left where Mackensen led the XVIIth German Corps. Heavy and continuous fighting developed on this flank, with the usual German tactical successes, captures of prisoners and cannon, but also with a sense of the constantly-growing weight descending upon them. The Second Russian Army irrupting from Warsaw in a south-westerly direction widely overlapped the German left. At the same time the four Russian armies arrayed behind the Vistula sought at many points to force a passage. A Caucasian corps, in which many Armenians served, actually established themselves across the river in the marshes of Koshenice, 10 miles north of Ivangorod. If the foothold could be made good and a bridge built, this passage, together with the permanent fortress bridge-head of Ivangorod, would secure to the Russian the means of debouching on a broad front. A continuous struggle developed in the swamps between the Caucasians striving to advance and the Germans to pin them to the river-bank. 'The Caucasians,' says Hoffmann, 'fought with surprising bravery.' 'The Russians' gun-trails were literally in the Vistula.' The survivors on both sides sustained a 'horrible impression' of this small protracted battle on the brink. Nothing could dislodge the Caucasians. They clung tenaciously to their lodgment; they built their bridge. Meanwhile farther to the south the whole of Dankl's First Army was gripped and menaced by another Russian army.

Thus hung the scales on the southward wing when the German left before Warsaw became at once weighed down and outflanked. On October 12 Mackensen's group of four divisions was within 12 miles of Warsaw, holding an important railway junction almost in its perimeter. But the Russian preponderance of numbers and length of front soon became irresistible. **H.** at Radom in fairly commodious quarters were now the centre of mental battles not less severe than those they were imposing physically upon their troops. Stubbornly they fought for victory. No general Austrian forward movement against the denuded Russian front across the San developed. The heavy rains flooded the countryside. Imperious demands upon Conrad for Austrian aid met with inadequate response. Dankl, instead of sending Austrian troops to the left, would do no more than lengthen the front of the First Austrian Army and release the right-hand German corps, the XIth, which was immediately transferred to the threatened left. **H.** with their four army corps were left locked in deadly battle with four whole Russian armies. Here we see with unmistakable plainness the ratios and values already established on the Eastern Front. The Germans fight with army corps and the Russians with armies thrice their number; and the battle is still obstinate!

But the moment came when flesh and blood could do no more; when the whole German front was racked and strained to within an ace of catastrophe, which nothing but their well-wrought plans for escape could avert. On October 17 **H.** dared persist no longer, and the orders for retreat were given. The withdrawal was speedy and deft. Through the sleet and slush of a Polish autumn the Ninth Army retired by forced marches upon Silesia, devastating the country and blowing up the roads and railways behind

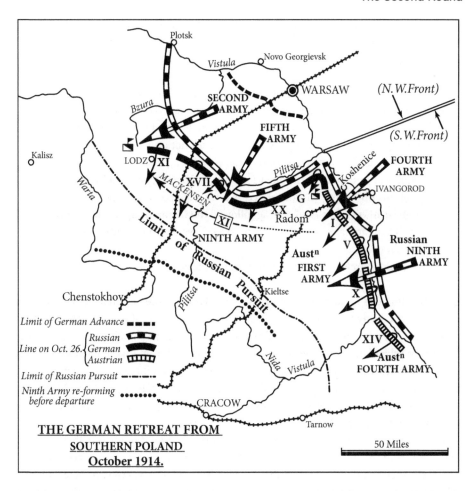

THE GERMAN RETREAT FROM SOUTHERN POLAND October 1914.

50 Miles

them. This movement was the signal for pursuit by all the Russian armies. From the 19th onwards the whole Russian front from Mlava to the San river was rolling westward with all possible diligence.

Says Hoffmann:

'I quite agree with the opinion of our eminently capable Quartermaster-General, Privy Councillor Dr. Keber, that the advance of a German army must come to a standstill when it gets about 100 kilometres from the railway. We calculated that by giving the Russians an additional 20 kilometres in consequence firstly of their exceedingly modest requirements, and secondly of their great want of consideration for their horses . . . we should be able to stop for a time the enemy advance while still on Russian soil to the east of the German frontier.'[38]

He reckoned on a halt of several days. This period the Ninth Army would have at its disposal to begin new operations, and the time must be fully utilized.

His calculation was vindicated. The Germans retreated, with more than one stubborn stand, in six days 60 miles, and by the end of October were, broadly speaking, back at their starting-point.

'At this point,' says Hindenburg, 'I cannot help admitting how much the punctual knowledge of the dangers that threatened us was facilitated by the incomprehensible lack of caution, I might also say *naïveté*, with which the Russians used their wireless. By tapping the enemy's wireless we were not only able to learn what the situation was, but also the intentions of the enemy. . . . Yet did it not look as if our final ruin had only been postponed for a time? The enemy certainly thought so and rejoiced. Apparently he considered that we were completely beaten . . . for on November 1 his wireless ran "Having followed the Germans up for more than 120 versts it is time to hand over the pursuit to the cavalry. The infantry are tired and supplies short."

'We could therefore embark upon fresh operations.'[39]

The recriminations incidental to failure were not lacking. The Germans reproached the First Austrian Army with having exposed their right at a critical moment by a needless retirement. They furthermore complained of the lack of any general advance across the San. Przemysl had, it is true, been temporarily disengaged from Russian investment, but otherwise in the main the spectacle of an energetic German force making head against heavy odds and difficult weather, while the very large armies of the Dual Monarchy seemed to palter with the weakened enemy upon their front, was vividly presented to the German mind and forcibly expressed to Austrian ears.

But what was the use of finding fault with Austria? For good or for evil, there she was in the War; and the sole first-class ally! The Germans could not afford to quarrel with the Austrians; they could only slave for them, and suffer from them and with them. Nor was this any temporary impatience to be restrained for a while. It had become the enduring condition of German war on the Eastern Front. Whereas the German troops were equal to two or three times their number of Russians, it was obvious that the Austrian armies were incapable of fighting the Russians, man for man.

No time was wasted in these sterile reflections. The need was urgent to rupture the impending Russian invasion of Silesia. The German Ninth Army had lost 40,000 men in its drive against Warsaw through South Poland. It must without delay strike again. But where? At the Conference at Chenstokhov on November 3 decision was taken. Hindenburg imparted it by a gesture. He raised his left hand. All present understood and assented. The German front which now faced north-east along the frontier from Posen to Cracow must be re-formed facing south-east from the level of Posen to the fortress of Thorn.

The change was made with almost incredible swiftness. Again the busy railways had to hum. Again the perfect organization for military purposes of these lateral communications was proved. Again locomotives, waggons, and sidings enabled Germany to multiply her army by two. Almost as soon as the Russians had exhausted their ardour of pursuit, the

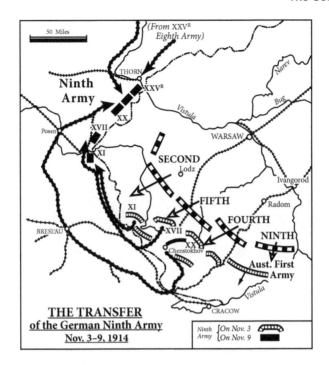

50 Miles

(From XXV^R Eighth Army)

Ninth Army

THORN
XXV^R
XX
XVII
Posen
XI

Narev
Bug
Vistula
WARSAW

SECOND
Lodz
Ivangorod
FIFTH
Radom
XI
FOURTH
BRESLAU
XVII
NINTH
XX
Chenstokhov
Aust. First Army
Vistula

THE TRANSFER
of the German Ninth Army
Nov. 3–9, 1914

CRACOW

Ninth Army { On Nov. 3 / On Nov. 9

Ninth Army had vanished from their front. By November 10 it was deployed anew on a 70-mile front from the fortress of Thorn southwards to the Warta river. The right-handed frontal punch towards Warsaw to the south had failed to revive the Austrian ally. A left-handed flank blow was now to be struck to save Germany herself from invasion. Within less than a fortnight from the end of the retreat in South Poland, the Ninth Army was ready to advance upon a new offensive in a different guise, purpose and direction, while the Russians were still sprawling in pursuit in regions where only ghosts remained.

CHAPTER XVI
THE BATTLE OF LODZ

On the morning of November 8 General von Falkenhayn in his new headquarters at Mezières consulted the Chief of the Field Railways upon the transport of important forces from the western to the eastern front. Colonel Groener informed him that it was possible to transport upon the four double tracks across Germany four army corps simultaneously. Each corps would require 40 trains daily and would arrive at its destination 4½ days later. The corps would have to be drawn two from the right wing, one from the centre and one from the left of the fighting front. In case of necessity he could even transport a fifth in the single sweep; but no doubt it would not be possible to withdraw so many units simultaneously from the line. The whole railway operation could be repeated in cycles as often as was desired.

There was certainly the gravest need for reinforcing the Eastern theatre. The repulse of the German army from Warsaw could only be the prelude of a Russian onslaught on the largest scale. The Austrians were in the depths of dejection and disorganization, and Conrad was unceasing in his reproaches for lack of help and even for breach of faith. **H.** had done wonders with their limited forces and would still strike many a shrewd, fierce blow; but the odds against them seemed overwhelming. From the third week in October when the retreat in South Poland was known to Supreme Headquarters, Falkenhayn had been left in no doubt of their need, and he felt it acutely. But meanwhile he was himself deeply involved in the endless battle of the Yser. He had curtailed his ambitions till they now flew no higher than the capture of Ypres. This would not be a strategical or even a tactical gain; it might indeed even be more advantageous to leave that shell-trap in enemy hands. But some definite indisputable event was required before the disastrous attempt against the Channel ports could be broken off. The capture of Ypres and the descent of winter would afford an indispensable pretext for closing down in the West. Ypres then it must be; and thereafter Groener's trains could carry at least four army corps to sustain and indeed restore the balance in the East.

But Ypres was stubborn. Haig and the 1st British Army Corps, long bombarded and tormented, held every point with constancy. The four new German Corps with their youthful volunteers had broken themselves in vain upon what seemed to be an inexpugnable defence. The German chief could not know how thin was the unyielding line of rifles, or how straitened their store of shells. Very nearly at Gheluvelt on October 31 had Falkenhayn gained the consolation prize. On that afternoon when for a time his front was actually broken, Sir Douglas Haig, there being no troops to send, had found it necessary to mount his horse and ride with half-a-dozen officers and his flag slowly forward amid the shells along the Menin road. On that, or a similar day, the survivors of a German company, penetrating a gap occupied only by the dead, had found themselves some distance inside the British front. They heard the battle going on behind them and conceived themselves in the midst of the hostile army. Their officer, forlorn, looked for some authority to whom to surrender. Eventually he laid down his arms to a sergeant and some hurriedly-armed cooks, and as the prisoners proceeded to the rear, he asked 'But where is your army? Where are your reserves?' His captors were too few to afford to tell him the truth!

But all Falkenhayn knew was that the young corps had been bloodily stopped. Now the best troops must be employed. A fresh Army Corps, containing a division of the Prussian Guard, was to make the decisive assault on the 10th (eventually the 11th) as a part of the final offensive in which 22 Divisions would march. That would finish with Ypres and then—'Eastward Ho!' So on this 8th day of November, having heard the report of his railway director, he despatched a trusted agent from Mezières to the Austro-Hungarian Headquarters at Cracow with an important message for Conrad.

We have heard of this agent before. He is the same Colonel Hentsch whose journey along the German line on September 9 had produced the general retirement which signalled the immortal end of the Marne. Here is the proof that Hentsch had not exceeded his authority on that occasion. We find him again, at the vital centre of affairs, charged with the most delicate and responsible duties. But this time his orders are in writing.

'Proceed at once to the Austro-Hungarian Headquarters and report the following by word of mouth to General Conrad von Hötzendorf. "I deeply regret that the whole course of our offensive in the West has only permitted me to send three cavalry divisions and 40,000 troops as reinforcements to the East. Any further weakening in the West would react very unfavourably on our condition without bringing about a decision in the East. Nevertheless I hope in about a fortnight to make five or six army corps available for the East. They must naturally be employed in the most effective direction, that is, . . . along the Vistula in co-operation with strong detachments of the German Eighth and Ninth armies. The first condition for the success of this operation is that the Austro-Hungarian army, together with the German forces fighting at its side, must hold the Russian armies on the left bank of the Vistula . . . and draw more forces towards it."'[40]

Colonel Hentsch arrived at Conrad's headquarters on the afternoon of November 10. What he said was recorded.

'General von Falkenhayn knows well how important it is to obtain a decision in Russia. But the whole German army is spread out from the Vosges to the coast, 100 to 200 yards from the enemy. The Germans want Ostend in order to make a war harbour there for U-boats. It is therefore important for the Supreme Command to drive the Allies back to Dunkirk. The Belgians have made inundations as a result of which the IIIrd Reserve Corps had to retire. We wish to take Ypres. If we do that, the English and French must go back. If the attack does not have the desired success, General von Falkenhayn will relieve certain forces and send them to the East. In this case, Germany would be leaving France the initiative. The German forces must therefore be grouped in depth, and the armies must have reserves behind them, in order to prevent a break through. The taking up of this formation in depth requires time. General von Falkenhayn hopes to be able to send five or six corps at latest in a fortnight. He thinks, moreover, that the Eighth Army, which has already parted with two corps, might give up some more, even at the cost of leaving East Prussia open. He hopes that the operations starting from the direction of Thorn with twelve Prussian army corps may bring about a decision.'[41]

Conrad asked when the German corps could be in the East. Hentsch replied: 'That would be about November 22. We can detrain four corps simultaneously.'

Conrad then said that the date of the advance of the German Ninth Army was already fixed for November 11. The question was whether this offensive should be carried out or whether it should wait until the German reinforcements arrived. Hentsch replied that his chief was still without knowledge of the offensive planned by the 'High Command East' (**HL**); but the Supreme Headquarters had thought of engaging five or six extra corps in the neighbourhood of Thorn in order to throw back the Russians towards the south-east by pressure from the north. 'It must be,' he opined, 'the same operation which the Ninth Army now wanted to make alone with thirteen or fourteen divisions. In these circumstances he could only inform General Ludendorff that in about a fortnight five or six corps would arrive with reinforcements, and leave it to him entirely whether to wait for them or not.'

The conversation shows either that Falkenhayn had not informed Hentsch of the 'already-decided and about-to-start manœuvre,' or that **HL** had kept their secrets to themselves. It shows also that once again Hentsch had been sent on a mission the wrong way round. In September he should have visited Kluck before Bülow. In November he should have seen Hindenburg before Conrad.

On November 9 **HL** begged the Supreme Command for reinforcements to carry out their new offensive. Hentsch was told to return via Hindenburg's headquarters, and discuss the situation. Falkenhayn replied on the same evening: 'I hope in a fortnight to make four more active corps available in the East. In the meantime,' he added inconsequently, 'any partial successes possible would be of great value.' **HL** had now to decide whether they would march unaided the next morning or wait a fortnight for a far more decisive operation with the promised reinforcements. The question was nicely balanced. Falkenhayn's telegram clearly placed the burden of decision on them. It must have been tempting to wait for the extra corps. By the time they arrived the Russians would have completely filled the bulge in the Polish salient and would probably already have penetrated some distance into Silesia. Any inertia by the Ninth Army would only encourage the Grand Duke in feeling that the Germans had been decisively beaten in the East. The whole impulse of the Russian army would be to press forward on to hostile soil, and in this mood they might well forget or put in the shade the perils they would run by a

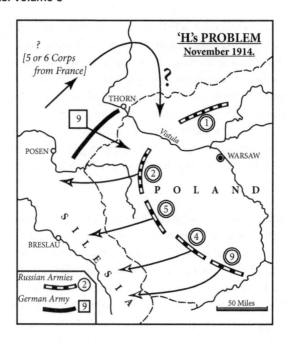

German counter stroke from the northern bastion. All the weight of the argument was in favour of delay till the enemy was more deeply involved and the strength of the German forces had doubled. But supposing they waited for the fortnight and the four corps did not arrive or only arrived piecemeal, then the inroad of the Russians would have become most serious. They would have established themselves in positions protecting their right flank. They would perhaps have interrupted some of the railways between Posen and Cracow. The danger would be all the greater and possibly the means of coping with it might be practically unimproved. Anyhow **H.** had timed their new offensive to start at daybreak. They decided to pursue unsupported their original plan. Events were to prove that they were wise to do so.

The final assault of the campaign of 1914 in the West took place on November 11. The Germans attacked the whole front from Bethune to the sea. The main force of the attack was concentrated upon the three sides of the Ypres salient. Twenty-two divisions converged upon the Ypres salient from Bixschoote to Frelinghien, supported by the greatest artillery fire yet heard. The Prussian Guard headed the onfall astride of the Menin road. Side by side twelve allied divisions, seven British and five French intermingled at many points, withstood the shock. Night fell upon severe losses but with the line virtually intact. This battle produced a change in Falkenhayn's outlook. He was forced to recognize that his campaign in the West must now end, and end in failure. His reaction however was no longer to send as many troops as possible to the East; on the contrary, he seems to have been apprehensive of his own weakness on the Western Front. His reports to the Kaiser at this time show that he regarded the German army as having sustained at least a moral defeat of the first order.

It was the duty of General von Plessen to summarize Falkenhayn's reports daily for the Kaiser. He has recorded his own impressions in his diary.

> On November 14 His Majesty is in a very depressed mood. Is of the opinion that the attack on Ypres has failed and come to grief and with it the campaign. At any rate the report of General von F[alkenhayn] that there are only six days' ammunition left, which means that to-day there are only four days' left, is absolutely overwhelming. If we leave this place without a decision in our favour it is a moral defeat of the first class, a very bad situation which will be made worse by our recent heavy losses!
>
> *November* 16. The Imperial Chancellor called me up. He is concerned about the enormous loss at Ypres. Wishes me to use my influence to stop further attempts to break through the position by main force. . . . I am of the same opinion. F. however will not abandon the attack on Ypres until the last heavy shell has been fired. Then four or five corps will be sent to the East.[42]

But **HL**, now at grips, requested precise dates for the arrival of the promised corps. Their telegrams of November 14 and 18 compelled Falkenhayn to come to a clear decision. On November 18 he wrote to Hindenburg a letter pregnant with consequences, revealing the change in his views. After rehearsing the reinforcements he had already sent, he said that the decision to send forces from West to East would be made easier 'if there was a well-founded hope that the arrival of fresh forces would, as far as could be foreseen, bring about a final decision in the East.' At present this hope seemed to have no foundation. In the most favourable circumstances the enemy might be drawn back behind the Narev and Vistula line and compelled to evacuate Galicia. This, although 'of great political importance,' would not be decisive. It would be of no value whatever if in the meantime their western enemies succeeded in driving the German forces back, or even in compelling them to give up the coast. '*For our most dangerous enemy is not in the East, but England, with whom the conspiracy against Germany stands and falls.** We can only injure her if we maintain our contact with the sea. Similarly Germany could only hold France in check if she maintained her present positions in the West. The injurious influence of even the smallest revival of French hopes had been shown after the German retirement in September, which was in the main ascribed to the weakening of the Western army in favour of the East.' The Chief of the Staff concluded with the assertion that 'the Supreme Command had decided in spite of the above objections to bring forces from the West . . . *but they could not be sent simultaneously and must arrive one after the other.*'[43] Such was the reaction upon the Eastern Front of the successful defence of Ypres. These second thoughts found **HL** in the heart of a desperate battle.

---

*My italics.—W.S.C.

The indefatigable German Corps opened their offensive into North Poland on November 10. Mackensen, whose conduct in the South Poland battles had retrieved any laurels lacking at Gumbinnen, was now placed in command of the whole Ninth Army. He advanced with his left hand on the Vistula, as if it were a balustrade. The impingement of the front was oblique, and the Russians, whose units of the Second and Fifth armies were streaming forward towards Silesia, suddenly found their right shoulders violently assaulted from the direction of Thorn. In three days Mackensen captured over twelve thousand prisoners and threw back, in much disorder, the Russian right, whose divisions, and even brigades, were encountered in detail by the German advance from this unexpected quarter. On the 15th and 16th the Vth Siberian, VIth Siberian, the IInd Corps of the First Army were all engaged and lost heavily, leaving, according to the German claim, twenty-five thousand prisoners in the enemy's hands. All these defeated troops fell back on and towards Lodz. Around this Cottonopolis of Central Europe a battle of extraordinary complication now impended. The Grand Duke disposed of numbers so superior that the Germans found themselves matched and baffled by the enormous masses directed and manœuvred, though with primitive mechanical efficiency, by a Headquarters' brain whose knowledge of the military art was not surpassed in Europe.

We shall now descend from the movements of armies and the sphere of strategy to a more detailed view of this remarkable battle.

* * * * *

The unexpected rapidity of **H.'s** advance brought their main forces into contact with the Second Russian Army during November 15. The Ist Reserve Corps and the Cavalry Division pierced the front of this Army, as a swimmer might strike out with a breast-stroke. The other four corps—namely, XIth, XVIIth, XXth, and XXVth (Res.)—swinging

to the right, were, by the evening of the 16th November, facing almost south towards Lodz. Here was the real break through, so long to be sought for on the Western Front. The front of the enemy is broken; the flanks are exposed on each side of the gap; while the intruding force prepares to rip and roll up the whole of the front. All the 17th and 18th November the Germans marched and fought in both directions; and two struggles developed on each side of the gap. With the northerly, and lesser, we need not much concern ourselves; the crisis was fought to the southward. By the end of November 18 the Germans had encircled Lodz, and perhaps a hundred and fifty thousand Russians defending it, on three sides. They were hopefully preparing to close their net, within which there struggled at least four Russian corps. The whole of these troops were, on the night of November 18, confined in an area about sixteen miles long by eight broad. Their destruction seemed imminent. It looked, to General Knox, as if Sedan and Tannenberg were to be repeated.

But meanwhile, amid the confusion of these unforeseeable events, and in spite of being continually beaten in each locality by much smaller numbers of Germans, the brain of the Russian High Command continued to function clearly and resolutely. The Grand Duke, on the night of November 17, while the climax was still impending, ordered the whole of the Fifth Army, which stood in the Russian line to the southward, to face about, counter-march and rescue the Second Army by driving back the left of the encircling Germans. The Fifth Army, therefore, marched north-eastward during the whole of November 19 and 20; they traversed the only unenclosed side of the oblong space in which the Second Army was imprisoned. During the 21st they came into heavy action with the German XXVth Reserve Corps, which formed the extreme point of the encircling movement. The Germans stood with their backs to Russia, and the Russians with their backs to Germany. On this day if a spectator had received a safe conduct to travel from north to south across the armies, he would in a journey of twenty-five miles have passed through eight separate fighting lines, back to back or face to face. Military authorities have pithily likened the situation to a Neapolitan ice. On the 19th November the Stavka heard from the Second Army 'that its right wing was completely enveloped and the enemy in possession of several localities south-west of Lodz; that the Second Army was on the defensive in every direction and all its reserves had been thrown in.' Thereafter all communication failed. The silence which enwrapped the Stavka left them the prey to terrible forebodings.

At the same time that the Grand Duke had ordered the Fifth Army to counter-march, General Ruzski, who commanded the North-West Front, had detached 3½ divisions from the left of his First Army to march south upon the backs of the Germans encircling the Second Army. This force—known as 'the Lovitch Force'—moved tardily and disjointedly. Its commander was changed the same evening that it started, and changed again next day. Nevertheless, by the afternoon of November 21, its leading division (the 6th Siberian) began to press upon the rear of the XXVth Reserve Corps at the same time that large masses of the Russian Fifth Army were attacking them from the opposite quarter. The position of the XXVth Reserve Corps and the 3rd Guard Division seemed now to be as fatally compromised as the Russian Second Army around Lodz had been

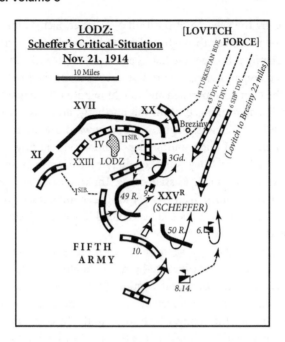

LODZ:
Scheffer's Critical-Situation
Nov. 21, 1914
10 Miles

[LOVITCH FORCE]

on the night of November 18. General Scheffer, who commanded, found that instead of enveloping and encircling the Russian masses in Lodz, he was himself surrounded and in the midst of enemies. The audacious German turning movement was not only attacked by superior forces in its front, but it was cut off from the rest of the Ninth Army and attacked in the rear by four Russian divisions who barred every avenue of retreat. The tables were thus completely turned. The stakes for which the Germans had played were the highest known in war. They had not succeeded, and when darkness fell on November 21, it looked as if the grim forfeit would be exacted.

It was in these conditions that Scheffer and his three German divisions fought on all fronts, facing in every direction, during the whole of the 22nd November. We do not know what reports (if any) he was able to send to his superiors, but at any rate the army commander Mackensen, and presumably Hindenburg and Ludendorff, realized that all chance of netting the Russians in Lodz had failed. Tannenberg would not be repeated there. At seven o'clock in the evening orders reached Scheffer to retire by the best route possible. A glance at the map will show that Scheffer's sixty thousand Germans were far more completely surrounded than Samsonov's army had been at Tannenberg. Moreover, they were surrounded by vastly superior numbers. So far as strategy can achieve or maps record a situation, their destruction seemed certain; in fact, trains to carry twenty thousand prisoners were already ordered at the Warsaw railway centre.

But now one of those homely truths of war proclaimed itself: a sharp knife will cut wood. By daybreak on November 23 Scheffer's well-knit organization was marching due north against the Lovitch Force. On this date he engaged the 6th Siberian Division. This division fought well all day. Its commander, seeing himself confronted with overwhelming German masses advancing upon him in three columns, cried out for help in all directions. Such was the confusion and failure of communications that he did not know that these German columns were themselves recoiling from the onset of the superior Fifth Russian Army which was following them up.

'The commander of the 1st Corps,' says Knox, 'was implored to move, but he and his troops, having been badly hustled, had been cowed into passivity. They—or, probably, only he and his staff—lacked the reserve of moral stamina for renewed effort. He hesitated (to pursue) and, finally, decided to ask the army commander. The latter did nothing.'

The 6th Siberian Division also called on the rest of the Lovitch Force to come to their assistance, but so predominant was the terror of the German armies at this time in the minds of Russian divisional and corps commanders that no effective measures were taken. Accordingly, on the 24th November, Scheffer destroyed the 6th Siberian Division.

'That Division, finding itself enfiladed in every direction and abandoned, retired during the morning of the 24th, and, finding Germans already in Breziny, dispersed in every direction.'

Barely fifteen hundred Siberians escaped. Scheffer then marched north-west and resumed his station between the 1st Reserve and XXth Corps of the German Ninth Army. His men had fought and marched continuously every day for at least nine days; they had almost encircled a Russian Army. Completely surrounded themselves by hordes of enemies, they had cut their way through, losing scarcely any guns or prisoners and carrying with them through the midst of these perils and manœuvres nearly all their own wounded and ten thousand Russian captives. It should be added that the weather during this period was exceptionally severe. The temperature at night fell to within ten degrees (F.) of zero. According to Danilov: 'The frost was becoming intensified, with icy winds, and with no prospect of snow and its accompanying rise in temperature.'

Thus ended the Battle of Lodz, in which a quarter of a million Germans were pitted against between five and six hundred thousand Russians; in which the Germans only just failed to surround and capture a hundred and fifty thousand Russians; and in which the Russians clutched, surrounded, but failed to hold sixty thousand Germans. No exact information of the casualties is at present to hand, but certainly we shall not exaggerate if we say that the Germans had thirty-five thousand killed and wounded and the Russians at least double that number, with twenty-five thousand prisoners taken in addition. Both sides shook themselves clear of this dreadful close. Breathless and exhausted, the Russians held Lodz until December 6, when they rearranged their line to the south of Warsaw. The Germans remained in close contact along their front and occupied Lodz in due course without further fighting.

All hopes of a Russian advance into Silesia had been effectually frustrated.

* * * * *

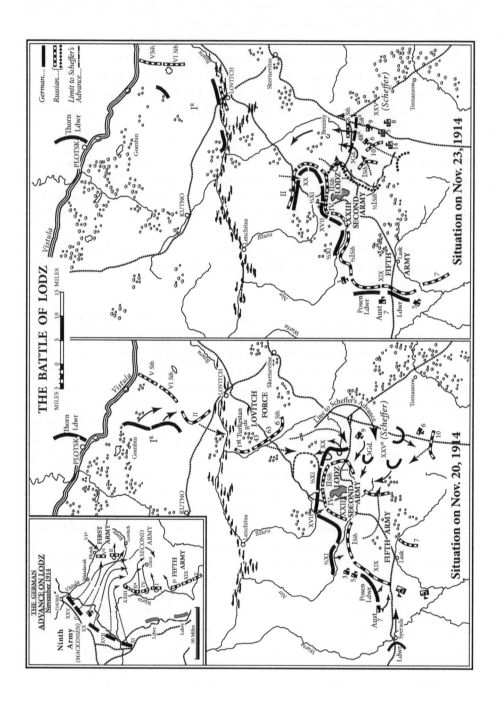

THE BATTLE OF LODZ

Situation on Nov. 23, 1914

Situation on Nov. 20, 1914

THE GERMAN ADVANCE ON LODZ
November 1914

All the Cabinets of the Allies had taken it for granted that Serbia would be destroyed in the Great War soon and easily by the might of Austria. However, when we left the Serbians in the last week of August, not a man of the Imperial armies remained on Serbian soil. The Austrians had rushed in, and had been flung out. They had wasted on the Drina and the Save the soldiers desperately needed in Galicia. There was a pause. Early in September Putnik's First Army raiding across the Save maintained itself precariously for a week on Hungarian soil. Potiorek was able to drive them out; but his further efforts in September foundered upon Serbian defensive tenacity. Whether he pressed with his Sixth Army across the Drina to threaten Putnik's left, or tried to cut in behind his right, or when he attacked in the centre, he was equally brought to a standstill, often in sodden, low-lying fields, always with grievous losses. Both armies—the Serbs had been fighting since 1912—were exhausted. Putnik, urged on by Russia to strike a further blow for the common cause, made by an excursion into southern Bosnia an alarming threat against the communications of the Austrian Sixth Army, with Sarajevo as his goal. It took Potiorek most of October to evict the raiders; but he could not drive them from Semlin which they had entered at the end of September, nor, worst of all, could the Austrian troops cope with the trench warfare which had developed all along the front.

By November Bosnia was cleared of its Serbian invaders, and both sides prepared themselves for a final effort. The Serbs were encouraged chiefly by rumours—the Russians, even the Greeks, were coming to their aid, some British sailors and naval guns had actually arrived. Putnik however, inferior in artillery, short of munitions, disorganized—several-fold decimated—determined to quit the dangerous angle of the great rivers and retire upon Valjevo and the Kolubara. The initiative passed to the Austrians. Potiorek's last chance had come. Using his unfading influence with the Emperor's circle, he scraped and scratched from Conrad's hard-pressed armies, and from their joint munitions supply, the means for a new offensive. He advanced on the familiar double-pincers plan. By November 15 Valjevo, Putnik's Headquarters in the

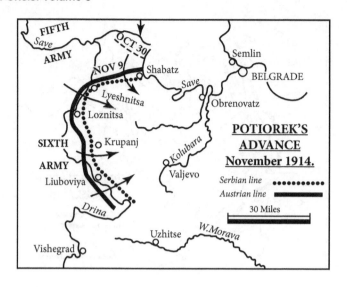

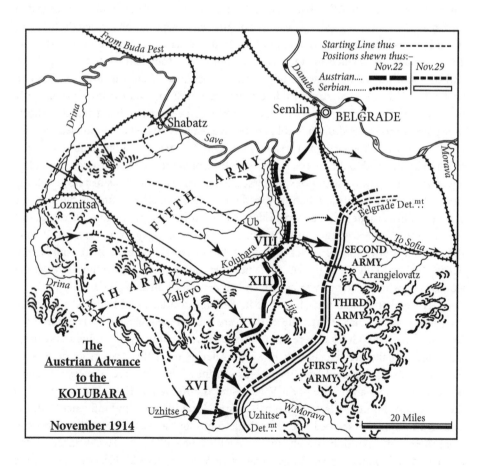

Jadar battle, fell to the Austrian Sixth Army. The Serbians recoiled before the onset, and by the 22nd Potiorek's line was established across the Kolubara and he had captured with hard fighting and heavy casualties eight thousand Serbian prisoners and forty guns. Here at any rate was a success, or something which might be represented as such. Here, as the Austrian history tells us, he might well have paused.

But Potiorek, though cautious of his person, was vigorous in thought. He saw the Serbs as a beaten enemy to be pursued. Belgrade lay near, and with it the longed-for railway which opened to the Central Powers the road to Turkey. And above all, almost within his grasp, the nearer Obrenovatz-Valjevo railway offered at last a new line of supply, a priceless relief to his present overtaxed and far-stretched communications running back behind the Drina. Despite deep snow in the mountains, rain below, appalling roads, shortage of food and an army dispirited, almost in rags, divided in its loyalties, he pressed on. In the battle of the Kolubara which followed, the Austrian armies drove forward another dozen miles.

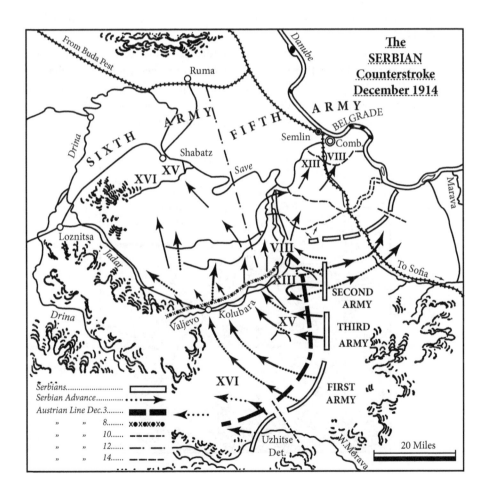

Putnik's leadership was not unworthy of his indomitable soldiers. Driven to the decision of a lifetime, he abandoned Belgrade. He swung back his right till it faced northwest. His left, the critical pivot, meant to hold fast at all costs, gave way under the pressure of the Austrian Sixth Army. But at the same time, when all seemed lost, the pursuing Austrians themselves subsided through sheer exhaustion: and from that moment the tide turned. Austrian troops might enter Belgrade; Potiorek, courtier like, might announce its capture to the Emperor as a greeting for his eighty-fourth birthday. But the Serbian nation, which was now its army, gathered itself for a supreme effort. Old King Peter, entering the trenches rifle in hand among his soldiers, appealed to his fierce countrymen. The Austrians were at the end of their tether; the Serbian counter-offensive began. On December 3 all their armies attacked; the First turned savagely on the Austrians in the hills, the Third advanced in the centre: the Second in the north met Potiorek's expiring effort to lap round their weak right wing. Irresistibly the north-west drive of the Serbian Second Army surged forward, threatening at once to cut off Potiorek's enveloping troops. On December 9, after nearly a week's confused but severe fighting, the outermost Austrian division was recalled. Said the telephone from Headquarters: "All has been in vain. Make no more efforts; we must go back; the order follows."

It was time. Potiorek's armies were cleft asunder. His Fifth army was bunched up around Belgrade; and his Sixth with the Serbians at their heels was in full flight for Shabatz. By December 15 the third Austrian assault upon Serbia had been flung back in utter rout across the river into the lands whence they came. The hated pig-farmers of Serbia, for the sake of whose punishment almost the whole world had been plunged

in war, had added to the Austrian annals this most ignominious, rankling and derisory defeat. It brought one advantage in its train. It was the end of Potiorek. The prodigy of the Serbian resistance was hardly comprehended by the busy world at war; but those who were best informed were the most astonished.

* * * * *

It is necessary to mention here the fortunes of the Turkish armies that invaded the Caucasus in pursuance of the long-cherished plan of Young Turkey. Enver Pasha, assuming direct command, concentrated at Erzerum the three corps (IXth, Xth, XIth) stationed in peace in Armenia, reinforcing them with a division from Bagdad, and bringing by sea from Constantinople the 1st Corps, two more divisions, to Trebizond. The Turkish Third Army so formed comprised nearly 150,000 men; while on the Russian side Voronzov, his forces depleted in order to swell the Galician armies, could muster but 100,000.

Voronzov had struck the first blow. In November he had thrust across the frontier to Koprikeui, 30 miles short of Erzerum. Here he had been confronted by Enver's XIth Corps. But Enver's plan was developing. The Russian army at Sarikamish was wholly dependent upon the railway from Tiflis and Kars. Enver, with Colonel von Schellenberg as Chief of the Staff, aimed the usual German turning movement at this vital line of communication. Holding the Russians frontally he sent his IXth and Xth Corps to turn their right and descend through the passes upon the Kars-Sarikamish railway. Meanwhile much farther to the north the Turkish Ist Corps drove down the Choruk valley, whence they too were to close in on the Tiflis railway. This plan in such a country and at this season was foolhardy. The Ist Corps in particular had to cross, at 8,000 feet in the depth of winter, the snow-bound passes leading down to Ardahan.

By the New Year the troops engaged in these desperate endeavours were in extremity. Struggling in snow-drifts through the rocky defiles by which alone advance was possible, lashed by incessant blizzard, in hideous privation, their columns were encountered each in turn by the Russians along the Sarikamish front. On New Year's Day Yudenitch, the local Russian commander, repelled the Xth Corps finally from his vital railway. The IXth thus stripped of support was enveloped and destroyed. Its commander and his staff surrendered. Fifty miles to the northward, the Ist Corps persisted in its fantastically-conceived mission. It actually succeeded in crossing the passes to Ardahan, to the amazement and alarm of the Russian headquarters. But there its effort died. A counter-attack drove the frozen and gasping Turks back into the icy wastes through which they had descended. Only the XIth Corps, for a while, played its part. Around Kara Urgan, in a gallant effort at least to cover the retreat of the remnants of the IXth and Xth, it made some headway; but by mid-January Yudenitch was able to concentrate against it. In a few days, after heavy loss, it was forced to retreat to Erzerum with the horrors of winter and famine added to military defeat.

Thus at length the skilful and determined Russian defence achieved a victorious fulfilment. By the last days of January the tables in this desperate game had been

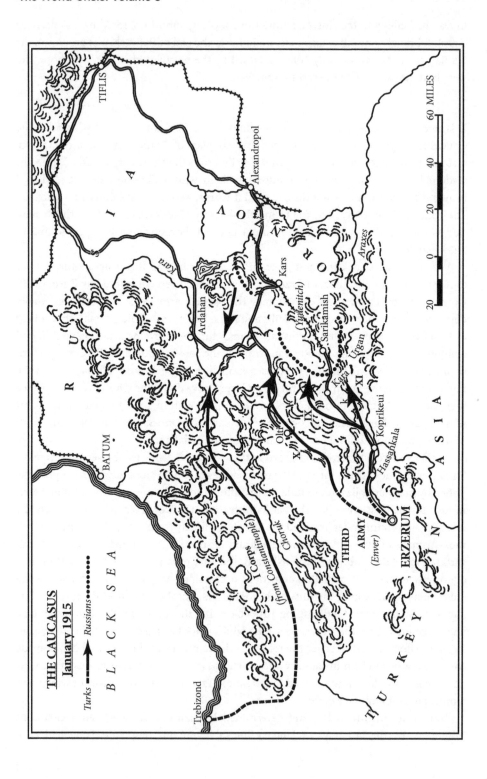

THE CAUCASUS
January 1915

Turks ▬▬■▬▬■▬▬ Russians ●●●●●●●

BLACK SEA

completely turned. Yudenitch, almost by standing still, aided by those elements the Turks had ignored, had robbed them of the rewards of their wildly audacious manœuvre and intense efforts. They perished in their attempt. Individuals escaped to tell the tale; but in the mountains above Sarikamish alone the corpses of 30,000 frozen soldiers were discovered and counted by the Russian patrols. Thus the situation in the Caucasus, which at the close of the year had seemed almost forlorn, was within a fortnight decisively retrieved.

CHAPTER XVII
EAST OR WEST?

The end of the year and the severities of winter closed what has been called 'The Second Round' of the struggle. In the West after the battle of Ypres, in the East after the battle of Lodz, the fronts became stationary in close contact behind ever-growing entrenchments. Sovereigns, statesmen and commanders on both sides surveyed the ghastly scene, weighed the results of all the battles, and set themselves to plan the future. An immense feeling of relief inspired the leaders of the Allies. The terrific onslaught of Germany upon France had failed. Time would now be given for the whole armed strength of the British Empire to be brought to bear. The naval victory of the Falkland Islands had exterminated the German cruiser warfare. The British command alike of the oceans and the narrow seas was absolute. Very large surplus naval forces released from the cruiser warfare came back into the hands of the Admiralty. The blockade of the enemy Empires was complete and its pressures began to grow.

Different indeed were the feelings with which the German Chiefs measured the past and faced the future. They had no illusions upon the results which had so far declared themselves. Although their armies stood almost everywhere on conquered soil and they disposed of enormous and still-growing resources, they cast about earnestly for some means of escape from the deadly toils into which they had incontinently plunged. The causes of British and French satisfaction were perfectly appreciated by them, and struck a knell in their hearts. To the problems of their Generals the German Chancellor and Foreign Office now made an unwelcome contribution. All hopes of inducing Italy or Roumania to join them had long vanished. On Christmas Day Count Czernin, Austrian Ambassador at Bucharest, had declared to Conrad that Italy and Roumania 'would enter the war upon the side of the Entente, unless the Central Empires could achieve a far-reaching victory by the spring.' Italy was pressing with increasing plainness and slowly unveiling menace her demands for grievous cessions of Austrian territory. Roumania seemed to be keeping step with Italy, and a hostile declaration by both Powers might well be simultaneous.

It became obvious that the attitude of the Balkan States was of decisive importance. Turkey—the one new adherent—had been defeated in the Caucasus, and was already in internal stress. No military communication existed between her and the Central Powers. Serbia had not been defeated, on the contrary, she was triumphant; Bulgaria had not been won over; Greece was adverse; and Roumania refused to allow the transport of munitions to Turkey. Already on December 14 General von der Goltz had written from Constantinople to Falkenhayn that the decision of the whole war rested with the small Balkan powers. Their by no means negligible forces and influence might turn the scale either way. It was evident to the German Foreign Office that the whole of the Balkan States and Italy might come into the war against the Teutonic and Turkish Empires. This would involve the speedy collapse of Austria-Hungary, the destruction of Turkey, and the final fatal isolation of Germany. All this pointed to the strongest action against Russia, to the imperative upholding of Austria, and to opening direct access to Turkey. To the East must the Germans go. Conrad, on December 27, telegraphed to Falkenhayn:

'Complete success in the Eastern theatre is still, as hitherto, decisive for the general situation and extremely urgent. . . . Rapid decision and rapid execution are absolutely necessary if the intervention of neutrals, which is certainly to be expected at the latest at the beginning of March, is to be forestalled.'

H. reinforced these claims by arguments of their own; and here we must note a real and only partly unconscious cleavage of interest and opinion which opened in the German supreme war-control. The German generals who had fought in the West had, since the French had turned at the Marne and begun to use their artillery and rifles, met with no success; and in war, which is always unfair, lack of success is serious. They had been unpleasantly surprised by the obstinacy of the French in defence. They had not believed them capable of such unsensational stubbornness. They were even more astonished by being forced to take the British Army seriously. They now realized that they were in the West confronted by troops and military organizations of the highest order. The German generals in the East, on the other hand, had gained splendid victories. There were no trench lines, no high-class riflemen, few machine-guns and only a comparatively weak artillery. There, was the opportunity for manœuvre, and for that large kind of tactics or battlefield strategy which manifests itself through the adroit use of a superior railway system. In the East great victories had been won, with hundreds of thousands of captives, and whole hostile armies destroyed, as the result of what were undoubtedly finely-conceived manœuvres modelled upon the classics of war. All Germany shone with the glory of Tannenberg. The Supreme Command, which had been thankful to see the failure of the Marne thus masked, now found with some disquietude that they cut a less impressive figure in the national eye than the triumphant warriors of the East. Hindenburg and Ludendorff, while comporting themselves with decorum, met in conferences men who, though in a superior station, bore the taint of failure. But the Supreme Command with its galaxy of Generals and Staff Officers, albeit discomfited, held nearly all the machinery of the German Army and five-sixths of its strength. Patriotism, public service, military discipline, personal courtesy, spread their emollients upon the sore places. Still the underlying facts remained; and the East said in unspoken words, 'Why don't you let us go on winning the war for you?' and the West replied by thunderous looks, 'Win the war! Why, you have only been collecting Russians!'

Even now the German Supreme Command had not divined the root fact that they were in the presence of an enormous inherent superiority of the defensive. At this time in the West, that is to say between armies of equal quality and in a theatre with closed flanks, the offensive could make no headway. Once the war subsided into the trench lines and barbed wire, the advantage of the defenders was overwhelming. The attacking troops had not got at this time the weight of artillery necessary to pulverize the trenches. Still less had they the volume of artillery capable of lining the whole front, so that an attack on a great scale could be launched on any one of three or four different sectors. The offensive therefore could not acquire the virtue of surprise. They had no tanks to crush down the barbed wire. They had not yet developed poison-gas. Even the creeping barrage was unknown. In short, the offensive possessed none of the processes or apparatus capable of making headway against a continuous line of bravely-defended trenches supported by the ordinary artillery of a field army, reinforced by many fortress guns. Falkenhayn did not understand this, nor did Joffre, nor did French, nor Foch, nor apparently any of the high military officers on either side. But it remained for several years the dominant fact in the Western theatre. With the armies matched as they were, no means of advance was open.

Falkenhayn throughout took the conventional military view, and adhered to it with perseverance. He did not believe that any manœuvres in the East would end the war. He had already reached the conclusion that so long as France, Russia and Great Britain held together, it was impossible to beat them sufficiently to attain a 'decent' victory, and Germany would run the danger of being exhausted. At this moment he sought nothing from Russia or France but an indemnity. He was no longer fighting for victory, but only for honourable escape. If, in order to find peace, Germany had to continue the war, the best chance was to press the struggle in the West. He was already busy planning a renewed offensive mainly against the British. Four new army corps would soon be ready in Germany. In January, or at the latest in February, his whole available force would be hurled upon the Northern sectors of the Anglo-French lines.

H. met him four-square in opposition. They were sure that the war could be won and ought to be won by making great efforts in the East, and that unless these efforts were made, it would be speedily and irretrievably lost by the apparition in the field of the armies of a Balkan block, and a separate peace by Austria. Conrad and the Austrian Headquarters reiterated these views with desperate energy. And now all the forces of high politics and diplomacy ranged themselves upon the Eastern side of the argument. The Chancellor and the German Foreign Office, rightly terrified at the prospect of Italy and a Balkan block being added to the hostile coalition, joined themselves to the victors of Tannenberg—the Great Twin Brethren of the East. 'The West has failed. The Schlieffen plan is burnt out. Smash Russia. Hold Austria up. Crush Serbia. Rally the Balkans and join hands with Turkey.' Thus arose a grim trial of strength between personages and policies of the highest consequence.

On New Year's Day Falkenhayn and Conrad met in Berlin. Ludendorff representing Hindenburg was also present. Tense discussions occupied the day. The conflict of wills and opinions rendered the conference abortive. Writing of it in after years, Ludendorff says that he received no clear answer and in effect that Falkenhayn adopted dilatory tactics towards Conrad's demands. 'It was all unsatisfactory and unmeaning. It was a contest of opinions settled beforehand.' On January 2 Falkenhayn confirmed his decision.

He telegraphed to Conrad, who had returned to Teschen, that the Kaiser agreed that troops could not at present be moved from the Western to the Eastern theatre. It would be time enough to settle the destination of the new troops now being raised in Germany in three weeks. And the next day he informed Hindenburg that to ear-mark the new formations for the East would be 'equivalent to renouncing all activity in the West for as long as could be forecasted, with all the serious consequences which that would entail; and these must not be lost sight of there.' Hindenburg thereupon took counsel with the Chancellor; and the latter, deeply impressed, proposed to the Kaiser Falkenhayn's removal from the Supreme Command.

On January 4 Conrad received a report from his military attaché in Rome that Italy was making all preparations to enter the war against the Central Powers, that the Italian army would be ready at the end of January and fully ready by the end of March. Berchtold, from Vienna, emphasized this formidable news and urged a speedy victory in the Carpathians as the only means of averting the peril. On this Conrad ordered the preparation of an offensive in Galicia and telegraphed both to the Supreme Command and to **H.** for the aid of four or five German divisions. Falkenhayn refused. He would not send troops from the West to the East, nor was he even willing that Hindenburg should send German troops from his own army to aid in an offensive in the Carpathians. If any troops were sent from the Ninth Army they should go to Serbia, rather than the Carpathians. 'Roumania's attitude, Bulgaria's possible accession and the extraordinarily important question of establishing communications with Turkey, are exclusively dependent on the situation in Serbia.' He added pointedly that 'In the view of German diplomacy, Italy could only be kept quiet by satisfying her wishes as soon as possible and not by driving the Russians out of the Carpathians.' To this Conrad retorted that the satisfaction of Italy was not to be thought of, and would it not be better for Germany to satisfy France (presumably in Alsace-Lorraine) 'and thus break up the Entente?' On this **H.** struck a decisive blow. They informed Berlin that they were in full accord with Conrad, and that they had already without consulting Falkenhayn promised to send several divisions to his aid. This independent action was a challenge of the first order to Falkenhayn's authority.

Both parties now clutched at the Kaiser. Hitherto he had stood by his new Chief of the Staff who was still also Minister of War; but the pressure had now become irresistible. The dismissal of Hindenburg and Ludendorff was impossible. All Germany would stand behind them. On January 8 the Kaiser decided in favour of Conrad's Carpathian plans and ordered the formation of a German Southern Army, the 'Südarmee,' under Linsingen. Falkenhayn, compelled to submit, was nevertheless strong enough to exact an important condition. He did not intend to be further surprised and defied by the Hindenburg-Ludendorff combination. He was resolved to break up the tremendous partnership which had already altered the centre of gravity of the German war control. He therefore obtained the Kaiser's assent to Ludendorff's appointment as Chief of the Staff to Linsingen. This invidious act was wrapt in a flattering reference to the Kaiser's special confidence in Ludendorff; but the motive was obvious. Hindenburg, deeply aggrieved, reported on January 9 directly to the Kaiser, saying that the success which he now expected in the Carpathians would be by no means an adequate cure for the difficulties of Austria.

'It must be combined with a decisive blow in East Prussia. Four new Army Corps will be ready at the beginning of February. The employment of these in the East is a necessity. With them it will not be difficult quickly to inflict on the enemy in East Prussia a decisive and annihilating blow and at last to free entirely that sorely afflicted province and to push on thence with our full force to Bialystok. . . . I regard this operation, with the employment in the East of the newly-raised forces, as decisive for the outcome of the whole war; whereas their employment in the West will only lead to a strengthening of our defence, or—as at Ypres—to a costly and not very promising frontal push. Our army in the West ought to be able to hold well-constructed positions sited in successive lines and to maintain itself without being reinforced by the new Corps until the decisive success in the East has been attained.'

He concluded with an impassioned appeal for the return of Ludendorff.

'Your Imperial and Royal Majesty has been graciously pleased to command that General Ludendorff should, as Chief of the General Staff, be transferred from me to the Southern Army. . . . During the days of Tannenberg and the Masurian Lakes, during the operations against Ivangorod and Warsaw, and in the advance from the Wreschen-Thorn line, I have grown into close union with my Chief of Staff; he has become to me a true helper and friend, irreplaceable by any other, one on whom I bestow my fullest confidence. Your Majesty knows from the history of war how important so happy a relationship is for the course of affairs and the well-being of the troops. To that is to be added that his new and so much smaller sphere of action does not do justice to the General's comprehensive ability and great capacity . . . '
'On all these grounds I venture most respectfully to beg that my war-comrade may graciously be restored to me so soon as the operations in the South are under way. It is no personal ambition which leads me to lay this petition at the feet of Your Imperial and Royal Majesty. That lies far from me! Your Majesty has overwhelmed me with favour beyond my deserts, and after the war is ended I shall retire again into the background with a thankful and joyful heart. Far rather do I believe that I am fulfilling a duty in expressing with all submission this request.'[44]

Meanwhile Falkenhayn had decided to attempt a personal settlement. On January 11 he reached Breslau and there met Conrad, Linsingen and Ludendorff. On the 12th he was at Posen and faced Hindenburg supported by Ludendorff and Hoffmann. These discussions only aggravated the existing differences, and an intense personal and technical crisis arose in Berlin. All centred upon the Kaiser. Hindenburg now openly joined the Chancellor in demanding the dismissal of Falkenhayn, the employment of the four corps in the East, and the reunion of Ludendorff and Hindenburg. The Kaiser, by the German Constitution Supreme War Lord, had to choose. He did not on this occasion fail the German people. He decided against Falkenhayn. The four corps were ordered to the East. Ludendorff after organizing the 'Südarmee' was to be returned to Hindenburg; and Falkenhayn was forced to resign the Ministry of War. In spite of these wounding blows, Falkenhayn was found still willing 'with a heavy heart' to remain Chief of the Staff of the Armies. Thus smitten in the foundations of his power, he nevertheless continued in the highest military office for nearly two years. He nursed for a time the idea that he himself might take command of the Eastern operations. Rebuffed again in this, he contented himself with a scathing commentary upon them. He doubted altogether 'the possibility of bringing to a combined result two decisive undertakings separated by a thinly-held gap of over 600 kilometres for which only limited forces were available.' He anticipated no more than 'fairly large local successes' in the Carpathians and in East Prussia. In this he was to be vindicated by the event. His authority had however received a mutilating blow, and henceforth there were two rival centres of power in the German army.

* * * * *

The severity of the war had already worn down the frail personality of Berchtold. The failure of Potiorek in Serbia had deprived him even of that local satisfaction he had purchased so dearly. The prospect of Italy joining the foes of Austria and adding a new front to the task of her crumbling armies was a strain beyond his nerve to bear. He who had been so rash and resolute in the crisis was the first to falter in the struggle. Tisza on the other hand, who had pleaded for caution and peace while time remained, now showed the stern strength of his character. Undismayed by events, he strove to infuse resource and energy into the leadership of the Empire. He resolved that Berchtold should give place to a more determined figure. The change was effected with an ease and politeness, with an absence of irritation or excitement thoroughly typical of the diplomatic circle in Vienna. On January 11 Tisza and Tschirschky lunched with Berchtold. The German Ambassador as usual pressed, and this time with harshness, that Austria should buy off Italy at all costs with territorial concessions. Tisza made it plain that this could not be done. After a long discussion between the three Tisza found himself alone with Berchtold for a few minutes before his audience with the Emperor. 'I told him,' he records, 'that I should be obliged to say to His Majesty that at the present moment I considered that the post of Foreign Minister should be occupied by a man of greater decision, who followed out his own policy with more consequence and energy.' Berchtold replied smiling, as was his custom, like a good child: 'I shall be very thankful if you really do say it, for I am always saying it; but he won't believe me. He will believe you.' Not disarmed by this engaging demeanour, Tisza repaired forthwith to the palace and proposed Berchtold's immediate dismissal to the Emperor. Francis Joseph did not demur. He had often, he remarked, thought the same thing. After Tisza had explained that he himself could not leave his post as Hungarian Minister and President, it was arranged that a man of the bureaux, a protégé of Tisza's, Baron Burian, should take charge of the foreign policy of the Empire. On January 13 Berchtold quitted the Ballplatz, and retired tranquilly to his estates, where he resides to this day. 'Leave me in peace,' he protested naïvely in 1916 to a friend, 'I got sick of the war long ago.'

* * * * *

We have witnessed the birth convulsions of the German plans for 1915. We shall presently follow their varied fortunes in the field. No one can now doubt that the decision wrung from the Kaiser, for which he deserves due credit, was right. The year that opened so darkly for Germany was to be for her the most prosperous of the war. In Artois and Champagne the French, at Neuve Chapelle and Loos the British, were doomed to wear themselves out upon the barbed wire and machine-guns of the German defence. With the loss of all her fortresses Russia was to be driven out of Poland and Galicia. Bulgaria was gained as an ally by the Central Powers; Serbia was invaded and for a space annihilated; Greece was distracted and paralyzed. While Roumania was awed into a continuing neutrality and Italy was left to break her teeth on the Isonzo, the German road to Constantinople was opened and Turkey, saved from destruction, fought on reinvigorated. To observe the other side of these surprising transformations and mighty achievements we must now repair to London.

The attention of France was riveted upon the Invasion. All French energies and thought were absorbed in the life-and-death struggle which for the moment had slackened, but must soon be renewed. Joffre, victor of the Marne, and his Grand-Quartier-Général, **G.Q.G.**, dominated the scene. France was hardly conscious of other scenes. Russia, Austria and the Balkans, all these were noticed only as a swordsman in the climax of a duel observes his seconds or the spectators. To strengthen the French army, to hold the front in France, to liberate the thirteen conquered departments from a hateful yoke— these were the war-plans of France. But in London, where the pressures were not so severe, a more general view was possible. A small group of men at or near the summit of the war-direction had been for some weeks gazing intently upon that same Eastern Front which was the subject of these lively discussions in Berlin.

The reader with all the facts laid bare before him must also realize how difficult it was in the Cabinet or at the Admiralty and War Office to learn and measure the facts and values of the episodes which this volume has already recorded. We had been absorbed in securing the command of the seas, in sending the British army to France and keeping it alive under the terrible hammer-blows which it endured; in gathering together the forces of the Empire, and in mobilizing for the struggle all the wealth, influence and manhood—not inconsiderable in any quarter of the globe—on which His Britannic Majesty could make a claim. The French told us little except their wishes, and the Russians less. We had sustained generally the impression that Russia had defeated Austria in a great battle called Lemberg, and that Germany had successfully defended East Prussia. We had the feeling that the Russian 'steam-roller' which the Western Powers had expected would smooth the path to victory, was moving backwards as well as forwards, as is indeed the habit of steam-rollers. But the full significance of Tannenberg was only gradually understood. Like the French, we were in contact with immeasurable events and occupied from hour to hour with vital details. Masses of information were provided in the Intelligence reports. Every day there lay upon my table twenty or thirty flimsies recording the ceaseless movement of troops to and fro across Europe and every kind of rumour true or false. From the Admiralty we asked the War Office repeatedly for general appreciations. But all the British General Staff had gone to the war, and had been entirely preoccupied ever since in keeping together the body and soul of the Expeditionary Army. No adequate machine existed for sifting, clarifying and focussing the multitudinous reports. Lord Kitchener, calm, Olympian, secretive and imperfectly informed, endeavoured in these months to discharge in his own person the functions of Secretary of State for War, Commander-in-Chief and of the collective intelligence of a General Staff.

Yet somehow things had not gone wrong. The seas were clear; the island was safe; the army had reached its battle station; the front was held; the Empire was forming in the fighting line. Therefore there was not at this juncture any very decided questioning of our impressions acquired from day to day, nor of our primitive methods of war-control. Indeed up to the end of 1914, we were, I feel, entitled to be proud of our conduct of the war. All our ships and men were being used to the full and in the right way.

No more elaborate organization would up to this point have produced better results. But a change had now come over the war. Its scale and complications grew ceaselessly; and we now had broadening surpluses of men and ships to employ. Here was the question which demanded scientific study.

Once we felt supreme and safe at sea, we looked almost instinctively to Turkey, Russia and the Balkans. During the whole of December Colonel Hankey, Mr. Lloyd George and I, working at first independently, became increasingly interested in the South-East of Europe. After war had been declared, diplomacy counted little with neutrals. They were no longer concerned with what was said or promised. The questions they asked themselves were, What was going to happen, and who was going to win? They were not prepared to accept British assurances upon either point. We were astonished to find that many of these neutrals seemed to doubt that Great Britain would certainly be victorious. One pitied their obliquity. But they persisted in it. The Foreign Office talked well; but it was like talking to the void.

However, by the first week in December, we three all separately reached the conclusions that the Western Front had frozen into a deadlock, that whoever attacked would get the worst of it, and that a great diversion or turning movement, diplomatic, naval and military, should be made through and upon the Mediterranean Powers. Little did we know how closely our thoughts corresponded to the pre-occupations of Berlin or to the conclusions of **H.** Behind the hostile fronts all was mystery. Behind the allied fronts, concerted action or machinery for such action was as yet in its infancy. On December 29 I wrote to the Prime Minister as follows:

'I think it quite possible that neither side will have the strength to penetrate the other's lines in the Western theatre. Belgium particularly, which it is vital for Germany to hold as a peace-counter, has no doubt been made into a mere succession of fortified lines. I think it probable that the Germans hold back several large mobile reserves of their best troops. Without attempting to take a final view, my impression is that the position of both armies is not likely to undergo any decisive change.'

On January 1 the Chancellor of the Exchequer, Mr. Lloyd George, circulated to the War Committee a paper drawing attention to the unfounded optimism which prevailed about the war, to the increasing failure of Russia as a prime factor, and to the need for action in the Balkan Peninsula, in order to rally Greece and Bulgaria to the cause of the Allies. On the same day Colonel Hankey circulated a masterly paper pointing to the Near East as the decisive theatre for our immediate allied action. These documents had been shown to me some days earlier, and on December 31 I wrote to the Prime Minister, Mr. Asquith, about them saying, 'We are substantially in agreement and our conclusions are not incompatible. . . . I wanted Gallipoli attacked on the Turkish declaration of war. . . . Meanwhile the difficulties have increased. . . .' On January 3, after continuous daily discussions at the Admiralty and with the Prime Minister, Lord Fisher wrote me a letter, already printed in the second volume of the *World Crisis*, in which he declared, 'I consider the attack on Turkey holds the field—but only if it's immediate!'

There is no doubt that had we known, as we know now, the nature of the discussions proceeding in Berlin, some plan of this kind could and would have been converted into coherent action. We had among ourselves divined the secret of success. Could we have obtained one commanding decision on the fundamental issue, and had there been a proper staff-machine to translate it into plans, it is certain that we could have intervened in the Eastern Mediterranean long before the Germans could have brought their forces to bear.

Sir Edward Grey argues in his book that the Germans were on interior lines and could thus frustrate all diversions. But this was not true of Turkey in this period of the war. On the contrary its untruth was the key to all the German perturbation. They could not aid Turkey for many months. Amphibious power could strike Turkey in a few weeks.

Our war-direction was not however upon that level. We have seen what struggles were called for from **H.**,—supported though they were by Conrad, by the whole influence of Austria and by the German Chancellor—to procure the transference of the war effort to the East, and only with what compromises they had succeeded. For all the power of the Admiralty we could only use arguments. We could not display the laurels of a naval Tannenberg. There was no supreme authority in London as in Berlin, to say Aye or No, right or left, west or east. It was only one man's opinion against another's. Still, from this moment the politicians on the War Council looked mainly to the East; while Sir John French and the British Army Headquarters fought desperately and naturally to have every man, gun and shell in France. Lord Kitchener with ever-changing mind was the battle-ground of these contentions. Sometimes one side prevailed with him and then again the other. There can be no doubt that if the 'Easterners' had only had to deal with the British army and its Headquarters staff, we could have given them orders. But behind

Sir John French and Sir Henry Wilson towered the mighty authority of General Joffre, victor of the Marne.

Joffre, like Falkenhayn, looked only to the Western Front, and like Falkenhayn believed in the superiority of the attack. There alone, in his judgment as in that of his opponent, lay in 1915 the decision of the war. Each was sure that he had only to gather a few more army corps and a few more cannon to break the opposing line and march triumphantly, as the case might be, to Paris or the Rhine. They were of course, as we now know, absolutely out of touch with the true facts and values. Neither of them, nor their expert advisers, had ever sufficiently realized the blunt truth—quite obvious to common soldiers—that bullets kill men. Against such an incubus we could make no headway. Every time Lord Kitchener was persuaded to the East—where indeed his instincts led him—and measures were taken in that direction, Joffre (with the French government working collaterally through the Foreign Office) descended upon him, so that he swung to and fro like a buoy in a tide-stream. Lots of people would no doubt have done the same. It must also be remembered that the British Empire was only at this time a subsidiary factor in the land war. France had ceded to us the decisive control of naval affairs, and some declared that it was our duty after expressing our views to conform to the military guidance of the chiefs of the great and heroic army at whose side our forces—only as yet a tenth as strong—were contending. As Lord Kitchener observed after one heart-shaking discussion: 'We cannot make war as we ought; we can only make it as we can.'

CHAPTER XVIII
THE WINTER BATTLE

Hindenburg had gained his way over Falkenhayn. He had now to make good against the Russians. No doubt in the course of the controversy which the last chapter has described both he and Ludendorff had been led to paint the successes which would reward their plans in glowing colours. All the German and Austrian armies on the Eastern Front were to join in an immense double offensive in East Prussia and far off in the Carpathians against the Grand Duke's northern and southern flanks. The Russian armies were to be seized, as it were, by a crab of monstrous size and gripped simultaneously with each of its two widely-spread claws. Falkenhayn had acidly pointed out that the two flanking attacks separated by 600 kilometres could not be brought into any effective relation. **H.L.** were under no delusions. The operations on which they had set their hearts lay in the north. Reinforced by the four corps wrested from the Supreme Command, they now controlled three Armies: their original Eighth, the Ninth with which they had made their two unsuccessful thrusts at Warsaw, and the three new corps now uniting as a Tenth Army under the command of General von Eichhorn. Their Eighth and Ninth Armies stood at the end of January along lines drawn after the battle of Lodz had ended in mid-December. The front of the Ninth Army running north and south faced Warsaw at about 40 miles' distance. The Eighth Army crouched behind the course of the Angerapp stream and the now frozen lakes. The interval of nearly 200 kilometres between them was filled by Landwehr and Landsturm troops, including Zastrow's corps, gathered at a second gleaning from the various German fortresses. **H.L.** now proposed to use all these forces in combination.

From what they had learned through the Russian wireless and other sources they credited the Grand Duke with 'a gigantic plan' of his own. They believed that as soon as the winter relented he would strike at East Prussia by an upward drive towards Thorn and simultaneously in the north from the direction of Kovno. They intended to forestall him. The Russian armies were in no lack of men. Limitless supplies of obedient peasants were training behind the Czar's frontiers, and as soon as uniforms, equipment and ammunition could be provided, refilled the shattered formations or added to their numbers. It was not men that Russia lacked; they were in fact the only resources she possessed in superfluity. Her armies filled their immense front, and on paper presented totals larger than ever before. But trained officers and educated non-commissioned officers and clerks of every kind were far below the proportions required to handle such masses of soldiery. Moreover, not only cannon of every calibre and ammunition of every kind, but even rifles were hideously deficient. Although the Grand Duke, Ruzski and Ivanov still nourished offensive schemes, they were painfully conscious

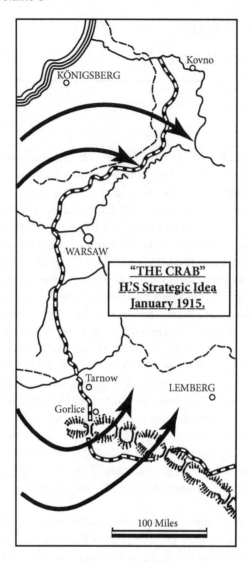

that the aggressive power of Russia had gravely declined since the early battles of the war. Ivanov, who already held the passes of the Carpathians, pressed the Stavka in long personal interviews to reinforce him for an invasion of the plains of Hungary. Ruzski, to whose opinion the Grand Duke leaned, preferred to renew the advance through Poland westward and north-westward towards the German frontier. All these discussions were abruptly terminated by German action.

According to the plan of **H⌐L**, the left claw of what I have called the 'Crab' was to reach suddenly forward through the Angerapp-Lötzen-Lakes line to seize and destroy all the Russians within its grasp. For this purpose the Ninth Army would move a part of its forces, mostly from the XXth Corps, northwards from the level of Warsaw to the neighbourhood of Ortelsburg and the fields where Tannenberg had been gained, while

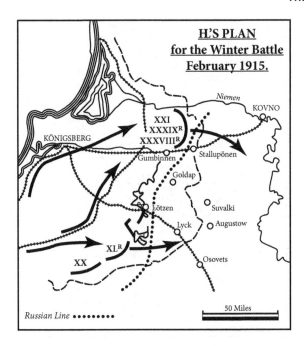

H'S PLAN
for the Winter Battle
February 1915.

the three corps forming the new Tenth Army would range themselves in the north in front of Insterburg. On the prescribed date the right of the Eighth Army would strike through Johannisburg towards Lyck, while the Tenth Army would march first north-east, towards Tilsit, then turning continually southwards, through Gumbinnen and Stallupönen towards Grodno. Both these movements as they developed would expose their outer flanks to Russian attacks, in the north from Kovno and the line of the Niemen, and in the south from the line of the Bobr, a tributary of the Narev. Not much danger was apprehended for the strong Tenth Army, but the German forces advancing south of the Lakes would be liable to heavy attacks on their right and right rear, and it was to protect them from this that the Ninth Army troops had been brought to the scene.

To mask the northward movement of these Ninth Army troops a sensational attack was made by the rest of the Ninth Army at Bolimov on January 31. A feature of this battle, intended to be much talked-of, was the first employment of 18,000 poison-gas shells. The greatest interest was taken in this improvident disclosure of a terrible secret. Hoffmann betook himself to the church steeple of Bolimov in order to witness the wholesale stifling of the Russians which the chemists had claimed would follow. He described the results as disappointing. The number of shells then thought magnificent was petty compared to later periods, and the intense cold robbed the poison gases of their expected diffusive power. Still on January 31 what the Kaiser afterwards decided to call 'the Winter battle in Masuria' was in fact begun by this fierce demonstration towards Warsaw.

It served its strategic purpose well. The Russian attention was violently drawn to this point, and they remained unconscious of the northward movement of troops from the Ninth Army. Even more remarkable is it that no inkling came to the Stavka of the

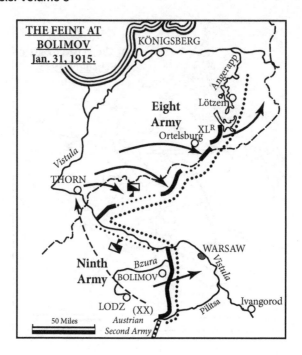

THE FEINT AT
BOLIMOV
Jan. 31, 1915.

KÖNIGSBERG

Angerapp

Eight
Army

Lötzen

XL^R
Ortelsburg

Vistula

THORN

Ninth
Army

Bzura

BOLIMOV

WARSAW

Vistula

LODZ (XX)
Austrian
Second Army

Pilitsa

Ivangorod

50 Miles

deployment and assembly in East Prussia of the four new army corps. They were all in their positions, three to the north and one to the south of the Lake line, in the early days of February, without any warning having reached their prey. Indeed the idea that any great operations could begin in such fearful wintry weather was scouted by the Russians' experience of their own climate. During February 5 and 6 tremendous snowstorms and blizzards lashed East Prussia. The cold was intense and the snow 'metre-deep,' or whirled into frozen drifts and hummocks. Even the stubborn wills of ⌐L hesitated before launching their hardy troops into the storm. But they steeled their hearts.

The immediate object of their design was the Tenth Russian Army, which sat in its trenches from Goldap to Johannisburg in front of the Angerapp-Lake line. They and their commander, General Sievers, suspected nothing of what was passing behind the shield of German fortifications. They passed the 6th and 7th in shovelling the snow out of their trenches. The right pincer of the German crab-claw began to move on the 7th. General Litzmann with the XLth Reserve Corps and the 2nd Division struck from Johannisburg towards Lyck. On the 8th the left pincer, the whole of the German Tenth Army, attacked between the Gumbinnen-Königsberg railway and the Memel river.

The three corps of this army (XXIst, XXXIXth Reserve and XXXVIIIth Reserve from north to south) drove the Russian covering troops before them and began immediately to turn the right and menace the Russian retreat. The enormous difficulties of the weather did not prevent the steady progress of the German Army. It continued to extend its enveloping movement around the Russian right, wheeling continually to the southward. On the night of the 9th–10th the XXIst Corps, after an uninterrupted march of 29 hours, had reached Schirwindt and Vladislavov. The centre corps had passed Pilkallen and the

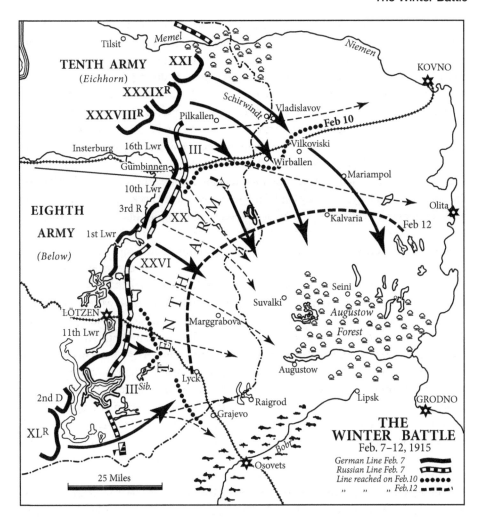

THE
WINTER BATTLE
Feb. 7–12, 1915

German Line Feb. 7
Russian Line Feb. 7
Line reached on Feb.10 ●●●●●
„   „   „ Feb.12 ▪▪▪▪▪

army front faced almost south at right-angles to the original Russian position. On the 10th the XXIst Corps reached Vilkoviski, cutting the railway to Kovno, and the XXIXth Reserve Corps in the centre reached Wirballen, where an entire Russian division which was in reserve was surprised and destroyed with a loss of 10,000 prisoners and 6 guns. Thus the line of retreat of the whole of the Russian right upon Kovno was severed. Vigorous attacks by Russian dismounted cavalry from Kovno upon the left and rear of the XXIst Corps were beaten off, but the threat from Kovno was considered sufficient to require the movement of a Landwehr division from the German right to ward off such interference. On the 12th the German Tenth Army front ran from Mariampol and Kalvaria to the neighbourhood of Goldap, and the Russian centre began to be seriously threatened. Indeed there were now left but two lines of retreat for the whole of General Sievers' army: the first towards the Niemen through Olita and the second through the Forest of Augustow.

Meanwhile in the south the XLth Reserve Corps was moving on Lyck to cut the Augustow road. Here they encountered tenacious Russian resistance. The road and railway junctions of Lyck were now vital. Bitter fighting with repeated Russian counter-attacks continued in this area in the most severe weather during the whole of the 12th. Valiantly the Russians continued to defend themselves. The German southern force, unable to make progress frontally, extended its right towards Grajevo. Meanwhile the whole front of the Eighth Army had broken out from behind the Angerapp position, and now fell upon the Russians in front of them. By the evening of the 13th they were close to Marggrabova—Sievers' old headquarters—and Suvalki. On this day the defenders of Lyck, with both their flanks turned and their rear menaced, withdrew in good order from the positions they had so bravely held. The Germans entered Lyck on the 14th, capturing 5,000 prisoners in the town. The Kaiser, closely following up the advance, visited the town that day and congratulated his victorious troops.

The pincers were closing fast upon the Russian Tenth Army. From the moment when these two great movements upon his flanks were revealed, General Sievers thought only of retreat. Burning villages behind them, but leaving nevertheless vast quantities of stores and provisions, over 350,000 Russians marched eastward as fast as possible. The roads became choked with transport in inextricable confusion. Infantry floundered through the snowdrifts. The wheeling advance of the German Tenth Army drove all these masses of men remorselessly southward. Large numbers of Russians broke and tore their way here and there through the encircling grip to the east and north-east. Masses of prisoners were taken; and always the main body of the Russian army was driven towards Augustow Forest. Everywhere the Russian rear-guards fought with the greatest stubbornness to secure the escape of their comrades; and as the Germans could only drag their artillery forward by using as many as eighteen horses to a single gun, their infantry were often stopped. The Russian counter-attacks from Kovno to prevent the imminent encirclement of General Sievers continued vigorously in the north. On the 13th in the south other strong efforts were made by Russian forces debouching from the small fortress of Osovets towards Lyck. These again were warded off by the Germans after hard fighting.

The frost had now broken and a sudden thaw converted the roads into quagmires of mud. By the night of the 15th the Russian IIIrd and XXVIth Corps had passed Augustow or traversed the forest with heavy losses and lay in great disorder, but outside the claw—around Grodno. But the Russian XXth Corps, with large numbers of stragglers and masses of transport and artillery, were still in the forest. Their rear-guards held its western edge with determination. And now Eichhorn, his right and centre arrested, resolved to repeat the audacious manœuvre which General von François had used at Tannenberg. He ordered his left corps (XXIst) to move southward round the northern side of the forest regardless of the peril which would threaten them in the rear from the fortress of Grodno. During the 15th, 16th and 17th this thin line of Germans, resolutely intent upon the encirclement of whatever Russians might be in their clutches, pressed continually forward, defending themselves both from the troops breaking out of the

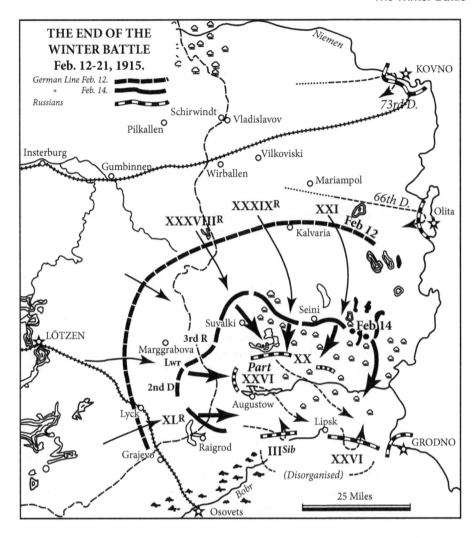

THE END OF THE
WINTER BATTLE
Feb. 12-21, 1915.

German Line Feb. 12.
»   Feb. 14.
Russians

trap and from the Russian counter-attacks from Grodno. On the 18th the forest was completely encircled.

Thus hopelessly trapped the Russian XXth Corps fought on with supreme devotion. For four days and nights they hurled themselves in vain against the thin invincible lines. On the 21st the crab-claw closed and seized its prey. 30,000 men, with 11 generals and 200 guns, laid down their arms, and many thousand German prisoners taken in the earlier fighting were also rescued by their countrymen.

Meanwhile the Eighth Army had advanced to the line of the Bobr, hoping to attack the fortress of Osovets. This small place played almost as important a part as Lötzen. Stoutly defended, it endured heavy bombardments and repeated attacks. Its forts were planted on the only eminences of the great plain in which it stood. The utmost efforts of the Germans were fruitless against it. To the southward behind the Bobr, strongly entrenched, the IIIrd Siberian Corps also resisted with constancy in what appeared to the Germans to be formidable entrenchments. Indeed the troops declared that they were semi-permanent works strengthened with concrete. Hoffmann disbelieved this and was in fact right; but it was thought impossible to demand further sacrifices from the willing but now completely exhausted Germans; and about the same time as the Russians in the forest were surrounded, the Winter Battle came to a close. The whole Russian Tenth Army had not been entrapped, but 110,000 prisoners and upwards of 300 guns were the prizes of the victors, and at least another 100,000 Russians had perished under the fire of the enemy, or sunk for ever in the snowdrifts or the mud. Although many had escaped and two corps still preserved some semblance of order, the Russian Tenth Army had ceased to exist as an effective fighting force.

This awful battle against the worst that nature or warring man could do constitutes an episode unparalleled in military history. Even the massive Hindenburg was chilled by its ghastly character.

'The name,' he says of the 'Winter Battle in Masuria,' 'charms like an icy wind or the silence of death. As men look back on the course of this battle they will only stand and ask themselves "Have earthly beings really done these things or is it all but a fable or a phantom? Are not these marches in the winter nights, that camp in the icy snowstorm and that last phase of the battle in the forest of Augustow so terrible for the enemy, but the creation of an inspired human fancy?"'

He adds further:

'In spite of the great tactical success ... we failed ... strategically. We had once more managed practically to destroy one of the Russian armies, but fresh enemy forces had immediately come up to take its place, drawn from other fronts to which they had not been pinned down. . . . We could not achieve a decisive result. The superiority of the Russians was too great.'[45]

Hindenburg could write thus of the Winter Battle, in spite of all its trophies. His confession of strategic barrenness applied even more forcibly to the Austrian operations at the other extreme of the Eastern Front. The southern claw of the crab had grasped nothing. Conrad's advance from the Carpathian passes was vigorously resisted. He failed even to cross the Dunajetz in force. Meanwhile, the Russian investment of Przemysl—siege it could not be called—continued. It appeared that that great fortress, the main base and depot of all the Austrian armies which had been ranged in Galicia at the outbreak of war, had only been victualled for three months. The temporary relief effected in October had not been sufficient to replenish its supplies. When the blockade closed again on November 9, the garrison was already straitened. Taught by their unsuccessful assault in October, the Russians patiently awaited the progress of famine. On March 18, the failure of the southern offensive being manifest, the Austrian garrison made, like Bazaine from Metz, a respectable but hopeless sortie, on the repulse of which the Commander proposed capitulation. This was a considerable event, and the prizes of the victors were impressive. Besides the stronghold with all its establishments, over 100,000 prisoners and a thousand guns were surrendered by Austria to Russia. The Russian investing army of the same size was liberated for further tasks. Thus, the grandiose operation, in the name of which **H.** had conjured Falkenhayn's army corps from the West, and in opposing which Falkenhayn had narrowly escaped dismissal, came to the sterile end he had predicted. He was near enough to the summit of power to be able, as occasion served, to point the moral. This was the first step in the revival of his assaulted reputation and impugned authority.

CHAPTER XIX
BEYOND THE DARDANELLES

Falkenhayn was a convinced and inveterate 'Westerner.' He believed that any great offensive against Russia would evaporate in the immense indefinite regions and measureless recesses to which the Russian armies could retire. Constantly before his mind's eye rose the warning pictures of the fate of Napoleon's Grand Army in the invasion of 1812. He did not choose to remember that Napoleon had no railways which could continually nourish large armies 1,000 or 2,000 miles from their home-base, and provide them with shelter from the winter and well-stocked depots at every stage of their advance. All his heart was in the war in France and Flanders. There alone, in his view could the supreme struggle be decided. There, was the proper and official theatre of war. There alone, could orthodox military principles receive their satisfaction. These strong professional views he shared with his leading opponents, with Joffre, with French, and after French with Haig. 'Better,' he might almost have exclaimed, 'be defeated in adhering to sound military doctrine, than conquer by "irregular" methods.'

However, as we have seen, the power and fame of Hindenburg, reinforced by the obtrusive influence of the politicians, had overruled his better judgment, forced him to smirch the purity of his creed, and make submission to 'the evil thing.' The four corps which he had longed to hurl into a new offensive in the West had been wrested from him. They had marched and fought in the Winter Battle, gaining new cheap laurels for his dangerous rivals, but producing as he had predicted no decisive strategic result. What was he to do? He must call a new army into being to replace the legions torn from his command.

On February 22 he confabulated with Colonel von Wrisberg, the head of the organizing department of the Ministry of War, upon the creation of a new reserve. New nine-battalion divisions were to be formed by taking three battalions from each of the divisions on the Western Front, and by reducing the number of guns in the batteries from six to four, and so on. The weakened divisions were each to be compensated with 2,400 trained recruits and additional machine-guns. This transformation was expected to take from six to eight weeks; and when completed Falkenhayn hoped to have at his disposal a free striking force of twenty-four new divisions. Actually from lack of equipment and other causes he had to content himself with fourteen, fit for service at the beginning of April. Upon these fourteen he was already building his plans. They should be formed into an Eleventh Army with the highly competent Colonel von Seeckt, afterwards better known as its Chief of Staff, under some figurehead. Early in March he set Seeckt, Krafft, Kuhl and Tappen to find the best place in the Anglo-French line for striking the longed-for blow. They made profound studies, replete with details and time-plans, of the requisite

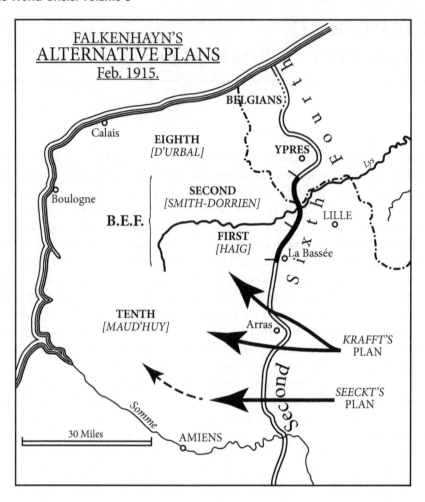

FALKENHAYN'S
ALTERNATIVE PLANS
Feb. 1915.

BELGIANS

Calais

EIGHTH
[D'URBAL]

YPRES

Lys

Fourth

Boulogne

SECOND
[SMITH-DORRIEN]

LILLE

B.E.F.

FIRST
[HAIG]

La Bassée

Sixth

TENTH
[MAUD'HUY]

Arras

KRAFFT'S
PLAN

Second

SEECKT'S
PLAN

Somme

30 Miles

AMIENS

number of divisions and guns. Seeckt selected that same front from Arras to the Somme which Ludendorff from 50 miles further back was to attack in 1918. Hohenborn, the War Minister, concurred in this, holding that 'it was the northern wing of the enemy front in the first place, [i.e. the British forces] which should be broken and crushed.' The right flank of the British then near La Bassée was to be assailed, and they were to be pushed north-west towards Boulogne and Calais, while a left-handed stroke swept the French to the southward. All these plans so busily prepared came to naught. Once again the East prevailed; but this time it was not the influence of **H**, but the force of events which plunged Falkenhayn into a new desertion of his favourite theories.

On February 18 a numerous and powerful British fleet, supported by a French squadron, opened fire upon the outer forts of the Dardanelles. The two seaward forts of the Gallipoli Peninsula were much damaged, and their guns were destroyed the next day by landing parties from the ships. As each successive day deliberate and methodical long-range bombardments accompanied by sweeping operations took place, it became evident that a serious attempt was to be made to force the Dardanelles. If this should succeed, Constantinople with the only Turkish magazines and arsenals would fall into the power of the victors, and the best that could be hoped for was that the Young Turk leaders would evacuate European Turkey, and continue the struggle as a purely Asiatic power. Thus the only ally the Teutonic Empires had gained would be irretrievably broken. Even more serious would be the political consequences. The spoils of the Turkish Empire would be at the disposal of the Allies. They could offer to Italy, Greece, and Roumania, all three already trembling on the verge of joining them, ample and highly-coveted rewards. They could act upon Bulgaria both by the threat of isolation amid a hostile Balkan Peninsula, and by potent bribes.

The reactions of the British thrust at Constantinople were immediately apparent upon all these four States. The demands of Italy and her preparations developed apace. Greece, torn between King Constantine and Venizelos, was apparently ready to supply an army to attack the Gallipoli Peninsula. King Ferdinand talked about joining the Allies, and refused to receive General von der Goltz in audience. Roumania froze into silence. Falkenhayn was forced to face the prospect of a complete adverse Balkan block which had everything to gain from the ruin of the Turkish and Austro-Hungarian Empires.

But all these direct impending consequences were in their turn dwarfed by the effect on Russia of full intimate contact with England and France, should the British Navy achieve the entry and command of the Black Sea. Russian troops would then flow freely southwards to animate the Balkan confederacy. British and French munitions with the world markets and the oceans behind them would revive and multiply the Russian armies. How to stop it? There were the strong defences of the Dardanelles, the forts, the mobile armaments, the mine fields, the adverse current, the great hazards of the adventure! It was a long-respected maxim that ships could not fight forts. But supposing the ships had guns which could destroy the forts and the forts had no guns which could reach the ships while so engaged, such a theory would evidently require modification. But worse lay behind. The power of the fortress cannon against the British fleet was severely measured by their supplies of armour-piercing shells. When these were exhausted, the forts had spoken their last word, and the advancing fleets would sweep the mine-fields, no doubt with loss, but also with certainty. Falkenhayn learned with distaste that the forts were ill-supplied with heavy ammunition and particularly with armour-piercing shells, and that no reserve of mines existed. On March 10 Admiral von Usedom, the German officer who had been appointed to command the water defences of the Straits, telegraphed: 'Despite the relatively small success of the enemy, the overwhelming of all the Dardanelles works cannot be prevented indefinitely, unless the munitions and mines now on order for months arrive soon, or the defence is sustained by submarines from home waters.' It could not take less than two months for submarines despatched from Kiel to make the perilous voyage. As for the shells and mines, how were they to reach the scene? Serbia was unconquered. Roumania, though professing friendship, was unwilling to transport munitions. In fact, although officers in plain clothes could travel to and fro across the neutral barrier, no munitions were allowed to pass from Germany to Turkey for nearly eight months. But who could tell what might happen in six weeks?

All these pressures developed upon the high strategic mind of Germany during February, March and April. On March 18 the hostile fleet made what appeared to be a resolute attempt to force the passage of the Straits. The great ships engaged the forts with vigour, and beat their gunfire down. The sweepers advanced towards the vital irreplaceable barrier of mines. However, luckily for **O.H.L.*** the last spare handful of mines had been laid parallel to the course of the fleet in an area which it had believed was swept, and two or three ships were sunk, one French ship with heavy loss of life. The British fleet, having itself suffered a loss of some forty lives, then withdrew, apparently baffled, from the contest, and the intelligence reports informed Berlin that a considerable army was collecting in Egypt for a land-attack on the Gallipoli Peninsula in concert with a renewed attack by the fleet. On the other hand, it was stated that as the Russians had now laid claim to Constantinople, the British were no longer in earnest about forcing the Dardanelles. As to the land-attack, the Turks, who had now crowded into the Gallipoli Peninsula and were under the command of General Liman von Sanders, professed confidence. But the difficulty about stopping the fleet consisted in the fact that the mine-fields could not be renewed if damaged in any way, and that there were less than 50 large armour-piercing shells for all the decisive guns of the forts together.

We can see these two opposing sets of circumstances maturing simultaneously in Falkenhayn's mind; the Eleventh Army gathering for use in the West, and this horrible intrusion upon Turkey from the south-east Mediterranean. In the fine brain of the supreme commander the two principles fought for mastery. In the end he decided of his own free will that the most urgent task was to crush Serbia and to open a road for munitions to Constantinople and the Dardanelles. Thus by the beginning of April when the new Eleventh Army was in being, Falkenhayn had already abandoned all his plans to use it in the West, and obeying the dominant strategic compulsion of the British attack on the Dardanelles, had decided to employ it against Serbia for the salvation of Constantinople and Turkey. While he was in this mood of concession to the Eastern heresy, another wave of pressures caught hold of him. Conrad had been cured by harsh experience of all desire for adventures against Serbia. He was clutching at the crests and passes of the Carpathians. At more than one point the Russian vanguards already overlooked the broad Hungarian plain. One more effort, one more success, and all the floods of Russian manhood would flow ravaging into the home-lands of Hungary. Such an event would rack the Empire to its foundations. Week by week the Russian flood mounted. The Austrian dykes and dams were already breaking. The major strategic values asserted themselves upon the Austrian Headquarters. Who now cared for Serbia, Italy and Roumania? Bulgaria and Turkey seemed relatively meaningless factors. At all costs the Carpathian front must be held.

To all German suggestions of a joint operation against Serbia, Conrad turned a dull ear. Nothing now mattered to him but the hour-to-hour defence of the Eastern Front, and for this he had a plan; a plan which in time, space and direction was the expression of

---

*Oberste Heeres-Leitung: the German G.H.Q.

his military genius. Somewhere on the Dunajetz river, say between Gorlice and Tarnow, there must be an efficient German thrust. Austrian troops would not suffice. There must be a German army capable of crashing through the Russian front and thus turning and undermining their whole line of battle along the summits of the Carpathians. Conrad saw that for him all might be regained by a punch with real Germans at this particular and deadly point. This then was what he urged, and to nothing else would he listen.

Falkenhayn had already relinquished his dreams of an offensive against the British in France. He had resigned himself to an Eastern campaign to relieve Constantinople. He now somewhat easily acceded to Conrad's demands. He certainly responded professionally to the strategic charm of his colleague's conception. He saw this was the place to hit. He saw that German troops alone could strike the blow. By this time the dreaded naval attack upon the Dardanelles had unaccountably dwindled and ceased. The danger was constant, but the urgency had abated; and Conrad pointed the path and clamoured for aid to his forces.

So, early in April Falkenhayn having first been drawn against his will to the East, decided to take all chances at the Dardanelles and succour Conrad. But he said, as Generals should always say, 'If this is worth doing, it is worth doing well,' and he said, what only those in the highest command can say, 'We will make a set-piece of it.' Four

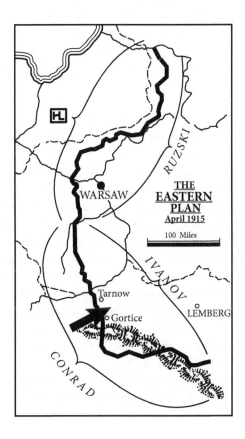

German divisions (which was all that Conrad had dared to ask) would be too few. Four corps might be enough. Conrad should have double what he asked. The new Eleventh German Army should be used between Gorlice and Tarnow.

In all this conflict of ideas and pressures, it is interesting to notice the part played by the German Crown Prince. No doubt he had accomplished military advisers, but certainly the tact and diplomacy which he employed deserve attention. On April 1 the Crown Prince had a long conversation with Falkenhayn. The Heir to the Throne, who had a considerable stake in all that was going forward, began by expounding the paramount importance of the Western Front. He declared his belief that the decision of the war could only be attained in France against the Western Powers, and that this would require the use of all the forces of the German army. In his view 'this fundamental idea must hold good during the whole war.' Thus he showed himself in the fullest accord with Falkenhayn's doctrine. For the present, however, he added, every attempt to reach a decision in the West now that the Austrian position had attained such importance was premature. The Russians must first of all be struck down and be made to make a separate peace. Falkenhayn's intention was merely to cripple the Russian power for some considerable time, and therefore not to use more forces against them than necessary. Not thus in the Crown Prince's view would the Germans attain the necessary freedom to enable them to carry out their main task, their final task in the West. Far rather was it necessary to put in such strong forces in the East that a decision might be attained there. Here was the policy of the 'Easterners' expressed in the language of the Western school. We have quoted Kuhl.[46] If the Crown Prince ever in fact used such arguments—and this is not yet disputed—he certainly wrapped the shrewdest military counsel in the coverings most likely to conciliate Falkenhayn. Falkenhayn was persuaded three-quarters of the way. He would not boldly seek the destruction of Russia and suffer all minor punishment elsewhere; but he agreed to throw his reserves upon the East rather than the West and he agreed further to throw them against Russia in the first instance, rather than against Serbia for the relief of Constantinople.

The plan which Conrad had conceived and which Falkenhayn had agreed to implement with doubled forces was a striking departure from the traditional German methods which **ᕼᒪ** had hitherto, with a single exception at Lodz, consistently employed. Instead of a wide enveloping movement directed against the flanks and rear of the enemy, it was a straightforward frontal attack. There was to be a break-through in the centre, or as the French call it, '*une percée*,' similar to those so often extravagantly bid for on the Western Front. The sector between Gorlice and Tarnow was about 30 miles wide. Behind the Austrian line between these two towns the German Eleventh Army began in early April to assemble. It was finally composed of four German Corps drawn from the French front; the Guard from Alsace, the Xth from the west of Rheims, the XLIst from Chaulnes, and a composite Corps from Lorraine. To these were added the Austrian VIth Corps and a Hungarian cavalry division; in all one cavalry and ten infantry divisions: about 170,000 men. The Eleventh Army had 352 field and 146 heavy guns, and the Austrian Fourth Army behind whom they were forming had 350 field and 103 heavy guns: that is to say a field gun to about every 45 yards and a heavy gun

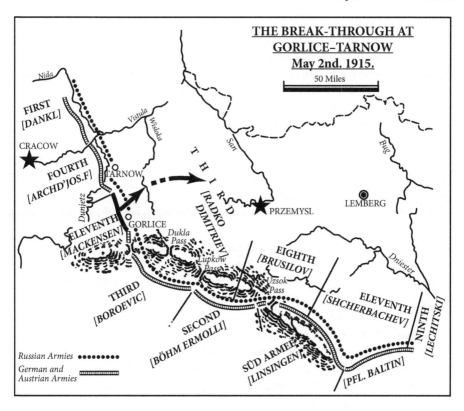

THE BREAK-THROUGH AT
GORLICE–TARNOW
May 2nd. 1915.

50 Miles

to every 132 yards. Although these proportions were far surpassed by both sides on the Somme in 1916, they represented in May 1915 the greatest artillery concentration yet prepared.

The direction of the Gorlice-Tarnow attack was to be north-east across the foothills between the Vistula and the mountains, and once the Russian line was broken, the Germans would wheel their front until they faced east, thus traversing, as may be seen by the map, the rear of all three Russian armies battling along the Carpathians to the southward. Indeed to make the operation fruitful in the highest degree, or as Falkenhayn expressed it, to improve the 'harvest prospects,' he suggested to Conrad that the Austrian armies holding the mountains should 'give way step by step drawing the enemy after them' into Hungary. But Conrad ignored the proposal. He could not bring himself to yield Hungarian soil. He had no desire to encourage his armies to retreat. His efforts had usually been required in the opposite sense.

To cover the withdrawal of such important forces from France 'lively activity' was prescribed along the entire Western Front. The gas attack at Ypres—not by shelling as at Bolimov, but by the continuous discharge of gas from cylinders—which began on April 22 was the most formidable of these distractive enterprises. The precipitate exposure of this deadly device at a time when no German reserves were at hand to exploit its surprising effects, was one of the debts which the Western allies owed to the

Eastern Front. **H.** were likewise ordered to make a diversion in their northern sphere. They seem to have viewed the Gorlice-Tarnow project with restrained enthusiasm. They had almost come to regard the Eastern Front as their preserve. The arrival of Falkenhayn and **O.H.L.** as prime actors in these scenes, furnished with the reinforcements for which **H.** had long pleaded in vain, could scarcely be welcomed. Moreover **H.** had only one method—a vast outflanking movement from the north. To march between Riga and Kovno and then drive southwards far behind the Russian front, cutting the main railways which sustained it, was their ideal conception. For this the forces were lacking. The most they could offer by way of diversion was a powerful raid by three cavalry supported by three infantry divisions into Courland and Lithuania. This operation began at the end of April and no doubt excited Russian concern.

Hindenburg's own remarks explain the direction in which his influence was exerted.

'My Headquarters was at first only an indirect participant in the great operation which began at Gorlice. Our first duty, within the framework of this mighty enterprise, was to tie down strong enemy forces. This was done at first by attacks in the great bend of the Vistula west of Warsaw and on the East Prussian frontier in the direction of Kovno, then on a greater scale by a cavalry sweep into Lithuania and Courland which began on April 27. The advance of three cavalry divisions, supported by the same number of infantry divisions, touched Russia's war zone at a sensitive spot. For the first time the Russians realized that by such an advance their most important railways which connected the Russian armies with the heart of the country could be seriously threatened. They threw in large forces to meet our invasion. The battles on Lithuanian soil dragged out until the summer. We found ourselves compelled to send larger forces there, to retain our hold on the occupied region and keep up our pressure on the enemy in these districts which had hitherto been untouched by war. Thus a new German army gradually came into existence. It was given the name of the "Niemen Army" from the great river of this region.'[47]

The Russian forces holding the front against which these dire preparations were progressing, consisted of the Third Army under General Radko Dimitriev, who had hitherto found no difficulty in containing the bulk of the Austrian Fourth Army. The greatest pains were taken to conceal from the Russians the gathering of the storm. All German reconnoitring parties were dressed in Austrian uniforms, and until within a few days of the battle, General Dimitriev was quite unaware of what impended upon him. Still less did he suspect its scale and intensity. The German Staff Officers climbing the hill-tops could see the Russian positions laid out before them as on a map. There were three lines of loop-holed trenches with overhead cover, constituting a single zone of defence. The German reconnoitring parties found the conditions very different from those of the Western Front. No-man's land was a wide space, three or four thousand yards across, through which occasional patrols wandered by night and in which the inhabitants cultivated their fields by day. The tranquillity of the countryside was broken only by an occasional splutter of rifle-fire or a few desultory shells. The first care of the Germans had been to remove all the inhabitants so that no tales could be told. Meanwhile enormous dumps of ammunition, 1,200 rounds for every field-, and 500 to 600 for every heavy battery were accumulated.

The delicate question of the command was adjusted in the following manner: the Eleventh Army, Austrian and German troops alike, and their offensive were entrusted to General von Mackensen with Seeckt as his mentor. Mackensen was placed under Conrad and **A.O.K.** But these in turn agreed not to give any orders to Mackensen which had not beforehand been approved by Falkenhayn and **O.H.L.** And then, lest this procedure should be dilatory, it was understood that in practice **O.H.L.** would tell Seeckt what to do direct, the formal orders reaching Mackensen as soon as possible through the prescribed ceremonial channel. Thus Austrian dignity was safeguarded, and no inconvenience arose.

The Eleventh Army had taken over the line by April 28, and on the same day Mackensen issued his warning order that the artillery would open on May 1 and that the assault would follow on May 2. The presence of Germans on the front was discovered by the Russians on the 25th, but no reinforcements were asked for by General Dimitriev. Even patrolling and vigilance seem to have sunk to a low ebb. Says Danilov: 'Our right front with its huge salient had many weak places. The Russian army was at the end of its power. The uninterrupted fighting in the Carpathians had cost it heavy losses. The deficit in officers and men in many units was terrifying. The lack of arms and munitions was catastrophic. In these circumstances the troops could still do something against the Austrians, but were incapable of stopping serious pressure from an energetic and determined foe.' Such was the situation on the eve of the attack.

The German artillery registration began during May 1, and gradually increased throughout the afternoon and night into a harassing fire to prevent the Russians from strengthening their defences. A two-hours' pause was made from 1 to 3 a.m. during the night, to give the German patrols opportunity for reconnaissance, and their engineers time to destroy wire and obstacles. At 6 a.m. on the 2nd, the four-hour intense preliminary bombardment began. At this time the storm troops were already in their assaulting positions, and behind them the successive waves of the attack, together with the field batteries destined to accompany it, deployed. In all ten divisions were marshalled, only the Xth Corps forming reserves upon either wing. The bombardment was crushing, the Russian overhead-cover of earth and sandbags supported on logs was everywhere smashed in by the German howitzers and trench-mortars. 'There was scarcely any reply from the hostile artillery. A few batteries that did attempt it were immediately silenced by overwhelming fire.' The German infantry instead of hugging the parapet stood upright, and almost unharmed watched the effects of the bombardment. When at 9 a.m. the trench-mortars developed their full intensity, the Russian wire and machine-guns flew into the air. At ten o'clock the trench-mortars ceased firing; the German artillery lifted on to the back lines, and through the dust and smoke, thirty or forty thousand assaulting infantry charged at a rapid pace. 'Here and there,' says the German account, 'loam-grey figures jumped up and ran back weaponless in grey fur caps and fluttering, unbuttoned greatcoats, until there was not one remaining. Like a flock of sheep they fled in wild confusion,' many to be caught on the next line of wire and there slain or captured.

Only where there were woods near the front line or where, owing to hilly ground, the bombardment had not done its work, was there any fighting. The front position was carried with a rush, and the Russian counter-attacks were hurled back upon their second line. After hard fighting all through May 2 this was stormed in its turn. On the 4th, the IIIrd Caucasian Corps sent from the Russian Army Group reserve attempted to counter-attack, but could do no more than cover the retreat. The Eleventh Army, drawing the Austrian armies on either side forward with them, had now broken completely through the Russian front. Dimitriev's army was annihilated. His divisions, after another week's fighting, could scarcely muster 1,000 men a-piece. 140,000 prisoners, 100 guns and 300 machine-guns fell during the whole operation to the victors, while the trenches were choked with dead and wounded. It had once more been proved that the Russian army in its weakened condition could not withstand the troops of any first-class nation. The whole of the Russian Carpathian front now became untenable, and everywhere along 100 miles of hard-won summits and passes, the Eighth, Eleventh and Ninth Russian armies retreated with the utmost speed, yielding up march after march the fair province which they had invaded nine months before and deemed their own for ever.

Meanwhile much had happened at the Dardanelles. The sudden and, as it proved, final cessation of all efforts by the British Navy to force the Straits, which had followed their repulse of the 18th of March, had been succeeded by a cloud of rumours of an impending land-attack upon the Gallipoli Peninsula. Very large British forces were known to be gathering in Egypt and the complete silence and passivity of the fleet betokened extensive preparations for a landing. Meanwhile the Turks under German direction worked feverishly to fortify all possible landing-places, and by the middle of April their army on the peninsula had been raised to eight divisions. Admiral von Usedom with scarcely any armour-piercing ammunition for his heavy guns, only the mines he had already sown and no hope of getting more of either, was fully conscious of his weakness in the face of a renewed naval effort. But the flower of the Turkish army was now gathering on the peninsula and Liman von Sanders, under whose orders stood the valiant Mustapha Kemal, awaited an impending descent by a hostile force with confidence and ardour. Indeed instructed military opinion in Turkish and German circles, as also at Sir John French's Headquarters, held that the operation of landing an army from open boats on beaches swept by machine-guns and modern rifle-fire was probably impossible. To the German Supreme Headquarters who, knowing the facts, watched the events, it must indeed have seemed strange that the British should be ready to face the appalling risks and sacrifices of a landing, while all the time the main fortress cannons which held the Straits could each count their armour-piercing shells upon a man's fingers. Perhaps however the British would attack by land and sea at the same time or in quick succession!

On April 25 the impossible was achieved. From earliest daybreak Liman von Sanders received the news of a series of landings and attacks on almost all the practicable beaches. Desperate fighting ensued, into which all the Turkish reserves at the end of the Peninsula were rapidly drawn. On the beaches, and amid the rocky scrub and ravines of the Peninsula a violent struggle at the closest quarters raged remorselessly, and by nightfall on the 26th after a loss of 20,000 men, more than 30,000 British, Australasian and French troops had established themselves upon the Gallipoli Peninsula. The assailants paused to land their artillery and supplies and Liman von Sanders hurried his remaining Turkish divisions to the scene. So critical was his need that he was forced to leave the isthmus of Bulair with its celebrated lines and his sole means of retreat utterly unguarded. On April 28 the British and French troops on the tip of the Peninsula resumed their advance and the furious first battle of Krithia was fought. The Turks withstood the invaders, weakened by their terrible losses and only lightly supported by field artillery, and yielded scarcely a mile of the precious ground. Still it seemed to the German-Turkish command that their enemies had overcome the main obstacle. They had established themselves on shore. All the Turkish reserves were engaged. The Turkish line of retreat could be cut at any moment by a further descent from the sea. No one could tell what reserves the ships might bring, or on what new point they would fall. There was nothing but to fight on stubbornly.

Europe therefore at the end of the first week in May took count of two new events of the first magnitude: the wonderful landing of the Allies upon Gallipoli and the crashing Russian defeat in North Galicia. 'As had been feared,' wrote Falkenhayn, 'the English set foot on the Gallipoli Peninsula on April 25. Italy's entry into the ranks of the enemy became daily more probable.' The negotiations between the Allies and Italy had in fact been virtually completed; but the naval and military conventions were still being settled in Paris. The naval arrangements which it had become my duty to conduct on behalf of the Allies presented no great difficulty. Our command of the sea at that time was absolute, and it was easy to give our hoped-for new ally whatever naval aid she might ask. But the essence of the military convention was that the Russians should maintain at least forty divisions in Galicia and should press the Austrians there with all their might. When the discussions began, the Italians might well have expected an immediate Russian invasion of Hungary. Before they ended, they were confronted with the apparition of Gorlice-Tarnow, and the spectacle of a general Russian retreat from the Carpathians. By the middle of May the magnitude of the Russian disasters in Galicia was plain. Moreover, the British attacks on the Aubers Ridge in France, upon which many vain hopes had been built, had also been easily repulsed with heavy slaughter. Everywhere the Germans struck or defended themselves with invincible strength and skill. Far larger Austrian forces would now be available to meet the Italian armies. The military position of the Allies had sensibly worsened.

There always however remained the ding-dong battle on the Gallipoli Peninsula, the military prodigy of the landing, and the apparent certainty that the amphibious power of Britain would enable her to beat down and break up the Turkish Empire with all that that would entail. The two events, the victory and the defeat balanced each other. The negotiations continued. The conventions were signed. On May 23 Italy ordered the general mobilization of her armies and declared war against Austria. At midnight on the 24th the Italian army which had long been on a war-footing crossed the Austrian frontier and a fourth Great Power joined the Allies.

CHAPTER XX
THE FALL OF WARSAW

We have now to chronicle the flood of disasters that the victory of Gorlice-Tarnow opened upon the Russians. During the whole of the summer and autumn of 1915 they had to face the almost ceaseless attack of nearly 40 German divisions and of nearly the whole of the Austrian armies. Already weakened in quality and structure by the injuries they had received, and in the worst phase of their munition supply, the armies of the Czar presented an 800-mile front to the successive German thrusts which now here, now there, broke the line or forced deep and rapid retirements. The consequences of such defeats wherever they had occurred, endangered the life of Russian armies far beyond the reverberations of the cannonade. We have the spectacle of the German warrior setting himself with prodigious energy to beat the life out of the Russian giant. The summer campaign of 1915 was the only time when very large German forces maintained a continuous, unrelenting offensive against the Russian front. Dragging along the Austrian armies with which they were often interspersed, the Germans marched forward into Russia, upon the kind of plans which had long been Conrad's dream, but which the armies of the Dual Monarchy could never have executed.

The tale is one of hideous tragedy and measureless and largely unrecorded suffering. Considering the state of their armies and organization, the Russian resistance and constancy are worthy of the highest respect. The strategy and conduct of the Grand Duke, bearing up amid ceaseless misfortune, with crumbling fronts, with congested and threatened communications, with other anxieties still further in rear, which most military commanders are spared, fills a chapter in military history from which a future generation of Russians will not withhold their gratitude. He yielded provinces; he yielded cities; one after another he yielded river lines. He was driven from Galicia; he was driven from Poland; in the north he was driven far back upon Russian soil. He gave up his conquests; he gave up Warsaw; he gave up all his fortresses. The whole defended front broke under the hammer. All its railways passed to the service of the invader. The entire population fled in terror and agony before the advancing storm. When at last the autumn rains choked the roads with mud, and winter raised its shield before a tortured nation, the Russian armies, extricated from their perils, stood along a still continuous line from Riga on the Baltic to the Roumanian frontier, with a future before them from which the hopes of general victory were not banished.

The easterly advance of the German Eleventh Army from the scene of its victory carried it by the end of May to Przemysl. The Grand Duke determined not to squander troops in the defence of the fortress. When the German and Austrian columns lapped it on both sides, the two army corps which it would have required to stand a siege withdrew towards Lemberg and other battlefields with which we are familiar. An attempt by the Austro-German Südarmee under Linsingen to envelop the extreme Russian left came to naught. Indeed it was decisively thrown back by a heavy counter-stroke. Meanwhile large Russian reinforcements drawn from their centre and north gathered in the path of the conquerors. Progress became slower and at the beginning of June the assailants paused for rest and reflection.

On June 3 High Conference at Pless! **O.H.L.**, **HL** and **A.O.K.**; Falkenhayn, Hindenburg, Ludendorff, Hoffmann, Mackensen, and Conrad; and over all the Kaiser! The whole situation was reviewed by the three or four chief captains with their principal officers within call. Italy had entered the war. Six or seven hundred thousand fresh troops already pressed against the Austrians upon the new fronts they had been forced to form along the Isonzo River and in Tirol. By September the Italian forces actually in the line would certainly be nearly a million strong. Conrad, voicing the sentiment of Vienna, wished above all to strike at the renegade ally, his hated foe who (in his view), after the basest blackmail, had stabbed a struggling neighbour in the back. He wished to dithdraw Austrian divisions from Galicia to nourish an offensive against Italy. The Germans demurred. Falkenhayn was still preoccupied about the Dardanelles. The battles on the Gallipoli Peninsula burned fiercely. The Turkish losses were enormous. The assailants, though never strengthened sufficiently to win, were constantly fed with reinforcements. It was rumoured that an entire new army was being prepared in England for a further descent. At any moment, moreover, the British fleet, which still lay idle, might resume its attack on Admiral von Usedom's unreplenished batteries. Hostile Serbia; neutral, doubtful Roumania still barred the passage of the vital munitions. The Serbs had sunk a ship carrying an ample cargo along the Danube. To crush Serbia, to rally Bulgaria and open the through route to Constantinople and the Dardanelles, filled the mind of the chief of the German General Staff.

But beneath all this lay always the supreme anxieties of the Western Front. Already there had been weighty French attacks from Arras and La Bassée. The French armies were re-gathering their strength after Foch's disastrous, prodigal spring offensive in Artois. Some potent enterprise must be expected from them in the autumn. The British army and artillery grew steadily in strength. The 30 or 40 divisions which had been raised from the eager volunteers of 1914 were now organisms of nine months' training. The wealth of Britain with the whole world at her disposal and all the seas and oceans under her control was surely equipping these new hosts with all they might require. The munition factories in England and America, adapted or expanded at the beginning of the War, would now begin to discharge an ever-broadening stream of rifles, cannons and shells. Falkenhayn must prepare himself to resist in the autumn efforts hitherto unequalled, and he wanted to withdraw immediately four German divisions from the Eastern Front. Lastly **HL** had their point of view. The Twin Brethren were still united. Their opinions and methods were unchanged. They had been amazed by the results of Gorlice-Tarnow. These had exceeded their hopes. They saw in what had happened the possibility of a super-Tannenberg embracing in its sweep the main mass of the whole Russian army.

Amid these varying schemes one plain question stood forth. Should Mackensen with the 'spear-head army' go on or stop?

Falkenhayn wished to stop. He wished to disengage his divisions. But to stop might not have that result. If the German forces in Galicia were seriously weakened, the Austrians would not be able even to remain stationary. They could not dispense with the full German aid. Until the Russians were beaten much lower, the German divisions must stay. If they stayed, must they not achieve something? Time was fleeting; if they were to advance, they would require further reinforcements. In the end it was decided, so far from weakening Mackensen, to reinforce him with four and a half divisions drawn from the north and rear of the Eastern Front. A general re-grouping of the armies was ordered. The Austrian Third Army was broken up, part being sent to Italy and the rest merged in the other armies. The Second and Fourth Austrian Armies on either side of Mackensen were placed under his command. With this great mass he would continue for the present to march East. These changes and the necessary replenishment of the armies were not completed till the middle of June. Mackensen was able to resume his advance on the 19th, and on the 22nd Lemberg passed into German hands.

After Lemberg, what to do? Falkenhayn posed the incessant question to **O.H.L.** 'How far do we mean to penetrate Russia? Where are we going to find a decision?' At this moment General Von Seeckt, Mackensen's Chief Staff Officer and professional guide, proposed that the whole of the Eleventh Army should wheel from the east to the north and should march due north between the Vistula and the Bug in the direction of Syedlets and Brest-Litovsk. Falkenhayn approved. The 'spear-head army' turned through a quarter-circle, and advanced over that same ground towards Lublin and Kholm across which only a year ago Dankl and Auffenberg had hopefully wended. In short, Conrad's original plan was renewed. But what was to be the co-operation from the north? Where was the other side of the pincer to be applied? In the south all was well; the Russian armies were staggering and mutilated; the upward thrust was to be made by German troops instead of Austrian. What would be sent to meet it from the north, and bite off the Polish salient? But here there were differences of view. On June 29 Falkenhayn wrote to Hindenburg that Mackensen had been ordered to advance between the Bug and the Vistula attacking the enemy 'wherever he found them.' This pressure, he said, would soon help Woyrsch (still forging slowly eastward along his original course). Now was the time for **H.** to move too. Obviously the Ninth German Army west of Warsaw could be depleted and its force used either from the south or the north. If from the north then surely the south-eastward thrust from Osovets and across the Narev would be the most effective. Thus Falkenhayn revived Conrad's first ideas.

But **H.** had more ambitious views. They sought a far wider sweep. They were sure that the Russian masses around Warsaw would escape a mere south-eastward scoop across the Narev. The fatal encirclement for the enemy lay in their judgment between Kovno and Grodno cutting the vital railway through Vilna and Dvinsk to Petrograd. Thereafter the northern German armies should turn southward and march between Brest-Litovsk and the Pripyat swamps, thus entrapping all foes at once. Falkenhayn had no mind for this far-flung operation. He had Serbia and the Western Front to consider. He resisted. Ludendorff proceeded to find all sorts of difficulties in the proposed more modest advance through Osovets. The swamps on either side of the little fortress would be embarrassing; the condition of the ground at this season of the year prohibitive. The resistance of Osovets would certainly be obstinate. **H.** could have no hopes of overcoming it. 'With the deepest regret I felt myself unable to agree to such an offensive even at the suggestion of General Headquarters.' In love with their gigantic conception **H.** riddled with solid technical criticism the more modest alternative.

Again high conference; again the Emperor. The same group minus Conrad; this time at Posen. **H.** and **O.H.L.** now face to face. Clash of argument, clash of wills, clash

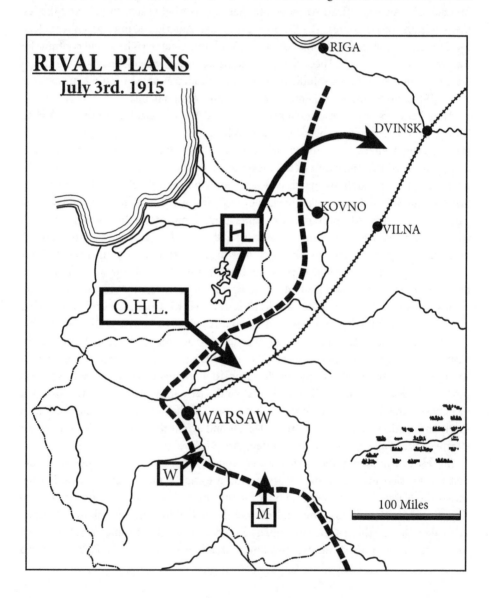

of interests, even—for the most noble military figures sometimes fall to the level of ordinary mortals. But the Kaiser ranged himself with Falkenhayn. Brought in as he often was to give a decision, as one might spin a coin, he ordered that the northern attack should be made between and across the Narev and not across the Niemen. Deference however was shown by way of compromise to General Ludendorff's objections to the advance by Osovets. Thus neither **H.** nor **O.H.L.** had their way. The front of the north attack was shifted further to the south and west. It therefore became less ambitious than even Falkenhayn had desired. But the decision had been taken; the All-Highest had pronounced it, and General von Gallwitz, who had hitherto commanded an army group or detachment, was placed at the head of a newly-combined Twelfth German Army.

On July 13 he struck with 12 divisions south-east towards the Narev through a town called Prasnish, which had already witnessed bitter fighting in the spring. In a week Gallwitz driving in the Russian front had reached the Narev and three days later his army had crossed it after overcoming the resistance of the minor fortresses of Pultusk and Rojan. At the same time the Niemen army made a further advance towards Mitau and Shavli, thus gripping the Russians on its front. Meanwhile Mackensen advancing from the south stood on the line Lublin and Kholm. The fall of Warsaw gleamed upon the German and glared upon the Russian headquarters. Even Falkenhayn scraped two more divisions from the Western Front to strengthen General von Gallwitz. At this stage the requests of **H.**, even though Hindenburg wrote direct to the Kaiser, that these two divisions should be sent to the Niemen army, and that further troops should be railed round from Mackensen's army to the same destination, were unceremoniously rejected. The blood of **O.H.L.** was roused. The hunt was keen.

But the Grand Duke was not caught. He retreated in good time. Warsaw was evacuated by the Russians on August 5. The cutting-off movement degenerated into a mere stern chase. The whole line of the Vistula was abandoned by the Russians; but they withdrew their armies in an orderly manner. The only fortress which the Grand Duke allowed himself to defend was Novo-Georgievsk. That he should have done so was an error: why he should have done so is a mystery. Novo-Georgievsk was the guardian of Warsaw. If Warsaw was to be abandoned, its significance was destroyed. Five years before the War, there had been an agitation in Russia to modernize the fortresses of the Vistula and the Narev. The Government had recognized the importance of this step. In order to lay down the new forts around Warsaw, they had swept away the old. The War had come before the new had been constructed! Novo-Georgievsk at least retained the defences of 1891, somewhat improved during the war period. It contained a garrison of over 90,000 men, only militia but still armed every one of them with a precious rifle. Perhaps to delay the German advance, the Grand Duke left these behind, and the siege of Novo-Georgievsk began.

For this task **H.** assembled some 80,000 men of various second-line formations; and they were furnished from Germany with a large part of the siege train including the Austrian howitzers which had previously demolished the outlying forts of Antwerp. Six 16-inch and nine 12-inch howitzers forming the 'very heavy artillery'; 44 8-inch howitzers with a few 9-inch and 8-inch guns and two companies of 10-inch mortars,

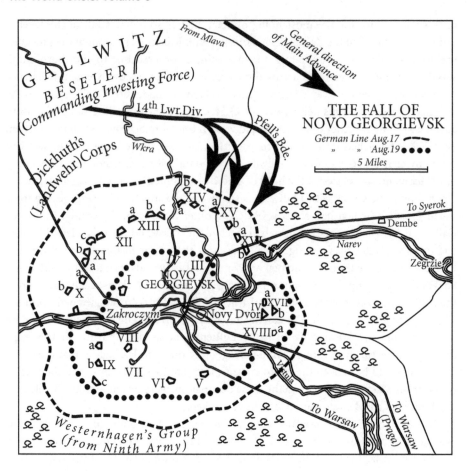

together with a respectable concourse of medium pieces, swiftly arrived upon the scene. General von Beseler, 'the hero of Antwerp,' took charge of the siege. The investment was completed on August 10 and the heavy batteries opened a few days later. The task of the attackers was lightened by good luck. The Chief Engineer of the fortress driving out to reconnoitre with all its plans in his motor-car had the misfortune to run into the advancing Germans and was duly captured with his documents!

The method of attack consisted in the destruction by overwhelming cannon-fire of one single sector of the defence, the ruins of which fort by fort were then to be stormed. But the militia men, 'bearded men going into action, pale with the thoughts of their wives and families,' developed a field position in front of the gap, which had first of all to be reduced. Thereafter six German battalions stormed fort XV.a and seven fort XV.b; and although eleven battalions were repulsed with much slaughter from fort XVI.a, the assailants were generally established in striking distance of the inner line by August 19. At 4 a.m. on August 20 Novo-Georgievsk, after slaughtering its horses and burning its stores, surrendered unconditionally. It had held out for thirty days from the first approach of the besiegers. 90,000 prisoners, including 30 Russian generals, over 700 guns and

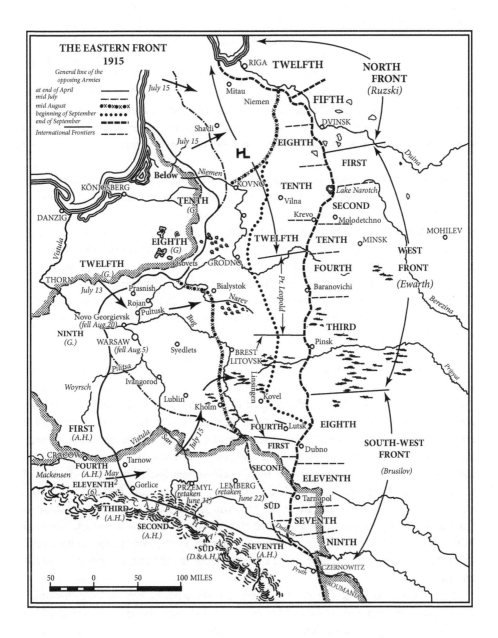

THE EASTERN FRONT
1915

General line of the
opposing Armies

at end of April
mid July
mid August ●x●x●x●x●x
beginning of September ● ● ● ● ● ●
end of September ▪ ▪ ▪ ▪ ▪
International Frontiers

July 15

RIGA TWELFTH NORTH
FRONT
(Ruzski)

Mitau FIFTH

Niemen

Shavli DVINSK

July 15 EIGHTH

HL FIRST

Below Niemen

KÖNIGSBERG KOVNO TENTH Lake Narotch

TENTH Vilna SECOND

DANZIG (G.) Krevo Molodetchno

EIGHTH TWELFTH TENTH MINSK MOHILEV

(G.) WEST

TWELFTH Osovets GRODNO FOURTH FRONT

(G.) Baranovichi (Ewarth)

THORN July 13 Prasnish Bialystok Narev Pr. Leopold

Rojan Pultusk

Novo Georgievsk Bug THIRD

(fell Aug.20) Pinsk

NINTH WARSAW Syedlets BREST

(G.) (fell Aug.5) LITOVSK

Pilitsa Linsingen Kovel EIGHTH

Woyrsch Ivangorod

Lublin Kholm FOURTH Lutsk SOUTH-WEST

FIRST FIRST Dubno FRONT

(A.H.) SECOND (Brusilov)

CRACOW Tarnow ELEVENTH

Mackensen FOURTH (A.H.) May Tarnopol

ELEVENTH² Gorlice PRZEMYL LEMBERG SÜD

(6.) (retaken (retaken

THIRD June 3⌐) June 22) SEVENTH

(A.H.) SECOND SÜD NINTH

(A.H.) SEVENTH CZERNOWITZ

SÜD (A.H.) Pruth

(D.&A.H.) ROUMANI

Vistula San July 15

Duina

Berezina

Pripat

Dnieper

50 0 50 100 MILES

many rifles were taken with the place. This may well prove to be the last defence of a first-class ring-fortress deprived of the support of a field army.

The general retreat of the Russian armies was accompanied by the flight of enormous masses of the inhabitants. Terrified by tales of German cruelty, millions of people fled from their homes dragging what belongings they could save along with them in vehicles of every kind. The roads were submerged by these slow-flowing streams of misery. The main current was between Warsaw and Brest-Litovsk. The Russian troops, whether in retreat or advancing to sustain their rear-guards, had no choice but to thrust these pitiful crowds from the highways often into the marshes which flanked them. Ludendorff says significantly on this subject: 'Many scenes in the Russian campaign have been indelibly imprinted on my memory.' The veteran General Gourko rejoices that he was not called upon to witness them as his duty lay in Galicia. But he writes:

> 'Still, men who had fought in several wars and many bloody battles told me that no horrors of a field of battle can be compared to the awful spectacle of the ceaseless exodus of a population, knowing neither the object of the movement nor the place where they might find rest, food and housing. Themselves in an awful condition, they increased the troubles of the troops, especially of the transport who had to move along roads filled with this disorganized human wave. Many a time our forces had to stop and fight a rear-guard action just to allow this crowd to make room for the troops. . . . God only knows what sufferings were endured here, how many tears were shed and how many human lives were given as victims to the inexorable Moloch of war.'

The crisis of the campaign was now over. The Russian armies were clear of the Polish salient on which they had counted so dearly, and for which they had sacrificed so much. Their situation was simplified. After August 18 when Kovno fell, the Eastern Front ran almost due north and south through Riga, Kovno, Grodno and Brest-Litovsk till it trailed along the Galician border to Roumania. In the year's campaign the Germans had killed or wounded nearly a million Russians, and had taken three-quarters of a million prisoners. But all chance of a mass encirclement had passed. **H.**'s dreams of a super-Tannenberg were ended. There was still a month's more fighting before the weather broke, and the steady advance of the whole German line pushed the Russian front and the fugitive population another 100 to 150 miles to the eastward. The final line at the end of September lay through Dvinsk along the Dvina, due south to the Pripyat marshes and thence through the southern corner of Galicia to the Roumanian frontier.

It was at this moment that the Czar indulged the wish he had so long cherished. Against the warning and appeals of his ministers, but with the ardent support of his wife, he assumed personal command of his Armies, and on September 5 took up his abode at the Stavka where he lived a quiet frugal life much preoccupied with the health of his young son. General Alexeiev conducted the war. The Grand Duke Nicholas was relegated to the command against Turkey in the Caucasus.

These tremendous events were watched by the western Allies with sorrow that they had happened, and with relief that they were no worse. The hopes of the French command and the anxious attention of their British ally were centred upon the impending great offensive in Champagne and at Loos, due to be launched on September 25. Marshal Joffre's attack in Champagne in which 50 divisions were to take part was confidently expected by the French, to rupture strategically the entire German front in the west, and to carry with it the consequences of Gorlice-Tarnow on three or four times its scale. These hopes were not to be attained. Italy also was at a standstill. On both the Isonzo and the Tirol fronts, the Austrian defence was maintained. Terrible battles involving the supreme efforts of the best and largest armies were fought out bitterly in France, as they had been in Russia: but the crowning episode of the year lay in the Balkans, and it is thither we must now proceed.

CHAPTER XXI
THE RECKONING WITH SERBIA

We have seen how Falkenhayn had first of all been drawn to the East in 1915 by the vital need which he recognized of opening through communications between Turkey and the Central Empires and thus relieving the Dardanelles, and how he had been forced to postpone this indispensable operation by the grievous state of the Austrian armies on the Russian front. **H.**, while welcoming the transference of effort to the East, urged the view that Russia should be made an end of once for all, by the use of even larger forces, and even wider movements. Falkenhayn did not agree. As soon as the Russians had been signally defeated and were in full retreat in Poland and Galicia, he returned with eagerness to his original plan. This involved the immediate total destruction of Serbia, and for this purpose the bringing in of Bulgaria upon the side of the Central Powers. During the whole of July, after various earlier efforts, negotiations were conducted at Sofia with King Ferdinand and his Ministers. The Bulgarian Government, always pro-German in their sentiments, were profoundly impressed with the disasters which had overtaken Russia and the vast recoil of all her armies. But the struggle upon the Gallipoli Peninsula dominated their actions. They knew that another great effort to storm the Peninsula and open the way to the fleet was imminent. Until this new battle had been fought, they would not take the plunge. If the Turks in Gallipoli were beaten, and the British Fleet arrived before Constantinople, an attack on Turkey offered them even far greater prizes than could be wrung from Serbia. Moreover, the elimination of Turkey from the European theatre, the opening of the Bulgarian southern frontier to the advance of an Allied army, and the opening of the Black Sea to the British fleet would almost certainly win Roumania and Greece to the Allies' cause, and thus expose Bulgaria to the gravest peril if she was found alone in the Balkans on the wrong side. Therefore Bulgaria, unmoved by the German victories in the east, awaited the issue of the battle in the south.

On August 6 a general attack by all the British, Australian and French forces began upon the Turkish positions, and simultaneously a large new British army descended upon the peninsula at Suvla Bay. The landing of 25,000 men was effected without serious opposition at a point where only a few Turkish gendarmes were watching the coast. The only Turkish troops available were three days' march distant at Bulair. However, owing to the incompetence of the British general commanding the landed force, and an unbelievable series of accidents and blunders, the troops remained upon the beaches and did not attack the high ground in earnest until powerful Turkish forces had actually arrived. The battle was then joined at all points and reached its climax on August 9, when the further advance of the Suvla army was arrested by the Turks; and when the British and Gurkha troops who had actually gained the key position of the Saribair mountain, were blown off the summit by the fire of their own naval artillery. By the 15th the British had been defeated all along the line with a loss of 20,000 men, and Bulgaria decided to join the Central Powers.

On September 6 a Convention was signed at Pless by Falkenhayn, Conrad, and General Gantschev, representative of Bulgaria, by which Germany and Austria-Hungary with six divisions each were to be on the Serbian frontiers ready for operations within thirty days, and Bulgaria with at least four divisions within thirty-five days. As the Bulgarian divisions were double the ordinary infantry strength, these arrangements concentrated against Serbia from three separate quarters the equivalent of at least twenty divisions. The failure of the Austrian offensive in Volhynia made it necessary for four Austrian divisions to be replaced with a like number of Germans. Thus no less than ten German divisions were to be employed. 'The Serbian troops,' says Falkenhayn, 'that were still fit for battle were estimated to number in all 190,000 to 200,000 men.* Our troops available against them were some 330,000 who in the main must have been superior in military value to the Serbians. The latter could hardly be expected to withstand the effects of massed heavy artillery or of trench-mortar batteries.' Such was the storm soon to break upon the violent small unhappy country.

The menacing attitude of Bulgaria riveted Serbian attention, and her military preparations were soon obvious. Great efforts were made by England and France to persuade Serbia to make concessions in Macedonia to Bulgaria which would avert the impending danger. But the Serbians with equal obstinacy and courage rejected these overtures and prepared themselves to meet the onslaught of their hated and deeply injured Balkan neighbour. Serbia began to mass her troops against a Bulgarian invasion from the east, and was altogether unaware of the terrible German thrust which was preparing from the north.

Not only had Falkenhayn to find his ten divisions against Serbia from the Austrian front, but he had also to meet the main offensive of France and England now rapidly approaching in the West. For both these needs he had to withdraw four divisions from the Russian front, including Hindenburg's command. **H.** had been authorized to begin their long-desired offensive through Kovno towards Vilna, and by the first week of September this was in full progress. Animated by Ludendorff, Hindenburg bitterly and fiercely resisted these withdrawals of his troops. Dominated by his local point of view, he fought for every division. His correspondence with Falkenhayn reveals the intensity of the struggle of these two powerful figures.

On August 27 the first German division had been taken from the Mackensen group and ordered to Orsova on the Danube, partly to bring it into the new theatre and partly to expedite Bulgarian decisions. At this time Conrad seems to have been drawn into the **H.** orbit. He supported the Hindenburg requests for the strengthening

---

*i.e. combatants.

of the Kovno-Vilna offensive. Falkenhayn gave a clear answer. 'A reinforcement of the Kovno Group is certainly to be desired, but it is incomparably more important that the Dardanelles should be secured and in addition the iron in Bulgaria struck while it is hot. Consequently the forces which we are able to withdraw from the region of Brest-Litovsk, without slackening our hold on the enemy's throat, must go to the Danube.' During the latter days of August and the early part of September no less than ten divisions were removed from the central and southern sectors of the Eastern front and sent either to the Danube or to meet the oncoming attack in France. These withdrawals were but the preliminary. 'Before very long,' says Falkenhayn, 'the necessity was bound to arise for ten or twelve divisions to be taken from the region of the army group in the north for use in other theatres of war.'

These transferences and the threatened minimizing of the eastern theatre were viewed with stern hostility by **H.** For them at the moment the Vilna offensive was the only object in the world. All their strategic convictions, all the fruits of their preparations, all their chance of winning distinction were equally at stake; and here was Falkenhayn and **O.H.L.** not content with coming over to the East, winning tremendous victories, and thereafter weakening the southern armies, but now actually withdrawing from **H.** the very divisions they were counting on for their promising operation in the north! Repeated warnings were given by Falkenhayn that whatever happened to the Vilna offensive, he meant to have all the troops he wanted to attack Serbia and meet the French. **H.** were bluntly told that they must adapt their plans to this condition. They were to give up two divisions in the middle of September and other forces would constantly be withdrawn from their command after a few days' interval. **H.** replied by counter-demands. They declared themselves in full battle, hopefully advancing on their left and heavily attacked on their right. They claimed in extreme urgency the Xth Corps withdrawn from Mackensen which was assembling at Bialystok for transport to the West. Let them have these for Kovno—even for a fortnight. Falkenhayn refused. The Xth Corps went to France.

On September 19 Falkenhayn informed Hindenburg that the removal of portions of the Twelfth and Eighth armies must begin, and that a division of the Twelfth Army in reserve, the 26th, must go at once. Six more divisions were to follow with all speed. **H.** complained about 'an interference' in their rights. They required these divisions for the capture of Riga, a main feature in their plans. This issue was fought upon the removal of the 26th Division. 'The division,' said Falkenhayn, 'is required for the Serbian front. Not one more day can be allowed.' Even when the 26th Division had been wrenched away, **H.** continued their resistance. They would, they said in a tone of independence, release the troops as soon as possible; but when they could release them, they could not say. They were being heavily attacked themselves. The whole of their plans would miscarry, if they were weakened at a moment when great results hung in the balance. 'I expect,' wrote Hindenburg, 'that I shall succeed in preventing the enemy from breaking through. It is impossible however at the moment to send off any more troops. This can only be done when the attack has been beaten off and after the front has been shortened by the taking of Smorgoni and the bridge-head of Dvinsk.' Falkenhayn replied brutally that the

Vilna offensive was of no consequence. What did it matter whether the line on which **H.** settled for the winter was drawn through Smorgoni or further back? He had to face the great French and British offensive in France and to nourish the all-important attack upon Serbia. 'The demand that your Excellency should transfer the first of these two divisions to the West as soon as it is possible to entrain them from Vilna, must therefore be adhered to.'

Hindenburg refused point-blank. He sent a letter to the Supreme Command challenging the entire past conduct of the campaign by Falkenhayn:

'The fact that further relinquishment of divisions is now meeting with difficulties is due to the plan of campaign favoured in the summer, which was unable to strike a deadly blow at the Russians in spite of the favourable circumstances and my urgent entreaties. I am not blind to the difficulties of the general military situation which have ensued, and if the Russian attacks are beaten off really decisively, I shall relinquish further divisions as soon as it seems possible for me to do so. . . . But I cannot bind myself to a definite time. A premature relinquishment would give rise to a crisis, such as is now being experienced, to my regret, on the Western Front, and in certain circumstances it would mean a catastrophe for the Army Group, as any retiring movement of my troops which are but weak in comparison with the enemy, must lead to very great harm being done to the formations, owing to the unfavourable condition of the terrain. I request that my views should be represented to His Majesty.'

Falkenhayn replied with vigour:

'Much as I regret that Your Excellency should without any cause consider the present moment suited for explanations of events of the past, which are therefore unimportant at the moment, I should not trouble to refute your statements, if they concerned only me personally. But as it amounts to a criticism of orders issued by **O.H.L.**, which, as is well known, have in all important cases met with the previous consent of His Majesty, I am unhappily compelled to do so. Whether Your Excellency agrees with the views of **O.H.L.** does not matter, once a decision has been made by His Majesty. In this case every portion of our forces has to adapt itself unconditionally to **O.H.L.**'

He then proceeded to make a highly controversial and at the same time masterly rejoinder to all the criticisms and insinuations which **H.** had put forward. He reflected acidly upon Hindenburg's operations, in the sense that he had been ready to put up with them so long as they did not obstruct larger possibilities. He concluded:

'I will report to His Majesty the scruples which Your Excellency raises against the withdrawal of the two divisions. I must refuse to bring the remaining points of your telegram to the knowledge of the Emperor, because they only concern past events . . . about which I do not intend in any case, to approach the Supreme War Lord in these grave days.'[48]

The clash was front to front; but the Emperor supported Falkenhayn, and Hindenburg bowed. It was well for his fame that he did so. He was taking a local view and a partisan interest. Had he and Ludendorff sat at the summit, they would have viewed a different scene. He suggests this himself quite simply in his memoirs.

On September 25 the British and French attacks in Artois and Champagne began. Sir John French fell on at Loos with his fifteen divisions and with severe losses stormed forward a mile and a half on a front of seven and a half. The French attack in Champagne, backed by thirty-four divisions, made great progress. Seventeen French divisions committed to the assault drove the remnants of two German divisions back two and a half miles on a front of about fifteen. Both British and French offensives had been prepared by a gunfire, the like of which human beings had never previously delivered or sustained. But once the troops sought to advance beyond the areas pulverized by their batteries, the machine-gun and the rifle asserted their then invincible power. General Joffre had evidently been impressed by the reports of the German break-through of Gorlice-Tarnow. The concentration of French infantry and artillery upon the front of attack was prodigious, and at the outset in the locality it was decisive. But the Germans were not the Russians. There was in fact not the slightest comparison between them. The great French mass instead of irrupting through the pierced German line and flinging back its wounded flanks on either side, found itself confronted with numberless obstinate resistances. On the 26th and 27th it came to a standstill. From that moment its very strength became its weakness. Its mass presented a hideous target to the swiftly-gathering German guns. The crater-fields which its own artillery had prepared became the tomb of tens of thousands of Frenchmen. The Xth German Corps, which had luckily been snatched from Hindenburg 'without one day's delay,' arrived on the scene at the critical moment. The German line, though dinted, was consolidated, and the French crowded together and unable to deploy were shot to pieces. The battle in Champagne was one of the most marked examples of the fallacious valuations of General Joffre and his Headquarters Staff. Even Loos with all its confusion and waste of young troops was a less blameworthy defeat.

By the early days of October both the French and British attacks had been definitely broken. They were only continued—unconsciously, no doubt—to save the faces of the High Command, and to allow the impression of defeat to evaporate in scrambling operations which the world could not follow. Nearly three hundred thousand French and British soldiers had been killed or wounded. The German front was everywhere intact; and not one single division did Falkenhayn remove from the mass he was gathering against Serbia. On the contrary at the height of the battle he even diverted the German Alpine Corps to replace the Austrian divisions who had failed to present themselves upon the Danube. We must consider this triple exercise of will-power, the stripping of **⊢**, the withstanding in the West, and the perfection of the preparations upon the Danube, all simultaneously proceeding, as the culmination of Falkenhayn's command.

All was now ready for Serbia. In the spring and throughout the summer the German Staff Officers had been intently studying the passages of the Danube and the Save. This work, entrusted to the peripatetic Colonel Hentsch, had been thoroughly done. Every battery position, every road, every bivouac, every billet, every water spring, all the islands, all the hills, all the railway possibilities had been examined with meticulous energy and the results woven into a complete texture of Staff knowledge. Four armies were now about to spring from three sides upon that small and fierce people on whom the guilt of Sarajevo had been fastened. One German and one Austro-German army were marching towards the Danube, Belgrade and the Save. The First Bulgarian Army ranged itself to strike towards the historic capital Nish. The Second Bulgarian Army prepared to lap round to the southwards and by severing the railway from Salonica isolate the doomed community from the world and from all forms of succour. The communiqués from the Eastern Front still depicted Mackensen fighting with his Army Group in Poland. Actually he had been for three weeks marshalling three of the four armies which were about to invade Serbia. One of these mornings, I see from the records of the British War Council, I drew the attention of my colleagues to a sentence amid scores of intelligence reports. 'Mackensen is at Temesvar.' It seemed to me, watching with attention from a situation of knowledge, but without executive authority, that the Bulgarian menace which was now so open must be a part of a general design against Serbia, and to clear a road for

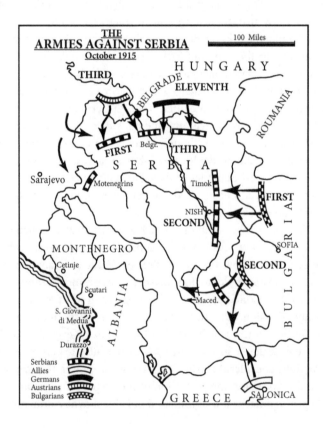

Germany to sustain the Turkish armies at the Dardanelles. Realization came a few days later. On September 20 our Military Attaché with the Serbians mentioned that there was more than the usual movement of troops and trains beyond the rivers, and on the 23rd he reported 'a steady increase' in the German and Austrian forces, beyond the Serbian frontier. On the same day the Bulgarian mobilization was announced. Still no one could tell how much Germany intended to do. Pressure and threats from the north by Austrian and German forces might be a sufficient assistance to a purely Bulgarian attack upon Serbia. Worrying always about the Dardanelles, I naturally credited the Germans with similar preoccupations. The words 'Mackensen is at Temesvar' seemed to glare from the pages and pages of stuff we had to read each day. All doubts were soon to be removed.

Mackensen's preparations were approaching completion. The most capable commanders were placed at his disposal. Gallwitz commanded the German Eleventh, and Kövess the Austro-German Third Army. It will be remembered that the earlier Austrian invasions of Serbia had been launched mainly from Bosnia across the Western frontier. The Austrians had considered the forcing of the Danube, often more than a thousand yards broad, too serious an operation. Potiorek had tried what he thought was an easier way. His experience had led him to remark to his successor at the moment of dismissal: 'If you ever have the chance again, go in by Belgrade.' The Germans were of this opinion too. In the early days of October they marched the Third and Eleventh Armies rapidly southward from the areas where they had been concealed to the selected passages of the Danube and the Save on either side of Belgrade.

Few indeed are the instances in history of a river-line athwart the advance of a superior army proving an effective defence. Mystifying bombardments at many points and an elaborate feint at Orsova baffled the Serbians. Almost to the last they remained in doubt of the actual points of passage, and altogether unwitting of the enormous forces which were rolling upon them. Two of their three small armies, the First and Third, at length faced the Austro-Germans, and their remaining Second Army stood between Nish and the rapidly-assembling Bulgarian First Army. Against the Bulgarian Second Army which to the southward threatened their sole railway-line for reinforcement or retreat, they could muster only detachments and volunteers.

On the 7th October both Teutonic armies began the passage of the rivers. Assisted by large islands, by the overpowering artillery which had opened on the 6th, and by the Austrian monitors, they soon established themselves after heavy fighting and several local repulses on the southern bank. On the 8th they were ferried across in great numbers. Belgrade fell to the Austrians on the 9th, and very large forces were dug in on Serbian soil along a 50-mile front on both sides of the city. The Serbians had placed their oldest men in the trenches and fortified positions from which the crossings were resisted. They now counter-attacked fiercely with both their northern armies. Hard fighting followed; but the weight and power of the Germans across the river grew continually. Mackensen had ordered the advance to begin on the 15th; but Gallwitz, visiting him personally, explained that his horses were not yet across. The general attack was therefore postponed till the 18th. On this day the battle began along the whole front. All day the Serbians held their positions, but on the 19th they were overwhelmed at many points, and by the

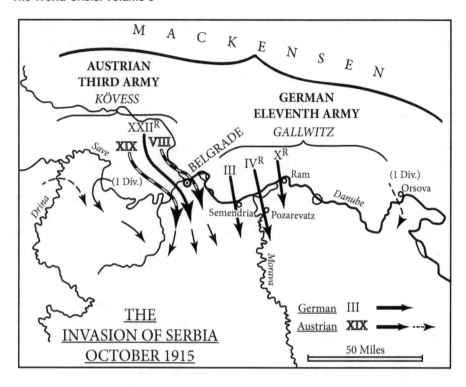

THE
INVASION OF SERBIA
OCTOBER 1915

24th both the Teutonic armies were advancing steadily into the centre of Serbia. It is surprising both that the two bridges across the Danube were not completed till the 21st, and that the invasion could be supplied in the interval entirely by boats. Mackensen had hoped that the Serbians would stand, and be surrounded at their arsenal and military centre of Kraguyevatz, but this temptation they resisted. Burning and blowing up their stores and depots, they continued their retreat to the southward.

They had need to do so. On the 23rd the Bulgarian First Army crashed upon them from the east, and a savage battle between armies whose soldiers hated each other with personal loathing, and the memory of recent bitter wrongs, began. Slowly but surely the fresher and far more numerous Bulgarians prevailed, and the Serbian Second Army retired towards their old capital. Meanwhile the Bulgarian Second Army, driving a weak opposition before it, had already captured Veles and Kumanovo by the 23rd, thus cutting the vital railway-line behind the forlorn people.

These tragic events as they swiftly developed produced emotion in the British Cabinet. Ever since the end of September there had been an intense desire among many of its leading members to save Serbia. Greece was by treaty bound to come to the assistance of her neighbour against a Bulgarian attack. But Greece, torn between the diverging sympathies of King Constantine and the Prime Minister, Venizelos, had no mind to plunge into the storm. The Greco-Serbian agreement had stipulated that the Serbians should assign 150,000 men to defend their southern province, and as these were all engaged against the Germans in the north, it was easy to declare that the *casus fœderis* had not arisen. The British and French Cabinets, animating each other, now saw the means of breaking off the attack upon Gallipoli and using the troops landed at Suvla Bay to stimulate Greek resolution and rescue the Serbs. At the end of September one French and one British division were shipped from the peninsula. After tangled negotiations they were landed at Salonica on October 5 upon the withdrawn invitation of Venizelos and the forthcoming protest of King Constantine. General Sarrail arrived from France to take command in this new theatre.

From the moment the Serbian government had realized the extent of their danger M. Pashitch had been ceaseless in his cries for help. The western Allies must send him 150,000 men or all was certainly lost. At the very least, he urged that the Allies should clear the railway-line and secure the escape of the Serbian army. The politicians then in the ascendant in London were eager to comply; but the General Staffs of Britain and France proved decisively that such an operation was not physically possible. The rolling-stock and capacity of the Salonica railway could not carry an army of such numbers and its supplies into Serbia within six or seven weeks. A single French regiment was for a moment to be sent to Nish and the streets were pathetically decorated to welcome them. Less sentimental counsels soon prevailed, and the western Allies declared they could only move northwards when they had concentrated an adequate force. The Bulgarians who had cut the railway at Veles caused the precipitate retreat of a French detachment which had ventured across the Greek frontier.

At first, during these painful days, the General Staffs had assured their governments that the real relief for Serbia would come from the great offensives of Artois and Champagne. They could not believe that in the face of such a threat, still less during the actual battle, the Germans could find any serious force to attack Serbia. Once the conflict was joined in the west, they were sure everything else would fade into insignificance. When this hope proved visionary, the only course which was considered was the breaking off of all offensive operations at Gallipoli, in order to reinforce Salonica. Whatever this policy might, or might not achieve, it obviously could bring no aid to Serbia in time.

The only chance of preventing the Bulgarians from declaring war was the use of the British fleet and French squadron to force the Dardanelles. The defences of the Straits had not only not been replenished with heavy shells and ammunition, but a large proportion of their mobile armament had been drawn into the fighting on the Gallipoli Peninsula. At any time during September a resolute attack on the forts, and the sweeping or breaking of the mine-fields, offered good prospects of success. The entry of the fleet into the Marmara would have destroyed the communications of the Turkish army in Gallipoli, and would almost inevitably have entailed their surrender. Failure would have meant heavy losses in the old and obsolete ships of which the fleet was solely composed, as well as the deaths of several thousand sailors. In spite of the vehement appeals of Admiral Keyes, Chief of the Naval Staff at the Dardanelles, who actually resigned his position and proceeded to London to plead his cause, the Admiralty would not face the responsibility of ordering the attempt.

I marvelled much in those sad days at the standard of values and sense of proportion which prevailed among our politicians and naval and military authorities. The generals were so confident of breaking the line in France that they gathered masses of cavalry behind the assaulting troops to ride through the huge gaps they expected to open on the hostile front. To sacrifice a quarter of a million men in such an affair seemed to them the highest military wisdom. That was the orthodox doctrine of war; even if it did not succeed, no error or breach of the rules would have been committed. But to lose one hundredth part as many sailors and a dozen old ships, all of which were in any case to be put on the Mother Bank in a few months' time, with the possibility of gaining an inestimable prize—there, was a risk before which the boldest uniformed grey-head stood appalled. The Admiralty and Generals had their way. The fleet continued idle at the Dardanelles. The armies shattered themselves against the German defence in France. The Bulgarians carried an army of 300,000 men to join our enemies; and Serbia as a factor in the war was obliterated. I found it unendurable to remain participant in such crimes against truth and reason.

No hope remained to the Serbian army and government but escape. Nish fell on November 5. The left of the Bulgarian Second Army was now advancing northward from Veles along the railway. At the other extreme an Austrian division invading from Bosnia had approached Vishegrad. The three armies of Mackensen now in one line drove all before them. The Serbian forces pressed together, retreated to the south and west carrying with them Prince Alexander, now become Regent, the civil government, the prostrated Voivode Putnik in a litter, a multitude of women and children and the 24,000 Austrian prisoners—hostages perhaps—they had captured from Potiorek in 1914. By the middle of November they had reached Kosovo Polye, the Field of the Blackbirds, where the earlier agony of their race had been endured. Although the valiant defence of the defile of Kachanik by two Serbian divisions had prevented the Second Bulgarian Army from making a complete encirclement, all chance of cutting a way out to the south was gone. The sole resource was flight in the depth of winter across the mountain tracks of Albania to the Adriatic and to the fleets of the Allies. At Prishtina the women and children were left behind and the remnants of the army, and as it seemed of the nation, ragged, exhausted, almost starving, with their last cartridges, plunged into the savage Albanian defiles, where dwelt a race their equal in fierceness and hunger.

The Germans and Austrians disdained to follow these remnants farther; but the Bulgarians, spurred by racial vengeance, pursued the melting columns like ferocious wolves. After harsh privations and the deaths of thousands from famine and exposure, 150,000 men, half of whom still preserved their military formation, arrived on the sea-coast at the port of San Giovanni di Medua. They were still in possession of 100 guns and of their 24,000 prisoners. Out of 425,000 men comprising the entire manhood of the country, borne on the ration-strength of the Serbian army at the beginning of October, over 100,000 had been killed or wounded. One hundred and sixty thousand more together with 900 guns had been captured by the enemy. The survivors had still a hard pilgrimage before they found sanctuary. San Giovanni di Medua was too near to the Austrian fleet at Pola to serve as a port of embarkation. During the whole of December the Serbians were toiling down the Adriatic coast painfully, and ultimately the survivors were transported to the island of Corfu.

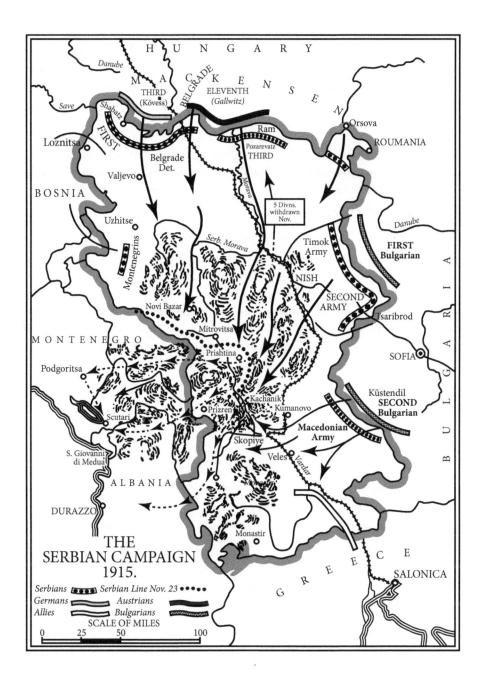

THE
SERBIAN CAMPAIGN
1915.

Serbians ▨▨▨▨ Serbian Line Nov. 23 ●●●●●
Germans ▬▬▬ Austrians ▭▭▭
Allies ▭▭▭ Bulgarians ▨▨▨▨
SCALE OF MILES
0   25   50   100

To celebrate these triumphs King Ferdinand entertained the Kaiser at a banquet in Nish. It was January 18, the 215th anniversary of the coronation of Frederick I as King of Prussia and of the institution of the Order of the Black Eagle. It was the 45th anniversary of the foundation of the German Empire. The guest, the scene and the occasion stirred the romanticism by which King Ferdinand was so often moved. Twice in the hopes of aggrandizement had he staked the Bulgarian Crown and people. Now, sure that victory had been won, he pronounced in the language, pomp and ruthless spirit of the Roman age, the following invocation:

'*Ave Imperator, Caesar et Rex. Vicor et gloriosus es. Nissa antiqua omnes Orientis populi te salutant redemptorem, ferentem oppressis prosperitatem atque salutem.*'
　'Hail Emperor, Caesar and King. Thou art victor and glorious. In ancient Nish all the peoples of the East salute thee, the redeemer, bringing to the oppressed prosperity and salvation.'

But the scroll of Fate was only half-unfolded. A hundred and twenty-five thousand ragged, war-bitten men, the survivors of an army, driven from their native land; homeless men whose families were in the power of their most hated foes, were gathered upon the island of Corfu. There, aided by England and France, they will reform the Serbian army. And upon their bayonets, while Ferdinand sits a dethroned exile, and Bulgaria is forever barred from greatness, the general victory of the Allies will found with a population of nearly twenty million souls, the Kingdom of the Serbs, Croats and Slovenes.

CHAPTER XXII
FALKENHAYN RETURNS TO THE WEST

Christmas had come again and Falkenhayn and Conrad surveyed the results of a crimson year. They had good cause to be thankful. The situation was transformed: Russia was broken, the Eastern Front stood almost everywhere on Russian soil. The whole strategic apparatus of the Russian defences, fortresses, railways and river-lines had passed into German hands. The enormous armies which a year before threatened East Prussia, Silesia and Hungary with invasion, had recoiled in awful slaughter and defeat. Austria, her territory freed, her armies sustained by German interpolations, had been able not only to play her part against Russia, but to ward off with considerable ease the once-dreaded Italian attack. The danger of a hostile Balkan confederacy was at an end. Serbia had been physically destroyed alike as a military factor and as a state. Bulgaria, showing herself convinced of German victory, had become an ally. A road had been opened to Turkey. A train could run from Hamburg to Baghdad across 2,200 miles of the earth's surface all under the control of Germany. The mere prospect of munitions streaming to the Dardanelles and Gallipoli had been sufficient to induce the British to evacuate the Peninsula in the ruin of all their hopes and sacrifice. The powerful force they had sent to the Mediterranean could now be contained by the Bulgarians in front of Salonica. Twenty divisions of the Turkish army released from the struggle upon Gallipoli were now free to threaten Egypt, to turn the tables in Mesopotamia, and to press the Russians in the Caucasus and Galicia. Fifteen British and five French divisions were for more than six months virtually out of action on the one side, and an almost equal reinforcement had been gained by the other. The balance between the opposing forces had been altered in Germany's favour to the extent of nearly 40 divisions or half the army of a first-class power. 'The year 1915,' says the Austrian writer Tschuppik, 'had opened gloomily, but it ended with the spectacle of military successes on a scale such as Europe had not seen even in Napoleon's time. The great change in the situation on the fronts roused a warlike spirit in Austria.'

Meanwhile in the West all the French and British attacks had been repulsed decisively with ghastly loss to the assailants, and 2¼ million Germans seemed able to hold in a deadlock nearly 3½ million Allied enemies. The will-power of the two Western democracies was still undaunted; the military strength of the British Empire still continued to grow steadily; the British command of the seas was still unchallenged; but it was not easy to discern how their purposes could be achieved. Victory seemed as far from their reach as peace from their resolves. Great strategic manœuvres against the Teutonic flanks in the Mediterranean or the Baltic were no longer open to them. There remained only gigantic frontal attacks upon the German fortified lines in France, and even for this many months of preparation must be required. When Falkenhayn contrasted this situation with the plight of Germany and Austria after the battles of the Marne and Lemberg, he had reason to be proud of his fifteen months' supreme command.

Moreover, in the personal sphere his position had been entirely restored. He had reasserted his authority over **H.** He had matched their tactical victory of Tannenberg with the far greater strategic consequences of Gorlice-Tarnow. His successes in the south-east against Serbia, rallying Bulgaria and frustrating the enterprise against the Dardanelles, had more than met the political requirements of the German Chancellor and Foreign Office. Bethmann-Hollweg had been detached from Hindenburg, and **H.** were in eclipse. The power to take the great point of view no longer lay with them. They were condemned to local operations against a frozen Russia, already in German opinion adjudged defeated. Their suggestions in the field of general war direction could now be regarded with the smile of superior achievement and knowledge, as well as with the hard stare of superior authority. They might brood on this in their winter quarters at Kovno. They might complain that the great opportunity to finish with Russia once and for all in 1915 had been lost. But Falkenhayn was lord of the ascendant. He alone held the baton and wore the laurel.

However, Falkenhayn rated his good fortune and services lower than did his Imperial Master, his own staff or the German people and their allies. He had been drawn to the East against his will. He had prospered beyond his hopes. He had been forced to quit the decisive theatre. He had been over-ruled into success. He was 'vainqueur malgré lui.' The brilliant operations which had restored the Teutonic cause were to his eye only of a secondary and even a meretricious character. As he had always said, they could never produce final results. The Russian army had escaped, as he had always predicted, that general encirclement at which Hindenburg would have aimed. Russia was still a first-class military factor. Her munitions crisis was passing, her front was everywhere maintained, and behind it lay indefinite distance and unlimited man-power. The Grand Duke dismissed, Warsaw taken, Serbia crushed, Bulgaria rallied, the Dardanelles expedition wrecked, and the British and French repulsed in Artois and Champagne—all these together could not compare in his mind with a successful German offensive in the West. There alone, in his conception, lay the hope of victory. Thither, now that he had regained his authority, would he return with all his strength. Unchanged in his convictions alike by his disasters at Ypres and on the Yser in 1914, or by his victories in the east and south-east in 1915, Falkenhayn now without apparent hesitation resolved upon a grand attack in France.

Those profound misunderstandings of the character of the war and misjudgments of its moral and technical factors, which led this soldier of genius but convention into so fatal an error, deserve closer examination. Between armies of anything like equal fibre an offensive requires superior numbers. Germany in 1916 could not hope to marshal superior numbers. On the contrary, she could never exceed in the West two-thirds of the forces of the Allies. Even with moderately superior numbers the strength of the defensive was at this time invincible. The French had found in Champagne that no massing of divisions and guns, no resources of valour, training or preparation could prevail. Even two

German divisions, when attacked by nearly twenty French, had resisted long enough for reinforcements to be brought to prevent the threatened breach. Falkenhayn had seen the magnitude of their efforts and of their failure, yet he was unchanged in his view. German troops and German methods would succeed where others had failed, and succeed even in the teeth of equal weapons and more numerous armies. He woefully underrated the morale and fighting qualities of his French and British opponents. He imagined political reactions in Paris and London as the result of a German onslaught, almost the reverse of those which were in fact produced. He ignored the unfavourable impression which the failure of Germany to gain complete success would produce upon an increasingly adverse world. He does not seem to have appreciated how easily even a most successful attack would be brought to a standstill after a few miles, nor that those who had lost ground would nevertheless be the victors if the battle were prolonged for several weeks. Anything less than absolute victory would count as a failure for Germany; but as long as the French and British fronts remained coherent the Allies would be the victors. Only one result, and that the most difficult, could achieve his purpose. A hundred variations would meet the modest requirements of his antagonists.

Such an adventure in the West even by itself was forlorn. But what opportunities and what dangers was he not leaving behind him in the East! The first and immediate opportunity was to bring Roumania into the German system. The collapse of the Allies at the Dardanelles, the accession of Bulgaria, the grisly fate of Serbia, and above all the weakness of Russia and the retreat or her armies from Galicia, left Roumania in a posture of almost intolerable isolation. Very little more pressure was required to compel from her the decision to which she had been formerly pledged, and on the verge of which she had trembled so long. To gain Roumania would, apart from distracted Greece, consolidate the whole of the Balkan Peninsula. It would add her army of twenty divisions to the forces against which Russia was contending in so much distress. It would place large resources of corn and oil at the disposal of the Central Powers. The very enterprise which above all others Germany should undertake in the south-east would at a single stroke draw in Roumania and afford her a fruitful and important field of action. The advance by German and Austrian troops into the Ukraine with Odessa as its main objective would open immense feeding-grounds to the blockaded Central Empires, would convert the Black Sea into a German lake, and with some German stiffening might carry the Turkish armies of the Caucasus almost to the oil-fields and broad waters of the Caspian basin. Germany, cut from the oceans by the British Navy, would regain in the vast continental spaces the means of continued life and power. Persia, Afghanistan and India would all in succession be violently excited by the rumour and fame of distant but steadily approaching legions. Great Britain, whose war-direction had now sunk to its lowest ebb, would be thrown on the defensive throughout the East and forced to divert to the plains and frontiers of India divisions now preparing for the fields of France. Nor were these great results to be achieved only by the employment of numerous forces. A dozen German divisions, far less than were to be consumed in a Western offensive, would have been sufficient to animate and guide the whole of the eastward march of Austrian, Turkish and Roumanian armies.

Meanwhile Hindenburg in the north would pin the Russians to the desperate defence of their remaining railways.

But Falkenhayn cared for none of these things. He had selected as his scene of the offensive perhaps the strongest point in the French front. The rugged, hilly, fortified salient, steel-tipped by the fortress of Verdun, was to be his battle-ground. It offered no line of advance to Paris; it was in fact the sector most remote from the capital. It struck at no joint between the British and French armies. A successful German advance of even 50 miles would drive the Allies back upon no vital communications. Even if the famous stronghold fell, and the vigorous field armies by which it would certainly be defended were forced to retreat so great a distance, they would only have shortened their fighting front and would still have 150 miles between them and the steps of Notre Dame.* Why then did this accomplished soldier, almost certainly the ablest brain which Germany employed in the whole war, plunge into courses of such surprising apparent perversity?

He had a plan of striking originality. Nothing like it has been found in the operations of any army in the Great War. Nothing like it was possible with the weapons of former wars. It was founded upon Falkenhayn's appreciation of French psychology and German artillery. He believed that the French regarded Verdun with sentiments which had no relation to material facts. Verdun was the historical scene of the triumph of the Gaul over the Teuton. It was regarded throughout France as the corner-stone in the French rampart against Germany. To preserve Verdun the French would, as Falkenhayn judged, make exertions which would exhaust their strength. Verdun would become the anvil upon which the remaining force of the French army would be pulverized in successive relays by the German heavy howitzers. They would be bled white; their hearts would be broken; honour would compel them to defend positions which a cool view of war would have yielded at a certain price. The brave would be slain, and Paris, accepting defeat, would sue for peace.

Here, be it observed, was no turning movement such as **HL** excelled in, nor any 'breaking through' like Gorlice-Tarnow. To force the French army to sacrifice itself in detail upon this grim altar was Falkenhayn's theme. He judged the French pride rightly. In the event they were to immolate nearly 400,000 men, the flower of 100 divisions, at Verdun. Actually the German attackers from the open field were to suffer less than the defenders of perhaps the strongest fortress-position in the world. In all the larger aspects he was wrong. He misjudged the heroic constancy of France and the stubborn fortitude of that old nation. And meanwhile he left behind him in the East not only lost opportunities but living perils. Russia was recovering her strength. A steady stream of munitions which the world had manufactured upon the authority of 700 millions of British wealth was now flowing towards Russia. All the year the armies of the Eastern Front might sway to and fro in indecisive warfare, but the Russian giant had still one mighty blow to strike.

---

*In France all distances are measured from these steps.

Another grave and undermining weakness lay in the conduct of Austria. The victories of 1915 on the Eastern Front, though won by German troops and skill, had raised the pride and self-confidence of **A.O.K.** Conrad felt himself a conqueror, at least by proxy. Had not his eye discerned the true point of attack on the Russian front; had not he rightly conceived its character? Relieved from immediate danger, in possession once again of the whole of Galicia, cheered by the prospects of a general victory, Conrad and the military circles over which he presided now assumed dominating power in the Dual Monarchy, and felt in a position to assert their independent judgment against their German ally. In their rejoicings over the campaign against Serbia there had mingled a strong strain of irritation. This longed-for event had in the end been a German achievement. They had felt themselves 'patronized' as well as commanded by **O.H.L.** In dark days, with the Russian bayonets bristling along the crests of the Carpathians, submission had been inevitable. Now that the tide had turned, their self-esteem mounted rapidly. An increasing tension developed between Falkenhayn and Conrad.

Personal friction was aggravated by diverging aims. Falkenhayn wished to gather the largest possible number of German divisions for the attack upon Verdun, and for this purpose he required Austria to exert herself continuously against Russia. Since he was going to the West, Conrad should throw his weight to the East, occupy the Russians and release a maximum of German troops. Conrad's ideas and Austrian inclinations were turned in the opposite direction. Their hatred of Italy was intense. Above all these things they desired to punish this 'perfidious' pirate nation. The Austrian troops themselves shared this mood. They understood the quarrel with the Italians; they always fought with keener spirit against them than against the Russians. A fierce offensive in Tirol was their heart's desire; and for this Conrad had a plan.

Falkenhayn deprecated this offensive. He was stiffly resisted. In order to frustrate it, he demanded the Austrian heavy howitzers for his attack on Verdun. He was refused. The most he could obtain from Conrad was a solemn undertaking that the Eastern Front should not be endangered by withdrawals for the campaign against Italy. This promise was not kept. While Russia gathered herself for a culminating effort, Austria steadily denuded her Eastern armies, and scraped every division and every gun to wreak vengeance against Italy in Tirol.

For these new excursions Conrad prepared himself by a merry event. He had long been a widower. His mother having died, he felt free to re-marry. When the news of his intention was brought to the Emperor, Francis Joseph manifested marked disapprobation. He deemed matrimonial adventures incongruous in a Chief of Staff in full crisis of war. His prejudices, unreasonable as they may have been, were shared by the Austro-Hungarian army and nation; and when Conrad's bride appeared in due course to do the social honours of the Headquarters at Teschen, even in that interlude of success, ungracious criticisms were rife. Conrad's popularity with the nation to whose service he was devoted was fatally affected. He was no longer in a position to sustain the renewal of defeat. There was a feeling that for great commanders Armageddon ought to be an all-sufficing occupation.

CHAPTER XXIII
BRUSILOV'S OFFENSIVE

The disasters which had befallen the Allies in every field during 1915 had forced them to a closer unity and more intimate consultation. Inter-allied conferences from henceforward began to play a prominent part. Intense effort was made to survey the war as a whole and to concert joint and simultaneous plans. There was at this time a strong reaction against what were termed 'side-shows.' For 1916 the supreme exertions were to be concentrated against the German fortified lines in the West. France and England were to assault together in the summer astride of the Somme, and Italy and Russia were to make great offensives at the same time. Thus on every front the Central Empires would be assailed.

Falkenhayn's attack upon Verdun on February 21 disturbed these elaborate preparations. It was necessary for the French to carry a whole army from their northern sector to Verdun; and the gap had to be filled by an extension of the British front. It has therefore been argued by the Falkenhayn school in every army that his irruption and seizure of initiative in the decisive theatre was thus vindicated. No doubt from the German standpoint this result was in itself good. But much easier and cheaper methods of deranging the impending Anglo-French offensive were to hand. If Falkenhayn had wished to pursue as the main feature of 1915 a far-reaching campaign in the East, he could evidently have minimized his dangers in the West by making the same kind of retirement in April, May or June, 1916, as Hindenburg and Ludendorff did when they were in control at the beginning of 1917. What was the use of all this French country which had been acquired so haphazard in the flux of the first invasion, if it were not to be sacrificed or sold back to its owners for a sufficient price in time or blood? The suggestion that, but for Falkenhayn's attack on Verdun and the consequent weakening of the summer thrust by the Allies along the Somme, the German Front in France must have been broken, is not one which can be accepted.

As the winter grudgingly withdrew the gigantic plans which both sides had evolved came into action. The Russians indeed, both in December and March, made heavy bloody and fruitless efforts with their northern armies. Their March attack near Lake Narotch seemed to be timed to catch the thaw, which at this season made the ground most painful to the infantry in assault and the roads impassable to the artillery and supplies in pursuit. The Narotch offensive, in which eighteen Russian divisions were engaged and where new, abundant supplies of shell and heavy shells were used, was repulsed by the Tenth Army under Eichhorn with a loss of upwards of 70,000 men.

The surprise cannonade of Verdun reverberated throughout the warring world, and from every theatre all eyes were turned upon the Homeric combats which raged round

Douaumont and Thiaumont and '304-metre hill.' The British hastened by every means the dispatch to France of all the 'Kitchener' armies for the forthcoming offensive on the Somme. It was expected that by the middle of June Sir Douglas Haig would have nearly fifty divisions, representing the fighting force of an army of two million men, at his disposal in France and Flanders. The Russians in that emulation of comradeship which was the characteristic of the Czar's armies concerted a new enormous onslaught. Their main attack, to which twenty-six divisions were assigned, was mounted on a 25-mile front to the north and south of the village of Krevo in the neighbourhood of Molodetchno. In order to hold their enemies upon the rest of the line and prevent the transference of reinforcements to the threatened sector, the High Command of the South-West Front was directed to prepare contributory offensives. General Ivanov had passed from the scene. He had been appointed to the 'Council of Empire'—an honorific method of compulsory and final retirement from executive authority. In his place sat General Brusilov, whom the reader will remember as the leader of the southernmost Russian Army in the battle of Lemberg now nearly two years gone by. Hitherto Brusilov, having always fought against Austrians, had borne all the tests of war. He will certainly go down in history as an officer of exceptional energy and comprehension. He was fortunate in having at the head of his four armies commanders of proved and real merit; Kaledin, Sakharov, Shcherbachev and Lechitski. All these men were fully abreast of the realities of modern war and accustomed to direct large operations. The South-West Front accordingly set itself to study its subsidiary role.

For nearly five months the Teutonic activities in the East had been in suspense. Apart from the two ill-starred Russian attacks a very tranquil form of trench warfare with, as was remarked, 'scarcely 100 to 150 casualties a day,' had smouldered from the Baltic to the Roumanian boundary. The breathing-space had been precious to Russia. Her armies had been refitted and replenished after the hideous retreat from the Polish Salient. The crisis of munitions was broken. From now onwards ammunition, guns, and above all rifles, were arriving in a growing stream. Our observer, General Knox, notes that nearly 1,200,000 rifles from the United States, from France, from Italy and Japan had reinforced the national production now expanded to 100,000 a month. Meanwhile the ranks had been refilled and large numbers of unarmed men stood behind every formation ready to relieve in turn the fighters of their rifles and their duties. The Russians thus contemplated resuming aggressive warfare upon the largest scale and throwing their whole front into full activity by about the middle of June. This general renewed onset from the East was to synchronize with the opening of the offensive of the western Allies upon the Somme. Of all this formidable recrudescence Falkenhayn and **O.H.L.** were unconscious.

Events were to precipitate the Russian attack. The drama of Verdun seemed to require from every ally of France competing sacrifices. But now on May 15 Conrad re-entered the scene. He was triumphant after his borrowed victories in Galicia. For long weeks he had been pining for the snows to melt, and open the hated Italy to his new offensive. We have seen how severely Falkenhayn had deprecated this diversion. The separation of the two Commanders was final. In the mountains of the Trentino, across almost the same ground where British and French divisions were to stand two years later, Conrad fell upon the Italians with superior forces and all the best Austrian artillery, of which the Austrian front against Russia had been denuded. He made immediately serious headway in the general direction of Verona. Italy raised the alarm. The King of Italy telegraphed personally to the Czar. The Stavka was moved to ask Brusilov whether he could do anything to take the pressure off the harassed ally. Nothing must of course prejudice the 'set-piece' attack impending near Krevo; but surely some forward movement was possible which would prevent further withdrawals of Austrian troops from Galicia to the Trentino? Brusilov replied that his armies could just as well make such a demonstration at the beginning of June as at the appointed time three weeks later, when they were to have conformed to the main Krevo battle scheme. Brusilov was authorized to strike for what he was worth; it being understood that only limited results could be expected.

It was this very derangement of the time-table that produced the greatest Russian victory of the war. By every maxim of military prudence the Stavka committed an error when they compromised their prospects in the battle planned around Krevo by loosing prematurely the offensives of their four south-western Armies. Yet it was this element of what is often called 'lack of clear thinking,' which imparted to Brusilov's attack the priceless quality of SURPRISE. Moreover, Brusilov's plan was well made. All the four Armies were to be launched at once. They were to attack without elaborate, noticeable preparation. A brief bombardment—only a single day, into which the ammunition of a whole fortnight's fighting was packed—was to be followed by a general incontinent walk forward of all the Russian forces along a line of nearly 200 miles. June 4 was fixed as the date; and the haste of the decision guarded its secret.

At the signal this broad though shallow battle burst upon the unsuspecting Austrians. Conrad, his gaze directed upon Verona, learned that all his Eastern Armies were ablaze. The next day the Russian infantry advanced. On the right Kaledin carried all the opposing trenches, progressing 10 miles on a front of thirty. On the left Lechitski was completely victorious. The successes of the two centre armies were less sensational; but in the main the Austrian troops either fled or eagerly surrendered in great numbers to the enemy. Bohemian regiments virtually fraternized with their fellow-Slavs. The resistance of the Austro-Hungarian Armies was broken upon the entire front and a gulf of 195 miles yawned in the Eastern defence of the Central Powers. Brusilov's contributory attack, launched prematurely and unrelated, had achieved results far beyond anything dreamt of for the great Russian 'set-piece' at Krevo. The Stavki showed itself capable of profiting by the gifts of fortune, and discarding all their long-cherished plans for the campaign, resolved to back the new success with every man and gun their railways could carry to the south. This transference of forces, hampered only by the meagre railways, was in full progress from the 9th or 10th June onwards. Meanwhile Brusilov was advancing. In the month that followed, the armies of Nicholas II, which had hitherto suffered unexampled miseries with patient fortitude, whom their conquerors had almost dismissed from their calculations, captured above 350,000 prisoners, nearly 400 guns, 1,300 machine-guns, and regained a tract of debatable ground 200 miles wide and in places nearly 60 miles in depth.

These disconcerting tidings reached Falkenhayn at the most awkward of moments. His attacks on Verdun had subsided into a prolonged concentrated struggle in the crater-fields around the fortress. Each side crammed new divisions into the limited arena of the death-grapple, and fed their guns with unstinted shells. The Germans had performed prodigies. Douaumont and Thiaumont and Vaux were in their hands. The possession of '304-metre hill' was disputed with blood and assertions. But the world sustained only one impression, namely that the French held Verdun; and that impression was grievous to the German cause. For over three months past there had been no question of an attack which could be broken off at pleasure. The prestige of the German army was engaged. The reputations of Falkenhayn, of **O.H.L.**, and indeed of the unlucky Heir to the Throne, were deeply involved. To gain some definite, indisputable success on this deliberately challenged battle-ground had become militarily and personally indispensable.

Meanwhile a hundred miles to the north all the new British Army, 30 or 40 divisions of them, every man a volunteer, with powerful French forces on their right, were obviously about to make their greatest attack in measureless force. The whole region before the German Somme front was lined with batteries; and air reconnaissance showed the enormous accumulation of munitions and the close-up camps of nearly a million men. This storm was about to burst. Falkenhayn had gone willingly—wilfully—to the West, and thus had he fared there.

Neither the German supreme commander nor his staff was unequal to the occasion. They took the decisions imposed upon them by events with cool and refined judgment. They yielded up their hopes of Verdun. They faced the approaching explosion on the Somme. They resolved to restore the Eastern Front.

Wherever in its turbulent advance the Russian waves had encountered German troops, they had swerved as from a rock. Bothmer with the Südarmee, its one German division stiffening nine Austrian, held his ground or receded slowly. Linsingen, opposite the extreme right of the Russian attack, covering Kovel and the important railways running back to Kholm and Ivangorod, maintained a stubborn posture. Now from every side Germans must be brought to regather the Austrian hosts and re-form the front. **H.** must send three divisions, two more must be scraped from local reserves; four must come from France at the very moment when they were most needed there. As for Conrad, caught in the act of having improperly and unfairly cast away the front which Germany had re-established for him, taken red-handed in the midst of an unwarrantable disconnected Trentino offensive, he must without compunction be brought under discipline. No more could the pretensions which **A.O.K.** had indulged after 1915 be tolerated. Unity of command was the penalty which **O.H.L.** exacted in return for their renewed valiant aid. Conrad's Italian offensive was immediately suppressed. Austrian divisions and Austrian artillery must recross the breadth of the Monarchy and help to stem the Russian flood. Brusilov's great battle now turned upon whether the Germans could arrive to succour Austria at a greater rate than Russians from the North could sustain him. Here the Russian railways showed their weakness. Moreover, the very quality of being launched on the spur of the moment which had favoured Brusilov's offensive, now deprived it of nourishment. There was no deeply-banked weight behind his attack. By the middle of

July the Teutonic Front was again continuous. Hard fighting with varying results burned all along the southern line, but it had once again become unbreakable.

Moreover, the great event had happened in France. On July 1 14 British and 5 French divisions with as many more in near reserve had begun the battle of the Somme. Although London and Paris were deluded or consoled by moderate captures of ground and prisoners, the general battle of the first day, never afterwards renewed on such a scale, was an unmistakable German victory. The French losses were not excessive for the results gained; but the British Army, the flower of the nation, was mowed down by the German machine-guns; and on the night of July 1 Sir Douglas Haig had to recognize his repulse at the cost of nearly 60,000 men. The Somme battle now developed into an inconceivably bitter and bloody struggle of divisions and corps, representing nations rather than armies, in pulverized fields and villages. It became to the German Staff a hideous preoccupation; but no longer a violent crisis. However, as it continued, the persistency with which regardless of losses the new British armies pressed forward over scores of thousands of corpses, and their vigour in the conflict began gradually to equalize the conditions. The German losses, at first disproportionately small, swelled savagely. All through July, all through August, through September the deadly duel continued. In October it spread from the Somme to the Scarpe; and even at the end of November, when the full rigours of winter in Picardy were added to the most intense horrors of war, Sir Douglas Haig was still possessed of ardent and stubborn divisions with which to strike new blows. The German losses now affected not only the man-power of the State, but the quality of the army. Never again, by the testimony of many of their own regimental histories, did they fight as they fought on the Somme.

Up till this moment Falkenhayn had survived the consequences of his decisions and the malicious strokes of fortune. But his mortal blow was now to come. So far the German people, though sorely tried and perplexed, had been up-buoyed by the reconstitution of the Eastern Front and the arrest of the British and French upon the Somme. So far **O.H.L.** could represent that 'all was proceeding according to plan.' But now Germany received a shock for which, though it had long been threatened, she was wholly unprepared. On August 27 Roumania declared war.

Throughout the winter of 1915 and far on into the summer of 1916, Hindenburg and Ludendorff had been marooned at Kovno. They disposed of four armies. Large local battles had been fought upon their front; but they were outside the stream of events. The World War had left them in a martial solitude. All their efforts to procure new forces for the East had been fruitless. They had watched with foreboding and disapproval Falkenhayn gathering his forces against Verdun, and Conrad gleaning the Eastern Front for the sake of the Trentino. Shrunken in authority, eclipsed by the brilliant episodes of 1915, they still sang their same old song, 'You should never go back to the West, till you have finished with Russia. Russia is only scotched, not slain. You could have finished her last year, if you had only allowed us to make the great encirclement by the North.' But while the dominating episodes of Verdun and the Somme filled all minds, nobody at the Supreme Headquarters paid much attention to **H.L.**

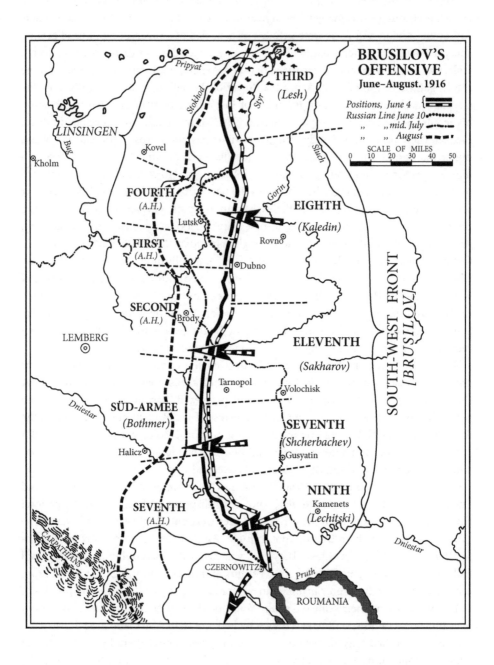

BRUSILOV'S
OFFENSIVE
June–August. 1916

Positions, June 4
Russian Line June 10
„ „ mid. July
„ „ August

SCALE OF MILES
0 10 20 30 40 50

Brusilov's victory had startled German military opinion. No one had believed that such an event could happen. No doubt **O.H.L.** was dealing deftly with the emergency. Still, there must have been serious miscalculation somewhere. Perhaps after all these Eastern Generals, the men of Tannenberg, were right when they cried repeatedly, 'Finish with Russia.'

The entry of Roumania as a German foe opened all men's eyes. Here was a small country desperately anxious to find the winning side, which in the third year of the war, even in the face of the Serbian Reckoning, now staked its all upon the ultimate victory of France, Russia and England. Less than a year had passed since Bulgaria had expressed in arms the contrary opinion. What had happened in the nine months to make so great a difference in German military credit? The battles, on the whole, had gone well. The public was saturated with tales of captured prisoners, cannon and territory; yet Roumania clearly thought that Germany was going to lose the war. The German armies had fulfilled every task set them. Someone had set them the wrong tasks. And thus there fell upon Falkenhayn a cataract of instructed or half-instructed displeasure. A tremor almost of panic swept the governing circles. The Crown Prince had expressed his views more than a year ago. They had certainly not been altered by the slaughters before Verdun, the responsibility for which had been unjustly thrown upon him. The Kaiser must have gone through great stresses to cast aside the accomplished, masterly Falkenhayn, the man who had retrieved the Marne and Lemberg. It was an awe-stirring act of state. Nevertheless, borne forward upon a tide of fierce opinion, Wilhelm II took the right decision.

On August 28 Hindenburg and Ludendorff were summoned to Berlin. That night, the chief of the Imperial Military Cabinet informed Falkenhayn that the Kaiser had decided to seek independent military advice. The Kaiser's letter to Falkenhayn tells its own tale.

August 28th, 1916.

The Chief of my Military Cabinet has informed me that you feel obliged to regard it as a sign of mistrust, to which you cannot submit, that I should consult F.-M. Hindenburg as to the present situation. You have also given expression to this standpoint in regard to myself in this evening's conversation. I can understand this from a theoretical point of view, as it is formally consistent with the position of trust of the Chief of the General Staff; I, however, as the Supreme Commander, to whom ultimately the Chief of the General Staff is himself subordinate, must claim to hear, when and as often as it seems right to me, the views of other high commanders in whom I have particular confidence, especially in so serious a situation as the present. But since I must fear that a constant source of dissension and friction is inherent in this conception of mine, I cannot, to my deepest regret, go against your wish to be relieved of your appointment. Meanwhile I thank you with a much-moved heart for all that you have accomplished in these two years of war, and I request you, until I have finally decided upon your successor, to continue your service. It will also be my care that your wish to find appropriate employment at the front shall be fulfilled.

Your well-disposed and grateful King

WILHELM.[49]

Thus did the 'Easterners' win the last round of their long duel. **HL** absorbed **O.H.L.** The massive figure of the aged Field-Marshal occupied the supreme military seat. At his side as vice-gerent, all-grasping, all-using, tireless and hazard-loving, General Ludendorff seized the control of Germany's destiny. Hoffmann would be left in the East. For the East indeed, no better choice could have been made. Yet now that we know so much that was hidden, it seems that a great triumvirate was broken when that wise mind was separated from Ludendorff's force and Hindenburg's prestige. Falkenhayn was sent against Roumania.

All through the autumn the Stavka steadily backed Brusilov. As the Germans gradually arrived upon the broken front, the Russian attacks became increasingly costly and barren. Nevertheless, they were continued with the ruthless prodigality of new hope. Their Russian operations were broadened by new offensive battles upon the Northern wing of the original attack. Heavy and bloody fighting raged along the Stokhod, throughout July, August and September. The Russian generals strove to make flesh and blood achieve the purposes of artillery. Wire entanglements, which there were no shells to cut, were traversed upon the heaps of dead which the German machine-guns piled upon them. This profusion in the commanders was equalled by the devotion of their troops. The Russian effort persisted in loyal accord with the British battles on the Somme and the Scarpe. The waste of human life in these unnoticed fields was scarcely exceeded in any period of the war. Brusilov's actual offensive had, up till the time when the Front was stabilized, cost him 350,000 casualties. Against this, he might set his equal number of Austrian prisoners, and probably an additional quarter of a million enemy killed and wounded. But the whole campaign in the Southern theatre, following in the wake of his offensive, involved Russian losses which approached a million. Against these there were no proportionate German casualties. Nevertheless, such was the indomitable vigour of the Russian operations in these months, that the German and Austrian forces in the East were raised under constant pressure from 1,300 to 1,800 battalions, an increase of 530 battalions, with all other arms in like proportion, while the German army in the West met the Anglo-French attacks at a uniform strength of approximately 1,300 battalions. This was the last effective military operation undertaken by the armies of the Czar.

The rest of the year witnessed the second of the great German recoveries. Although not on the same vast scale as after Lemberg and the Marne, the paroxysm of German war-energy manifested at the end of 1916 astounded the Allies. London and Paris had been led to believe that the Germans were in extreme distress upon the Somme, that Austria had been mortally stricken by Brusilov, and that the Roumanian declaration was the beginning of the end. Instead they were to endure, before the end of 1917, the total destruction of their small new ally, the final collapse of Russia, and the rout of Italy at Caporetto.

Although the preliminary arrangements to cope with Roumania had been foreseen and prepared by Falkenhayn—were in fact executed by him in person—the credit of that act of retribution was naturally ascribed to the new commanders. I have, in an earlier volume, described in some detail the campaign which overran Roumania, destroyed or scattered her armies, occupied her capital, and drove the remnants of the Roumanian state to shelter and to starve through a cruel winter within the Russian lines in Bessarabia. The swift ruin of Roumania produced almost the same consternation among the Allies as her arrival in the field had created in Berlin. This little country seemed to have been quite fruitlessly consumed. Indeed the only result of her immolation was a most inconvenient extension of the Russian front by more than 400 miles, and the diversion of nearly twenty Russian divisions. Bucharest fell on December 6, and the Somme battle subsided in the frost and sleet of December.

* * * * *

The time was now come for the Emperor Francis Joseph to die. He had witnessed with frigid satisfaction the vast recoil of Russia in 1915. The dismissal of the Grand Duke Nicholas from the command of the Russian armies had seemed to him a signal of Teutonic victory more indubitable even than the fall of Warsaw. He had followed with measured approval the over-ripe, but at last condign chastisement of Serbia. He had welcomed the Kaiser on his way to the celebrations of that joyous event. All was then a feast of mutual congratulation. Yet intimate observers had noticed that the high spirits of both potentates had seemed rather forced, and Baron Margutti, to whose records we are indebted, felt at the time that both really wanted peace. They looked upon victory as the means of gaining peace, not, like their generals, as the means of further victories. They had pre-occupations not shared by their servants. Nations may fall and rise again; but dynasties in modern times can only stand or fall. Still, at the beginning of 1916 the sun shone so brightly on the bristling bayonets of the Central Empires that the general staffs were everywhere in the ascendant. Falkenhayn, it was said, had new wonders to produce, and Conrad too, as we have seen, had his plans.

The Emperor lived long enough to endure the news of Brusilov's offensive, to receive the Roumanian declaration of War which he had so long dreaded, to see Falkenhayn, the glittering deliverer of the spring, dismissed by the Kaiser in the autumn. The old man's inveterate pessimism and deeply-ingrained expectation of misfortune returned with doubled force. How often had he not seen these false dawns before? True, the Prussian military flame seemed unquenchable, and Roumania was already suffering the penalty of her faithlessness. But the clouds had gathered again. The summer of success had been bright, but also brief. Evidently, as he had always been convinced, and so often declared, the road was to be uphill to the very end. The end had now come for him.

Since the War began, he had scarcely been seen in public. He refused all holidays and ploughed methodically through his daily routine at Schönbrunn. The care of the Court Chamberlain had forbidden the Park before the Imperial windows to the public. It was widely rumoured that the Emperor was already dead, and was being preserved as a fetish and a symbol. Unpleasant details about the social and economic life of his Peoples were

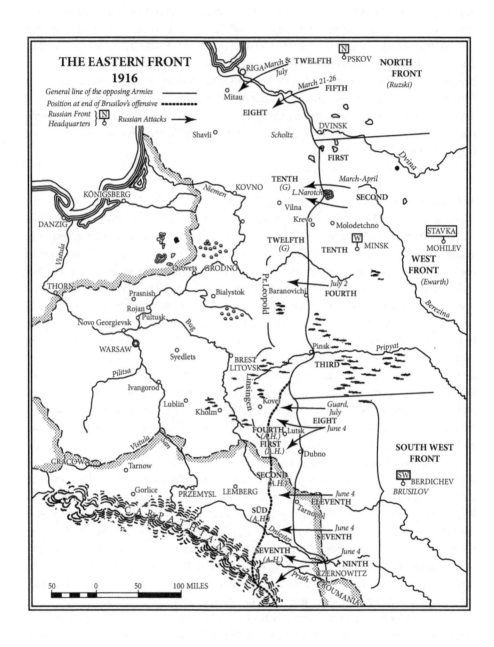

THE EASTERN FRONT
1916

General line of the opposing Armies ——————
Position at end of Brusilov's offensive ••••••••••
Russian Front } [N]
Headquarters } → *Russian Attacks*

sedulously kept from him: but his immense experience enabled him to understand better than his courtiers or his generals how grave the food-shortage and popular discontents had become; and when his Prime Minister, Count Stürgkh, was pistolled to death by the son of the leader of the Democratic Party, Francis Joseph formed a perfectly clear resolve to make peace as soon as possible. He determined to make peace by any means at latest in the spring of 1917. As a first step he replaced his murdered minister by a politician of the Left, Koerber, a man who was honoured by the hungry millions, and distrusted by the well-fed tens of thousands. This was his last contribution to the affairs of the Austro-Hungarian Monarchy.

Bronchitis at 85 is always serious. The Emperor coughed much and passed bad nights. Nevertheless, the dawn of November 20th saw him already seated in his old blue uniform at his writing-desk. It was the practice to send him three portfolios a day. The first was punctually discharged. Before the second was completed his condition of weakness and fever was such that his granddaughter brought him a special blessing from the Pope and persuaded him to receive the sacraments. Four chickens were made into a broth for him at noon. He could not eat it. But the midday files were duly despatched to the Departments. In the afternoon the doctors succeeded in inducing him to go to bed. He rose from his table, but had to be supported to the neighbouring room. The immense fatigue of years of care overwhelmed him. Sleep and death drew quickly near. With an effort he said to his valet, 'Call me at seven. I am behindhand with my work,' and sank almost immediately into coma. The Departments inquired about the evening portfolio. The aide-de-camp on duty replied that it would not be delivered that night. A few hours later, the sixty-six years' reign of Francis Joseph was completed. He died in harness.

Although the War weighed oppressively upon Vienna, the funeral of the departed ruler was magnificent. The populace, sorely-tried, silent, helpless, hungry, understood that a long chapter in the history of Central Europe had closed. New pages must be turned; nay, a new volume must open. The aged Count Paar would not see this volume. 'I died yesterday,' he said to Margutti on the morrow of his master's death. In fact, he expired during the memorial service two days later. The ties of a lifetime which had been snapped were also the heartstrings of this faithful servitor.

But the war rolled on.

CHAPTER XXIV
THE RUSSIAN COLLAPSE

During the afternoon of March 13, 1917, the Russian Embassy in London informed us that they were no longer in contact with Petrograd. For some days the capital had been a prey to disorders which it was believed were being effectively suppressed. Now suddenly for a space there was a silence. Volumes have been written upon the causes and consequences of this silence. For us it draws the curtain upon the tale.

The Allies, startled and disappointed by the German recovery at the end of 1916, had planned in closer concert than ever before what they hoped would be the decisive operations of the coming year. Each and all of the Allies were to attack at the selected moments upon all their fronts—French, British, Russian, Italian, Roumanian, Salonican. The prospects were good. The Allies now disposed of a superiority of nearly five to two, and the factories of the whole world outside enemy territory were pouring munitions and implements of war to them across the seas and oceans. Russia, from whose fathomless man-power so much was still hoped, was for the first time since the opening battles to be properly equipped. The doubled broad-gauge railway to the never-ice-bound port of Murmansk on the White Sea was now at last completed. The labours, the sufferings and dying gasps of thousands of prisoners-of-war intermingled with criminals and Chinese, toiling for months in perpetual night, had built these sixteen hundred miles of line across the frozen plains and marshes; and Russia was now for the first time in permanent contact with her Allies. Nearly 200 new battalions had been added to her forces; and behind the armies large deposits of all kinds of shell had been amassed. There seemed to be no military reason why the year 1917 should not witness the final triumph of the Allies, and bring to Russia the reward which she had sought through infinite agonies.

Now suddenly there was this silence. The great Power with whom we had been in such intimate comradeship, without whom all plans were meaningless, was stricken dumb. With Russian effective aid, all the Allied fronts could attack together. Without that aid it might well be that the War was lost. It was therefore with strained attention that we watched for the reopening of the telegraph lines to Petrograd.

* * * * *

Many streams had flowed together to bring the deluge. The Russian revolution was begun by social, military and political forces which within a week were left aghast behind it. In its opening paroxysm all conscious Russia participated. It was primarily a patriotic revolt against the misfortunes and mismanagement of the War. Defeats and disasters, want of food and prohibition of alcohol, the slaughter of millions of men, joined with inefficiency and corruption to produce a state of exasperation among all classes which had no outlet but revolt, could find no scapegoat but the Sovereign. For a year past the Czar and his wife had been the objects of growing universal resentment. The fond, obstinate husband and father, the absolute monarch obviously devoid of all the qualities of a national ruler in times of crisis, bore the burden of all the sufferings which the German Armies had inflicted on the Russian State. Behind him the Empress, a still more hated figure, dwelt in her tiny circle listening only to her cronies—her lady companion Madame Virubova, her spiritual adviser the sensual mystic Rasputin—and presumed thence and on such promptings to sway the whole policy and fortunes of the tormented Empire.

In vain the Imperial family, deeply concerned for their own existence—apart from all other issues—approached their Head. In vain the leaders of the Duma and every independent figure in Russia made their protests. In vain the Ambassadors of the Allied Powers dropped their elaborate hints, or even uttered solemn and formal warnings under the direction of their Governments. Nicholas II, distressed, remained immovable. He saw as clearly as they did the increasing peril. He knew of no means by which it could be averted. In his view nothing but autocracy established through centuries had enabled the Russians to proceed thus far in the teeth of calamity. No people had suffered and sacrificed like the Russians. No State, no nation, had ever gone through trials on such a scale and retained its coherent structure. The vast machine creaked and groaned. But it still worked. One more effort and victory would come. To change the system, to open the gate to intruders, to part with any portion of the despotic power, was in the eyes of the Czar to bring about a total collapse. Therefore, though plunged daily deeper in anxiety and perplexity, he was held alike by all his instincts and his reasoning faculties in a fixed position. He stood like a baited animal tied to a stake and feebly at bay.

It is easy for critics never subjected to such ordeals to recount lost opportunities. They speak lightly of changing the fundamental principles of the Russian State in the stress of the War from absolute monarchy to some British or French parliamentary system. It would be a thankless task to assail convictions so confidently asserted. Nevertheless, the martial and national achievements of Russia in the three terrible campaigns this volume has described constitute a prodigy no less astounding than the magnitude of her collapse thereafter. The very rigidity of the system gave it its strength and, once broken, forbade all recovery. The absolute Czar in spite of all his lamentable deficiencies commanded Russia. It can never be proved that a three-quarters-Czar or half-Czar and the rest a Parliament, could in such a period have commanded anything at all. In fact, once the Czar was gone, no Russian ever commanded again. It was not until a fearsome set of internationalists and logicians built a sub-human structure upon the ruins of Christian civilization, that any form of order or design again emerged. Thus it is by no means certain that the generally-accepted view upon the practical steps is right, or that the Czar for all his errors and shortcomings was wrong. After all, he was within an ace of safety and success. Another month and the accession of the United States to the cause of the Allies would have brought a flood of new energy, encouragement, and moral stimulus to Russian society. The certainty of victory, never again lost, was to dawn like a new sun beyond the wastes of Asia and the Pacific Ocean. Only another month till daybreak! Only another month and the world might have been spared the tribulations of the two most grievous years of the War. That month was lacking. A brief but hideous hiatus marred the scene. Meanwhile Nicholas II, casting his eyes now towards the Providence he sought to serve, now towards the family group he loved so well, clung chained to his post.

All sorts of Russians made the revolution. No sort of Russian reaped its profit. Among the crowds who thronged the turbulent streets and ante-rooms of Petrograd in these March days with resolve for 'Change at all costs' in their hearts, were found Grand Dukes, fine ladies, the bitterest die-hards and absolutists like Purishkevitch and Yusupov; resolute, patriotic politicians like Rodzianko and Guchkov; experienced Generals; diplomats and financiers of the old regime; Liberals and Democrats; Socialists like Kerenski; sturdy citizens and tradesfolk; faithful soldiers seeking to free their Prince from bad advisers; ardent nationalists resolved to purge Russia from secret German influence; multitudes of loyal peasants and workmen; and behind all, cold, calculating, ruthless, patient, stirring all, demanding all, awaiting all, the world-wide organization of International Communism.

Actually the deposition of the Czar was effected by the Chiefs of his Army. Nicholas was at his Headquarters at Mohilev when on the afternoon of March 11 the first telegrams about the disorders in Petrograd began to flow in. It was reported at first that they were of no great consequence. Had he been in his Capital accessible to all the moderate forces now inflamed, there might still have been time, not indeed as we hold to avert disaster, but to lessen its shock. But he was at Mohilev, and the Grand Duke Nicholas who should have ruled the Armies was far off in the half-banishment of Tiflis. On the morning of the 11th Rodzianko, President of the Duma, confronted with a swiftly mounting crisis, sent the following telegram to his Master:

'Position serious. Anarchy in the capital. Government paralyzed. Arrangements for transport, supply and fuel in complete disorder. General discontent is increasing. Disorderly firing on the streets. Part of the troops are firing on one another. Essential to entrust some individual who possesses the confidence of the country with the formation of a new government. There must be no delay. Any procrastination fatal. I pray to God that in this hour responsibility fall not on the wearer of the crown!'

He repeated this to the Commanders-in-Chief on all the Army-group 'Fronts,' and to Alexeiev at the Stavka, with a request for their support; and next day, the 12th, he telegraphed again to the Czar:

'The situation is growing worse. Immediate steps must be taken, for to-morrow will be too late. The final hour has come when the fate of the country and the dynasty must be decided.'

To such grave tidings was added scarcely less disturbing news from Tsarskoe Selo. The Royal children had sickened of the measles. The Czar replied to his counsellors with hard defiance, and to his wife with overflowing sympathy.

As the day wore on Alexeiev took to his bed with anxiety and fever. The Czar called for the Imperial train. His duties as a Sovereign and as a father equally demanded his return to the seat of Government. The train was ready at midnight; but it took six hours more to clear the line. The Dowager-Empress had arrived. Mother and son travelled together. The next afternoon the train stopped at Dno. Impossible to proceed! A bridge had been, it was said, blown up or damaged. The Czar indicated an alternative route, and for the first time came in contact with naked resistance. Such authority as now reigned in Petrograd refused to permit his further approach. Where to turn? Some hours passed. Back to Mohilev? We do not know how far he tested this possibility. Perhaps he had been conscious of the unspoken reproach with which the atmosphere of the Stavka was loaded. To the North-West Front then—to General Ruzski. Here at least he would find a trusty commander, whose armies lay nearest to the rebellious capital.

The train reached Pskov. Ruzski was there with grave salutes. But with him also very soon were Guchkov and Shulguin as a deputation from the Duma. Here were able, determined public men with plain advice: immediate abdication in favour of his son, and the Regency of his brother, the Grand Duke Michael Alexandrovich. The Czar appealed to Ruzski. Ruzski, anticipating his responsibilities, had felt that the matter was too serious for him. Already before the Czar's arrival he had consulted the Stavka and the other commanders. Accordingly fateful telegrams had been despatched through the Stavka along the whole length of the Russian front. All the Army Group Commanders, Brusilov, Ewarth, the Grand Duke, and finally, with many reservations, Sakharov from distant Roumania, declared in favour of abdication. The document was drawn. Guchkov presented the pen. Nicholas was about to sign. Suddenly he asked whether he and his family could reside in the Crimea, in that palace of Livadia whose sunlit gardens seemed green and calm and tranquil. Bluntly he was told he must leave Russia forthwith, and that the new sovereign must remain among his people. On this his fatherly love triumphed over his public duty and indeed over his coronation oath. Rather than be separated from his son, he disinherited that son. The paper was redrafted and Nicholas II abdicated in favour of his brother. Thus all claim of legitimacy was shivered; and everything in a second stage was thrown into redoubled confusion.

However, it is over now. The Czar has ceased to reign. The brother, around whom everything is melting, fears to seize the abandoned reins of power without the vote of a National Assembly, impossible to obtain. Nothing could ever bring stabilizing ideas together again. We cannot here follow the long, swift, splintering, crashing descent which ended, as it could only end, in the abyss. The dynasty was gone. Vainly did leaders of the Duma and the Zemstvos strive to clutch at hand-holds. In their turn they broke. Vainly did Kerenski with his nationalist democracy try to stop the fall a long leap lower down. Vainly did the great men of action, Kornilov the warrior, Savinkov the terrorist patriot, strive to marshal the social revolutionary forces in defence of Russia. All fell headlong into the depths where Lenin, Trotski, Zinoviev and other unnatural spirits awaited their prey.

We are here concerned only to notice the ruin of those brave armies which had hitherto guarded the Russian land. On March 15 the Petrograd Soviet issued the fatal historic 'Order No. 1' which destroyed the discipline of the troops, and delivered the Russian Army in the full storm of war to the rule of elected committees. Nothing mattered any more after that. The soldiers ceased to fight the foreign invaders. Their energies and hatreds were turned upon their own officers. The ignominious tragedies of the Kerenski offensive and the flight from the Riga bridge-head deserve no place in this account. Russia became incapable of offence, of defence or even of retreat. Peace at any price was the only resource. It needed all Lenin's cold massive logic to compel even the most extreme of those who had laid Russia low to accept the consequences of their acts. An armistice was arranged in November and the Treaty of Brest-Litovsk was signed the following March.

The uncertainties and obscurity of the Russian situation, and memories of their painful surprise at Brusilov's hands, held a large but mainly motionless force of Austrian and German troops upon the Russian front until the Armistice. Even in October, 1917, there were still eighty Teutonic divisions in the East. But in November Austria with German backing threw her main strength upon Italy at Caporetto, and at the close of the year Ludendorff requested Hoffmann to arrange the transport of a million men—fifty divisions and five thousand guns—from Russia to the Western Front. The gigantic heart-shaking battles of 1918, involving the death or mutilation of upwards of two million of British, French and German soldiers, followed their appointed course. The Eastern Front was at an end.

APPENDIX I

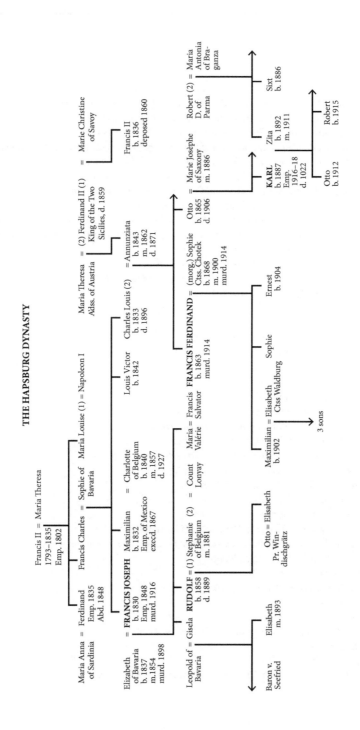

THE HAPSBURG DYNASTY

APPENDIX II
SOME AUTHORITIES CONSULTED

EDMONDS. *Military Operations, France and Belgium* (British Official History).
ASPINALL-OGLANDER. *Military Operations, Gallipoli* (British Official History).
GOOCH and TEMPERLEY. *British Documents on the Origins of the War.*
Les Armées françaises dans la Grande Guerre (French Official History).
CHAPOUILLY. *La Grande Guerre: Relation de l'Etat Major russe* (Russian Official, translated).
Die Grosse Politik der Europäischen Kabinette (German Official Documents).
REICHSARCHIV. *Der Weltkrieg, 1914–1918* (German Official History).
Zur Vorgeschichte des Weltkrieges (German Official Committee of Inquiry).
Oesterreich-Ungarns Aussenpolitik (Austrian Official Documents).
KAUTSKY. *Die deutschen Dokumente zum Kriegsausbruch* (German Official Documents).
KRIEGSARCHIV. *Oesterreich-Ungarns Letzter Krieg, 1914–1918* (Austrian Official History).
GOOCH. *Recent Revelations of European Diplomacy.*
SCHMITT, BERNADOTTE E. *The Coming of the War, 1914.*
HÖTZENDORF, CONRAD VON. *Aus meiner Dienstzeit, 1906–1918.*
KNOX. *With the Russian Army, 1914–1917.*
IRONSIDE. *Tannenberg.*
HINDENBURG. *Out of my Life.*
LUDENDORFF. *My War Memories, 1914–1918.*
FALKENHAYN. *The General Staff and its Critical Decisions.*
HOFFMANN. *War Diaries and Other Papers.*
GOURKO. *Russia in 1914–1917.*
BRUSILOV. *A Soldier's Note-book.*
TSCHUPPIK. *The Reign of the Emperor Francis Joseph.*
MARGUTTI. *The Emperor Francis Joseph and His Times.*
JASZI. *The Dissolution of the Hapsburg Monarchy.*
GLAISE-HORSTENAU. *The Collapse of the Austro-Hungarian Empire.*
SUKHOMLINOV. *Erinnerungen* (German translation).
MARCHENKO. *La Catastrophe austro-hongroise.*
FEYLER. *Les Campagnes de Serbie.*
LARCHER. *La Grande Guerre dans les Balkans.*
DANILOV. *Russland im Weltkriege, 1914–1915* (German translation).
DOBROROLSKI. *Die Mobilmachung der russischen Armee* (German translation).
MONTGELAS. *Leitfaden zur Kriegsschuldfrage.*
KUHL. *Der Weltkrieg, 1914–1918.*
SCHWARTE. *Der grosse Krieg, 1914–1918.*
ELZE. *Tannenberg.*
ZWEHL. *Erich von Falkenhayn.*
GALLWITZ. *Meine Führertätigkeit im Weltkriege, 1914–1916.*
BARBY. *L'Epopée serbe.*
PITREICH. *Lemberg.*
AUFFENBERG. *Aus Oesterreich-Ungarns Teilnahme am Weltkriege.*

APPENDIX III
REFERENCES

Note.—The following abbreviations are used for the titles of the works from which passages have been quoted. In each case the title-symbol is followed by the number of the volume and of the page or document.

'A'   Austrian official History, *Oesterreich-Ungarns letzter Krieg.*
'B'   *British Documents on the Origins of the War.*
'C'   Conrad, *Aus meiner Dienstzeit.*
'D'   *Die grosse Politik.*
'E'   Elze, *Tannenberg.*
'F'   Falkenhayn, *The General Staff and its Critical Decisions.*
'G'   German official History, *Der Weltkrieg* (Reichsarchiv).
'H'   Hindenburg, *Out of my Life.*
'Hm' Hoffmann, *War Diaries and Other Papers.*
'J'   Regimental History, 41st (v. Boyen) Infantry Regiment.
'K'   Kuhl, *Der Weltkrieg.*
'Ky' Kautsky, *Die deutschen Dokumente.*
'O'   *Oesterreich-Ungarns Aussenpolitik.*
'P'   Pierrefeu, *Plutarque a menti.*
'R'   Russian official History, *La Grande Guerre* (Chapouilly).
'T'   Tschuppik, *The Reign of the Emperor Francis Joseph.*
'Z'   Zwehl, *Erich von Falkenhayn.*

Reference No.

1. D., XXVI (i), doc, 9026.

2. B., V, doc. 768.

3. B., V, doc. 764.

4. C., II, p. 282.

5. C., II, p. 284.

6. C., IV, p. 34.

7. O., VIII, doc. 9984; Ky. I, doc. 13.

8. C, IV, pp. 36–8.

9. O., VIII, doc. 10,118; C., IV, pp. 44–51.

10. O., VIII, doc. 10,146; C., IV, pp. 57–9.

11. O., VIII, doc. 10,145.

12. C., IV, pp. 61–2.

13. E., pp. 158–160.

14. Z., p. 56.

15. Ky., I. doc. 271.

16. Ky., I, doc. 293.
17. Ky., I, doc. 332.
18. Ky., I, doc. 335.
19. Ky., I, doc. 390.
20. C., IV, pp. 110–111.
21. Ky., I, doc. 503; C., IV, p. 156.
22. C., IV, p. 113.
23. C., IV, pp. 164–5.
24. C., IV, pp. 193–5.
25. C., IV, pp. 203–4.
26. C., IV, pp. 388–9.
27. C., IV, p. 390.
28. C., IV, pp. 391, 393.
29. C., IV, p. 467.
30. C., IV, pp. 507–8.
31. R., p. 133.
32. C., IV, pp. 551–3.
33. C., IV, pp. 701–2.
34. P., pp. 236–7.
35. J., p. 23.
36. A., I, pp. 344–5.
37. H., pp. 118–119.
38. Hm., II, p. 62.
39. H., p. 123.
40. G., VI, pp. 3–5.
41. G., VI, p. 5.
42. G., VI, p. 93.
43. G., VI, pp. 95–6.
44. G., VII, pp. 11–12.
45. H., pp. 137–8.
46. K., I, p. 184.
47. H., p. 139.
48. F., pp. 145–8.
49. Z., p. 213.

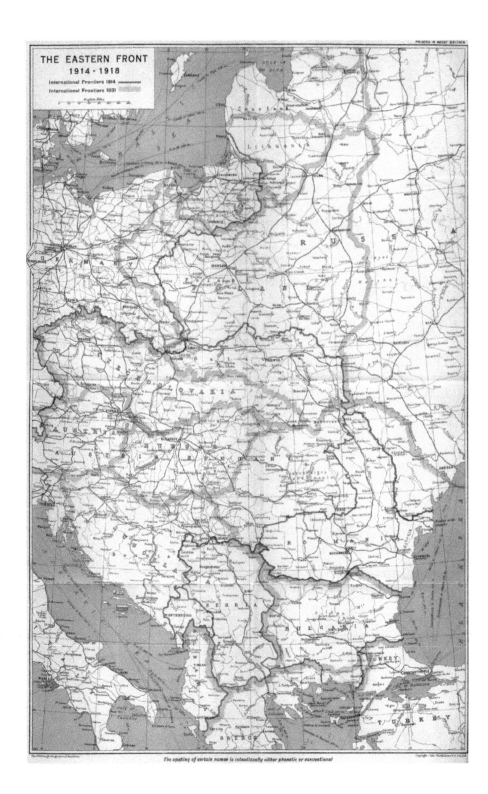

THE EASTERN FRONT
1914 - 1918

International Frontiers 1914 ——
International Frontiers 1931 ▓▓▓▓

English Miles

The Edinburgh Geographical Institute

The spelling of certain names is intentionally either phonetic or conventional

Copyright John Bartholomew & Son Ltd.

INDEX

Index

Index

Index